COUNTRY

A Regional Exploration

Recent Titles in
Greenwood Guides to American Roots Music

Jazz: A Regional Exploration
Scott Yanow

Folk Music: A Regional Exploration
Norm Cohen

GREENWOOD GUIDES TO
AMERICAN ROOTS MUSIC

COUNTRY
A Regional Exploration

Ivan Tribe

Norm Cohen
Series Editor

GREENWOOD PRESS
Westport, Connecticut • London

781.642
T82c

cat

Library of Congress Cataloging-in-Publication Data

Tribe, Ivan M.
    Country : a regional exploration / Ivan Tribe.
        p.   cm.—(Greenwood guides to American roots music, ISSN 1551–0271)
    Includes bibliographical references (p.   ) and index.
    ISBN 0–313–33026–3 (alk. paper)
    1. Country music—History and criticism.   I. Title.   II. Series.
ML3524.T739   2006
781.64209—dc22   2005034851

British Library Cataloguing in Publication Data is available.

Library of Congress Catalog Card Number: 2005034851

ISBN: 0–313–33026–3
ISSN: 1551–0271

First published in 2006

Greenwood Press, 88 Post Road West, Westport, CT 06881
An imprint of Greenwood Publishing Group, Inc.
www.greenwood.com

Printed in the United States of America

The paper used in this book complies with the
Permanent Paper Standard issued by the National
Information Standards Organization (Z39.48–1984).

10 9 8 7 6 5 4 3 2 1

To
Deanna, Dorothy, Abby, Donna,
Lori—the ladies in my life.

Contents

Series Foreword

If present trends are any indication, soon anyone with access to the Internet will be able to tune in to music from any part of the world. When that happens, listeners may well find Kentucky bluegrass bands playing Tex-Mex music along with banjo tunes and gospel favorites, while musicians in India may intersperse elements of American rap music with their own native raga traditions.

It's difficult to predict right now, but even to understand the significance of this revolution requires an appreciation for the fact that until recently all musical genres, like every aspect of human activity, were associated with relatively compact geographic regions, bounded not only by national boundaries but also by the more limiting barriers of language, religion, geography, and cultural heritage. In the United States, regional boundaries might enclose an area as large as the vast Southwest or as small as the immediate environs of Galax, Virginia.

This series of musical studies seeks to describe American musical traditions that are, or once were, associated with geographic regions smaller than the nation as a whole. These musical varieties include jazz, blues, country music, Hispanic American music, Irish American music, polka music, Franco-American music (including Cajun and Zydeco), Native American music, and traditional folk music. Jazz music originated in New Orleans and other cities along the lower Mississippi River in the early 1900s, but by midcentury it was equally at home in New York and San Francisco as in New Orleans or Memphis. Jazz was in turn heavily influenced by blues music, an African American creation born in the broader regions of the Deep South.

Country music of recent decades is a merger of two regional Anglo-American musical traditions, one from the Appalachians and other southeastern states, and the other from the southwestern plains. Its earlier name of country-western music reflects more clearly that parentage. Irish American music, brought to these shores mainly in the 1840s and later by emigrants from Ireland, flourished best in the big cities where the Irish made their new homes: Boston, New York, Philadelphia, and Chicago.

Hispanic (Latino, Tex-Mex) music migrated north from Mexico and other Latin American countries. In the early 1900s it could be heard only in Texas, New Mexico, and California; a century later, Spanish language radio stations reach almost everywhere in the lower forty-eight. Polka music was brought to the New World by musicians from Central Europe—Germany, Switzerland, and what used to be Czechoslovakia. It was fruitfully transplanted to the Midwestern states from Texas north to Nebraska and the Dakotas.

The music of First Nations (Native Americans) was spread across the continent in varieties associated with particular groups of peoples, but as a result of ethnocentric federal policies that forced their relocation to "Indian Reservations," was subsequently located in regions that were often at great distances from the original homelands. Traditional folk music, the product of evolved music of European American and African American immigrants, had developed distinct regional characteristics in the New World by the eighteenth and nineteenth centuries, but as a result of internal, primarily western migrations, had changed considerably by the early twentieth century.

Four of these musical styles—jazz, blues, country, and traditional folk—are treated in separate volumes; the other "ethnic" traditions (Hispanic, Cajun/Zydeco, Polka, Irish, and Native American) are presented together in a fifth volume.

American music continues to evolve. Readers of these volumes can doubtless think of changes in music that have taken place in their own lifetimes. The many musical heritages of the nineteenth and twentieth centuries laid the foundations for today's music. The advent and growth of national media—radio, television, digital recordings, Internet—exert powerful forces on the nature of musical genres that were once regional. Ironically, national media permit two contradictory phenomena. At first, they introduce listeners to the regional musical forms that a wider audience otherwise might never have known about. Eventually, though, they provide the mechanism for the scrambling and cross-pollination of what were once distinct styles.

This does not mean that American musical regionalism is gone forever, doomed to a homogeneous culture that is the same in Key West, Florida, as in the San Juan Islands of Washington. If the past is any guide, new regional styles will continually emerge, gradually to become part of the national mix. As long as immigration to these shores continues, the influx of new musical styles will contribute to and invigorate the old. It is an exciting prospect.

Norm Cohen
Portland Community College, Oregon
Series Editor

Preface

From as far back as I can recall, my musical preferences have always been for some form of country. The first singer I remember on radio was the yodeling cowboy vocalist Kenny Roberts at WLW Cincinnati. By 1950, I was tuning in to the *Grand Ole Opry* at WSM Nashville at the time when Hank Williams began to sing "Long Gone Lonesome Blues." I also listened to other radio stations, including WPDX in Clarksburg, West Virginia, where deejay "Cherokee Sue" (Hattie Graham) favored more traditional songs by the likes of Molly O'Day, the Bailes Brothers, and the duo of Wilma Lee and Stoney Cooper. At the hometown station, WATH in Athens, Ohio, deejay Ted Covert played all the honky-tonk favorites. When I was in high school, Elvis and the other rockabilly figures took my attention, and about the time I entered college the Kingston Trio introduced me to commercial folk music. As a historian, this led me to old-time music and rekindled my interest in bluegrass. I bought all the Jimmie Rodgers and Carter Family albums that were coming out in the early 1960s. Soon I found out about County Records and its reissues of Charlie Poole and other early figures.

Those pioneer artists from the early decades of country music really stirred my interests, and I endeavored to learn more about them. I began to correspond with Dorsey Dixon. Collector Robert Nobley furnished me with tapes of Ernest Stoneman and Fiddlin' John Carson among others. I journeyed to Ohio State University, where I attended concerts by Doc Watson, Clint Howard, Fred

Price, and also the New Lost City Ramblers. I saw and heard Bill Monroe for the first time in September 1969 and thereafter began to attend bluegrass festivals. In 1973, I wrote my first articles for *Bluegrass Unlimited* and the *JEMF Quarterly*. Still later, I authored two books on country music history: one a study of the music within a state and the other of a family's life in music.

Late in 2002, Norm Cohen, editor of the *Greenwood Guides to American Roots Music* series, asked if I might be interested in writing the *Country* volume in the Greenwood series. After some thought, I accepted since I knew that a broad survey of this nature within a regional context would be challenging, yet intellectually rewarding, and very much needed. It has taken the better part of three summers and much of two springs to get this accomplished. It has been a long and, at times, tiresome journey, but I hope readers will find the end product a satisfactory and useful one.

Acknowledgments

In writing a book that is based largely on secondary sources, this list is shorter than it has been in earlier books. Still a few notes of appreciation are in order. The first goes to series editor Norm Cohen and acquisitions editor Debra Adams of Greenwood Press for giving me the opportunity to contribute a volume to what I hope will become a memorable collection of musical history. My first opportunity to work with Norm dates back to 1973 when I did my first article for *JEMF Quarterly* on songs and ballads of the Silver Bridge Disaster, and even before then I was familiar with his early chronicles of the Skillet Lickers. In the ensuing years, I also became acquainted with Archie Green, Neil Rosenberg, Charles Wolfe, Gus Meade, Tony Russell, Wayne Daniel, Bill Malone, Nolan Porterfield, W. K. McNeil, and Pete Kuykendall, among others, in the small but growing group of country music historians who I believe exerted positive influences on my own work including this one.

Closer to home, I owe much assistance to my wife, Deanna, and her secretary, Lois Campbell, who came to my rescue more than once in my ongoing struggle with the technology of the computer. Roger Van Dyke, a fraternity brother of long standing, patiently proofread the entire manuscript and caught many typographical and grammatical errors. At the University of Rio Grande, my colleagues in history Sam Wilson and especially Ellen Brasel, shouldered a disproportionate share of departmental duties to free up more time for me to work on this volume. I also appreciate the understanding of Department Chair Barry Thompson and Judithe Thompson of the Honors Program. My recently graduated office computer assistant Joshua Price also deserves acknowledgment.

Chronology

1922   First country music played on WSB radio in Atlanta and WBAP Fort Worth. Eck Robertson records for Victor Talking Machine.

1923   Fiddlin' John Carson and Henry Whitter record for OKeh. William Houchins records for Gennett.

1924   Gid Tanner and Riley Puckett, Samantha Bumgarner, Eva Davis, and Ernest Thompson all record for Columbia. George Reneau, Uncle Am Stuart, and Uncle Dave Macon all record for Vocalion. Tweedy Brothers and David Miller record for Gennett. Marion Slaughter, A.K.A. Vernon Dalhart, records "The Prisoner's Song"/ "Wreck of the Old 97" for Victor, giving country music its first megahit. Radio station WLS Chicago begins what becomes *National Barn Dance.*

1925   Ernest Stoneman for OKeh and Charlie Poole for Columbia begin recording careers. Radio station WSM Nashville begins what becomes *Grand Ole Opry.* Carl Sprague records cowboy songs.

1926   Gid Tanner, Riley Puckett, and Clayton McMichen form nucleus of Skillet Lickers, a string band that records first for Columbia and later for Bluebird. Bradley Kincaid begins singing at WLS Chicago. Numerous new country artists begin recording.

1927   First recordings made in Bristol, Tennessee, by Victor of the Carter Family and Jimmie Rodgers, among others. Recording boom continues.

1928   Harry McClintock makes first records. Recording boom still continues.

1929   Jimmie Davis and Gene Autry make first recordings for Victor. Stock Market crashes in late October; within months record sales decline.

1930   Cliff Carlisle makes first recordings. W. Lee O'Daniel hires Bob Wills and Milton Brown and sponsors them on radio for Burris Mills as Light Crust Doughboys.

1931   Charlie Poole dies. Delmore Brothers make first recordings.

1932   A. P. and Sara Carter separate but continue to record. Bob Wills and Milton Brown record as Fort Worth Doughboys and soon leave O'Daniel to start own bands.

1933   President Roosevelt introduces his New Deal. Radio Station WWVA in Wheeling begins *Jamboree* program. Jimmie Rodgers dies. Repeal of Prohibition Amendment leads to increasing number of jukeboxes in cafes and nightclubs throughout South and Midwest. Victor Company initiates budget-priced Bluebird label.

1934   Decca Records enters American market. Bill Boyd and Milton Brown record for Bluebird, and Sons of the Pioneers record for Decca. Callahan Brothers begin recording.

1935   Bob Wills and Texas Playboys and Mainer's Mountaineers make first recordings. Gene Autry begins to make musical westerns. Patsy Montana records "I Wanna Be a Cowboy's Sweetheart." Elvis Presley born in Tupelo, Mississippi.

1936   Milton Brown dies from auto wreck injuries. Monroe Brothers, Blue Sky Boys, and Dixon Brothers all begin recording for Bluebird. Tex Ritter becomes second singing cowboy film star. Roy Acuff makes first recordings for American Record Corporation. Ernest Tubb makes first recordings, and Hank Snow begins recording in Canada.

1937   Roy Rogers begins solo recording and making singing cowboy films.

1938   Monroe Brothers split. W. Lee O'Daniel elected Governor of Texas, initiating entry of country music personalities into serious politics.

1939   *Grand Ole Opry* has half-hour segment sponsored by Prince Albert Smoking Tobacco broadcast over NBC Radio Network, greatly enlarging its audience.

1940   First peacetime draft in United States inspires songs like "I'll Be Back in a Year." Republic Pictures makes film *Grand Ole Opry* starring the Weaver Brothers and Elviry with appearances by Roy Acuff, Uncle Dave Macon, and George D. Hay.

1941   Japanese bomb Pearl Harbor, bringing United States into World War II. Shellac shortage will soon hamper record manufacturing as war will dampen market for phonograph records. Ernest Tubb records his signature song "Walking the Floor over You" for Decca.

1942   Capitol Records launched in California and soon joins Victor, Columbia (ARC), and Decca as major recording company. Tex Ritter is its first country and western artist. WWVA Wheeling becomes 50,000-watt station, but *Jamboree* discontinues as live audience program for duration of war. Elton Britt records "There's a Star-Spangled Banner Waving Somewhere," which becomes best-known country song of World War II era. American Federation of Musicians (AFM) recording ban in effect from August 1, 1942, until September 1943 further curtails recording activity. Acuff-Rose becomes first major music publishing company in Nashville.

1943   King Records, launched in Cincinnati in November by Syd Nathan, becomes key independent label for next decade.

1944   Eddy Arnold makes first recordings for RCA Victor. Hill and Range Publishing Company established. Jimmie Davis elected Governor of Louisiana.

1945   World War II ends; postwar prosperity boom begins. Four Star Records started in California. Mercury Records started in Chicago, gains major label status within a few years. Recording activity booms. Spade Cooley dominates western swing scene in California.

1946   Hank Williams makes first recordings for Sterling. Bill Monroe records first bluegrass music on Columbia with Lester Flatt, Earl Scruggs, and Chubby Wise as part of his Blue Grass Boys band. Wheeling Jamboree resumes live audience broadcasts. Molly O'Day begins recording for Columbia.

1947   M-G-M records launched; Hank Williams becomes its most significant country artist. Bob Wills also signs with the new label. Tex Williams gives Capitol Records its first million-record seller.

1948   Second AFM recording ban in effect from January 1 until December 14. Among the few recordings made that year are some of the first records by Lester Flatt and Earl Scruggs on Mercury, who made peace with the AFM early, and Hank Williams recording of "Lovesick Blues" for M-G-M on December 22. KWKH radio in Shreveport begins *Louisiana Hayride* as live audience country show. Roy Acuff loses bid for Tennessee governorship.

1949   Hank Williams joins cast of *Grand Ole Opry*.

1950   Lefty Frizzell and Carl Smith make first recordings for Columbia. Hank Snow has major hit with "I'm Movin' On."

1951   Lefty Frizzell has four of the top ten country hits at one time in April.

1952   Hank Williams fired from *Grand Ole Opry*; returns to *Louisiana Hayride*. *Town Hall Party* becomes leading country show on West Coast, broadcast from KFI before a live audience in Compton, California. Stuart Hamblen is Prohibition Party Presidential candidate.

1953   Hank Williams dies early on New Year's Day (or perhaps New Year's Eve 1952).

1954   Elvis Presley makes first recordings for Sun; incites development of rockabilly movement. Webb Pierce has signature hit with "Slowly" and gives impetus to use of pedal steel guitar.

1955   Presley's contract purchased by RCA Victor. First recordings by Patsy Cline. Tennessee Ernie Ford has crossover hit with "Sixteen Tons."

1956   Johnny Cash has first number one hit with "I Walk the Line."

1957   Jerry Lee Lewis records "Whole Lotta Shakin' Goin' On" and "Great Balls of Fire."

1958   Country Music Association (CMA) established.

1959   Marty Robbins records signature song "El Paso," as does Jim Reeves with "He'll Have to Go."

1960   Porter Wagoner begins syndicated television program. Loretta Lynn makes first recordings. Patsy Cline records "I Fall to Pieces."

1961   Jimmie Rodgers, Hank Williams, and Fred Rose are first persons elected to Country Music Hall of Fame.

1962   George Jones has major hit with "She Thinks I Still Care." Roy Acuff becomes first living Country Music Hall of Fame member.

1963   Patsy Cline, Cowboy Copas, and Hawkshaw Hawkins killed in plane crash. Buck Owens has first number one hit, soon makes Bakersfield Sound a significant musical force.

1964   Jim Reeves killed in plane crash. Dolly Parton, fresh out of high school, leaves Knoxville for Nashville. Buck Owens has four number one hits.

1965   First bluegrass festival at Fincastle, Virginia.

1966   Tammy Wynette makes first recordings for Epic. Carter Stanley dies. First popular history of country music, *The Country Music Story* by Bob Shelton and Burt Goldblatt, published.

1967   Dolly Parton joins cast of Porter Wagoner's TV show. Merle Haggard has first number one hit. Country Music Hall of Fame opens.

1968   Johnny Cash records live album at Folsom Prison in California. Ernest "Pop" Stoneman dies. First scholarly history of country music, *Country Music, U.S.A.* by Bill Malone, published.

1969   *Johnny Cash Show* on prime time ABC television (until 1971). *Hee Haw* debuts on CBS-TV. George Jones and Tammy Wynette marry.

1970   Ricky Skaggs and Keith Whitley serve musical apprenticeship as Ralph Stanley's band members.

1971   Tom T. Hall has signature hit with "The Year that Clayton Delaney died."

1972   Donna Fargo has signature hit with "Happiest Girl in the USA."

1973   Double album *Bean Blossom* recorded live at Bill Monroe's bluegrass festival in Indiana.

1974   Hank Snow has last number one hit with "Hello Love."

1975   Willie Nelson has first number one hit with "Blue Eyes Crying in the Rain." Bob Wills dies.

1976   Willie Nelson and Waylon Jennings have signature hit with "Good Hearted Woman."

1979   Lester Flatt dies.

1980   Group known as Alabama has its first number one hit. Loretta Lynn's life story, *Coal Miner's Daughter*, becomes hit motion picture.

1982   Ricky Skaggs has three number one hits, inaugurating boom in neotraditional country.

1983   The Nashville Network (TNN) established.

1984   Reba McEntire wins first of four awards as CMA Female Vocalist of the Year.

1986   Randy Travis has first number one hits with "On the Other Hand" and "Diggin' Up Bones."

1988   Kathy Mattea has signature hit with "Eighteen Wheels and a Dozen Roses."

1989   Keith Whitley dies.

1990   Release of Garth Brooks album *No Fences*, which goes on to sell thirteen million copies.

1991   Alan Jackson has three number one hits, most notably "Don't Rock the Jukebox."

1992   Billy Ray Cyrus has major hit with "Achy Breaky Heart."

1993   Conway Twitty, who had forty number one country hits, dies.

1995   Debut of Shania Twain's album *The Woman in Me*, which goes on to sell nine million copies.

1996   Tim McGraw marries Faith Hill. Bill Monroe dies.

1998   Tammy Wynette and Grandpa Jones die.

1999   Martina McBride wins first of four CMA Female Vocalist of the Year awards.

2000   Film *O Brother, Where Art Thou?* generates widespread interest in grassroots music. George Strait has thirty-sixth number one hit; becomes the all-time leader of neotraditional country.

2001   September 11 attacks on the World Trade Center and the Pentagon inspire Alan Jackson's "Where Were You (When the World Stopped Turning)" and Charlie Daniels' "This Ain't No Rag, It's a Flag."

2002   Wave of patriotic songs continue with Toby Keith and Darryl Worley having respective hits with "Courtesy of the Red, White, and Blue" and "Have You Forgotten?"

2003   June Carter Cash dies on May 15, and Johnny Cash dies on September 12.

2004   George Jones celebrates fiftieth anniversary as a recording artist.

2005   "Whiskey Lullaby," written by Bill Anderson and John Randall and performed by Brad Paisley and Allison Krauss, wins CMA Song of the Year Award. Johnny Cash motion picture biography *Walk the Line* is released.

1

A Brief Survey of Eighty Years of Musical History

An amateur historian writing a somewhat pedestrian article on country music once penned the sentence, "There were no country music stars before the recording industry came into existence." He continued, "before that time . . . country music was unknown. It was simply music of the rocking chair, the harvest, and the worship from rural America."[1] This author stumbled on to a simple truth: country music as known for the last eight decades is a commercial art form born of the phonograph and radio. To be sure, that commercialism had folk roots in the simple tunes and songs that folks played for home entertainment on their porches and living rooms, at rural dances, and in their worship services in local churches and revival meetings. This music derived from Anglo-Celtic fiddle tunes and ballads and other sounds originating in Europe. Over the years, these influences received supplemental infusions from nineteenth-century show tunes, the minstrel stage, the emerging popular music industry on "Tin Pan Alley," shape-note hymnals together with singing schools, and cross-cultural contacts with African Americans.

THE BIRTH OF COUNTRY MUSIC

One could therefore date the birth of country music from the time it was first heard on radio and on phonograph records in the early 1920s. The pioneering radio efforts apparently took place on WSB Atlanta and WBAP Fort Worth.

More significant for the airwaves, however, were the regular "barn dance" programs on WLS Chicago from April 1924 and WSM Nashville from November 1925, which took the respective names *National Barn Dance* and *Grand Ole Opry*. The seemingly unexpected large audiences that these broadcasts attracted demonstrated that the music had appeal. Both station managers and aspiring musicians made the most of the situation, and country music became a regular feature on the radio, particularly to outlets that catered to a rural and working-class audience. By and large the music appealed mostly—but not exclusively—to white rural southerners, but it also had appeal to Midwesterners, rural New Englanders, urban migrants, and a scattering of others.

Since phonograph discs are better preserved and therefore more easily documented than radio programs (unless recorded in some manner for posterity) that once played but are lost to future generations, the development of country music on sound recordings is much better known to history. The first known examples date from June 30, 1922, when the Victor Talking Machine company recorded a pair of traditional fiddlers: thirty-five-year-old Eck Robertson from Texas and septogenerian Henry Gilliland from Oklahoma, who were fresh from playing at a Confederate Veteran's Reunion in Richmond, Virginia. Then in mid-1923, Ralph Peer of the General Phonograph Company's OKeh Records made some discs in Atlanta by a traditional fiddler and vocalist known as Fiddlin' John Carson (he had earlier played his fiddle on WSB radio). The Carson efforts stimulated further endeavors to find similar talent, not only by Ralph Peer, but by rival record firms as well. In addition to Victor and OKeh, Columbia, Vocalion, Brunswick, Gennett, and Paramount soon got into the act. A few companies, such as Edison, showed minimal interest in the new form. The country music industry thus grew into a significant business and recognized mode of entertainment from these modest beginnings.

The early recording companies labeled their newfound music by such names as "old-time tunes," "songs from Dixie," and "familiar tunes—old and new." However, for better or worse, the term "hillbilly" soon came to be applied, a name that sometimes had negative connotations. Simultaneous with the recording business learning about the new musical form, so too did the song publishers. While the earliest recordings tended to feature either traditional material or pop songs from a prior generation, the driving forces of the market soon led to a need for both newer artists and newer songs to enhance the record companies and the song publisher. Ralph Peer, in particular, got into the publishing business almost as soon as he became a talent scout or, as they were known in the trade, "A&R Men" (for artist and repertoire). Throughout the 1920s, country music as an art form and a business expanded steadily.

While nothing quite like a "star system" (as it would later be termed) existed in the early years of country music, some early recording artists and groups did achieve more prominence than others. Outside of the recording studios in New

York and such additional locales as Camden, New Jersey, for Victor, Richmond, Indiana, for Gennett, and Port Washington, Wisconsin, for Paramount, companies held field sessions in such locales as Atlanta with some regularity and less often in Bristol, Johnson City, Memphis, and Nashville, Birmingham, San Antonio, Dallas, Charlotte, Chicago, Asheville, and Ashland. Local musicians would come in prompted by either newspaper ads or suggestions made by local wholesale distributors and retailers who recommended that an individual or groups might wish to audition. Those musicians who seemed most promising usually had opportunities to record again.

From the beginning, OKeh Records had Fiddlin' John Carson as its prime artist and, to a lesser degree, Henry Whitter and Ernest Stoneman. When Peer departed to work for Victor in 1926, Stoneman went with him and could be termed Victor's top country artist until Jimmie Rodgers and the Carter Family arrived on the scene after their initial recordings made at Bristol in July and August 1927. The top country artists at Columbia were Gid Tanner and the Skillet Lickers, Charlie Poole and the North Carolina Ramblers, Smith's Sacred Singers, and Riley Puckett (who also worked with the Skillet Lickers). Vocalion and Brunswick had Uncle Dave Macon, the Kessinger Brothers, and the blind duet of Lester McFarland and Robert Gardner. Gennett had various combinations of Fiddlin' Doc Roberts and his son James along with guitarist/vocalist Asa Martin, together with several of the WLS radio artists—most notably, Bradley Kincaid. Somewhat outside the system and yet part of it too was Texas-born Marion Slaughter, who recorded for all of the above companies under a variety of pseudonyms—most notably, Vernon Dalhart and Al Craver. Slaughter could be called country in a sense, although he might be termed as a crossover artist who turned to performing such material to revitalize his career as a popular singer. However one categorizes him, his 1924 recording under the pseudonym Vernon Dalhart of "The Prisoner's Song"/ "Wreck of the Old 97" ranks as the biggest selling country record of the music's first decade.

THE GREAT DEPRESSION

The Great Depression ended the first era of hillbilly music and ushered in what might be termed the second. Many record companies endured bankruptcies and reorganizations while sales took a significant nosedive, partly because the principal buyers of their product faced dire economic times. The number of new recordings decreased and sales plummeted. For instance, the best-selling Jimmie Rodgers record and his second release from late 1927, "Blue Yodel"/"Away Out on the Mountain" (Victor 21142), had racked up sales of 454,586 while his last Victor release (24456) in 1933 "The Cow Hand's Last Ride"/"Blue Yodel #12" sold only 1,115 copies. Those artists who were established on radio, such as Uncle Dave Macon at WSM's *Grand Ole Opry* and Bradley Kincaid at WLS, fared somewhat better economically but were hardly getting rich. Some, like Ernest Stoneman, plunged into dire poverty. Many of the older artists ceased recording altogether and found other ways to support themselves. Other new artists kept entering the field and trying, and eventually the country music business experienced a modest recovery. More modest priced records (generally thirty-five cents), typified by Victor's budget label Bluebird, the English company Decca, and the variety of labels owned by the American Record Corporation, also helped because buyers could no longer afford the seventy-five-cent discs.

WESTERN MUSIC AND SINGING COWBOYS

The biggest new success of the 1930s, Gene Autry, attained his fame and fortune in Hollywood as the star of a series of low-budget western films as the first and most acclaimed of the "singing cowboys." Prior to the mid-1930s, he had enjoyed a career as a recording artist and radio performer at the *National Barn Dance*, often recording blues material not unlike that of Jimmie Rodgers. However, his songs from motion pictures and other cowboy material helped make western music part of the genre. Cowboy songs had been around since the mid-1920s, performed by Carl Sprague and Jules Allen, among others, but the songs of Autry and his successors, such as Tex Ritter, Roy Rogers, Jimmy Wakely, and Rex Allen, gave country music a whole new dimension and image. Not all of the western music was made by individual vocalists, as some of it was performed by singing groups such as the Sons of the Pioneers.

While the singing cowboy films placed a new emphasis on western music, a parallel movement in Texas, Oklahoma, and the Southwest occurred. The "Big Band" sound had become a major force on the popular music scene, and the country version of it evolved into a musical form initially known as "hot string bands," but soon came to be called "Texas-swing" or "western swing." The style combined elements of country fiddle bands, jazz, and popular music and came to be played in the large dance halls of the Southwest region. Early examples of the fiddle bands included such groups as Prince Albert Hunt's Texas Ramblers and the East Texas Serenaders, but two individuals who really made western swing a musical style had initially been part of a flour company-sponsored outfit called the Light Crust Doughboys: Milton Brown and Bob Wills. However, the sound did not completely jell until each had their own bands—the Musical Brownies and the Texas Playboys, respectively. Brown, a vocalist, worked on radio out of Fort Worth and worked dances at a place outside of town called the Crystal Springs Dance Pavilion. Between 1934 and 1936, his Musical Brownies placed 100 numbers on Bluebird and Decca Records and would have done more had not his career ended in 1936 with his tragic death in an automobile accident. Wills, a fiddler, survived in Waco and then found true success at KVOO Tulsa and Cain's Dancing Academy while making numerous recordings for the American Record Corporation.

Since Wills kept his Texas Playboys together well into the 1950s, his sound is the best known in the field, but there were others. The more notable included Bill Boyd's Cowboy Ramblers—based at WRR Dallas—who led the Bluebird label's best-known swing band, but there were also the Tune Wranglers and Jimmie Revard's Oklahoma Playboys in San Antonio. After Brown's death, Decca's best-known group was led by former Brownie sideman Cliff Bruner, who was usually based in Beaumont, but there were other groups led by Dickie McBride, Leon Chappelear, and Bob Dunn. In addition to the Texas Playboys, the American Record Corporation's stable of swing bands also included the Light Crust Doughboys, the Hi-Flyers, Roy Newman's Boys, W. Lee O'Daniel's Hillbilly Boys, and Shelley Lee Alley's Alley-Cats. Adolf Hofner's band recorded for Bluebird, Decca, and American Record Corporation at one time or another in his long career and sometimes combined western swing with German and Bohemian music. Bob Skyles and his Skyrockets worked on both Bluebird and Decca and combined western swing with a variety of novelty sounds.

By the early 1940s, western swing had become big in California, with Wills relocating to the West Coast and groups led by Spade Cooley and Tex Williams making their mark on the music. Some swing groups flourished in the Southeast, too, such as Claude Casey's Pine State Playboys and Hank Penny's Radio Cowboys, although Penny eventually followed the others to the far West. The *National Barn Dance* at WLS Chicago had the popular group the Prairie Ramblers, composed largely of Kentuckians who incorporated elements of western swing into their sound. The Ramblers also furnished musical support for Arkansas-born Ruby Blevins, who under her stage name "Patsy Montana" became the first notable female in country music and who sang songs heavily laden with western and cowboy themes.

THE SOUTHEAST IN THE DEPRESSION YEARS

For the most part, country music in the Southeast remained closer to its original roots. String bands retained a rougher sound, such as those of J. E. and Wade Mainer (both together and seperately), who gained popularity on radio in the Carolinas and recorded for Bluebird. The American Record Corporation boasted of Roy Acuff and his Crazy Tennesseeans (soon renamed the Smoky Mountain Boys), initially based on radio in Knoxville but later based at Nashville and the *Grand Ole Opry*, which by the 1940s had become the leading country music program on the airwaves. Also attaining popularity were harmony duet groups accompanied by their own guitars or guitar and mandolin. Alton and Rabon—the Delmore Brothers—dominated the twin guitar duos, while Bill and Charlie—the Monroe Brothers—and the Blue Sky Boys (Bill and Earl Bolick) used the mandolin as lead instrument. Other brothers who made a notable impact bore such surnames as Anglin, Callahan, Dixon, and Morris. Cliff and Bill Carlisle sang both in the duet style and with their own group, retaining more than a touch of the blues-influenced Jimmie Rodgers-styled music. A few noted duets who were not brothers were the Chicago-based but Kentucky-born team of Karl Davis and Harty Taylor and West Virginia's Bill Cox and Cliff Hobbs. In Texas, Bob and Joe—the Shelton Brothers—had a sound somewhat more akin to western swing. Some brother teams gained popularity in the 1940s and 1950s, including the Bailes, the Louvin, and the Wilburn Brothers, as did the brother-in-law combination of Johnnie Wright and Jack Anglin.

By the end of the 1930s, individual vocalists with small instrumental groups that used electrically amplified instrumental backing began to emerge as a major force in country music. Electric lead guitars and steel guitars—initially used by western swing bands—augmented by fiddle became most common, partly because jukeboxes in nightclubs and bars that catered to country music fans demanded recorded music with sufficient volume that could be heard over the noise. The resulting style was termed "honky-tonk."

THE HONKY-TONK SOUND

Decca Records pioneered these sounds on disc with such individuals as Louisiana's Jimmie Davis, who had initially, like Gene Autry, come out of the Jimmie Rodgers–white blues tradition. Buddy Jones, a Davis protégé, usually recorded with western swing accompaniment and sang the type of double-entendre songs that Davis increasingly eschewed as his political star began to rise and music attained a wider audience (he eventually served two terms as governor). Alabama-born Rex Griffin made an impact as both vocalist and writer. Floyd Tillman had been a member of the Texas-swing group Leon Selph's Blue Ridge Playboys prior to embarking on a solo career that emphasized his original songs that would make him a major force by the late 1940s. Hank Thompson maintained a large enough band to qualify as western swing but also had a honky-tonk sound, maintaining a base in Texas and Oklahoma and doing most of his recording in California. However, by far the most significant exponent of the honky-tonk style was Texas-born Ernest Tubb, who emerged from a brief career as a singer in the Jimmie Rodgers tradition to become Decca's major artist during the 1940s and inspired those vocalists who would become the major stars of the pre-rock-and-roll era of country music.

The continuing influence of the radio jamborees continued to be the driving force for general audience listeners. The *Grand Ole Opry* and the *National Barn Dance*, portions of which were heard on the networks, maintained their reputations as the premier programs with such figures as Acuff and Tubb at the former and the husband-wife duo of Lulubelle and Scotty Wiseman at the latter. Others entered the field during the 1930s and 1940s. Radio station WWVA in Wheeling, West Virginia, started its *World's Original Jamboree* in January 1933. The *Jamboree* initially—like the *Opry*—featured local amateurs but soon began to attract professional and aspiring professionals, such as the Tweedy Brothers

Although he had no hit records, Grandpa Jones had one of the longest and most notable careers in country music. He is shown here on stage at the Ohio State Fair, August 1982.
Courtesy of Deanna Tribe.

fiddle band; the trio of Cap, Andy, and Flip; Hugh and Shug's Radio Pals; Grandpa Jones; and the most durable of all, Doc Williams and his Border Riders. The Border Riders, made up in part of persons from East European immigrant families, mixed mainstream hillbilly music with polkas and other sounds, which helped make them more acceptable to those not of Anglo-Celtic backgrounds. John Lair, once associated with WLS, developed the *Renfro Valley Barn Dance*, the one show of its type to actually be broadcast (after temporary homes in Cincinnati and Dayton) in 1939 from a rural setting in east-central Kentucky (via WHAS Louisville and a portion on the CBS Network). Powerful WLW in Cincinnati then started *The Boone County Jamboree*, later restyled as *The Midwestern Hayride*. Both the *Barn Dance* and *Hayride* featured some performers once associated with WLS, along with some newer talent.

WORLD WAR II

The World War II years broadened the audience for country music, partly because those who found the music appealing became more geographically dispersed and gained a degree of affluence that they had lacked during the Great Depression. The transplanted Okies and other "dust bowl" refugees finally found the opportunities that had initially eluded them in the Golden State. Bob Wills and the Texas Playboys relocated to California, and new bands, such as those led by Spade Cooley, found an audience there. Vocalists Jack Guthrie, Merle Travis, and Wesley Tuttle joined older West Coast singers, such as Stuart Hamblen, and the movie cowboys on the California scene. Many of these individuals soon signed with Capitol Records, a new firm that soon became a major force on the national scene in both the pop and hillbilly markets.

Since many soldiers were of rural and Southern backgrounds, they, too, favored country as their music of choice. According to one apocryphal story, Japanese soldiers are alleged to have taunted Americans with such insults as "to hell with Roosevelt, to hell with Babe Ruth, to hell with Roy Acuff." Ironically, in later years numerous Germans and Japanese became country music fans. The wartime shortages did curtail record manufacturing as shellac became a scarce commodity. Gasoline rationing made tours next to impossible, but country music via radio helped keep morale high among both civilian and military personnel, and songs like "There's a Star-Spangled Banner Waving Somewhere," "Smoke on the Water," "Rainbow at Midnight," and "Stars and Stripes on Iwo Jima" contributed to the culture that helped inspire victory.

The immediate aftermath of the war witnessed a resurgence of activity with new record firms and new radio barn dances arriving on the scene. Mercury Records in Chicago, King Records in Cincinnati, and M-G-M, a recording division of the Metro-Goldwyn-Mayer film studios, were just three of the more significant new record companies. New show venues included *The Big D Jamboree* from KRLD Dallas, the *Louisiana Hayride* from KWKH Shreveport, and the *Tennessee Barn Dance* from WNOX Knoxville. These locales contributed a number of vocalists and instrumentalists who went on to win wider acclaim in Nashville. Southern California boasted the *Home Town Jamboree* and *The Town Hall Party*, the latter a television program.

THE POSTWAR DECADE

The decade that followed the war saw the honky-tonk style of country music reach its height of popularity. Eddy Arnold began to vie with Tubb and Acuff as the *Opry's* top star, and by the end of the 1940s, Hank Williams, an Alabama native, moved from the *Louisiana Hayride* to join the *Opry's* ranks. Hank Snow, a transplanted Canadian, began his climb to legendary status as well. Williams, in particular, had a short and tragic career, dying en route to a personal appearance on New Year's Day of 1953, but his style and original songs earned him a status among fans that probably makes the single best-known figure in country music history. Others who came to prominence in this era included Little Jimmy Dickens, Lefty Frizzell, George Morgan, Webb Pierce, Marty Robbins, Carl Smith, and Kitty Wells, who was memorable as the first female solo vocalist to attain an enduring star status.

The 1950s were also a time of technological change. At the beginning of the decade, the ten-inch 78-rpm record still dominated. However, the smaller seven-inch 45-rpm record made the older type of disc virtually extinct by 1959. Increasingly, the twelve-inch 33-rpm disc, usually containing twelve songs (but sometimes fewer and sometimes more), became the significant factor, especially

Eddy Arnold, also known as the "Tennessee Plowboy," got his start as a hillbilly country singer. His songs later evolved into a pop country style, which helped him to have 145 songs on the *Billboard* Country charts.
Copyright © Corbis.

among adult record buyers. Attractive packaging of the long play album with multicolored photos or other intricate designs also helped to determine a record's success.

Cultural tastes change with the times, however, and country music is no different. A younger generation of rural southerners, most born during the Depression decade, not only appreciated the country music with which they grew up but also found that the sounds of the African American music known as rhythm and blues appealed to them, particularly from those musicians who music historian Arnold Shaw termed the "honkers and shouters."[2] Some of this music probably had some influence on those who performed the up-tempo "country boogie" songs that attained some popularity from the late 1940s. The boogie numbers were popularized by artists ranging from veteran performers, such as the Delmore Brothers with numbers like "Hillbilly Boogie" and "Pan American Boogie," to relative newcomers, such as Tennessee Ernie Ford with "Shot Gun Boogie" and "Blackberry Boogie." Out of this amalgam emerged a sound that would be known as "rockabilly." This music bridged a three-way gap between older country, rhythm and blues, and what was quickly becoming the dominant style in pop music, rock and roll, or, as it would simply be known by the 1970s, rock.

ROCKABILLY

An early exponent of rock and roll was a Michigan-born, Philadelphia-based singer of country-western songs named Bill Haley, who had a moderate hit in

1954 with "Rock Around the Clock," a song that reentered and remained atop the *Billboard* pop charts for eight weeks the following year. However, he was soon eclipsed by four Memphis-based southern musicians who made their initial recordings for Sun Records. Tupelo-born Elvis Presley cut his first discs in Memphis but soon moved on to RCA Victor, and with songs such as "Don't Be Cruel," "Hound Dog," and "All Shook Up," he took the entire nation (or at least the youth market portion of it) by storm. Louisianan Jerry Lee Lewis was perhaps the wildest of all with his pumping piano and songs like "Whole Lotta Shakin' Goin' On" and "Great Balls of Fire." In addition to their stylings, their free-wheeling stage antics often offended the sensibilities of the older generation and contributed to the feeling of rebelliousness that they generated. Arkansan Johnny Cash strayed less from his country roots than the others, while Carl Perkins's auto accident prevented him from attaining as much success as the others. Outside the Memphis circle, the Everly Brothers attained the most acclaim with their harmony duets of such songs as "Bye Bye Love" and "Wake Up Little Susie."

Dozens of young rockers tried to duplicate the success of Presley and his protégés, although few experienced long-term stardom. These performers included such figures as Johnny Carroll, Joe Clay, Janis Martin, Billy Lee Riley, Ronnie Self, and Andy Starr. Some, such as Cash and Conway Twitty and even Jerry Lee Lewis, eventually returned to a more country orientation and achieved legendary status. Mainstream country star Marty Robbins adapted easily to rockabilly, and even western-swing veteran Moon Mullican came up with credible rock-and-roll entries, although he was a bit beyond the age of being a teenage idol. Most major figures recorded at least a few songs with a rockabilly feel, although their songs of this type tended to become collector's items in later years rather than major hits at the time. Still, later country music continued to retain rockabilly influences. For a time, it seemed that country music of the pre-1955 variety would vanish, but eventually it bounced back, albeit in a modified form.

THE NASHVILLE SOUND

The resurgence of country music derived from what became known as the "Nashville Sound." The Nashville Sound was so called because it was developed in the recording studios of that city by such record producers as super-guitarist Chet Atkins, Owen Bradley, and Don Law. It removed some of the hard edge from the older hillbilly and honky-tonk instrumentation and made some accommodation to popular music in order to broaden the audience potential. Strings, pedal steels, drums, and occasionally even horns as well as choral back-up could be heard on recordings made in Nashville. Some of the earliest hit records that could be so labeled included "Crazy Arms" and "City Lights" by Ray Price on Columbia, "Four Walls" and "He'll Have to Go" by Jim Reeves on RCA Victor, "Alone with You" and "Hello Walls" by Faron

Young on Capitol, and "Still" by Bill Anderson on Decca. George Jones, a straight Texas honky-tonk singer—who made minor forays into rockabilly—hit his peak in 1961 but would continue to symbolize country music for some four decades despite periodic battles with alcoholism. Older stars such as Hank Snow and Ernest Tubb managed to adjust to the smoother sound, and while traditionalists viewed the newer sounds with suspicion, country music seemed more popular than ever and also began to take steps toward gaining more acceptance and recognition from the musical mainstream. A number of noted syndicated television programs produced in what was becoming known as "Music City, U.S.A.," such as those of Porter Wagoner, the Stoneman Family, Ernest Tubb, and the Wilburn Brothers, further reinforced the image of the Tennessee capital as the preeminent country music center.

Although death at age thirty in a 1963 airplane crash ended her career during the early years of the growth of the Nashville Sound, Patsy Cline's life and influence merit special attention. A native of Winchester, Virginia, Cline (born Virginia Hensley) had her first hit record in 1957 with "Walking After Midnight," but several more in the early 1960s, including "I Fall to Pieces," "Crazy," and "She's Got You," elevated her to star status. Overall, Cline had far fewer hits than Kitty Wells, but like Hank Williams, an early demise, together with those later female stars who credited her with a strong impact on their own rise to prominence, such as Dottie West and Loretta Lynn, probably helped her gain legendary status.

OTHER CENTERS

While the Nashville Sound became the dominant force in the country music mainstream, events elsewhere often made a major impact on the idiom. For instance, the southern California city of Bakersfield had become a center for such West Coast–based figures as Ferlin Husky and Tommy Collins in the mid-1950s. However, the emergence of such major stars as Wynn Stewart and especially Buck Owens and Merle Haggard as superstars of the mid- and late 1960s really put Bakersfield on the country music map. Likewise, in the early 1970s, Austin, Texas, also made a pitch for dominance, but in the final analysis, neither become a serious rival to Nashville. Branson, Missouri, with its numerous theaters featuring country music, also became a haven for many country stars, especially those who seemed a little past their prime.

THE COUNTRY MUSIC ASSOCIATION

The Country Music Association (CMA), a trade organization founded in 1958, had a great deal to do with creating the new portrait of country while dispelling the old hillbilly image. Because, with a few exceptions such as the *Grand Ole Opry*, live country music as radio entertainment largely disappeared during the 1950s, the CMA began to push for all-country-music radio stations utilizing disc jockeys who played records all day long. By the end of the 1960s, virtually every major city in the United States had at least one country radio station, and numerous other broadcast outlets featured several hours of country music on a daily or weekly basis. The CMA also began giving annual awards and opened the Country Music Hall of Fame and Museum in the section of Nashville where many of the recording studios and publishers congregated. Initial inductees into the Hall of Fame in 1961 were deceased musical legends Jimmie Rodgers and Hank Williams together with songwriter-publisher Fred Rose. In 1962, Roy Acuff, who had been the premier musical figure at the *Grand Ole Opry* during the 1940s, became the first living inductee. Former Hollywood singing cowboy Tex Ritter relocated from California to Nashville and became a key spokesman for the CMA during its formative years.

One apparent casualty of the new image created by the CMA was a tendency to ostracize and segregate the more traditional styles of music. Such was

especially true of the acoustic music that had grown out of the older string band and harmony-duet style known as bluegrass. When Bill and Charlie Monroe went their separate ways in 1938, Bill kept a band that featured acoustic instruments built around his own mandolin, a frequent lead fiddle, and rhythm provided by guitar and an upright bass. In 1945, he hired a three-finger-styled banjo player, the young North Carolinian Earl Scruggs, for the Blue Grass Boys. Their *Opry* and concert appearances together with their Columbia Recordings gave rejuvenation to the older style (termed "folk music with overdrive" by Alan Lomax[3]). During the next few years, additional bands emulated this style, giving their own distinctive touch to the music. Among the most influential were Lester Flatt, Earl Scruggs, and the Foggy Mountain Boys, who went on their own in 1948; the Stanley Brothers and the Clinch Mountain Boys; Don Reno, Red Smiley, and the Tennessee Cutups; and Jim and Jesse and the Virginia Boys. Although the major record labels dropped most of their bluegrass

Lester Flatt (left) and Earl Scruggs (right) teamed up together as one of the most successful bluegrass duos of all time. *Copyright © Corbis.*

acts—they never had many—the music flourished in spite of this, with companies such as County, Rebel, Rounder, and Sugar Hill becoming increasingly skilled at marketing their product.

BLUEGRASS

Although bluegrass music was increasingly segregated from the mainstream Nashville Sound that dominated the country radio stations, it nonetheless managed to survive. It did so partly because many fans of the folk music "revival" that engulfed many a college campus in the late 1950s and early 1960s embraced it. It also flourished as a result of the growing popular phenomenon of weekend bluegrass festivals from the mid-1960s that were initially promoted by such astute individuals as Carlton Haney and Bill Monroe himself. Since the 1970s, bluegrass festivals have sprouted up during the warmer months throughout the South, Midwest, and even the Northeast and far West. In addition to the above mentioned groups who were exponents of what would become known as "traditional" bluegrass, another form developed largely by bands in the Washington, D.C., area, such as the Country Gentlemen (led by Charlie Waller, John Duffy, and others), became known as "progressive" bluegrass and borrowed elements from urban folk music and even rock. Both types of bluegrass would thrive over the next three decades even as time took its toll on its initial practitioners, including Carter Stanley, Flatt, Reno, Smiley, and ultimately Bill Monroe himself, in 1996, passed away into history. Meanwhile, in 1985, musicians and persons connected with the business of bluegrass founded the International Bluegrass Music Association (IBMA), which by 1990 sponsored an awards program, festival, trade show, and museum in Owensboro, Kentucky. Later in the decade, all but the museum and executive offices were moved to Louisville. Bluegrass also found some outlet for airplay on some of the public stations that had limited programming of alternative and roots music because their management viewed it as less commercial than mainstream country. Ironically, one of the biggest boosts for traditional bluegrass and even old-time music came from the 2000 hit motion picture *O Brother, Where Art Thou?*, which provided younger audiences with an unexpected and well-received glimpse of the musical heritage of the rural South.

SACRED MUSIC

Sacred songs have always been a significant part of country music—with the exception of western swing, which was driven largely by the dance hall business and the jukebox trade—and gospel songs have often been among those most frequently requested by radio listeners. In the Columbia 15,000 series, religious quartets with piano accompaniment, such as Smith's Sacred Singers, have been among the best-selling discs. Much of this gospel music was an outgrowth of the nineteenth-century singing-school tradition that was promoted by the publishers of paper-cover shape-note hymnals that were common in the rural South. By the early 1900s, companies such as the James D. Vaughn Music Publishing Company of Lawrenceburg, Tennessee, began to hire quartets to promote songbook sales.

Vaughn's quartets and those of the Stamps-Baxter Company of Dallas both entered the recording studios during the 1920s. Over the next few years, other quartets, such as the Blackwood Brothers and the Speer Family, entered the field as musical professionalism merged with evangelistic zeal. By the end of World War II, Atlanta began to emerge as a center for this music, with such groups as the Homeland Harmony Quartet, the Swanee River Boys, the Statesmen Quartet with Hovie Lister, the Bill Gaither Trio, and the LeFevre Trio becoming among the most influential. The syndicated television programs *Gospel Singing Caravan* and *Gospel Singing Jubilee* brought the music into thousands of private homes.

The same trappings of musical professionalism that country music had acquired soon were manifest in the sacred field—for example, the Gospel Music Association (GMA) which was formed in 1964. Radio stations specializing in southern gospel music began to compete with other types of specialty programming on the airwaves. In 1969, the GMA instituted the "Dove Awards" to recognize achievement within its industry. Some years later, a degree of dissension led in 1995 to the formation of the Southern Gospel Music Association, a parallel organization that in 1997 started its own awards program and, in April 1999, opened a museum and Hall of Fame within the Dollywood theme park complex at Pigeon Forge, Tennessee. By the end of the century, such television programs as those associated with Bill Gaither brought numerous figures together for televised programs featuring their music, and the producer not only could buy the time to broadcast them over cable networks, but the subsequent sales of videocassettes would yield profits as well.

NEOTRADITIONAL COUNTRY

Meanwhile, country music as a commercial musical art form continued to grow and expand in popularity. Although traditionalists could complain with considerable justification that as country became more "cool" (to paraphrase a 1981 hit by songstress Barbara Mandrell), it became less country. Much of this resulted from the fact that country music tended to appeal mostly to adults, and perhaps consciously or unconsciously, country sounds often absorbed a portion of the popular music of an earlier era, just as country music in the 1920s incorporated influences from the early Tin Pan Alley and the minstrel stage. Older country fans often saw the stars of an earlier era, such as Hank Snow and Ernest Tubb, pushed aside with their records seldom receiving airplay, while newer stars, such as Ronnie Milsap or Anne Murray, seemed only marginally country but often dominated the charts. Still, unapologetic country figures like Loretta Lynn and Dolly Parton could become virtual national institutions, although the musical arrangements on their hit songs often veered in the direction of pop music.

In the early 1980s, however, something of a neotraditional trend began to develop. Ricky Skaggs, an eastern Kentucky native and onetime member of Ralph Stanley's Clinch Mountain Boys, experienced a string of hits with a combination of bluegrass and western swing accompaniment, some of them older standards from the best-known bluegrass artists of the 1950s, while others either were new or came from such older practitioners of honky-tonk country as Webb Pierce. Soon, other newer artists, including Randy Travis, Dwight Yoakum, Patty Loveless, Reba McEntire, and George Strait—all of whom but the latter two were reared in the heart of Appalachia—found success with such material. While the music of the neotraditionalists may have lacked the rough edge of a Hank Williams, it still remained unabashedly country.

The music remains in a state of flux, and the constant search for new stars has led to an industry where one usually experiences some degree of career decline after a few years in the limelight. Few seem to sustain themselves at the top for more than seven years. As recordings become ever more expensive to produce, fewer discs appear on the market. In the 1960s, a popular artist such as Bill Anderson or Porter Wagoner might have two or three vinyl albums released in a year, each bearing one of his hits as the title cut. However, by the mid-1980s, as many as four or five charted hits might appear on a single album, cassette, or compact disc. One album release a year (or even less often) became the standard. By the end of the decade, the vinyl album was rapidly facing the same fate as had befallen the 78-rpm single three decades earlier.

Be that as it may, a number of newer stars emerged at the end of the 1980s. Some such as Alan Jackson and Travis Tritt fell clearly into the neotraditional mold. Others, most notably Garth Brooks, fit more into what those in the industry termed "high-speed country-rock." Performers such as Joe Diffie and Aaron Tippin rank somewhere in the middle of these two styles. Among the new female stars, Shania Twain fits into the same category, and many critics, while conceding that

After his first eight albums sold close to 60 million copies, Garth Brooks became the most successful artist country music had ever seen.
Copyright © Corbis.

Twain surpasses many of her rivals in the glamour field, have been hard-pressed to find much evidence of country in either her vocals or her musical arrangements. Loveless and McEntire continue to rank high among the more traditional-sounding female country singers, while Martina McBride and Faith Hill are—to quote a 1960s song—"Somewhere Between."

Obviously, country music has undergone considerable change in the seventy-five years that elapsed from the time of Fiddlin' John Carson's first recording of "Little Old Log Cabin in the Lane" and Henry Whitter's "Lonesome Road Blues" to Garth Brooks's "She's Gonna Make It" and Shania Twain's "Don't Be Stupid." Even the latest from Alan Jackson or Reba McEntire bears little resemblance to the first efforts of Ernest Stoneman or Roba Stanley. The nature of record buyers and radio listeners probably exhibits more continuity. The common folk of the rural South and Midwest who bought those early discs or listened to early broadcasts probably have grandchildren and great-grandchildren who are fans of Garth Brooks and Reba McEntire but whose parents may have favored George Jones or Loretta Lynn. Many likely have only a vague awareness of the metamorphosis that has transpired over the decades.

Commenting on the cultural changes that have transformed American music, historian Russel Nye wrote "each era [meaning generation] chooses its own songs to express itself."[4] The early balladeers, fiddlers, and string band musicians who dominated the earliest country markets had to make room for and accommodate Jimmie Rodgers and the Carter Family after 1927. In the depths of the Great Depression, both had to give way to the "hot string bands" of the Southwest and the harmony duets. For a generation, hillbilly musicians found themselves dressing like Gene Autry even though cowboys or the West may have never been mentioned in their song lyrics. Electric instruments and increasingly complex sound systems took on a greater significance, and the music moved farther away from its origins, yet the society that produced the first musicians and fans—or at least the second generation—moved with it. As Bill Malone states, "Many have followed the music through the last forty years, and are as easily reconciled to Garth and Shania as they were to the stars that preceded them."[5] The tenant farmers, textile workers, and coal miners of the 1920s may have become industrial workers in the defense plants and auto workers a generation later. Their children may have gone to college and listened to the latest hits from Nashville, attended bluegrass festivals, or even abandoned country for what their urban peers termed more sophisticated music. Yet the changes occurred at a slow pace, and a high degree of continuity made them hardly noticeable to the casual fans.

The music may have changed a great deal. To the scholar, it may seem virtually unrecognizable. But to the great majority, it may not seem that different. As Malone points out, "the percentage of native born southerners who perform [and hear] country music remains remarkably high" and "the 'twang' is still there."[6] In other words, the term country remains relevant. After all, even the country is not what it once was. Most rural households now have electricity and conveniences once common only in an urban environment. Persons who may talk about preserving a rural environment often lack an awareness that the country atmosphere they want to maintain vanished a generation ago. Just as the country music of an earlier era has changed, so has its audience. Still enough remains of the old that the term remains relevant. The venerable Hank Williams is alleged to have said that "to sing like a hillbilly, you have to have lived like a hillbilly.... You had to have smelt a lot of mule manure."[7] Hank has been dead for a half century; not many of today's country musicians or even their fans have smelled much—if any—mule manure. Yet the culture created by that world of smelling "mule manure" has demonstrated remarkable persistence.

NOTES

1. LeRoy J. Davis, "The History and Growth of Country Music," *Miscellanea* 13:4 (1995), 29–32.

2. Arnold Shaw, *Honkers and Shouters: The Golden Years of Rhythm and Blues* (New York: Collier Books, 1978).

3. Alan Lomax, "Bluegrass Background: Folk Music with Overdrive," *Esquire* 52 (October 1959), 108.

4. Russel Nye, *The Unembarrassed Muse: The Popular Arts in America* (New York: Dial Press, 1970), 359.

5. Bill C. Malone, *Don't Get Above Your Raisin': Country Music and the Southern Working Class* (Urbana: University of Illinois Press, 2002), 258.

6. Ibid., 254.

7. Rufus Jarman, "Country Music Goes to Town," *Nation's Business* 41 (February 1953), 51.

2

Southeastern Dominance: The Early Years of Hillbilly Music, 1922–1941

Traditional rural musicians took the first steps toward making their music of choice a commercialized art form in 1922 and 1923, when they began playing and singing it on the radio and in the recording studios. Until then, only fiddlers who played for rural dances or competed for prizes in contests could be called semiprofessional. Blind street musicians so earned their living by necessity. Perhaps the same could be said for those who might entertain in medicine shows or to attract crowds at political rallies.

The first commercial radio station KDKA began in November 1920 in Pittsburgh, and in less than two years, country music was heard on the airwaves. Not much is known about the early radio broadcasts, but it would seem likely that WSB in Atlanta, Georgia, and WBAP in Fort Worth, Texas, were two of the first—and perhaps the first—radio stations to feature country musicians. Fiddlin' John Carson (c. 1868–1949), a mountaineer from Fannin County, had moved to the city in 1900 and played at WSB in September 1922. Carson, a middle-aged house painter and former textile-mill worker, gained a local reputation for his down-home music in the working class section of Atlanta known as "Cabbagetown." The Texas pioneer Moses J. Bonner (1847–1939), an older man who had once been a captain in the Confederate army, fiddled on WBAP on January 4, 1923. He found so much favor with listeners that the station became the first to feature a regular "barn dance" program. The first radio fiddlers were also among the first to make phonograph records. Fiddlin'

John went on to make well over 100 recordings between 1923 and 1934. Bonner made only two sides of the same disc in 1925.[1]

The honor of being the first actual country recording artist goes to another Texas fiddler who became well known for his prowess with the bow. Alexander Campbell "Eck" Robertson (1887–1975) of Amarillo had been filmed with some friends by the Fox Movietone News. Seeing this silent footage in a theater led him to think that he might have a wider commercial potential for his music. In June 1922, he went to Virginia to play at a Confederate veterans reunion. While there, he and another veteran of the "Lost Cause," Henry Gilliland, decided to visit the Victor studios and try to make a record. They journeyed to New York and auditioned for Victor. On June 30, 1922, the pair made four fiddle duet recordings, of which "Arkansas Traveler" and "Turkey in the Straw" subsequently appeared on disc. On July 1, Robertson returned to the studio and made additional recordings: two solo numbers, "Sallie Gooden" and "Ragtime Annie"; and two with piano accompaniment, the "Done Gone" reel and a medley of "Sally Johnson/Billy in the Low Ground." Two additional masters were never released. At the end of the decade, Robertson recorded again for Victor. After Eck's 1922 efforts, Victor officials showed relatively little interest in their new music until 1924 when one of their popular artists, Marion Slaughter (as Vernon Dalhart), who had some rural roots, made a couple of recordings that would become the first certified million seller in the emerging country field.[2]

ATLANTA AND NORTH GEORGIA

The real boom, such as it was, began the following year in the spring of 1923 when Ralph Peer journeyed to Atlanta to make some field recordings by local African American musicians for the newly discovered market in what had been termed "race music." The local furniture dealer—and regional distributor—Polk Brockman wanted Peer to cut some discs by the aforementioned John Carson. The latter had a following for local entertaining among working-class folk in Atlanta and had made numerous appearances in fiddling contests. Brockman believed that recordings by Carson would be purchased by the same people who enjoyed his somewhat rough fiddle and vocal style. Peer initially (on June 14 or June 19) cut masters for two songs, "The Little Old Log Cabin in the Lane," an 1870 sentimental song by Will S. Hays, and a traditional tune with some lyrics, "The Old Hen Cackled and the Rooster's Going to Crow." Whether a surprise or a calculated risk, the Carson recording sold well, and Fiddlin' John went back to the studio, this time to New York, to make a dozen more numbers. A second release, "You Will Never Miss Your Mother Until She's Gone" and "Papa's Billy Goat," did equally well and Carson's career as a professional entertainer soon extended beyond Atlanta and its environs. Fiddlin' John was not a star in any modern sense of the word—far from it. Yet he did pursue professionalism to a degree and played shows over North Georgia and adjacent states in the South and through central Appalachia.

Fiddlin' John painted his name on his automobile identifying himself as an OKeh "record artist" and sometimes appeared with a larger band called the Virginia Reelers and sometimes with his attractive daughter Rosa Lee Carson, who became known as "Moonshine Kate." One of his cohorts, Earl Johnson (1886–1965), even carved out a recording career of his own. Through 1931, Fiddlin' John had recorded some 140 songs and tunes for OKeh, and in 1934, he and Kate did another eighteen numbers on Victor's budget label Bluebird. As he grew older, Carson became increasingly involved with the Georgia populist Democrat politician Eugene Talmadge, entertaining on behalf of his campaign and subsequently holding such jobs as elevator operator at the state capital and doorkeeper at legislative sessions. He continued this with Eugene's son Herman Talmadge, who also became governor.[3]

The honor of being the first woman to make a solo country recording, however, goes to Roba Stanley (1910–1986), a teenager who did a few numbers for OKeh in 1925. Her most memorable song, "Single Life," took an assertive point of view, with the memorable line "I am single and no man's wife, and no man can control me." Ironically, Stanley married the next year and terminated her musical career at her husband's request, only to be rediscovered in old age and become a symbolic figure.[4]

Given the success that OKeh experienced with Fiddlin' John Carson and to lesser degrees with Earl Johnson and the blind newsboy-songwriter Andrew Jenkins, it stands to reason that other record companies would seek talent in that portion of Georgia. Columbia had especially good fortune in discovering a blind street singer named Riley Puckett (1894–1946), who would become its principal vocalist on the emerging country music scene. It also found something of a rival to Carson in the personage of James Gideon "Gid" Tanner (1885–1960), a chicken farmer from rural Dacula. Tanner's fiddle skills may have been limited, but combined with a younger master of the bow named Clayton McMichen (1900–1970), Riley Puckett, and a scattering of other musicians, such as fiddlers Lowe Stokes (1898–1983) and Bert Layne, and banjoist Fate Norris, they formed a popular and charismatic string band. Gid Tanner and the Skillet Lickers ranked among Columbia's most popular rural groups, and Puckett continued to record solo and duet material as well. Tanner and Puckett recorded from 1924 as a team, but that ended when the Skillet Lickers came together as a team in 1926. Their repertoire included fiddle breakdowns, a variety of songs, and a series of comedy skits interspersed with short musical interludes that came to be known as "rural drama." The best known of these latter efforts was the "Corn Licker Still in Georgia," a series that ran to fourteen sides. Nearly as popular was "A Fiddler's Convention in Georgia," which extended to four. The others consisted of two each and included titles that also offered vignettes of rural life as typified by "Possum Hunt on Stump House Mountain," "Hog Killing Day," and "A Bee Hunt on Hell-for-Sartin Creek." The rural dramas had a precedent that probably went back to the comic monologues and occasional skits by Cal Stewart, with his "Down East" or rural New England characters—chiefly Uncle Josh—from the fictional Vermont community of Punkin Centre that had been popular on record in the early 1900s. However, the rural dramas proved to be among the best-selling Skillet Licker discs and soon spawned imitators on other labels, including some by the Stoneman group on Victor that bore such titles as "Possum Trot School Exhibition" and "Old Time Corn Shuckin'."

In all, the Skillet Lickers recorded eighty-eight numbers on Columbia, plus another thirty-six sides of rural dramas. Their first fourteen single releases sold over a million discs for the company, with their coupling of "Bully of the Town"/"Pass Around the Bottle" totaling sales of 207,149, while "Hand Me Down My Walking Cane"/"Watermelon on the Vine" did almost as well with 181,675. In addition, each member of the group recorded, both by themselves and in combination with others inside and outside the regular band members, with Puckett having nearly 200 sides either by himself or with such duet partners as Tanner, McMichen, or Hugh Cross.

In 1934, the Skillet Lickers regrouped with Gideon Tanner, his son Gordon Tanner, Puckett, and mandolin picker Ted Hawkins comprising the band and did twenty numbers for Bluebird and four skit sides. Tanner and Puckett did a few more numbers together. Riley Puckett continued to make solo numbers until 1941, mostly for Bluebird, but also did twelve songs for Decca in 1937. McMichen formed a new group called the Georgia Wildcats and did numerous numbers in more of a swing vein as well as traditional fiddle tunes. Both Puckett and McMichen made a considerable impact on country music's first generation in addition to the work they accomplished with the Skillet Lickers.[5]

Country music continued as a cultural phemomenon in the Atlanta area throughout the Depression years with radio programs such as *The Crossroads Follies* in the 1930s and the *WSB Barn Dance* in the 1940s. Others programs would flourish on other stations such as WGNT. The city also continued as a significant recording locale with Columbia, Victor, and Brunswick/Vocalion holding periodic sessions there. Some of the musicians hailed from the local region, including Earl Johnson, Herschel Brown, and John Dilleshaw, but there were also others from other subregions, such as the Deep South to the west and the Appalachian and Piedmont areas to the north. In fact, most of the major figures in the first two decades of country music growth, including the Carter family, Jimmie Rodgers, Ernest Stoneman, Mainer's Mountaineers, and the Delmore Brothers, made at least some of their recordings in the Peach State metropolis. Not until the 1950s would Atlanta and North Georgia decline as a music center. The area continued producing significant musicians, but they would go to Nashville and elsewhere to achieve their mark in the business.[6]

APPALACHIA AND THE PIEDMONT

Another fertile region for southern music could be found in the highland region and the adjacent Piedmont, where numerous mountain folk had migrated to work in the textile mills. John Carson shared some of the honors as the OKeh recording pioneer with Henry Whitter (1892–1941), a Fries, Virginia, textile worker who in March 1923 journeyed to New York on his own to attempt to place his music on disc. The General Phonograph Company gave him an audition but demonstrated no interest in him until after the first Carson release. At this point, he was recalled to the studio, and on December 10, 1923, he made several recordings beginning with "Lonesome Road Blues"/"Wreck on the Southern Old 97," the latter a ballad about a 1903 railroad accident that had taken place near Danville, Virginia. Subsequent covers of the train wreck song—particularly the one on Victor by Vernon Dalhart—would generate considerable controversy over the authorship of the song lyrics and result in litigation.

Whitter sang with accompaniment provided by his own guitar and harmonica. Most critics viewed Whitter's music as mediocre in quality, with the exception of his harmonica solos, but he continued to make recordings. In 1927, he formed a partnership with G. B. Grayson (1887–1930), a virtually blind fiddler and ballad singer from Laurel Bloomery, Tennessee, and the pair recorded a number of old ballads, chiefly for Victor but a few for Gennett, that have been rated as among the best ever made. These included such traditional murder ballads as "Ommie Wise," "Rose Conley," "Tom Dooley," and "Banks of the Ohio" (as "I'll Never Be Yours"); British ballads such as "I've Always Been A Rambler" and "Handsome Molly"; temperance songs typified by "I Saw a Man at the Close of Day" and "Don't Go Out Tonight My Darling"; and even original fiddle tunes like "Going Down the Lee Highway" ("Lee Highway Blues") and "Train 45." Grayson's death in an unusually bizarre truck accident in 1930 ended his career, and Whitter's career faded thereafter.[7]

A third significant figure, Ernest Stoneman (1893–1968), recorded for OKeh beginning in 1924. However, his most significant efforts came on other labels, such as Victor, Gennett, and Edison. Stoneman, a carpenter by trade, hailed from Galax, Virginia (near Henry Whitter's home in Fries), and journeyed to New York because he thought that he could sing better than Whitter. Stoneman met with Peer, and his second recording of "The Titanic," a ballad about the 1912 ship disaster accompanied by his own autoharp and harmonica, struck a favorable chord with listeners, and he had additional sessions with OKeh. When Peer transferred to Victor in 1926, Stoneman seems to have gone along, although he still cut discs for OKeh through mid-1927. As string bands with fiddle, banjo, and guitar became more common, Stoneman added others to his entourage, such as Kahle Brewer, Eck Dunford, Bolin Frost, and his cousin George Stoneman, appearing under such collective names as the Dixie Mountaineers and the Blue Ridge Corn Shuckers. The Galax area produced some of the more remarkable talents in traditional Anglo-American music, and that Blue Ridge community

Ernest Stoneman (seated, with guitar) banded together with fellow guitarists, fiddlers, and banjo players to form the Dixie Mountaineers.
Courtesy of the author.

eventually became the site of the most significant Fiddler's Convention in America. Many of Stoneman's recordings tended to be covers of songs recorded by other artists, but some such as "The Fate of Talmadge Osborne" and "The Old Hickory Cane" were virtually unique to his repertoire. Stoneman's career stalled from 1929, and once the Great Depression hit, he and his large family plunged into deep poverty, living mostly in the Washington, D.C., area. However, in the 1950s, his career began to resurge, and with the help of his children, he staged a remarkable comeback that ended with his death in 1968.[8]

Like Ernest Stoneman, the band that named the music, the Hill Billies, started on OKeh but soon moved to another label. This group had its origins with a singer-pianist and organizer named Al Hopkins (1889–1932), a native of Watauga County, North Carolina, who had some experience with both the traditional music of the mountains and more contemporary popular music picked up from a residence of several years in Washington, D.C. In 1924,

Hopkins moved to Galax, Virginia, to help a relative run a medical clinic. He soon struck up friendships with a local barber and fiddler named Elvis "Tony" Alderman (1900–1983) and an old-time banjo picker, John Rector, who had recently made a trip to the recording studios with Henry Whitter. Forming a band with Hopkin's brother Joe on guitar, the four believed they could do better than Whitter's Virginia Breakdowners and soon set off for the OKeh offices to make their point. On January 15, 1925, they cut six sides—instrumentals with some vocal refrains—including tunes that became standard: "Old Joe Clark," "Cripple Creek," and "Sally Ann." When Ralph Peer inquired as to how they should be billed, Hopkins or someone else suggested that as they were just a bunch of hillbillies from the Blue Ridge, they should be called the "Hill Billies." Their later recordings, from April 1926 through 1928, bore the credit "Hill Billies" on the Vocalion label and "Al Hopkins & His Buckle Busters" on Brunswick. Personnel varied on the recordings, but usually the Hopkins boys (there were three) and Alderman were key figures along with Tennessee fiddler Charlie Bowman (1889–1962) and banjoist Jack Reedy (c. 1900–1940). Unlike some of the other early artists, the Hill Billies made some radio appearances on stations in New York and Washington and also toured on the vaudeville circuits. Fiddle band fare usually with vocal refrains dominated their repertoire, which eventually numbered about seventy sides. Although they stopped recording after December 1928, they continued as a working band until Hopkins died in an automobile wreck in the latter part of 1932, and the group soon dissolved without his leadership.[9]

Columbia found other early-day musicians in the highland and Piedmont areas of North Carolina. In 1924, it recorded a few sides by the female fiddle-banjo duo of Samantha Bumgarner (d. 1960) and Eva Davis and more in two sessions by a blind musician named Ernest Thompson (1892–1961), who had a high-pitched vocal style and played several instruments. However, the real discovery in the Carolinas appeared in the studio in mid-1925. A string band trio that styled themselves the North Carolina Ramblers proved to be the only real rival of the Skillet Lickers and even then could not match them in record sales. Unlike the freewheeling undisciplined sound perfected by the Georgians, the North Carolina Ramblers had a tightly knit sound that featured a single fiddle lead and rhythm support by banjo and guitar. The Ramblers hailed from the cotton mill area around Spray and Eden, North Carolina, and were led by Charlie Poole (1892–1931), a hard-drinking banjo picker who admired the classic banjo styles of Fred VanEps and Vess Ossman, both influential turn-of-the-century vaudeville and stage performers. Poole also did most of the singing. The original guitar player, Norman Woodlieff, was replaced by Roy Harvey (1892–1958) of Beckley, West Virginia, who also recorded for Brunswick, Paramount, and Gennett with his own band of North Carolina Ramblers. The fiddle work was ably handled initially by Poole's brother-in-law, Posey Rorer, and then by another West Virginia native, Lonnie Austin. Odell Smith played fiddle on their last two Columbia sessions in 1930. The first Columbia release,

"Don't Let Your Deal Go Down Blues"/"Can I Sleep in Your Barn Tonight, Mister," proved to be one the best sellers in Columbia's Old Familiar Tunes Series and racked up sales of just over 102,000 copies. The second release, "I'm the Man That Rode the Mule 'Round the World"/"The Girl I Left in Sunny Tennessee," sold 65,500 copies. Two releases from 1926 exceeded the latter number, with respective sales of 81,000 and 76,000. However, as more North Carolina Rambler records came on the market, sales slacked off somewhat as record buyers had a wider variety of their discs from which to choose. Generally speaking, numbers with singing sold more than did purely instrumental tunes, a fact that characterized Skillet Licker sales as well.

Like Ernest Stoneman and the Skillet Lickers, the Great Depression proved harmful to the career of the North Carolina Ramblers. While Stoneman turned back toward carpentry and other labors to support his large family and the Skillet Lickers went their separate ways, Poole reacted by increasing his alcohol consumption, a circumstance that led to his early death at age thirty-nine on May 21, 1931. Roy Harvey made a few more recordings that sold poorly in spite of their high quality, and he eventually returned to railroading. The others drifted into other occupations.[10]

Another early recording artist, Kelly Harrell (1889–1942), ranked as one of the best old-time ballad singers. Hailing from the same general area as Whitter and Stoneman and a textile mill worker by trade, Harrell worked in the mills at Fries and later moved to Fieldale, near Martinsville. He did four sides for Victor on January 7, 1925, but returned the following year and redid them as recording technology had improved during the interim. Harrell's early sessions for Victor used studio musicians for backup, since he played no instrument himself, so when he recorded eight songs for OKeh that August, Henry Whitter supplied the music. Beginning in 1927, he brought local musicians to the studios, including North Carolina Rambler fiddler Posey Rorer, and they recorded as the Virginia String Band. With more familiar support, the Virginia balladeer reached his zenith on such murder ballads as "Henry Clay Beattie" and "Charles Giteau," old love songs typified by "Shadow of the Pine" and "I Love My Sweetheart the Best," such songs of understated humor as "My Wife, She Has Gone and Left Me" and "My Name Is John Johanna," and the sacred duets with Henry Norton on tenor vocal "Row Us over the Tide" and "I Have No Loving Mother Now." A final trip to the studio in 1929 yielded four more songs, including another humor classic, "The Henpecked Man," and the vision of a dying child, "I Heard Somebody Call My Name" (more commonly known as "Little Bessie"). Like many other early day musicians, the Great Depression brought an end to Harrell's recording career, but he continued to work in the Fieldale mills until his death.[11]

Some of the old-time recording artists of note did not fit into convenient-to-classify categories. For instance, the Carolina Tar Heels did not use a fiddle but still rank as a string band of sorts. Banjo player Doc Walsh (1901–1967) was the constant member of this group, which also included some combination of

Clarence Ashley (1895–1967), Garley Foster (1905–1968), and Gwen Foster. A harmonica usually figured heavily in their sound, and many of their novelty songs on Victor had a blues flavor. Ashley and Walsh made some solo recordings as well.[12]

As other record companies sought rural talent for recording purposes, they explored other portions of the mountain South. The Aeolian Company that owned the Vocalion label found talent in the state of Tennessee with the help of management from the Sterchi Brothers Furniture Company, in the persons of a blind street singer, an aging traditional fiddler, and a banjo-picking vocalist much influenced by the nineteenth-century minstrel show tradition. The first two—Blind George Reneau (1901–1933) from Knoxville and Uncle Am (for Ambrose) Stuart from Morristown—had relatively short careers. Stuart, who was in fact already seventy-three, passed away shortly after his only recording session. Reneau made several trips to the studios, but in fact, at least some of the vocals billed under "the Blind Musician of the Smoky Mountains" were actually by pop vocalist Gene Austin, and Reneau played only guitar and harmonica.[13]

Columbia, OKeh, Victor, and Vocalion were all New York-based firms. Smaller but nonetheless significant businesses based in the Midwest also engaged in recording activity. The most important of these, Gennett, the recording division of the Starr Piano Company, was based in Richmond, Indiana. Early talent for this company hailed from the Cumberland and Allegheny Plateau regions of the Kentucky hill country and to a lesser degree from West Virginia. The first to cut discs from the Bluegrass State, William B. Houchins (1884–1955), a Kentucky migrant to Ohio, recorded a number of fiddle tunes with piano rhythm in Gennett's Richmond studios as early as September 22, 1922. Harry and Charles Tweedy, sons of a country doctor, from near Wheeling, West Virginia, also did fiddle tunes with piano as early as June 14, 1924. Little is known of Houchins, but the Tweedys embarked on a brand of primitive professionalism by bolting a piano to the back of a flatbed truck and entertaining at fairs, carnivals, and other gatherings throughout West Virginia and Ohio and passing the hat amongst the crowd to earn money. Starr donated Charles's piano, which they so advertised, and Harry fiddled, sometimes using such things as a large piece of wood carved in the shape of a banana and painted yellow or a large wooden spoon for a bow. On some of their later sessions, a third brother, George, joined to play second fiddle. On December 16, 1924, in its Cincinnati studio, Gennett recorded the first country vocalist from West Virginia, a former National Guardsman named David Miller (1893–1959), who lost his eyesight and was billed as "The Blind Soldier." Like Puckett and Reneau, Miller usually earned his living as a street singer in Huntington. Although the Tweedys and Miller recorded several sessions and did programs on radio, neither ever had the impact or success that the better known artists on the New York–based labels experienced.[14]

The real find for Gennett was a Madison County, Kentucky, fiddler named Phil "Doc" Roberts (1897–1978) and a clique of musicians who accompanied him to the studios. A local would-be talent scout named Dennis Taylor conceived the idea of transporting local musicians to Indiana and recording them, usually under the name Taylor's Kentucky Boys. Roberts soon found that Taylor enjoyed all the profits from such arrangements and was really not necessary. Roberts had several associates: Edgar Boaz, Ted Chestnut, Welby Toomey, Green Bailey, Roy Hobbs, and Dick Parman, among them. However, his major partners were his own son, James Roberts (b. 1918), and a singer-guitarist from nearby Estill County named Asa Martin (1900–1979). Their recordings were divided between traditional—and often unusual—fiddle tunes and vocal numbers usually featuring James and Asa in duet. On the vocal numbers, Doc played mandolin. After Gennett became less active, the threesome moved on to the reorganized American Record Corporation and recorded more numbers in 1933 and 1934. Since Gennett recordings were leased to the Sears, Roebuck and Company for use on a variety of labels bearing names like Silvertone, Supertone, Challenge, and, later, Conquerer, these records usually sold better than those on Gennett and its budget label, Champion. While their sales could seldom equal those of the more mainstream labels like Victor and Columbia, the Martin–Roberts aggregation nonetheless managed to preserve a sizable amount of good music on disc.[15]

One significant pair from Huntington, West Virginia, Frank Welling (1898–1957) and John McGhee (1882–1945), had a style that may have been a little too sophisticated for country purists. Nonetheless, much of their material was tradition rooted, except for some of the church hymns. Not confining themselves exclusively to Starr-related labels, they also did sessions for Brunswick-Vocalion, Paramount, and the American Record Corporation. Welling helped to popularize both the Hawaiian guitar and the sentimental recitation in country music. After their recording career ended in 1933, Welling moved on to Charleston for a lengthy stint as an announcer and occasional performer at WCHS radio where he also created a comic alter ego known as "Uncle Si."[16]

Welling and McGhee also made numerous recordings for Paramount, a subdivision of the Wisconsin Chair Company, based in Port Washington, Wisconsin (near Chicago). Paramount had much success with their recordings of African American music, particularly with blues and gospel items. Paramount's hillbilly series, which ran from 1927 to 1932, left a great deal to be desired, but over a period of years, it had over 300 discs released. Many of its more significant artists also cut masters for Gennett. Many of the musicians on its label came from the upper South but did include a string band probably from West Virginia called the Fruit Jar Guzzlers and the eastern Kentucky balladeer Emry Arthur, who first recorded "I Am a Man of Constant Sorrow." Paramount had a subsidiary label called Broadway, which seems to have been marketed through the mail-order firm of Montgomery Ward.[17]

Among other Appalachian musical figures, the Monticello, Kentucky, team of Richard Burnett (1883–1977) and Leonard Rutherford (c. 1900–c. 1954) could be counted among the more notable. Burnett lost his eyesight at age twenty-four and, like Miller, Puckett, and Reneau, turned to music for survival. He became adept on fiddle, banjo, and guitar and had a fine singing voice. He also composed songs that included the now famous "I Am a Man of Constant Sorrow," which he termed "Farewell Song," but never actually recorded it (Emry Arthur did). In 1914, he met a boy fiddler named Leonard Rutherford who became his guide and protégé. The two developed a highly proficient if somewhat archaic style. After some years of plying a trade as street singers in the mountain towns of Kentucky and West Virginia, they met a record retailer who arranged for them to go to Atlanta and record six numbers, including "Lost John," for Columbia in November 1926. The following year, they returned to make eight more numbers, including the old ballad "Willie Moore" and what some consider their masterpiece, "Ladies on the Steamboat." The two later recorded for Gennett and with other partners before drifting back into obscurity after 1930. Collectors found Burnett still very much alive and still residing in Monticello in the early 1970s, but old age and death soon caught up with him.[18]

Eastern Kentucky produced another superb old-time musician in Buell Kazee (1900–1976), a native of Magoffin County, who had gained a college education and eventually spent some thirty-nine years as a Baptist minister. However, in his youth, the young mountaineer learned to pick the banjo and sing the old ballads. After high school, he went to Georgetown College in central Kentucky and studied for the ministry. Kazee also had some formal music training, but when he went to record for Brunswick in their New York studios in April 1927, he was disappointed that they wanted not his "good voice" or trained voice, but his "folk" voice. Nonetheless, he went back to New York again the following year and to Chicago in 1929, placing some fifty-eight sides on disc, fifty-two of which were actually released. Many of Kazee's songs were traditional ballads, such as "The Wagoner's Lad," "The Butcher's Boy," and "The Little Mohee," but they also included composed songs from earlier generations, such as "The Faded Coat of Blue," "Snow Deer," and sacred numbers from the Vaughn songbooks. When Brunswick went under during the Great Depression, Kazee went into the ministry full-time as he pastored churches in Morehead and Lexington. In his later years, folklorists rediscovered him, and Kazee recorded again.[19]

Another unusual early-day artist, Frank Hutchison (1897–1945), billed by OKeh Records as the "Pride of West Virginia," ranks among the early practitioners of "White Blues." A native of Raleigh County but a resident of Logan, Hutchison's music demonstrated a considerable degree of African American influence, which he apparently learned from black railroad laborers during his youth. He began recording in 1926, making such numbers as "Worried Blues," "Train That Carried the Girl from Town," and "Stackalee." However, his best-known song, "Coney Isle," resurfaced in 1960 with only a few words changed as "Alabam," a major hit for country singer Cowboy Copas. By that time, Hutchison was long dead. Like others, he recorded no more after 1929 and drifted into obscurity dying in Dayton, Ohio, toward the end of World War II, virtually forgotten by an industry he had helped to create.[20]

An uncle-nephew duo, Clark (1896–1975) and Luches Kessinger (1906–1944), from St. Albans, West Virginia, billed as the Kessinger Brothers, first recorded at field sessions in Ashland, Kentucky, in February 1928. Over the next two-and-a-half years, the Kessingers placed seventy numbers on disc, all of them fiddle tunes of excellent quality, although a few of the earlier ones had square dance calls on them. The bankruptcy of Brunswick Records ended the Kessingers career on disc, although Clark would be rediscovered in the early 1960s and rejuvenated some of his fame.[21]

Although country music was a growing part of the record market throughout 1926, some scholars and local boosters have looked for a "big bang." Not satisfied with the early and evolving development of Atlanta as a focal point for early recording, they have concentrated their attention on Bristol, Tennessee, as a key locale. This theory developed because the sessions held there in late July and early August 1927 resulted in the first recordings of the two real superstars of the decade. Although most dedicated scholars know better, the emphasis on Bristol is based on the first recordings by the legendary Carter Family and the Mississippi Blue Yodeler Jimmie Rodgers. Others recorded there, too, including Henry Whitter and especially an entourage led by Ernest Stoneman, both being seasoned veterans of the city studios. In addition to Atlanta, record companies held recording sessions in such locales as Asheville, North Carolina, and Dallas, Texas, to find regional talent and would later hold them in other cities scattered across the South. However, according to oral tradition among his children, Ernest Stoneman convinced Ralph Peer that Bristol would be an excellent place for recording because many back-country musicians could not be persuaded to go to such faraway spots as Atlanta, New York, and Camden, New Jersey. However, they would come to a smaller regional city such as Bristol, which straddled the Tennessee–Virginia border in central Appalachia. Stoneman brought some new musicians from the Galax area, including the droll singer-raconteur Uncle Eck Dunford, Walter Mooney, Tom Leonard, George Stoneman, Edna and Kahle Brewer, and Irma Frost. All told, Stoneman groups recorded sixteen masters and Henry Whitter added two harmonica pieces. Many new individuals and bands did come to the sessions, including the West Virginia balladeer Blind Alfred Reed; East Tennessee singers the Johnson Brothers (Charles and Paul); a powerful sacred singer from Kentucky, Alfred G. Karnes; Ernest Phipps and his Holiness Quartet; the Shelor Family; the Tenneva Ramblers; and another harmonica player, El Watson. However, those most remembered are the Carters and Rodgers.[22]

Of the emerging stars, the Carters, who lived in Scott County, Virginia, must have made the greater impression at the time because Peer took six numbers from them. A. P. Carter (1891–1960), his wife Sara (1898–1979), and sister-in-law Maybelle (1909–1978) made up this ensemble. Sara sang and played autoharp, Maybelle sang and played guitar, and A. P. chimed in on occasional vocals. A. P. and Sara had been married for a dozen years, but the Carters had come together as a threesome only a year before when Maybelle had married A. P.'s brother Ezra. With guitar lead, two female vocalists, and an emphasis on song lyrics, the Carters had something a bit different to offer listeners who had become accustomed to fiddle bands, solo vocalists with self-accompaniment on guitar and harmonica, or spirited fiddlers. Although some of their songs, like "Bury Me Under the Weeping Willow," had been recorded before, others, like "The Storms Are on the Ocean," "Poor Orphan Child," "Little Log Cabin By the Sea," and Sara's vocal on "Single Girl, Married Girl," were new to listeners. The only prior version of "The Wandering Boy" had yet to be released. Small wonder that the Carters were called back by Peer to record again, cutting a dozen more numbers the following May. With Peer venturing into music publishing, the promise of new material to copyright (even if some of it was old forgotten material that A. P. had picked up in oral tradition) made the Virginia threesome even more attractive. Only fragmentary information is available on their record sales, but their coupling of "Wildwood Flower"/"Forsaken Love" sold somewhat over 120,000 copies. Over the next seven years, Victor would collect a total of 132 numbers from this threesome, including such classics as "Keep On the Sunny Side," "Foggy Mountain Top," "Homestead on the Farm," "Jimmie Brown, the Newsboy," "My Clinch Mountain Home," and numerous others that made the Carter family so significant in country music annals.

After leaving Victor in 1934, the Carters continued making records, although in 1932, Sara and A. P. separated and eventually divorced. They had sessions for the American Record Corporation in 1935 and again in 1940. In between, they cut sixty numbers for Decca (1936–1938) and went back to Victor in 1941 for their final efforts, which appeared on the Bluebird label. They also journeyed to Texas over the winters of 1938–1939 and 1939–1940, where they did radio programs on the powerful Mexican border stations and made numerous transcriptions. By that time, some of their children were also in the group. Sara remarried during their stay in Texas and eventually moved to California. The three original Carters did their last live radio work in 1943 at WBT Charlotte. After that, all except Maybelle and her daughters retired from music, but their musical legacy still looms large.[23]

At radio station WLS in Chicago, a key country music showcase called the *National Barn Dance* began in 1924. Many of its early artists came from the upper South—such as Chubby Parker—and its few recordings appeared on Gennett-related Sears-Roebuck labels. But the first real star at WLS, the "Kentucky Mountain Boy" Bradley Kincaid (1895–1989), constituted its first real star. Kincaid was a native of Garrod County, Kentucky and had been an illiterate mountaineer until late adolescence when he got belated schooling at Berea Academy. He then secured a part-time position with the YMCA in Chicago that allowed him to attend college there. Starting out as a part-time performer at WLS with his folk songs, he became so popular that he allegedly had to sing "Barbara Allen" every Saturday night for four years. Of course he sang other songs, too, and he became the first country artist to cash in on mail-order songbooks through his programs. Kincaid always sang in a plain and unadorned but clear vocal style that reflected his settlement school and Berea background. And in spite of his popularity, he did not inject a great deal of emotion or personality into his performance. After finishing college in 1928, he remained at WLS for another year and then moved on to WLW in Cincinnati in 1929 and to KDKA Pittsburgh in 1931. He would play fairs and theaters in the immediate vicinity of the stations where he worked, moving on to a new locale after about eighteen months. He also published new editions of his songbooks. Kincaid's later work took him eastward to WGZ Boston, WGY Schenectady, WEAF New York and the NBC Network, WTIC Hartford, and WHAM Rochester. Initially working by himself, he added a young Grandpa Jones and Bashful Harmonica Joe Troyan to his act. He came back to Cincinnati in the early 1940s and finally worked at WSM Nashville and the *Grand Ole Opry* from 1944 to 1949. He came to WWSO Springfield, Ohio, in 1949, took over ownership of the station, and also operated a music store in that city in later years. Meanwhile, he continued to record for Brunswick in 1930, for Bluebird in 1933 and 1934, for Decca in 1934 and 1935, and for Bullet and Majestic in the 1940s and made his last commercial recordings for Capitol in 1950. While his records obviously sold, radio and songbooks were always his main forte. In retirement, he made a few appearances and recorded a series of albums for the collector label Bluebonnet, still singing in the simple style that had carried him through a quarter century of radio stardom.[24]

After Kincaid, other musicians came and went from the *National Barn Dance*, but by the mid-1930s, the most popular act on the program was an Appalachian North Carolina duo who retained their mountain image and probably still rank as the premier husband-wife team in country music history, Lulubelle and Scotty. The latter—Scott Wiseman (1909–1981)—had attended college at Fairmont State in West Virginia and worked on local station WMMN until graduating in 1933 and coming to WLS. Initially known as "Skyland Scotty," he had made some recordings prior to meeting Myrtle Eleanor Cooper (1913–1999). John Lair, director of the program, had given her the nickname "Lulubelle" and paired her as the mountaineer girlfriend of Red "Burrhead" Foley. This stage adaption of "Lulubelle and Burrhead" was short lived as she and Scotty soon became a team, marrying on December 13, 1934. From January 1935 until they retired in 1958, they were among the most popular acts on the program, except for an eighteen-month stint when they went to WLW Cincinnati in the early 1940s. They also appeared in several motion pictures, among them *Swing Your Partner* for Republic. While they waxed some sixty-four songs for the American Record Corporation, Vogue, and Mercury during their radio days, they never really had what could be termed a major hit, although Scotty's original song "Have I Told You Lately That I Love You" became a major hit for other artists.[25]

The end of the 1930s brought more change and stardom for another mountain musician. Roy Acuff (1903–1992), the man most associated with making WSM and the *Grand Ole Opry* a major country center in later years, joined the program in March 1938, ironically as a replacement for the suspended Fiddlin' Arthur Smith. An East Tennessee native, Acuff had been on radio at WNOX Knoxville for some time and had been recording rather frequently for the American Record Corporation since 1936. With his band the Crazy Tennesseans, soon renamed the Smoky Mountain Boys, Acuff became the dominant figure on the Nashville program and reached his zenith of popularity during World War II. He eventually became known as the "King of Country Music." Most of his songs had a fiddle and resonator guitar prominent in their accompaniment and favored what could best be described as a mountain sound. His best-known hit in the early years was a sacred lyric of holiness or pentecostal origins, "The Great Speckled Bird," which

Roy Acuff, known to most as the "King of Country Music," was honored in 2003 by being one of the few country singers to have his picture on postage stamps. *Courtesy of Photofest.*

was inspired by a vague phrase from the Old Testament Book of Jeremiah. He soon added more, such as "The Precious Jewel," "Wreck on the Highway," "Come Back Little Pal," and a number of train songs, including "Wabash Cannonball," "Night Train to Memphis," "Freight Train Blues," and "Tennessee Central No. 9."[26]

Much of Acuff's rise to prominence derived from his being the featured act on that half-hour portion of the *Opry* that was broadcast over the NBC radio network beginning in October 1939. This additional exposure soon prompted Republic Pictures to make a movie titled *Grand Ole Opry*. Although the real stars of the film were the old vaudeville act the Weaver Brothers and Elviry, Roy Acuff had the opportunity to sing a few songs, Uncle Dave Macon got to perform one of his numbers and do his banjo tricks, and George D. Hay also had a role. Although WSM was already a powerful station, the network and movie exposure (or at least Hollywood's view of it) gave more people the opportunity to hear and see the program that in the immediate postwar years would become the dominant country music radio outlet.[27]

Through the 1930s, harmony duets often performed by brothers played a prominent role in country music, and many of these groups came from the Highland and Piedmont areas. For instance, in 1934, the American Record

Corporation signed the Callahan Brothers. Homer (1912–2001) and Walter Callahan (1910–1971) came from the Asheville, North Carolina, area and had a few original songs to contribute to the genre, such as "Curly Headed Baby" and "Little Poplar Log House." The Callahans usually had two guitars for instrumentation, although they sometimes added a mandolin as well (usually played by a third person, although Bill could play it after a fashion). Not quite as musically proficient as their rival artists on Victor's Bluebird label, the Callahans also forged out a career in radio for themselves in such locales as Asheville and Louisville before eventually finding a permanent home in Texas (usually Dallas) where they took the first names of "Bill" and "Joe." In 1941, the Callahans shifted to Decca and back to Columbia for a final session in 1951. In between, they continued in radio and made a motion picture, *Springtime in Texas*, with singing cowboy Jimmy Wakely in 1945. After Walter retired from music, Homer continued for many years as a comedian.[28]

If the Callahans were the first notable Appalachian duet, the Blue Sky Boys, whose names were Bill (b. 1917) and Earl Bolick (1919–1998), exhibited the softest, smoothest, and most technically proficient vocal harmonies. Natives of Hickory, North Carolina, the Bolicks received the name "Blue Sky Boys" from Bluebird A&R man Eli Oberstein, who believed that there were too many "brothers" going by that name on record labels. Working from various radio stations in the Carolinas, Atlanta, and Bristol, the Blue Sky Boys placed over 100 numbers on disc with Bluebird from 1936 through 1940. After wartime military service, they continued with RCA Victor through 1951 and then dissolved their act. Their repertoire consisted of a combination of old traditional ballads and songs, hymns, and a few newer "heart" songs. Many of them seem to have come directly from a 1936 songbook by M. M. Cole Publishing in Chicago, *Doc Hopkins and Karl and Harty of the Cumberland Ridgerunners: Mountain Ballads and Home Songs*. According to the generally accepted line, the Bolicks chose to retire rather than accommodate to changing styles and modernization. However, some degree of internal dissension also played a role in their decision. They reunited for a few later concerts and record sessions in the 1960s and 1970s, but never really emerged from their retirement.[29]

Other duet acts had varying degrees of commercial success. For instance, Dorsey (1897–1968) and Howard (1903–1961), the Dixon Brothers, had a guitar–steel guitar-backed duet that demonstrated considerable appeal, despite a rougher singing style. Like many other natives of the Carolina Piedmont, the Dixons emerged from a textile mill worker culture that they never quite escaped for more than short periods of time, despite frequent radio appearances on such important radio stations as WBT Charlotte and WPTF Raleigh and some sixty Bluebird recordings that included a large number of original and reworked traditional songs. Numbers such as "Weave Room Blues," "Weaver's Life," "Sales Tax on the Women," "The Old Home Brew," and "The Intoxicated Rat" have been popular among those who cherished the subtle wit with a hint of protest in their lyrics. Their song "Down with the Old Canoe" recently inspired a title for a book dealing with the culture of the *Titanic* disaster. Perhaps their biggest legacy came with Roy Acuff's 1942 cover of their 1938 original "I Didn't Hear Anybody Pray," retitled "The Wreck on the Highway" which went on to become an all-time country classic.

Another couple to record for Bluebird, Wiley (1919–1990) and Zeke (1916–1999), the Morris Brothers, formed, disbanded, and re-formed several times over a period extending from 1936 into the early 1950s. In between, Zeke, the more active brother, spent stints with both J. E. and Wade Mainer and Charlie Monroe's band after the breakup of the Monroe Brothers. Eventually, they settled for part-time music status and operated an auto body repair shop in Black Mountain, North Carolina. Like the Dixons, Wiley and Zeke bequeathed an enduring classic song, "Salty Dog Blues," to the bluegrass world and are remembered as giving banjo legend Earl Scruggs his first professional job. Other brother duets of some significance included the Anglin Twins (not really twins but brothers), the Crowders, and the Halls. The next decade would see other brother duets come to the forefront.[30]

Not all the significant duet acts of the Depression decade were brothers. Chief among them was the Kentucky-born, Chicago-based team of Karl (1905–1979) and Harty (1905–1963), who first gained prominence on WLS and later on WJJD. This duo contributed several noted songs to the genre, especially "I'm Just Here to Get My Baby Out of Jail," with their American Record Corporation offerings and later with Capitol. Another duet with an extensive disc resume, Bill Cox (1897–1968) and Cliff Hobbs (1916–1961), placed sixty-six sides on record. A native of Kanawha County, West Virginia, Cox had worked on local radio in Charleston and initially did covers of Jimmie Rodgers songs for Gennett as well as other white blues and comedy songs. In 1933, Cox moved to the American Record Corporation and continued in this style, taking Hobbs as a duet partner in 1936. Cox's career probably suffered from his own rowdy lifestyle, but it also inspired such tongue-in-cheek humorous lyrics based in part on his own experience, such as "The Jailor's Daughter," "Alimony Woman," and "Rollin' Pin Woman." He has been most remembered for his topical songs typified by "N.R.A. Blues," "Franklin D. Roosevelt's Back Again," and "The Democratic Donkey." Cox and Hobbs also contributed two classics to the genre with Cox's reworking of the Spanish American War song "Filipino Baby" and his original "Sparkling Brown Eyes."[31]

The other brother team to reach prominence never recorded together after their first two sessions and then never sang together. Mainer's Mountaineers often used harmony duets within a larger string band. Joseph E. "J. E." Mainer (1898–1971) played fiddle, led a band, and occasionally did vocal solos or joined in on a chorus. Younger brother Wade Mainer (b. 1907) played a two-finger banjo style and did most of the singing, sometimes in duet with young Zeke Morris. Mainer's Mountaineers was rounded out by "Daddy" John Love (c. 1907–c. 1963), who played rhythm guitar and sang Jimmie Rodgers–styled solo blues numbers. A native of the mountainous region near Weaverville,

J. E. left home in early adolescence and settled in Concord, working in a cotton mill. Wade came out of the mountains some years later, and both worked in the mills, forming their band about 1932 to play for fiddler's contests and local dances. When the Crazy Water Crystals Company needed musicians for radio sponsorship at WBT Charlotte, it hired Mainer's Mountaineers to play on its programs. Their first Bluebird session at Atlanta in August 1935 yielded their biggest hit, "Maple on the Hill," which featured Wade and Zeke in duet. By the time of their next session, they had split up, with Wade briefly forming a duet with Zeke, and then a band, the Sons of the Mountaineers. In the remaining years before World War II, both Mainers played radio stations in the Carolinas and adjacent states with separate bands that could best be described as "pre-bluegrass." Important musicians who worked with them at one time or another included Boyd Carpenter, Howard Dixon, Tiny Dodson, Jay Hugh Hall, De-Witt "Snuffy" Jenkins, Steve Ledford, Clyde Moody, George Morris, Jack and Curly Shelton, Homer Sherrill, Leonard Stokes, and Norwood Tew. Some of these persons also recorded on their own—in particular, Jenkins and Sherrill, who formed the nucleus of the Columbia, South Carolina–based band Byron Parker's Mountaineers. In essence, the Mainer-led groups could best be termed transitions between those string bands of the 1920s, such as the North Carolina Ramblers, and the bluegrass bands that developed in the post–World War II years. Both Mainers remained musically active, although their period of prominence faded. J. E. led a band until he died, recording in every decade except the 1950s. Wade moved to Flint, Michigan, in 1953 but continued to sing in churches after a conversion experience and to record for King. After retiring from General Motors in 1972, he rejuvenated a career with his wife Julie, played numerous festivals, received the National Heritage Award, recorded numerous albums, and even made an appearance on the *Grand Ole Opry* at the age of ninety-five.[32]

Another carrier of the string-band tradition, Roy Hall (1907–1943), might have had as significant a career as the Mainers had he not died in an automobile crash. Hall, a native of Waynesville, North Carolina, made a few duet recordings with his brother Jay—a Mainer sideman—on Bluebird but had greater success with his band, the Blue Ridge Entertainers. Built around the fiddle of Tommy Magness (1909–1971) and the resonator guitar of Bill Brown, the Blue Ridge Entertainers made their name on radio at WAIR Winston-Salem and at WDBJ Roanoke. With a 1938 session for the American Record Corporation and two for Bluebird in 1940 and 1941, Roy Hall and the Blue Ridge Entertainers popularized such songs as "Don't Let Your Sweet Love Die," "Can You Forgive," and "I Wonder Where You Are Tonight," all songs that would later become bluegrass standards. They also introduced "Please Come Back Little Pal" prior to Roy Acuff making it his own. The Blue Ridge Entertainers also recorded "Orange Blossom Special" (which was not released until sixty years later) before anyone else and helped to make "Wabash Cannonball" the quintessential railroad song.[33]

There were other string bands in the Carolinas, including J. H. Howell's Carolina Hillbillies, the Dixie Reelers, and the longtime radio gang the WBT Briarhoppers. The latter also boasted the quality harmony mandolin-guitar duet of Whitey and Hogan (Roy Grant and Arval Hogan) within their ranks, but none east of the Appalachians had the impact of the Mainers and their associates. By the same token, none west of the Appalachians had the impact of Roy Acuff and his Smoky Mountain Boys.[34]

One other string band—the Coon Creek Girls—merits discussion: John Lair (1894–1985), who served as musical director at WLS and later organized *The Renfro Valley Barn Dance* in rural Kentucky, conceived of the idea of an all-girl mountain string band and recruited young Lily May Ledford (1917–1985) of Powell County, Kentucky, a talented fiddler and banjo picker, to lead it. He filled it out with her sister Charlotte "Rosie" (1915–1976) on guitar and two Mid-westerners, Esther "Violet" Koehler (1916–1973) and Evelyn "Daisy" Lange (b. 1919) on bass. He gave the other girls stage names of flowers, and they worked on WLW and later with Lair at *Renfro Valley*. They recorded sparingly for the American Record Corporation in 1938, and Lair even took them to the White House, where they played for the Roosevelts and for King George VI. The original members broke up in 1939, but Lair kept others in the act, always giving them flower names—most notably, Minnie Ledford (1923–1987), who became "Black-Eyed Susan." They remained at *Renfro Valley* for a number of years and provide an example not only of skilled female mountain musicians but also of the skills of Lair in the development of image in radio acts.[35]

THE UPPER SOUTH (AND A BIT OF THE MIDWEST)

The third Tennesseean to record for Vocalion (after the mountaineers Reneau and Stuart), David Harrison "Uncle Dave" Macon (1870–1952) enjoyed a lengthy and colorful professional career that lasted until his death in 1952. Macon hailed from Middle Tennessee, rather than the Appalachian highlands, and had actually spent much of his youth in Nashville, where his parents ran a hotel. Accordingly, he learned a great deal of current commercial music traditions from the minstrel and vaudeville performers who passed through the establishment. This provided him with opportunities for cultural growth that exceeded even those of the blind performers who were more dependent on music for their livelihood. When Macon grew to adulthood, he played mostly for local entertainments, farmed, and ran a horse-drawn wagon freight business near his home in Woodbury, Tennessee. However, with such modern conveniences as automobiles and trucks squeezing his transport business, Macon went on a Keith circuit vaudeville tour about 1918 that put show business in his blood to stay. Opportunities to make records in 1924 further infused him with musical professionalism, and in 1926 he began appearing on the *Grand Ole Opry* radio broadcasts before a live audience from WSM Nashville and in a sense became its first real star in the pre–Roy Acuff era.

A 1933 letter indicates that Uncle Dave looked forward to adding television to his résumé. Although that never happened, he did become a featured performer in the 1940 Republic picture *Grand Ole Opry* and continued on the radio broadcasts from WSM until a few weeks before his death.

As a recording artist, Macon steadily made discs for Vocalion and Brunswick (Aeolian merged with Brunswick-Balke Collender Company in 1925) through 1929. After that he did sessions with OKeh in 1930 and Champion in 1934. From 1935 to 1938, Macon again had regular sessions for Bluebird, ultimately placing about 175 masters on disc. His repertoire varied from old minstrel and popular songs, many of them humorous, to sentimental songs and originals, all of which he gave his own special touch. Like Carson and others, he brought several associates to the studios as accompaniment, fiddler Sid Harkreader (1898–1988) and the brother duo Sam (1894–1975) and Kirk (1899–1983) McGee ranking as the most significant, and who made recordings under their own names as well. Sam McGee, in particular, ranked as an outstanding guitarist. Like Macon, these individuals also favored radio station WSM with their music and rank among the early *Grand Ole Opry* artists.[36]

The radio program *Grand Ole Opry* dated from November 1925 and eventually became the nation's premier country radio program. It was the brainchild of George D. Hay (1895–1968), a young journalist known as "the Solemn Old Judge" who had moved into radio at Memphis in 1923, then became an announcer at WLS, where he emceed its *Barn Dance* for a few months, and came to WSM Nashville in early November 1925. Before the month ended, on November 28, he had started a barn-dance-type program that featured an archaic fiddler, Uncle Jimmy Thompson (1848–1931). The program soon expanded to include other central Tennessee musicians, such as Dr. Humphrey Bate (1875–1936) and his Possum Hunters and already accomplished recording artist Uncle Dave Macon and his sometime associates Fiddlin' Sid Harkreader and the brothers Sam and Kirk McGee.[37]

By the time Hay named the program *Grand Ole Opry* in 1927, other performers included the African American harmonica player DeFord Bailey (1899–1982) and other area string bands, such as the Crook Brothers, the Binkley Brothers, George Wilkerson's Fruit Jar Drinkers, the Pickard Family, Theron Hale and Daughters, and Paul Warmack's Gully Jumpers. With the exception of Macon and his immediate associates, none of these persons were any more than semiprofessional musicians. Several made their only commercial recordings in 1928 when Victor held sessions in Nashville.[38]

With the passing of time, other musicians became affiliated with the increasingly popular program. One of the most influential was Arthur Smith (1898–1971), a fiddler from Humphries County and a railroad worker who had made semiregular appearances on the program from December 1927 through 1930. In May 1932, Smith became an *Opry* regular as part of a band with the McGee Brothers known as the Dixieliners. For the next six years, this threesome ranked among the more popular acts on the show as Smith became known for his deft bowmanship on such traditional tunes as "Blackberry Blossom" and numbers more specifically identified with him as "Pig in the Pen" and "Walking in My Sleep." In 1935, he began to record for Bluebird but used the Delmore Brothers for rhythm support. Smith began to sing on some of his recordings in 1936, again with help from the Delmores, and had some real signature songs to his credit, such as "There's More Pretty Girls Than One," "Chittlin' Cookin' in Cheatham County," and "Beautiful Brown Eyes." Unfortunately, Smith also had a reputation as a hard drinker, and one such incident in February 1938 led to a three-month suspension from WSM. Nonetheless, he worked a few more times at the *Opry* until mid-January 1939, continued to record for Bluebird through 1940, and worked around on various radio stations in Alabama and West Virginia. In 1946, he went touring to Hollywood, cutting some more records for Black & White and Capitol, and making movies with Jimmy Wakely. By 1951, Fiddlin' Arthur was back in Tennessee and spent the rest of his life as a freelance fiddler, occasionally gaining some recognition for his achievements.[39]

Another key act on the *Opry* during the Depression decade was the afore-mentioned Delmore Brothers, who had much impact through their recordings as well as radio. Alton (1908–1964) and Rabon Delmore (1916–1952) hailed from Elkmont in north Alabama and made their first recordings for Columbia, recording two sides during the dark days of 1931. They finally got on the program as regulars in April 1933 and remained until September 1938, but somehow in spite of their popularity with audiences and on records (they had regular sessions on Bluebird from December 1933), the Delmores never really felt accepted by the management. Their soft, smooth harmonies, intricate guitar work, and original songs—typified by "Brown's Ferry Blues," "Blue Railroad Train," and "Gonna Lay Down My Old Guitar—all proved endearing and helped cement their place in musical history. Some impact of the Del-mores on other musicians can be found in the number of duets that emulated their style, such as the Andrews, the Philyaws, and the Milo Twins, who found their way onto major record labels prior to 1940, and lesser knowns, such as the Stepps, Blankenships, Hamricks, and Mayse Brothers, all of whom played on West Virginia radio stations in the later 1930s. Finally, late in 1938, Alton and Rabon departed from WSM for WPTF in Raleigh, never to return except for two guest appearances. Over the next several years, they had brief stints at various radio stations, including WCHS Charleston, WMC Memphis, and WLW Cincinnati. Their records on Bluebird, Decca, and finally King con-tinued to do well, and at the latter label, they helped initiate the country boogie fad of the late 1940s. They also put together a quality gospel quartet, the Brown's Ferry Four, that included Grandpa Jones and Merle Travis. But they never again had a long-running radio home like the *Opry*.[40]

At the time, Arthur Smith, the Delmores, and even the aging but ever popular Uncle Dave Macon were overshadowed by a highly polished but now nearly forgotten trio known as the Vagabonds. Composed of Curt Poulton

(1907–?), Dean Upson (1900–1975), and Herald Goodman (1900–1974), the Vagabonds had forged a career in radio dating back to 1927. Even before, Upson and his brother Paul had sang as students in 1926 at Otterbein College in Ohio. Poulton joined them in 1927, and they appeared on WLS Chicago as the Three Hired Men and then as the Vagabonds. They recorded for Brunswick in 1928, prior to Paul Upson leaving in February 1929 to be replaced by Goodman. They worked regularly for about two years at KMOX St. Louis before coming to WSM in August 1931. Unlike the weekend pickers and semiprofessionals associated with the *Opry*, the Vagabonds were young adults but seasoned professionals and salaried staff musicians. Before coming to Nashville, they were more of a pop music trio, but they increasingly redirected themselves toward nostalgia and home songs typified by "Lamp Lighting Time in the Valley" and their own "Little Mother of the Hills." Quite popular for a time, they made some custon recordings in the Gennett studio for their "Old Cabin" label, sold songbooks, and in 1933 began recording for Bluebird. They broke up in 1934, although Goodman and Poulton later led bands that performed there for a time. In retrospect, their chief contribution to the program was to move it along the road to greater professionalization.[41]

A fourth act at WSM had some impact by producing the first and, in a sense, only true child star in country music. Asher Sizemore (1906–1975) and his son Little Jimmie (b. 1928) hailed from mountainous eastern Kentucky. About 1930, Asher became a radio singer, and young Jimmie soon joined him singing children's songs. Like Bradley Kincaid, the Sizemores did especially well with songbooks and put out several editions through the decade. Although they played on several stations over the years and made numerous transcription programs, their main bases for operations tended to be dividing their time between WSM and the *Opry* and WHAS in Louisville. Charles Wolfe has documented their stays at the *Opry* as beginning in September 1932 through most of 1933 and January 1934. Thereafter, they played only a few times yearly through April 1939. The Sizemores recorded sparingly on Bluebird in 1934 and eventually settled down in Arkansas, where Asher had a radio station in DeQueen and Jimmie had one in Jacksonville.[42] The *Grand Ole Opry* also featured a number of musical groups that hardly recorded at all. For instance, Jack Shook and His Missouri Mountaineers straddled the line between pop and country. Shook also served as part of the trio of Nap, Jack, and Dee that sang Sons of the Pioneers-like material. Jack Shook (1910–1986) did eventually do a great deal of session work as a rhythm guitarist after Nashville emerged as a recording center after World War II. The Golden West Cowboys, beginning in June 1937 and led by Wisconsin-born Pee Wee King (1914–2000), played a brand of western swing not altogether to the liking of Judge Hay. Only after World War II did they become recording stars. The program also had a number of comedians during the 1930s—most notably, the duo of Sarie and Sally (Edna Wilson and Margaret Wilson) and the former minstrel show men "Lasses" White (1888–1949) and "Honey" Wilds (1902–1982) as blackface comics. After White left WSM in 1936 to work in Hollywood, Honey Wilds took on new partners who took the stage name "Jamup" (first Tom Woods and then Bunny Biggs), and they remained on the program until the early 1950s.[43]

Although the *Opry* eventually became the most important of the radio jamborees, the program was initially overshadowed by the *National Barn Dance*, broadcast from the decidedly non-Southern locale of Chicago. When record sales slumped during the hard times that characterized the 1930s, radio took on an increasing significance. The percentage of households with radios had increased during the later 1920s, and when ordinary folks lacked the funds to continue purchasing records at seventy-five cents each (or even thirty-five cents and less), they usually still had their radios. While WSB in Atlanta and WBAP in Fort Worth had pioneered in broadcasting country music, two other stations—one in Chicago and one in Nashville—soon had a greater impact at creating major performers through regular programming. Radio station WLS in Chicago was owned until 1928 by the retail mail-order giant Sears, Roebuck and Company and then by the agriculture periodical *Prairie Farmer*. On April 19, 1924, the station began its *National Barn Dance*, which attracted a large audience in the upper South and, incidently, the Midwest. While not exclusively country (i.e., Henry Burr, Grace Wilson), the *Barn Dance* was predominantly so and remained the dominant country music radio show until the 1940s and was on the air at WLS until 1960. From March 19, 1932, the program played to a live audience at the Eighth Street Theater in downtown Chicago. From 1933 until 1946, the NBC network carried a half-hour of the program, as did ABC from 1949 until 1960. Most of the *Barn Dance* regulars also made recordings but tended to credit whatever degree of stardom they possessed to radio rather than to their phonograph discs. Since Sears-Roebuck leased recordings from the Starr Piano Company for its own labels, many of the early *Barn Dance* performers did much of their recording for Gennett even though the records might appear only on Silvertone, Supertone, Challenge, or Conquerer. Later the American Record Corporation's masters dominated the Conquerer releases. Except for the aforementioned acts that hailed from the central Appalachian highlands—Bradley, Kincaid, Lulubelle and Scotty, and those associated with John Lair—most of the artists and the program came from such upper South locales as Western Kentucky, Arkansas, southern Illinois, and, in one case, Oklahoma.

Always seemingly in the shadow of larger name acts on the *National Barn Dance*, but its longest running performer, Luther Ossenbrink (1907–1981) was billed as "Arkie, the Arkansas Woodchopper." Working on the show from 1929 until it folded in 1960 and then again on the revived *WGN Barn Dance*, which was also syndicated on TV, Ossenbrink, who had started on radio at KMBC Kansas City, soon moved to WLS and became a fixture on Chicago radio for over four decades. His recordings for Gennett, Columbia, and the American Record Corporation contributed but little to his career success.

Unlike Kinkaid, he did project personality and laughed easily, often while being needled by fellow performers.[44]

One popular duo on Vocalion and Brunswick did not began recording in 1926 but, like Uncle Dave Macon, gained more fame via radio. Lester McFarland (1902–1984) and Robert Gardner (1897–1978), a pair of blind musicians who first met at the school for the blind in Louisville, accompanied themselves on mandolin and guitar and sang in a style that might be termed a bit too formal for hard-core hillbillies. Yet Mac and Bob, as they were known on radio in locales ranging from Knoxville to Pittsburgh, probably gained their greatest fame at WLS, and the *National Barn Dance* from 1931 had a repertoire of old sentimental songs and traditional ballads that could hold their own with any of the hard-core purists.[45]

From 1933 until 1946 and again from 1949, portions of the five-and-a-half hour show were heard on the NBC Network, and the program became more popular than ever. In 1931, Gene Autry (1907–1998), a Texas-born, Oklahoma-reared former telegraph operator who had been making records since 1929, joined the cast, remaining until 1934, when he went to Hollywood and motion picture stardom. However, as Jon Guyot Smith has pointed out, it was during his Chicago radio days that Autry began—under WLS tutelage—to recast his image in the western mode. Other WLS artists also began developing a western image, including Milly and Dolly Good, two sisters from Mt. Carmel, Illinois, who became famous as the Girls of the Golden West; the Girl from Hope, Arkansas, who gained renown as "Patsy Montana"; and the string band from Kentucky who transformed themselves into the Prairie Ramblers.[46]

The *National Barn Dance* boasted several other noted acts in the pre-World War II years. Among them were young George Gobel (1919–1991), who later became famous as a stand-up comedian but was billed at the time as the "Little Cowboy"; the comic novelty foursome of the Hoosier Hot Shots; a string band, the Cumberland Ridge Runners, whose membership included Red Foley (1911–1968), who would later become a star on the *Grand Ole Opry* and the *Ozark Jubilee*; the mandolin-guitar duet of Karl Davis (1905–1979) and Harty Taylor (1905–1963); and the tragic Linda Parker (1912–1935), who died young with peritonitis. All recorded for the American Record Company in the 1930s, but only Foley after he left Chicago would ever be a major force in recording. Perhaps more than any other locale, the *National Barn Dance*, by virtue of attracting a nationwide audience as well as performers from several regions, contributed to an eventual blending of musical style.[47]

By the end of the 1930s, other radio jamborees could be found on the radio dials, most of which would have more influence in later years. These included the *Renfro Valley Barn Dance* from really rural Renfro Valley, Kentucky, the *Boone County Jamboree* (later renamed the *Midwestern Hayride*) from WLW Cincinnati, the *Sunset Valley Barn Dance* from KSTP in St. Paul, the *World's Original Jamboree* from WWVA Wheeling, the *Old Farm Hour* from WCHS Charleston, and the *Sagebrush Roundup* from WMMN Fairmont, the latter three in West Virginia. In addition, numerous stations featured live country music acts, usually for quarter-hour segments in the early morning hours when farmers and factory workers would be preparing to go to their labors. Some also had programs around lunchtime when working people might be more able to listen during their midday meal either at home or at work.

Still another influential radio outlet for country music could be found on the powerful radio stations that operated just south of the Mexican border and were not subject to regulation by the Federal Communications Commission, although their programs could be widely heard in the United States, especially during the late night hours. While the station's advertising frequently pushed dubious products, listeners found their entertainment enjoyable. The Carter Family probably heads the list of significant country groups who played on "border radio," but at one time or another so did J. E. Mainer's Mountaineers and unrecorded cowboy singers, such as Roy Faulkner and the much-loved Nolan "Cowboy Slim" Rinehart (1911–1948), who died in an automobile crash.[48]

Also by the mid-1930s, the phonograph record business had made a modest recovery, based primarily on the low-priced disc—typically thirty-five cents—less than half of what they had sold for in the prosperous 1920s. The English firm Decca entered the market in 1934 and soon had its country-oriented 5,000 series. Victor retained its main label priced at seventy-five cents, but only the more affluent-audience-oriented items appeared on it. Mainstream pop, African American, and country material came out under the budget-priced Bluebird name. The Montgomery Ward chain store leased Bluebird material. What had once been Columbia, OKeh, Brunswick, and lesser firms merged into the American Record Corporation. Its principal labels bore names such as Melotone, Vocalion, and Perfect, but it also had labels affiliated with a variety of chain stores, such as Oriole (McRorys), Banner (S. S. Kresge), Romeo (S. H. Kress), and Conqueror (Sears, Roebuck and Company). In 1940, this company lost the rights to use the Vocalion name, so it revived the OKeh label for these issues. From a low of 275 new releases in 1933, the record industry rebounded to have about 375 new releases by 1936. In addition, records on the mainstream labels that had sold poorly at the higher price were being rereleased on the budget labels and selling better. For instance, two of the more memorable Jimmie Rodgers songs, "Mother, the Queen of My Heart" and "Peach Picking Time in Georgia" on their original Victor releases sold 6,385 and 2,621 copies, respectively. When reissued on Bluebird back to back a few months later, the disc sold 25,206 copies. Still, good-selling discs hardly matched those of earlier years. The Delmore disc of "Brown's Ferry Blues" reportedly sold about 100,000. For instance, one of the better selling hillbilly records from 1935, "Maple on the Hill"/"Take Me in the Lifeboat" by J. E. Mainer's Mountaineers," is alleged to have sold about 60,000 copies, much less than say the 100,000 that the better selling Rodgers and Carter discs were selling before the Great Crash of October 1929.[49]

The popularity of harmony duet acts (usually brothers) has already merited some discussion. Alton and Rabon Delmore, the Alabama duo who had two sides on Columbia followed by eighty on Bluebird while appearing regularly on the *Grand Ole Opry*, led the way in establishing this trend along with the team of Karl Davis and Harty Taylor, who emerged from the Cumberland Ridge Runners on the *National Barn Dance*. While the Delmores favored guitar and tenor guitar instrumentation, the mandolin and guitar backup music that Karl and Harty preferred usually provided a more spirited sound. Aside from those associated with the Carolina Piedmont and mountain areas, a pair of teams from western and central Kentucky contributed much to the style.[50]

The Monroe Brothers ranked as the most exciting of the new teams with their dynamic mandolin picking supplying the sound. Charlie Monroe (1903–1975) with his lead vocal and rhythm guitar together with younger brother Bill (1911–1996) on tenor vocal and mandolin had been born in Rosine, Kentucky. Moving to Hammond, Indiana, for industrial work, the Monroes came under the influence of radio WLS and the barn dance in nearby Chicago. Their initial radio programs took place in such unlikely locales as Nebraska and Iowa and came to full maturity in the Carolinas. The first Monroe record release was a hymn from 1912, "What Would You Give in Exchange for Your Soul" backed with "This World Is Not My Home." Historian Charles K. Wolfe speculates that this disc may have outsold "Brown's Ferry Blues." By the time the Monroe Brothers went their separate ways in 1938, they had recorded sixty songs (half of them sacred), many of which went on to become standards in country and bluegrass music. These numbers included "My Long Journey Home," "Foggy Mountain Top," "Nine Pound Hammer," "New River Train," "Banks of the Ohio," and "Roll in My Sweet Baby's Arms." Although not many of their songs were truly original, having been earlier recorded by other groups, their high-powered treatment helped preserve them for later bluegrass repertoires. As Charles Wolfe states, "With their heartfelt...harmonies, their stunning instrumental virtuosity, and their penchant for dressing up old gospel and sentimental songs, the Monroe Brothers were soon the talk of the Carolinas" and other southern and midwestern areas. Both brothers later had significant individual careers, but Bill went on to attain a degree of musical immortality as the creator of bluegrass.[51]

Another brother pair that usually worked apart but teamed ups at times were the Carlisles. Kentuckian Cliff Carlisle (1904–1983) started his career on WHAS Louiville and began recording in 1930 with Gennett, singing Jimmie Rodgers-type material and playing a resonator guitar, frequently in the company of a second guitarist, Wilbur Ball. Cliff even accompanied the Blue Yodeler on a Victor session in 1931. In addition to blues material (sometimes risqué, such as "Tomcat Blues" and "Ashcan Blues"), Carlisle sang numbers with train, hobo, and cowboy themes, as did Rodgers. Headquartered at a variety of radio stations through the decade, Carlisle moved to the American Record Corporation in 1932, and in 1933 his brother Bill (1908–2003) joined him, sometimes recording with Cliff but more often by himself. Both brothers signed with Bluebird in 1936 and then went to Decca in 1938 and 1939, returning to Bluebird again in 1941 when they recorded a memorable blues lyric, "Sugar Cane Mama." During a radio stay in the Carolinas, Cliff took on additional recording partners for a few songs, including Fred Kirby, Leon Scott, and Claude Boone. He also made some recordings with his son Tommy. Bill added a band member named Shannon Grayson, who also recorded with both brothers on Decca. During much of the 1940s, the brothers were based at WNOX radio in Knoxville and continued recording. Bill also developed a comedy role in the character of "Hot Shot Elmer." Cliff began to ease his way out of the entertainment world about 1950 and settled in Lexington. Bill went on to the *Grand Ole Opry* and had some major hits in the 1950s, usually with humorous novelty material.[52]

HILLBILLIES IN THE DEEP SOUTH

Deep South country musicians frequently—although not always—demonstrated more African American and blues influence than did those from other subregions of the Southeast. No musical figure illustrates this more than the Mississippi Blue Yodeler Jimmie Rodgers, who Ralph Peer had initially recorded at the aforementioned Bristol sessions. Virtually all of the other hillbilly artists at recorded Bristol were mountain folks, but Rodgers proved to be the major discovery of the week.

As for Jimmie Rodgers (1897–1933), Peer took only two numbers, "The Soldier's Sweetheart" and "Sleep Baby Sleep," the latter being a cover of a lullaby-type number from 1886 that earlier had been recorded on Columbia by Riley Puckett. Rodgers, a native of Meridian, Mississippi, had been a railroad brakeman plagued by poor health and infrequent employment and had been trying to make it as a vocalist with little success. In fact, until just prior to recording, he had been part of the band known as the Tenneva Ramblers, but they had split the night before their sessions and each recorded separately. However, brisk early sales (they would eventually total 152,038) prompted Peer to bring Rodgers back for another session on November 30, 1927. This session resulted in his biggest hit, "Blue Yodel (T for Texas)"/"Away Out on the Mountain," which would sell 454,586 copies over the next few years. His second best seller, "Blue Yodel # 4 (California Blues)"/"Waiting for a Train," reached 365,604 copies sold; and the third, "Daddy and Home"/"My Old Pal," sold 264,711 copies. The total of these three single discs passed a million in sales. Seven other releases had sales in excess of 200,000 copies each, totaling over 1,500,000 more, or an excess of 2,600,000 for ten releases. Six additional releases had sales in excess of 100,000 each. Once the Great Depression hit, Rodgers's sales dropped off considerably. His last Victor release, "The Cow Hand's Last Ride"/"Blue Yodel No. 12," sold only 1,115 copies, but Rodgers discs still sold better than most. Although much has been written about the

African American blues influence in Rodgers's music (especially the blue yo-dels and other blues numbers), about as many if not more of his songs derived from Anglo-American and Tin Pan Alley traditions.[53]

Another way to measure the impact of the Mississippi Blue Yodeler would be to look at the number of new recording artists whose own styles—at least in the beginning—closely resembled that of Jimmie Rodgers. Although Gene Autry, Jimmie Davis, Bill Carlisle, Cliff Carlisle, and Billy Cox would begin their careers on the Rodgers model, they eventually carved out their own persona. Most of the earlier recordings of Frankie Marvin were covers of Rodgers and Rodgers-like songs. Ernest Tubb and Hank Snow had their first sessions three years after Rodgers died, and although they found real success only after they developed their own styles, they began in the lingering shadow of the "Singing Brakeman." Others like Bill Bruner made only a slight impact on the market, but in more distant parts of the English-speaking world, folks like Wilf Carter, Tex Morton, and Buddy Williams showed the influence.

Independent of Rodgers, the duo of Tom Darby (1890–1971) and Jimmie Tarlton (1892–1979) hailed from Columbus, Georgia, and Phenix City, Ala-bama, respectively. Their blues-flavored songs had a standard guitar and Ha-waiian slide-guitar instrumentation. Recording on Columbia between 1927 and 1930 and briefly for Victor and the American Record Corporation in 1932 and 1933, they did some sixty songs together despite a cantankerous rela-tionship. Their best-known songs, "Birmingham Jail"/"Columbus Stockade Blues" sold nearly 200,000 copies and provided the traditional music world with two of its more memorable classics.[54]

An Alabama native, Alsie "Rex" Griffin (1912–1957), did radio work in locales extending from Georgia to Texas, recording some thirty-six (thirty-four of his own composition) sides for Decca between 1935 and 1939 and con-tributing such original songs as "The Last Letter," "Everybody's Trying to Be My Baby," "Beyond the Last Mile," and "Just Call Me Lonesome from Now on" (the latter of which he never recorded). Griffin's 1939 version of the 1923 pop song "Lovesick Blues" also provided postwar star Hank Williams with one of his biggest hits. His career also suggests the increasing need for new songs that had begun to drive the country record market. Increasingly plagued by drinking problems, Griffin's career declined to making transcriptions in 1944 and a session for King in 1947. When remembered at all in later years, it has been for his songwriting.[55]

The most significant new solo vocalist during the 1930s (other than Gene Autry) was a former schoolteacher, politician, and court clerk who lived in Shreveport and pursued only a part-time career in music during his years of greatest popularity. James Houston "Jimmie" Davis (c. 1900–2000) had one of the most remarkable lives of any American in the twentieth century. Like other country music pioneers, Davis emerged from the southern plain-folk working-class culture. Born in Beech Springs, Louisiana, Davis came from a family of poor sharecroppers, but unlike most of his peers, he pursued formal education, becoming the first person in his community to graduate from high school and to pursue a college education. After graduating from Louisiana College at Pineville in 1924, he taught school and did graduate work at Louisiana State University, completing a master's degree in 1927. That fall he took a teaching job at Dodd College in Shreveport. He also took began singing on KWKH radio. In 1928, Davis also made some custom records for the Doggone label, owned by W. K. Henderson, an avowed enemy of chain stores. The songs, with piano accompaniment, were more pop than country, but one was a cover of the back side of Jimmie Rodgers's biggest hit, the Kelly Harrell composition "Away out on the Mountain."

Leaving his teaching job, Davis took a job as a criminal court clerk in Shreveport. While this position provided him with a steady income, it also allowed time to pursue music as a sideline. A December 4, 1928, session in Dallas for Columbia resulted in only two rejected masters, but another for Victor in Memphis on December 19, 1929, placed four songs on wax, of which the two record releases sold more than 7,200 copies each, a good beginning in a declining market. Through August 1933, Davis would have more than sixty songs released on Victor and Bluebird. While none could be classified as hit of the magnitude of "Blue Yodel" or "Wildwood Flower," many more than held their own in the depressed market of the early 1930s. For instance, his best-selling Victor releases from a November 1930 session, "Bear Cat Mama from Horner's Corners" and "She's a Hum-Dum Dinger," sold 9,653 and 8,098 copies, respectively. Paired on a Montgomery Ward release, the two songs chalked up another 6,148 sold. By 1933, they were not doing that well, some recordings failing to reach 1,000, but few were selling more by this time. Most of the Davis recordings from those early years were clearly in the Jimmie Rodgers shadow. Some numbers with titles like "Organ Grinder Blues" were packed with double-entendre, but others like the "Gambler's Return" were sentimental tearjerkers.

In September 1934, Davis signed with the new Decca label and over the rest of the decade had more releases on that label than anyone else. Some of his earlier releases for the new company, such as "Jellyroll Blues" and "Shirt Tail Blues," mirrored his Victor efforts. However, the success of "Nobody's Darling But Mine"/"When It's Round-Up Time in Heaven," his fourth Decca release, soon steered him in other directions. After 1936, the more rowdy numbers were left to his former sideman Buddy Jones, and Davis went with more sentimental and romantic fare—songs like "My Brown-Eyed Texas Rose," "My Mary," and "In My Cabin Tonight." Even his prison ballads like "Moonlight and Skies (No. 2)" and "Shackles and Chains" were largely sentimental. He still did the rowdier songs such as "Goodbye Old Booze" with choral support in 1937, but these were hardly sung in the convincing manner of Charlie Poole's version of a decade earlier. Davis hardly ever played an instrument—the guitar often seen in photos seems to have been essentially a stage prop. The blues accompaniment on his Victor sides sometimes was played by jazz guitarist "Snoozer"

Quinn and sometimes by African American blues musicians like Oscar Woods and Ed "Dizzy Head" Schaffer, who were replaced by a small western swing combo led by Charlie Mitchell on electric steel guitar. The Louisiana singer also increasingly appeared for publicity photos in cowboy clothing and interspersed western themes in his song repertoire. Jimmie Davis continued to record and later held public office. In 1938, he was elected to the position of Commissioner of Public Safety, which in essence put him in charge of the police department. By the beginning of World War II, Davis had placed over 150 masters in the Decca vaults, including his February 5, 1940, rendition of "You Are My Sunshine." This upbeat love song would propel him to virtual superstar status and would eventually elevate him twice to the Louisiana governorship, becoming the subject of a biographical motion picture.[56]

None of this is to suggest that the "Rodgers effect" overpowered the market. Several string bands continued to record and have good selling records. For instance, a Mississippi string group, the Leake County Revelers, led by small-town hardware man R. O. Mosley (1885–1937) and fiddler Will Gilmer (1892–1960), who worked in a drug store, made four sides in New Orleans for Columbia in April 1927. Their second release, a slow-paced instrumental string quartet coupling of "Wednesday Night Waltz" and "Good Night Waltz," released in December 1927 sold nearly 200,000. A few of the Reveler numbers had vocals, but they continued with their brand of music through December 1930, having a total of forty-four sides in the catalog. Another fiddle-guitar team, the Stripling Brothers—Charles (1896–1966) and Ira (1898–1967)—hailed from Pickens County, Alabama. Charlie's fiddle first played in a makeshift Birmingham studio in November 1928, and his tune "Lost Child" would be one of the best new tunes on disc (readapted a few years later as "Black Mountain Blues" and "Black Mountain Rag"). Unlike the Revelers, the Striplings continued to record well into the 1930s, managing to hook up with the new Decca label for sessions in 1934 and 1936. In all, Charles and Ira had forty-two released tunes to their credit. Initially part of the brother duet tradition, Bob (1909–1983) and Joe (1911–1980), the Shelton Brothers (their real surname was Attlesey) had notable radio stints at WWL New Orleans and KWKH Shreveport, recording extensively on Decca from 1935. Eventually they returned to their home state of Texas and moved toward western swing accompaniment.[57]

COUNTRY MUSIC OUTSIDE THE SOUTHEAST

Although most country music in the early years emanated from the South, a few areas in other parts of the country also made contributions to the musical culture. Edison Records, one of the pioneer companies in the recording field, had begun to fade by the 1920s but continued to issue both cylinders and thick discs. Compared with the aforementioned firms, Edison displayed less interest in down-home rural music but did not wholly neglect it either. Even before the real boom started, it had recorded traditional fiddlers like John Baltzell of Knox County, Ohio, and Jasper Bisbee of Paris, Michigan, with a New England background. Ernest Stoneman made a number of Edisons between 1926 and 1928. There were also country dance bands in rural portions of northeastern states, such as Woodhall's Old Time Masters, who had played dances from their home in Elmira and made eight instrumentals for Victor in 1941. However, the most frequently recorded artist in the entire field was the "citybilly" Vernon Dalhart.[58]

In 1924, Marion Try Slaughter (1883–1948), known usually as Vernon Dalhart but sometimes as Al Craver, Tobe Little, Jep Fuller, Jeff Calhoun, or some other pseudonym, had some success in New York. This Texas-born popular vocalist recorded a cover of "Wreck of the Old 97" backed by a set of floating lyrics he called "The Prisoner's Song," which contained the memorable line "If I had the wings of an angel, over these prison walls I would fly." Not quite country yet not exactly pop music either, the disc took off like no other and became what is widely accepted as the first certified million seller (the Victor version) in the fledgling country music industry. It also gave Dalhart a new lease on life and made him the leading artist in the field for the next few years even if he was never quite part of it. He had a follow-up hit in 1925, with the topical song "The Death of Floyd Collins," a lyric about the amateur cave explorer who became trapped and expired before he could be rescued. Composed by Andrew Jenkins (1885–1957), the blind newsboy-preacher of Atlanta who had also written songs for Fiddlin' John Carson and recorded for OKeh, it set off a near fad in topical songs about significant current events, crimes, executions, and, occasionally, historic events. Song topics ranged from current tragedy like "The Lost French Flyers" to the New Mexico outlaw of forty-five years earlier, "Billy the Kid." Jenkins wrote a few of the Dalhart songs, and even more came from Carson Robison (1890–1957), a Kansan who played guitar on many of the recordings and sometimes served as a duet partner. Although topical songs continued to be a country music staple into the twenty-first-century (i.e., "Saving Private Lynch" by Joe Price), the market became virtually glutted with them in the later 1920s, and few achieved hit status after that time. As Dalhart's luster faded, Robison continued by himself with a band and a new partner, fellow Kansan Frank Luther (1901–1980). Robison recorded into the 1950s, one of his last efforts being titled "Rockin' and Rollin' with Grandma" in 1956 on the M-G-M label.[59]

The radio station that played the biggest role in the dissemination of country music in the northeast was actually located in the upper Ohio Valley at the edge of Appalachia. Radio station WWVA in Wheeling, West Virginia, took the air in 1926 and, when George Smith became program director, began to play music that appealed to rural listeners. In addition to daily programs, he initiated the Saturday night *World's Original Jamboree* beginning in January 1933. Early artists included the aforementioned Tweedy Brothers and the trio of Cap, Andy, and Flip (i.e., Warren Caplinger, Andy Patterson, and William "Flip" Strickland). By 1937, the cast included Cowboy Loye (Pack), Grandpa

Jones, Big Slim, the Lone Cowboy (Harry C. McAuliffe), and longtime stalwarts Doc Williams and His Border Riders. Their largest audience undoubtedly was in rural Pennsylvania, but when the station went to 50,000 watts in 1942, the *Jamboree* found additional receptive audiences in upstate New York, rural New England, and adjacent parts of Canada.[60]

True country music also made its appearance in the far West. In 1919, a family of transplanted Appalachians named Crockett settled in Fresno, California. They brought their musical culture with them, and in 1923 son Johnny made his first appearance on local KMJ radio; by 1926, his parents and other family members had joined him. The Crocketts soon moved to KNX in Los Angeles and began recording for Brunswick in 1928. Other early country folk on California radio included Logan Laam and his Happy Hayseeds in Stockton, Len Nash and his Country Boys in Los Angeles, and Harry "Haywire Mac" McClintock in San Francisco. By 1930, hillbilly music in California had begun the process of amalgamation with the songs and music associated with the Far West, especially real and reel cowboys.[61]

IN SUMMATION

The above discussion makes up but a small proportion of the early hillbilly and old-time musicians who made some contribution to the country sounds of the pre–World War II years. Many others entered the radio and recording studios to make their voices and instruments heard. Some found a degree of commercial success while others met with disappointment. Some stayed closer to their traditions while others adapted and borrowed from other styles. For better or worse, all played a role in the development of what became an important part of the nation's musical heritage.

The progress of Jimmie Davis from sharecropper's son to becoming Decca's top recording artist in the field in a sense parallels the changes that had taken place in the nearly twenty years since Eck Robertson and John Carson had first played their fiddles for recording equipment. While country music as an industry remained primitive compared with New York's Tin-Pan Alley and developments in the motion picture world, it had also become increasingly commercialized through the recording industry's continual search for new songs and new talent. Song publishers such as Ralph Peer controlled the copyrights of big sellers like Jimmie Rodgers and the Carter Family, and the M. M. Cole Company of Chicago had an in with the songs and writers associated with the *National Barn Dance*. Through daily morning and midday programs, along with the Friday and Saturday night jamboree shows—especially those on the 50,000-watt stations and network connections like the *National Barn Dance* and the *Grand Ole Opry*—country music had become a staple for radio entertainment and furnished regular and part-time employment for hundreds of musicians. The recording business had prospered somewhat in the 1920s and managed to survive the Great Depression in diminished fashion. By the early 1940s as the economy began to show signs of real recovery, fueled in part by increased defense expenditures as war clouds began to loom on the horizon, country music—still called hillbilly—began to experience a widening audience. The latter was fueled to some extent by the growth of two distinct musical subtypes that merit closer examination.

NOTES

1. Bill C. Malone, *Country Music, U.S.A.*, 2nd rev. ed. (Austin: University of Texas Press, 2002), 32–34.

2. Charles Wolfe, *The Devil's Box: Masters of Southern Fiddling* (Nashville: Country Music Foundation Press and Vanderbilt University Press, 1997), 12–29.

3. For background on the birth of hillbilly records, see Archie Green, "Hillbilly Music: Source and Symbol," *Journal of American Folklore* 78 (1965), 204–228. For a broader look at the life of Carson, see Gene Wiggins, *Fiddlin' Georgia Crazy: Fiddlin' John Carson, His Real World and the World of His Songs* (Urbana: University of Illinois Press, 1987).

4. Charles Wolfe et al., "Roba Stanley: The First Country Sweetheart," *Old Time Music* 26 (Autumn 1977), 13–18.

5. Norman Cohen, "The Skillet Lickers: A Study of a Hillbilly String Band and Its Repertoire," *Journal of American Folklore* 78 (1965), 229–244, remains the best study, although some minor corrections are found in Norm Cohen, "Early Pioneers" in Bill C. Malone and Judith McCulloh, eds., *Stars of Country Music* (Urbana: University of Illinois Press, 1975), 27–34.

6. For a thorough study of country music in the Atlanta area, see Wayne W. Daniel, *Pickin' on Peachtree: A History of Country Music in Atlanta, Georgia* (Urbana: University of Illinois Press).

7. Norm Cohen, "Henry Whitter—His Life and Recordings," *JEMF Quarterly* 11 (1975), 80–91; Kip Lornell, *Virginia's Blues, Country, & Gospel Records, 1902–1943: An Annotated Discography* (Lexington: University Press of Kentucky, 1989), 208–216; Wolfe, *The Devil's Box*, 61–65.

8. Ivan M. Tribe, *The Stonemans: An Appalachian Family and the Music That Shaped Their Lives* (Urbana: University of Illinois Press, 1993).

9. Green, "Hillbilly Music: Source and Symbol," 211–215; Lornell, *Virginia's Blues, Country, & Gospel Records*, 99–107.

10. Kinney Rorrer, *Rambling Blues: The Life & Songs of Charlie Poole* (London: Old Time Music, 1982).

11. Tony Russell, "Kelly Harrell & the Virginia Ramblers," *Old Time Music* 2 (Autumn 1971), 8–12.

12. For the Carolina Tar Heels, see Archie Green and Eugene Earle, *The Carolina Tar Heels* (Folk-Legacy Records FSA-24, 1965), inside liner booklet.

13. Green, "Hillbilly Music: Source and Symbol," 215–217; Charles K. Wolfe, "George Reneau: A Biographical Sketch," *JEMF Quarterly* 15 (1979), 205–208.

14. See Rick Kennedy, *Jelly Roll, Bix, and Hoagy: Gennett Studios and the Birth of Recorded Jazz* (Bloomington: Indiana University Press, 1994), 139–175, for a general account of the role of Gennett Records and the Starr Piano Company in the development of country music.

15. Charles Wolfe, *The Devil's Box*, 66–78, contains the best account of this group.

16. Ivan M. Tribe, "John McGhee and Frank Welling: West Virginia's Most-Recorded Old Time Artists," *JEMF Quarterly* 17 (1981), 57–74.

17. Norm Cohen, *Paramount Old Time Tunes* JEMF 103 (1976), liner notes.

18. Charles K. Wolfe, "Man of Constant Sorrow: Richard Burnett's Story," *Old Time Music* 9 (Summer 1973), 6–9; "Part 2," ibid. 10 (Autumn 1973), 5–11.

19. Loyal Jones, *Buell Kazee: Biographical Notes* (June Appal LP 009, 1978), liner notes.

20. A good introduction to Hutchison's music is Tony Russell, "Frank Hutchison: The Pride of West Virginia," *Old Time Music* 1 (Summer 1971), 5–7, but more detailed biography is found in the album liner notes by Mark Wilson, *Frank Hutchison: The Train That Carried My Girl from Town* (Rounder 1007, 1973).

21. Wolfe, *The Devil's Box*, 99–112.

22. See Charles K. Wolfe, "Ralph Peer at Work: The Victor 1927 Bristol Sessions," *Old Time Music* 5 (Summer 1972), 10–15, for the best account of the Bristol happenings from contemporary sources.

23. Mark Zwonitzer with Charles Hirshberg, *Will You Miss Me When I'm Gone? The Carter Family and Their Legacy in American Music* (New York: Simon & Schuster, 2002), is likely to become the definitive work on the Carters, although it lacks scholarly trappings and should be balanced with Charles Wolfe, *The Carter Family: In the Shadow of Clinch Mountain* (Hamburg, Germany: Bear Family Records BCD 15865, 2000).

24. Loyal Jones, *Radio's Kentucky Mountain Boy: Bradley Kincaid* (Berea, KY: Appalachian Center, 1980). For a good brief history of the *National Barn Dance*, see James F. Evans, *Prairie Farmer and WLS: The Burridge D. Butler Years* (Urbana: University of Illinois Press, 1969), 165, 213–321.

25. For Lulubelle and Scotty, see William E. Lightfoot, *Wiseman's View: The Autobiography of Skyland Scotty Wiseman* (Boone, NC: North Carolina Folklore Society, 1986), 1–13. Unfortunately, the unfinished autobiography ends at the point where Scotty joins WLS. The introduction contains more information on the Wisemans' professional life.

26. For Acuff, see Elizabeth Schlappi, *Roy Acuff: The Smoky Mountain Boy*, 2nd ed. (Gretna, LA: Pelican Publishing, 1993).

27. Charles K. Wolfe, *A Good Natured Riot: The Birth of the Grand Ole Opry* (Nashville, TN: Country Music Foundation Press and Vanderbilt University Press, 1999), 254–265.

28. Ivan M. Tribe, "Bill and Joe Callahan: A Great Brother Duet," *Old Time Music* 16 (Spring 1975), 15–22. For a general discussion on the popularity of duets in the 1930s, see Bill C. Malone, "Brother Duets," in Paul Kingsbury, ed., *The Encyclopedia of Country Music* (New York: Oxford University Press, 1998), 56.

29. Wayne W. Daniel, "Bill and Earl Bolick Remember the Blue Sky Boys," *Bluegrass Unlimited* 16 (September 1981), 14–21.

30. Mike Paris, "The Dixons of South Carolina," *Old Time Music* 10 (Autumn 1973), 13–17; Wayne Erbsen, "Wiley and Zeke, the Morris Brothers," *Bluegrass Unlimited* 15 (August 1980), 40–50. The Shelton Brothers have received less attention, but a brief sketch is on a set of liner notes by Ivan M. Tribe, *The Shelton Brothers: A Collection of Song Hits* (Old Homestead OHCD 4201, 2000), based largely on an

interview of Joe Shelton by Bill C. Malone. It lacks information on Bob Shelton's death.

31. Charles K. Wolfe, "Whatever Happened to Karl and Harty," *Bluegrass Unlimited* 18 (October 1983), 26–32; for Cox and Hobbs, see Tribe, *Mountaineer Jamboree: Country Music in West Virginia* (Lexington: University Press of Kentucky, 1984), 35–37.

32. Ivan M. Tribe and John Morris, "J. E. and Wade Mainer," *Bluegrass Unlimited* 10 (November 1975), 12–22.

33. Ivan M. Tribe, "Roy Hall and His Blue Ridge Entertainers: Almost Bluegrass," *Bluegrass Unlimited* 13 (September 1978), 44–49.

34. Only the careers of the Briarhoppers have been documented; see Ivan M. Tribe, "The Briarhoppers: Carolina Musicians," *Bluegrass Unlimited* 12 (March 1978), 31–38.

35. See Lily May Ledford, *Coon Creek Girl* (Berea, KY: Berea College Appalachian Center, 1980). See also Ivan M. Tribe, *The Coon Creek Girls: Early Radio Favorites* (Old Homestead OHCS 142, 1982), liner notes.

36. Ralph Rinzler and Norm Cohen, *Uncle Dave Macon: A Bio-Discography* (Los Angeles: John Edwards Memorial Foundation, 1970); Charles Wolfe, "Uncle Dave Macon," in Malone and McCulloh, *Stars of Country Music*, 40–63. An updated version is in Charles Wolfe, *Uncle Dave Macon*, Rutherford County Historical Society Publication No. 35 (Murfreesboro, TN: Rutherford County Historical Society, 1995).

37. Charles K. Wolfe, *A Good Natured Riot*, 3–25, 43–118.

38. Ibid., 119–153, 166–178. For a more thorough study of Bailey, see David C. Morton, *DeFord Bailey: A Black Star in Early Country Music* (Knoxville: University of Tennessee Press, 1991).

39. Wolfe, *The Devil's Box*, 113–150.

40. The best source on the Delmores is Alton Delmore, *Truth Is Stranger Than Publicity* (Nashville, TN: Country Music Foundation Press, 1977); although it was completed only to 1945, a brief postscript by Charles Wolfe fills in the Delmore story to its conclusion.

41. Wolfe, *A Good Natured Riot*, 179–189.

42. Ibid., 162–165.

43. Ibid., 225–253.

44. Brief sketches of Ossenbrink are found in Charles K. Wolfe, "Arkie, the Arkansas Woodchopper," in Barry McCloud, ed., *Definitive Country* (New York: Perigee Books, 1995), 22; and Wayne W. Daniel, "Arkie the Arkansas Woodchopper," in Kingsbury, *The Encyclopedia of Country Music*, 15. The former contains more depth, but the latter has his correct birthdate.

45. No definitive account of the careers of Lester McFarland and Robert Gardner exists, but a brief sketch is found in a reissue CD liner note: Ivan M. Tribe and Robert R. Olson, *Mac and Bob* (Old Homestead OH CD 4158, 2000).

46. Quoted in Jonathan Guyot Smith, "Gene Autry," in Kingsbury, *The Encyclopedia of Country Music*, 22–23. For a more detailed look at western music at WLS, see Chapter 3.

47. For Karl and Harty, see Wolfe, "Whatever Happened to Karl and Harty," 26–32.

48. See Gene Fowler and Bill Crawford, *Border Radio* (Austin: Texas Monthly Press, 1987), 77–143, 219–244, for those portions most relevant for music scholars.

49. Cohen, *Long Steel Rail*, 32, 37–38; Nolan Porterfield, *Jimmie Rodgers: The Life and Times of America's Blue Yodeler* (Urbana: University of Illinois Press, 1992), 59; Wolfe, *A Good Natured Riot*, 217. The sales figure on the Mainer disc comes from an interview of Wade Mainer by Eddie Stubbs on WSM radio, c. 2002.

50. Wolfe, "Whatever Happened to Karl and Harty," 26–32.

51. For the Monroe Brothers, see Richard D. Smith, *Can't You Hear Me Callin': The Life of Bill Monroe, Father of Bluegrass* (Boston: Little, Brown, 2000), 28–46. For Charlie Monroe's later career, see Ivan M. Tribe, "Charlie Monroe," *Bluegrass Unlimited* 10:4 (October 1975), 12–21; Charles K. Wolfe, *Bill Monroe: Blue Moon of Kentucky, 1936–1949* (Hamburg, Germany: Bear Family Records, 2002), 9.

52. Charles Wolfe, "Cliff Carlisle," *Bluegrass Unlimited* 12 (December 1984), 41–45; Wayne W. Daniel, "The Traditional Roots of Jumpin' Bill Carlisle: Veteran Singer of Novelty Songs," *Bluegrass Unlimited* 26 (June 1992), 41–44.

53. Porterfield, *Jimmie Rodgers*. For data on record sales, see Nolan Porterfield, *Jimmie Rodgers* (Hamburg, Germany: Bear Family Records, 1992), 59.

54. Ed Kahn, *Darby & Tarlton: Complete Recordings* (Hamburg, Germany: Bear Family Records BCD 15764, 1995), inside liner booklet.

55. Ronnie Pugh, "Rex Griffin: Passing on the Rodgers Legacy," *Mid-America Folklore* 16 (Fall 1988), 72–79.

56. There is no adequate biography of Jimmie Davis. His authorized biography, Gus Weill, *You Are My Sunshine: The Jimmie Davis Story* (Gretna, LA: Pelican Publishing, 1991), falls far short. For his music, the best available are the two booklets that accompany the boxed sets of his early recordings: Tony Russell, *Governor Jimmie Davis: Nobody's Darlin' But Mine* (BCD 15943) and *Governor Jimmie Davis: You Are My Sunshine* (BCD 16216) (Hamburg, Germany: Bear Family Records, 1997). Data on Davis's Victor sales are from Tony Russell, "Jimmie Davis: An Annotated Discography, The Early Years, 1928 to 1933," *Old Time Music* 41 (Spring–Autumn 1985), 17–19. A forthcoming study by Kevin S. Fontenot promises to fill this gap in scholarship.

57. Tony Russell, "The Leake County Revelers: Waltz Kings of the Old South," *Old Time Music* 20 (Spring 1976), 26–35; Charles Wolfe, *The Devil's Box*, 99–112; Graham Wickham, "Interview with the Stripling Brothers," *JEMF Newsletter* 4 (March 1968), 15–22.

58. For a discussion of some of these individuals, such as Baltzell and Bisbee, see Simon J. Bronner, *Old-Time Music Makers of New York State* (Syracuse, NY: Syracuse University Press, 1987), 29–41.

59. Walter Darrell Haden, "Vernon Dalhart," in Malone and McCulloh, *Stars of Country Music*, 64–85. See also Robert Coltman, "Carson Robison: First of the Rural Professionals," *Old Time Music* 29 (Summer 1978), 5–13.

60. Tribe, *Mountaineer Jamboree*, 43–62.

61. Gerald W. Haslam, *Workin' Man's Blues: Country Music in California* (Berkeley: University of California Press, 1999), 25–31, 168.

3

Cowboys and the West:
Real and Reel

The western frontier and the life of the American cowboy have captured the imagination of the American people for more than a century. The mythical exploits of frontiersmen such as Daniel Boone and Davy Crockett along with the fictional characters in the novels of James Fenimore Cooper and the dramas of James Kirke Paulding provided a degree of fascination for both children and adults even before Anglo-Americans began to settle in Texas and other parts of the trans-Mississippi west. Perhaps because they were mounted on horses, cowboys soon outstripped the gold seekers, miners, and homesteaders among the occupational groups that peopled this frontier. Many cowboys in reality lived lives of dull drudgery and hard work in a dry and often hostile environment. In many instances, the myth of the cowboy also incorporated music into the lifestyle. Even before motion pictures reinforced this image—sometimes to the ultimate in the twentieth century—cowboys were often viewed as singing to calm their herds and modify the loneliness of frontier life. Likewise, songs of cowboy and frontier life also entered American culture, popular and otherwise. Books containing cowboy songs had been published in 1908 and 1916.[1]

No one can identify the first cowboy singer on phonograph disc with certainty. Fiddler Eck Robertson often appeared in cowboy-styled clothing but did not sing. Some have advanced a claim for Charles Nabell (1885–1977), an otherwise unknown person who died in Joplin, Missouri, but recorded a number of songs for OKeh in November 1924 and March 1925, none of which made much of an impact on either the industry or the market. Others would credit Texas-born Marion Slaughter, who as Vernon Dalhart recorded "Way Out West in Kansas" in August 1924 at the same session that produced "The Prisoner's Song" and "Wreck of the Old 97," the first certified "country million seller."[2]

TEXAS AND ELSEWHERE IN THE REAL WEST

While he may not have quite been first, the case for initiating a trend in recording songs of the cowboy can be credited with certainty to another Texan, Carl T. Sprague (1895–1979). Although not a working cowboy, Sprague had grown up on a ranch near Alvin, Texas, where he learned a great many of the songs and on August 5, 1925, recorded "When the Work's All Done This Fall" for Victor, a song that derived from an 1893 poem by a Montana cowboy named D. J. O'Malley. Other cowboy songs made by Sprague over the next four years established his reputation as a cowboy vocalist, although he had no aspirations to make a career out of music. Living into the 1970s, this pioneer western singer recorded again in 1972.[3]

Others with a touch of realism followed in Sprague's footsteps. Another Texan, Jules Verne Allen (1883–1945), had more actual experiences as a cowboy and recorded more cowboy songs for Victor in 1928 and 1929. Allen styled himself "the Original Singing Cowboy" and worked on a number of radio stations in such locales as Dallas, Los Angeles, and San Antonio. He also wrote a book about cowboy life and songs, *Cowboy Lore* (1933). Harry McClintock (1882–1957) worked on radio at KFRC in San Francisco, singing a mixture of cowboy, hobo, and railroad songs. In 1928, he began recording for Victor, turning out such numbers as "Get Along Little Doggies," "Billy Venero," "The Trusty Lariat," and "Goodbye Old Paint." His delivery was as authentic as those of Sprague and Allen. Overall, he still remained better known for his songs of hobo life, such as "The Bum Song," "Hallelujah! I'm a Bum," and "The Big Rock Candy Mountain" (which reappeared in 2000 on the sound track of the motion picture *O Brother, Where Art Thou?*). Sometimes overlooked is the Dallas radio singer "Peg" (for his wooden leg) Moreland, who billed himself as "King of the Ditty Singers" and recorded a number of ballads, many of them of or about cowboys. Victor made other recordings of cowboy songs, including those of "Powder River Jack" and Kitty Lee, Jack Webb, Paul Hamblin, Arthur Miles, J. D. Farley, the Cartwright Brothers (who also had a session on Columbia), and Billie Maxwell, who deserves to be remembered as the first singing cowgirl.[4]

Other companies also had singers of cowboy songs, most of whom remain virtual unknowns. These included Marc Williams, who billed himself as the "Cowboy Crooner" and made a number of recordings for Brunswick; Edward L. Crain (or Crane), who cut several cowboy songs, including the first version of the traditional "Bandit Cole Younger"; Rex Kelly; Leon Chappelear; Jack

Weston; and the duo of Patt Patterson and Lois Dexter. Perhaps the most significant of these was the somewhat better known Goebel Reeves (1899–1959)—often billed as the "Texas Drifter"—who, like Harry McClintock, favored hobo songs but also included some cowboy material, including "Cowboy's Lullaby," a seeming rewrite of his own "Hobo's Lullaby."[5]

In addition to the individual cowboy songsmiths, a number of groups also gained some significance with their singing. Perhaps the most important of these, at least in the beginning, was the Oklahoma Cowboys, initially led by Billy McGinty but taken over around 1926 by Otto Gray (1884–1967), a nonperforming leader with some management skills who got his entourage on vaudeville circuits until 1932 when they dissolved. Ironically, on the basis of the few recordings they made for OKeh, Vocalion, and Gennett, very little of their material was western or cowboy in content but included generally comic novelties, such as "Adam and Eve" and "Don't Try It 'Cause It Can't Be Done." However, they dressed the part of cowboys and provided show business entry for such figures as country comedian Ben Ford (the Duke of Paducah), and such western-style singers as Zeke Clements and Walden Whytsell (as Don White).[6]

COWBOYS GO HOLLYWOOD

As a western singing group, the Beverly Hill Billies of KMPC radio in Los Angeles ranked among the first to set a style in tight vocal three-part harmony. Membership in the group changed from time to time, but when they made their first recordings for Brunswick, which included such songs as "Red River Valley" and "When the Bloom Is on the Sage," members included Tom Murray, Lem Giles, Cyprian "Ezra" Paulette, and Zeke Manners. They recorded again in 1932, but their discs tend to be rare and scarce. The Hill Billies made their biggest impact on radio in California. By 1935, some of them relocated to New York for a time. Over the next few years, several persons who would later make names for themselves in the western field spent some time with them, including such luminaries as Ken Carson, Curley Bradley, and Jack Ross, who would later become the nucleus of the Ranch Boys. Those who made a name for themselves individually included Wesley Tuttle, Stuart Hamblen, and Elton Britt. The Beverly Hill Billies managed to inspire a number of other vocal groups to develop in southern California, but most tended to be short-lived.[7]

However, the Sons of the Pioneers became the western vocal group that ultimately dwarfed all the others. The nucleus of the Pioneers was their trio—Bob Nolan (1908–1980), Tim Spencer (1908–1974), and Leonard Slye (1911–1998)—who were supplement by instrumentalists Hugh Farr (1903–1980) on fiddle and his brother Karl Farr (1909–1961). The trio after a number of reorganizations and false starts came together in 1933 and made their first recordings for Decca in August 1934. Spencer left for a year in 1936 and was replaced by Lloyd Perryman (1917–1977). When Leonard Slye left to become a successful cowboy movie star under the name "Roy Rogers," Perryman remained as part of

In the 1930s, the Sons of the Pioneers became one of the most well-known western vocal groups. Though the members changed throughout the years, the group had a continuous existence for close to 70 years.
Courtesy of Photofest.

the trio. Over the next thirty-two years, the Sons of the Pioneers recorded an immense volume of songs for Decca, for the American Record Corporation (briefly), and for RCA Victor. Spencer and especially Nolan were gifted writers who, according to cowboy music historian Douglas B. Green's book, *Singing in the Saddle*, had talent for "Painting the West in Song" with their lyrics, which emphasized the beauty of the wide-open spaces. Songs like "Tumbling Tumbleweeds," "Blue Prairie," "Cool Water," "Moonlight on the Prairie," and "The Touch of God's Hand" all demonstrate Green's point.

In addition to their radio and recording work, the Sons of the Pioneers also appeared in numerous western films. Beginning with *Gallant Defender* in 1935, they provided musical interludes in Charles Starrett movies for about five years. After a year in Chicago, they came back to Hollywood and performed a similar role in Roy Rogers pictures. Personnel changes took place over the years as members came and went. Spencer dropped out after a religious conversion in 1948, and Nolan departed the next year but did return for some recording sessions. Perryman remained until his death while others, including Ken Curtis, Tommy Doss, Rusty Richards, Ken Carson, Shug Fisher, and Pat Brady, all spent time with the group. For the last half-century, Dale Warren has provided the continuity for the legendary group that seemingly goes on forever.[8]

While numerous musical acts appeared in a few western films, no other acts were regulars at it until the mid-1940s. The most notable were Foy Willing (1915–1978) and his Riders of the Purple Sage, who flourished from 1944 to 1952 making numerous pictures with Roy Rogers. They also recorded for Capitol, Majestic, and Decca and cut numerous radio transcriptions. Another 1940s vocal team, Andy Parker (1915–1977) and the Plainsmen, appeared in films with Eddie Dean and Ken Curtis, among others, while recording many sides with Capitol. The Cass County Boys were a radio combination in Dallas and after World War II appeared as regulars on Gene Autry's *Melody Ranch* program, toured with him, and worked in several of his films.[9]

The entry of the Sons of the Pioneers into film may have been the musical and artistic zenith of cowboy song in Hollywood. As early as 1929, Academy Award-winning Warner Baxter in his role as the Cisco Kid delivered a song, "My Tonia," in Fox's *In Old Arizona*. Action stars Bob Steele in *Oklahoma Cyclone* and Ken Maynard in *Sons of the Saddle*, both from 1930, featured some singing. Steele never sang again, but Maynard's rough but authentic vocal was heard in a few more of his films—in one he also played the fiddle. In addition, Maynard recorded eight songs for Columbia on April 14, 1930 (only two released at the time). In *The Strawberry Roan* (1933), he sang the title song in a trio with Frank Yaconelli and Charles King (the latter best remembered for his numerous roles as an outlaw). Maynard may have aspired to other roles as a singing cowboy, but fate—augmented by the star's temperament and attitude problems—decreed otherwise.[10]

Another Ken Maynard film, *In Old Santa Fe* (1934), was the first motion picture to feature the man who did become the ultimate singing cowboy. Gene Autry (1907–1998) was born in Texas, reared in Oklahoma, and learned the skill of a telegrapher, which he plied on the Frisco Railroad. According to an oft-told tale, the noted celebrity Will Rogers walked into the workplace to send a telegram and heard young Autry strumming his guitar and singing. He suggested that Autry should get on records. Inspired by this suggestion, the young telegrapher went to New York, where he made the acquaintance of Frank (1904–1985) and John (1897–1943) Marvin, who had some experience in the field. Told that he needed more experience, Autry came back in 1929 and had more success. In the coming months, he made records for many companies ranging from Gennett to Victor. Many of his early efforts were covers of Jimmie Rodgers and Jimmie Davis songs, but by the fall of 1931, he had begun to carve out a more distinct identity for himself and joined the cast of the *National Barn Dance*. Some of his early recordings were duets with another railroader and his future wife's uncle, Jimmy Long (1889–1951), including the real major hit among his early efforts, the sentimental favorite "That Silver Haired Daddy of Mine."

In 1934, Autry came to Hollywood to try his luck in films and was initially cast in a featured role in the aforementioned Maynard picture. Whether the credit for launching the success of Autry and the singing cowboy movie goes to record producer Art Satherley, to soon-to-be-ousted Mascot Studio head Nat Levine, to Republic Studio tycoon Herbert Yates, to Autry himself, or to some combination of these has yet to be determined. However, the first Gene Autry-starred picture proved the financial correctness of the formula. Estimates of the film's cost ranged from $15,000 to $18,000, while those of the gross take varied from $500,000 to nearly $1 million. For the next few years, Autry appeared in anywhere from three to nine films a year, continued to turn out hit records, and did extensive tours between movie shooting. In 1940, he added a weekly CBS

Legendary Gene Autry began his career as a telegrapher for the Frisco Railroad, until his musical hobby landed him in the music and television world as a singing cowboy. *Courtesy of Photofest.*

network radio program, *Melody Ranch*. By July 1942, when he entered military service, his annual income was estimated at $600,000. No other person with a country-western background had ever enjoyed such financial success.

Out of the service in 1946, Gene Autry developed better plans to ensure his financial future. He soon managed to escape Republic Pictures and negotiate a new deal with Columbia. He and the tightfisted Herbert Yates had already had more than one contract dispute. After making only one film each year for Columbia in 1947 and 1948, he settled into a comfortable routine of six pictures a year through 1953, by which time changing tastes had brought singing cowboy movies and indeed the B western to an end. By the beginning of the 1950s, he had expanded into television as well. During those years, he not only continued to make hit records but scored his biggest hits with children's songs, such as "Here Comes Santa Claus," "Rudolph, the Red-Nosed Reindeer," "Peter Cottontail," and "Frosty the Snowman." Throughout the 1950s, Autry became less and less of an entertainer and more and more of a businessman. The details of his entrepreneurial endeavors are beyond the scope of this study, but, suffice to say, he remains the ultimate musical success story in his field.[11]

It did not take long for the Autry phenomenon to make an impression on other motion picture executives. While none did as well as the original singing cowboy, some did indeed have some remarkable achievements. Those who did best, like Gene Autry, sang convincingly, how the public thought that real cowboys might sound. Those who sang in a semi-operatic style did not do so well. The second singing cowboy, Dick Foran, is a case in point. Foran possessed a fine singing voice, but his style was too fancy and unconvincing. His first film, *Moonlight on the Prairie*—also released in 1935—and several more that followed for Warner Brothers made money, but they failed to generate the excitement that Gene Autry's pictures did. Those others who sang in the Foran manner, typified by Fred Scott, George Houston, James Newill, Smith Ballew, and Jack Randall, faced a similar fate. Persons who watched western films were not the same audience that watched operettas where people sang like Nelson Eddy and Jeanette McDonald in *Rose Marie*; audiences wanted entertainers who sang like down-home men of the West.[12]

Those who sang like cowboys might have sang, did better in films. Tex Ritter (1905–1974) probably had the most convincing cowboy singing voice, in spite of a college education, and was already an experienced recording artist via sessions for the American Record Corporation and Decca. He also had stage experience in New York and had hosted his own radio programs on various stations in New York City, such as *Tex Ritter's Campfire* and *Cowboy Tom's Roundup*. Coming to Hollywood in mid-1936, Ritter contracted with independent producer Edward Finney, who arranged for his films to be released by Grand National, a new company on somewhat shaky financial footing. Herbert Yates might have been a tightwad, but the early Autry pictures still had budgets in the $15,000–$18,000 range. Ritter's efforts were made with an $8,000–$12,000 budget range, and the results showed in spite of Tex's potential strength as a singing cowboy. The obvious use of old stock footage for distance scenes, some dating back to 1912, was obvious. While the twelve Tex Ritter movies did not pack the theaters with the same gusto as did those of Gene Autry, they did well. Tex had some outstanding leading ladies, including nineteen-year-old Rita Hayworth in *Trouble in Texas* and such remembered rangeland sweethearts as Eleanor Stewart, Iris Meredith, and Marjorie Rey-

nolds in others, but it was not enough to keep Grand National from going under. In mid-1938, before the roof fell in, Finney managed to take his cowboy singing star to Monogram, where Ritter chalked up twenty more films through 1941. In the most memorable of these, *Take Me Back to Oklahoma* (1940), movie audiences had the first opportunity to see western swing legends Bob Wills and the Texas Playboys on the silver screen. Tex continued to record for Decca through 1939 but did not really have what might be termed hits until he signed with Capitol in 1942.

The remainder of the Ritter films saw him sharing star credit, except for three motion pictures he made at Universal Studios in 1943 and 1944, which probably rank as his best. After leaving Monogram in 1941, he did eight pictures with action-star Bill Elliott at Columbia and seven with Johnny Mack Brown at Universal. The first four costarring Ritter and Brown all bore the names of songs. Ritter closed out his declining movie stardom at PRC (Producer's Releasing Corporation), sharing honors

Best known for his theme song to the critically acclaimed film *High Noon*, Tex Ritter enjoyed his career as one of Hollywood's famous singing cowboys. *Courtesy of Photofest.*

with Dave O'Brien and sidekick Guy Wilkerson in the last eight films of the "Texas Ranger" series. His fans found them pleasant and enjoyable but relatively undistinguished.

If Tex Ritter's movie career declined sharply in the latter half of World War II, his singing efforts reached new heights. Beginning with the cowboy-flavored "Jingle Jangle Jingle," he enjoyed a string of hits on the newly formed Capitol Records. As Doug Green points out, all of his later hits were far more "country" than western in terms of song content, but his image as an on-screen singing cowboy was pretty well set by this time. For the remainder of the 1940s, he turned out hits typified by "There's a New Moon over My Shoulder," "Jealous Heart," "I'm Wasting My Tears on You," and "You Two-Timed Me Once Too Often," which stayed atop the charts for eleven weeks. He also made new versions of some of his earlier traditional songs, like "Rye Whiskey," "The Old Chisholm Trail," and Everett Cheetham's "Blood on the Saddle." Somewhere in between was his rendition of the "Bo-Weevil." Ritter remained with Capitol for the rest of his life, but the most significant of his later recordings was probably "High Noon," the theme for the 1952 classic Gary Cooper western of the same name, which also launched Grace Kelly on the road to film immortality. He also hosted *The Town Hall Party* from 1953 to 1959, which was probably the principal country-western live show on radio and television (the latter syndicated as *Ranch Party*). Touring heavily, Ritter took an active interest in the formation of the Country Music Association and served as an early president. This circumstance led to his move to Nashville, early selection to the Country Music Hall of Fame, and affiliation with the *Grand Ole Opry*. A failed 1970 entry into politics as a U.S. Senate candidate did not hurt his musical popularity, although it may have drained much of his finances. He continued to tour and place songs on the lower rankings of the *Billboard* charts until his death at age sixty-eight.[13]

Bob Baker (1910–1975) had a brief career as a singing cowboy and had the advantage of being a credible western singer. Born Stanley L. Weed in Iowa, Baker grew up there and in Colorado and Arizona. He had experience as a radio singer in El Paso and for several months at WLS in Chicago. In 1937, he became Universal's singing cowboy through a dozen starring roles, beating out Leonard Slye in a screen test. After suffering an injury, the studio demoted Baker to a subordinate role under Johnny Mack Brown, and he never got top billing again. Unlike the other singing cowboys, he never got a recording contract, which is regrettable. Baker eventually returned to Arizona, where at various times he served on the Flagstaff police force, ran a dude ranch, and became a leather craft expert.[14]

In terms of movie stardom, the singing cowboy who most nearly rivaled Gene Autry, Roy Rogers (1911–1998), had originally been Leonard Slye of the Sons of the Pioneers. Born in Cincinnati, Slye grew up in rural southern Ohio, but in 1930, his family moved to California in search of a better life. When Gene Autry gave Republic Studios and Herbert Yates contract problems in

1937, the tightfisted studio head decided to develop another singing cowboy star, and Slye was given the role and a name change. His first film, *Under Western Stars*, proved to be a success, and Rogers went on to star in some eighty westerns, all for Republic, although he did not surpass Autry in popularity until 1943, when the original singing cowboy was in military service. Then Roy earned the sobriquet "King of the Cowboys." After the war, some of the Rogers films had bigger budgets, many of them costarring Dale Evans (1912–2001), who also became his wife in 1947.

Roy Rogers's solo vocals found their way onto American Record Corporation discs by the end of 1937, and in 1940, he moved on to Decca. Although his recordings did well, Rogers really had no major successes until after World War II, when he went with RCA Victor. By this time, like those of Gene Autry many of his recorded songs bore the same titles as his films. Examples include "Along the Navajo Trail," "Home in Oklahoma," "Night Time in Nevada,"

Known as the "King of the Cowboys," Roy Rogers enjoyed a long career of singing and acting with his wife Dale Evans. *Courtesy of Photofest.*

"Roll on Texas Moon," and, perhaps the best-known of all, "Don't Fence Me In." Still, Roy Rogers—although a fine singer, yodeler, and successful recording artist—never really had the hit songs experienced by Autry, Ritter, or another prominent singing cowboy, Jimmy Wakely.

The King of the Cowboys remained with Republic Studios until 1951 when he closed out his second seven-year contract and eighty-first starring role with *Pals of the Golden West*. He then went into television, making 100 half-hour dramas geared to the juvenile market through 1957. Afterward, Roy and Dale continued to tour and to make guest appearances for some years. In the 1970s, they recorded several albums for Capitol and even made another movie. In later years, he opened a museum in Victorville, California, made an album singing duets with various country stars, and died at the ripe old age of eighty-six.[15]

Four more singing cowboys made their appearance on film in the waning days of World War II and immediately thereafter. The first and most significant of these, Jimmy Wakely (1914–1982), had been a featured singer with small film parts since late 1939. Born in Arkansas and reared in Oklahoma, he began radio work in a trio group that included Johnny Bond and Dick Reinhart before going to Hollywood. In addition to small musical roles in films, Wakely—known initially as the "Melody Kid"—appeared with the trio on Gene Autry's *Melody Ranch* CBS network program and became a Decca recording artist in August 1940, having his first hit with a song called "Too Late," but a Bond composition, "Cimarron (Roll On)," probably had the most impact in the long run.

Jimmy Wakely finally got his own series for Monogram Pictures in 1944, beginning with *Song of the Range*. Over the next five years, he starred in a total of twenty-eight musical westerns, which were all pleasant if not particularly outstanding. In the earlier ones, former minstrel star Lasses White served as sidekick and also sang a bit from time to time. Wakely had a clear, smooth vocal style acceptable to both pop and country ears, hardly semi-operatic like Dick Foran, but considerably smoother than Tex Ritter. Many observers put him in the same vocal style as Gene Autry, but Wakely also mentioned listening faithfully to western swing vocalist Milton Brown in his early adulthood.

After thirty-four sides with Decca through 1944, Wakely signed with Capitol in 1947 and enjoyed his biggest hits with that company, including two that went number one, "One Has My Name (the Other Has My Heart)" and "I Love You So Much It Hurts," both in 1948. Ten more made the top ten. In addition, between 1949 and 1951, Jimmy and pop vocalist Margaret Whiting had nine additional top ten hits, three of which made the top ten on the *Billboard* pop charts. Their best-known song, a cover of country songwriter Floyd Tillman's "Slipping Around," stayed on top for seventeen weeks. While he continued to do songs with western themes, all of his major hits came with mainstream country material. Wakely remained with Capitol until 1953 and then went to Coral and back to Decca.

Wakely had a network radio show from 1952 through 1958, after many network radio programs had been discontinued. One advantage this indirectly provided him was that ownership of the tapes of these shows supplied him with much material that he later released on his record label Shasta. In addition to his own record label, which also featured recordings by Tex Williams, Johnny Bond, and Eddie Dean, among others, Wakely had a program on armed forces radio and continued touring until not long before his death at age sixty-eight.[16]

For all its brevity, the film career of Wakely outlasted that of Eddie Dean (1907–1999). Born in Texas, Eddie and his older brother Jimmy (1903–1970) began singing on radio in locales extending from Chicago to smaller markets, such as Shenandoah, Iowa, and Yankton, South Dakota. The brothers had recorded for Decca in 1934, but the material could hardly be termed western. Eddie came to Hollywood and worked clubs until he finally landed some small movie roles and worked on Autry's *Melody Ranch* series and then on Judy Canova's radio program. He had sessions back with Decca in 1941 and 1942, with eight sides released, including one of his own signature songs, "On the Banks of the Sunny San Juan." However, his big break occurred in 1944 with a strong appearance in Ken Maynard's last starring film, *Harmony Trail*. This led to a musical series for low-budget studio PRC (later Eagle-Lion). The Dean series lasted through eighteen pictures (nineteen if counting one edited slightly and rereleased under a different title), the first four shot in Cinecolor. Although Dean looked sufficiently heroic, he never seemed comfortable and relaxed on the screen. He had a good strong voice that held up until he was in his eighties. While Dean managed to get on some major labels, including Mercury and Capitol, his recordings were no more than average sellers, and the two really outstanding songs he composed were on a smaller label and became major hits when recorded by Wakely and Ritter. Nonetheless, he managed to earn a decent living with his music into the 1990s and was a familiar sight at western film fairs until advancing age slowed him down.[17]

Monte Hale (b. 1919) had a pleasant voice that brought him a series of nineteen starring films at Republic. Oklahoma-born and Texas-reared, Hale came to Republic at the behest of Herbert Yates in 1945, allegedly to keep Roy Rogers in line, just as Rogers had been brought in to keep Autry in line. With the passage of time, the singing in his films diminished, and in 1950, both ended. He recorded for the small Belltone label and had a number of pleasant releases on M-G-M. His most notable song, the patriotic "Statue in the Bay," ranks as a credible tribute to the Statue of Liberty and was also recorded by the Sons of the Pioneers. Hale also toured for a time as a singer but eventually drifted out of entertainment and into real estate and other forms of livelihood. Unlike Ritter and Wakely, who sustained lifetime careers out of their songs, Hale seemed uninterested, perhaps because he never had that big of a hit. He jokingly has said that he made more money from the popular line of *Monte Hale Western* comic books that came out from 1950 to 1955 than he did from his motion pictures. Universally admired by all who know him, Hale has one consolation: he has outlived all of the other western movie stars and cowboy singers of his generation.[18]

Unlike Monte Hale, his replacement at Republic studios and the last Hollywood musical cowboy, Rex Allen (1920–1999), experienced a long singing career. Allen, a native of Wilcox in Cochise County, Arizona, had a natural style and as authentic a western background as any movie cowboy ever in the business. Winning a local talent contest prompted him to seek a living in music. After a few false starts, he found himself a regular radio program at the unlikely location of WTTM Trenton, New Jersey, and also with the Sleepy Hollow Gang in Philadelphia. *Grand Ole Opry* star Roy Acuff met Allen in 1944 and urged him to try out at a major station. He lost his chance at WSM to the newly emerging Eddy Arnold but succeeded at WLS and the *National Barn Dance* in Chicago. He also began singing for the newly established Mercury Records in Chicago, and by the end of the 1940s, he had a string of successful—if not really super hit—recordings on the market, some with western and cowboy themes.

Along with the discs and a well-established reputation as a *Barn Dance* star, Allen attracted the attention of Republic's Herbert Yates, who thought the public would still accept a singing cowboy. Yates offered Allen a contract; Allen was reluctant to enter films but eventually relented. His first picture, *The Arizona Cowboy*, came out late in 1950, and from then until 1954, Rex Allen starred in a total of nineteen pictures. His series ended with *Phantom Stallion*, the last musical B western ever made. Meanwhile, he moved to Decca Records and had his biggest hit in 1953 with "Crying in the Chapel." In 1956, he had an excellent album of western songs with orchestral accompaniment. Back at Mercury in 1961, he had his biggest hit with a western flavor, "Don't Go Near the Indians." In addition to music, Allen's later career also included voice narration for such Disney nature films as *Charlie, the Lonesome Cougar*. He also narrated the Hanna-Barbara cartoon feature *Charlotte's Web*. Rex Allen had increasing visual problems as he grew older, which may have contributed to his accidental death on his Arizona ranch.[19]

While only the eight aforementioned movie cowboys qualify as approaching anything akin to stardom, a few others merit discussion. Ken Curtis (1916–1991), who also spent some time with the Sons of the Pioneers, had top billing in eight Columbia B musicals with western settings prior to gaining a greater fame as a character actor with his portrayal of "Festus Haggen" for many years in the TV western drama *Gunsmoke*. Ray Whitley (1901–1979) made a number of shorts for RKO Radio Pictures and sang in a few others during the late 1930s and early 1940s. Whitley also made some recordings for both the American Record Corporation and Decca in the same period. Probably his greatest contribution to the field was his primary authorship of "Back in the Saddle Again," which he recorded for Decca in 1938, but it became much better known when Gene Autry covered it and also became his radio theme song. In 1950, Tex Williams (1917–1985), who already had several hit records, made some fifteen shorts for Universal. Although actually a jazz singer, Herb Jeffries (b. 1911) made four musical B westerns in the late 1930s with all-black casts for showing in segregated African American theaters.[20]

Leading ladies in westerns films occasionally did a bit of singing. Only Dorothy Page (1904–1961) ever had a series, and it ended after three films. Although she had a pleasant voice, like Bob Baker she never recorded. Dale Evans, who played the leading lady in twenty-seven Roy Rogers pictures and on his TV shows, sang in a number of his films and made solo recordings for Majestic, RCA Victor, Capitol, and Word. She also contributed to the authorship of his radio theme, "Happy Trails to You." Carolina Cotton (1925–1997) sang in numerous Columbia western films and recorded for M-G-M, King, and some smaller labels. Jane Frazee, Jean Porter, Ruth Terry, and Penny Singleton sang in a few films but were really pop singers. Mary Ellen Kay sang duets with Rex Allen in a few of his motion pictures.[21]

Cowboy stars, whether they sang or not, were usually accompanied by a "sidekick" who primarily did comedy parts. A few of these contributed vocal numbers from time to time—most notably, Lester "Smiley" Burnette (1911–1967), who had the sidekick role in numerous Gene Autry and Charles Starrett films and also did a few with Sunset Carson and Roy Rogers. Burnette also had a recording career with the labels Capitol and Starday. Most of his original songs, such as "Hominy Grits" and "It's My Lazy Day," had little to do with the

West, but a few, such as "Jackass Mail," did. Others including Lasses White, Fuzzy Knight, and "Arkansas Slim" Andrews sang a bit from time to time but experienced no singing career as such.[22]

Although Charles Starrett—most famous as the "Durango Kid" in pictures— did not sing, most of his 125-plus starring films had musical moments first furnished by the Sons of the Pioneers and then by a variety of guests. Some were mainstream country stars, such as Ernest Tubb, Elton Britt, Jimmie Davis, and guitar innovator Merle Travis. Most, however, were small country and/or western groups with regional name recognition, such as the Columbus, Ohio-based Georgia Crackers or the Charlotte, North Carolina–based Tennessee Ramblers. Others were more obscure, like Ozie Waters and his Colorado Rangers or Shorty Thompson and his Saddle Rockin' Rhythm. These musical acts worked into the dramas in such roles as saloon entertainers who could also double as posse members to help round up outlaw gangs at the precise moment.[23]

At least three individuals who played minor roles in pictures had substantial careers on the California country and western music scene. Texas-born Stuart Hamblen (1908–1989) had first recorded for Victor in 1929, and after brief service with the Beverly Hill Billies had a more than twenty-year life as a major figure on Los Angles radio with his Lucky Stars. His western songs included "Poor Unlucky Cowboy" and his classic, "Texas Plains," which made up both sides of Decca's first country release. Most of Hamblen's better known songs were more country than western, and after his conversion around 1949, he turned his focus to sacred music, authoring such notable songs as "It Is No Secret (What God Can Do)" as well as the secular "This Old House." Johnny Bond (1915–1978) came to Hollywood as part of the Jimmy Wakely Trio but also had a long association on radio with Gene Autry. As a vocalist, he recorded for many years each for Columbia and Starday and composed such western favorites as "Cimarron (Roll On)." A man with scholarly insight into the significance of his peers, Bond wrote extensively in his later years, authoring a biography of Tex Ritter, his own autobiography, and a still unpublished manuscript that many people think may be the definitive work on Gene Autry. Wesley Tuttle (1917–2003) also had a short stint with the Beverly Hill Billies and worked in numerous films as a support musician. He also had a successful recording career with Capitol records beginning in 1944 and had numerous charted hits, most notably "With Tears in My Eyes." In the late 1950s, he, too, turned to sacred music and worked many years as an active minister but continued to make religious albums, many of them duets with his wife, the former Marilyn Myers.[24]

CHICAGO COWBOYS

While Hollywood singing cowboy movie stars and their associates may have dominated the western music scene and set the pattern for stage clothing, listeners probably heard more of the music on radio at the time. Outside of the

West Coast, the largest number of influential western vocalists was undoubtedly concentrated in Chicago. As Douglas Green has pointed out, the only real challengers among singing trios to the Sons of the Pioneers came from the Ranch Boys, consisting of Curley Bradley, Ken Carson, and Jack Ross, who sang on network radio and had about thirty sides released on Decca by 1937. When the trio disbanded in 1941, Carson went with the Sons of the Pioneers for a time while Bradley continued on in Chicago in various radio roles and also as the radio voice of Tom Mix.[25]

The other Chicago acts were associated with WLS and the *National Barn Dance* at one time or another. Ruby Blevins became known to the musical world as Patsy Montana (1908–1996). A native of Hope, Arkansas, she went to California to enroll in a music school but soon dropped out to work briefly with Stuart Hamblen. She also worked with a local trio known as the Montana Cowgirls, from whence she acquired her stage name. Coming briefly to KWKH Shreveport, Patsy shared a record session with Jimmie Davis. She then went to Chicago to appear at the 1933 World's Fair, which led to an audition at WLS where the Kentucky Ramblers were looking for a female singer.

This band soon changed their name to the Prairie Ramblers and recorded for Bluebird. With the exception of the year from December 1934 to December 1935, when they were at WOR New York, this group would be associated with WLS until the 1950s. While on the East Coast, the Ramblers converted totally to the western look. They also began extensive work with the American Record Corporation, where on August 16, 1935, Patsy recorded what would be her defining career song, "I Wanna Be a Cowboy's Sweetheart." Reputedly the first million-selling disc by a female in the country and western field, it became in the minds of many her only notable song, which is unfortunate because Patsy Montana had many outstanding numbers. Of some sixty recordings Patsy made with the support of the Prairie Ramblers, more than two-thirds had western themes and featured her spirited singing and yodeling. Many reflected a strong feminine viewpoint, such as "The She Buckaroo," "A Rip-Rip Snortin' Two Gun Gal," "I Wanna Be a Western Cowgirl," and "Rodeo Sweetheart." Others simply expressed a more romantic look, typified by "I Want to Be a Cowboy's Dream Girl" and "Little Sweetheart of the Ozarks." Others simply illustrated the continuing love for the west, like "Old Nevada Moon," "Back on Montana Plains," "I'm a Goin' West to Texas," and "Out Where the West Begins." Patsy also traveled to California, where she made one movie with Gene Autry, *Colorado Sunset* in 1939.

Patsy Montana left WLS and the Prairie Ramblers in 1940 and switched to Decca Records in 1941, where she had musical support from the Light Crust Doughboys and the Sons of the Pioneers in successive sessions. Her songs continued to be flavored with western material, including "Shy Anne from Old Cheyenne," Gallopin' to Gallup," "Sunny San Antone," and the current pop favorite "Deep in the Heart of Texas." Doing her part for military morale, her last Decca release was "Good Night Soldier" and "Smile and Drive Your Blues

Away." After the war, she returned to RCA Victor and continued to record for smaller labels into the 1970s, remaining semiactive until well past the normal retirement age.[26]

The Prairie Ramblers, with or without Montana, continued to play, sing, and record western material as well as swing-flavored, pop, humorous, sacred, hard country, and—as the Sweet Violet Boys—risqué and double-entendre songs for the jukebox trade. The original foursome of Chick Hurt (1901–1967), Jack Taylor (1901–1962), Salty Holmes (1909–1970), and Shelby "Tex" Atchison (1912–1982) proved to be one of the most versatile in country music history. After Atchison and Holmes departed, Hurt and Taylor recruited Alan Crockett (1915–1947) and Rusty Gill (b. 1919) as replacements. Following World War II, they continued to record on the Mercury label and in the 1950s evolved into a polka combo, at which time they became known as Stan Wolowic and the Polka Chips and had the honor of being the first polka band in 1956 to have a prime-time network television program.[27]

Patsy Montana was not the only yodeling cowgirl to join the *National Barn Dance* in 1933. That year the cast also gained the soft-voiced harmony duet known as the Girls of the Golden West. Natives of Mt. Carmel, Illinois, Mildred (1913–1993) and Dorothy Good (1915–1967) had brief radio experience at KMOX in St. Louis before arriving at Chicago and WLS a few months before Patsy Montana joined the Prairie Ramblers. From 1933 until 1938, they also recorded sixty-four songs, mostly for Bluebird but also a few for the American Record Corporation. About two-thirds of their songs were western in content, and most of the remainder were old favorites, such as "When the Bees Are in the Hive." They split their western material between such traditional songs as "Get Along Little Doggies" and "Bucking Broncho" to newer songs typified by "I Want to Be a Real Cowboy Girl." The latter is notable because it suggests that the term "cowgirl" may have not yet been in general use (Patsy Montana's "I Wanna Be a Western Cowgirl" was made in 1939). Milly and Dolly sang and yodeled in soft but tight harmony that in retrospect sounds somewhat like a feminine version of brother duets, except that the girls used only a simple guitar accompaniment.

When John Lair left WLS in 1937 to go to WLW Cincinnati and pursue his dream of creating his *Renfro Valley Barn Dance*, he dipped deeply into the *National Barn Dance* talent pool, including the Girls of the Golden West. However, when Lair moved again to rural Kentucky in 1939, Milly and Dolly remained in Cincinnati, where Milly's husband had a position with WLW. The Cincinnati station had their own *Boone County Jamboree* (known after 1942 as the *Midwestern Hayride*). Although they made no more recordings until 1963, by which time they had been long retired, the Goods continued to play and tour the area through 1949, by which time their style had become dated, as honky-tonk-flavored music seemed to be taking over much of the Midwest and upper South. They did a series of albums for Bluebonnet in 1963, sounding virtually the same as in 1938, but Dolly's death in 1967 ended the possibility of any comeback. Milly lived on for another generation, during which time she informed researchers that the girls had not come from Muleshoe, Texas, as the WLS publicity department had earlier claimed, and that their original surname had been Anglicized as well. The only thing really western about them had been their costumes and their music, which—in the final analysis—was what really mattered.[28]

If the image of the Girls of the Golden West had been largely manufactured, no real need existed to do so for the other major western act in Chicago. The Massey Family originally hailed from Hunt County, Texas, where Henry Massey's oldest daughter, Victoria Louise (1902–1983), was born. After moving to Midland, two additional children were born—Allen (1907–1983) and Curt (1910–1991)—and around 1914, the family took up ranching near Roswell, New Mexico. Dad Massey also developed his children into a family music group with himself as the fiddling leader. Louise sang and played piano while Allen played guitar and young Curt also fiddled and played the trumpet. When Louise married Milt Mabie (1900–1973), he became their bass player. About 1928, the Masseys went professional, touring on the Chautauqua circuit and then doing radio for a year at WIBW Topeka and then at KMBC Kansas City. At the latter locale, the Westerners added accordion player Larry Wellington (1903–1973) to their entourage. About the time they came to the *National Barn Dance* in 1933, Dad Massey retired, but he did fiddle on some of their sessions for the American Record Corporation as late as 1937. Like the Ramblers and Patsy Montana, the Westerners went to New York for a time and then returned to Chicago. The Massey's music tended to be a bit more formal than that of the other Chicago groups but was still firmly in the western category.

From 1939, the group became known as Louise Massey and the Westerners. Not all of their songs had a cowboy or western flavor, such as their 1942 hit, "The Honey Song," although many did. They contributed several originals—most notably, Curt's "Ridin' Down That Old Texas Trail" in 1934; "When the White Azalia's Start Blooming"; and Louise's classic, "My Adobe Hacienda" in 1941. The Westerners made a film appearance in Tex Ritter's Monogram film, *Where the Buffalo Roam*, in 1938. Louise and Milt eventually retired back to New Mexico, although Allen and Curt—who composed the themes for both the *Beverly Hillbillies* and *Petticoat Junction* television shows—remained in music in various capacities.[29]

In 1949, the *National Barn Dance* contributed its last major figure to the cowboy genre in the person of Bob Atcher (1914–1993), who had already been an accomplished veteran of the Chicago and network radio scene for a number of years. A native of Hardin County, Kentucky, Atcher may or may not have spent part of his boyhood in North Dakota and was adept at rendering older folk songs, cowboy numbers, contemporary country, and even a touch of humor, particularly with his version of "Thinking Tonight of My Blues," through which he shed a number of satirical tears. His recording career began with the American Record Corporation, and continued with the company after it became Columbia. Many of his early discs were duets with Loetta Applegate, who was billed as "Bonnie Blue Eyes." In the early 1940s, Atcher appeared in two Columbia pictures, *Panhandle Trail* and *Hail to the Rangers*, both with Charles Starrett. In the late 1940s, he had two ten-inch albums on Columbia, one of cowboy material, *Songs of the Saddle*, and another titled *Early American Folk Songs*. He switched to Capitol in the early 1950s, but did straight country material. During his barn dance years, Atcher was known for his well-tailored western clothing. The year before the WLS program ended, he branched into local politics, becoming mayor of suburban Schaumberg, Illinois, a position he held for sixteen years. When the program moved to WGN, he remained with it throughout that period, by which time he had become known as the "Dean of Cowboy Singers" and cut a new Columbia album of that name. After retirement Atcher moved back to Kentucky, where he spent his declining years.[30]

The postwar *National Barn Dance* leadership assembled a western vocal group called the Sage Riders composed of Dolph Hewitt, Don White, Ray Klein, and Red Blanchard. All were radio veterans, and White had been in three films as a member of the Charlotte-based Tennessee Ramblers. The Sage Riders made no commercial recordings but cut numerous transcriptions, many of which featured White's pleasant vocals on such western songs as "There's a Blue Sky Way out Yonder." When the group dissolved at the end of the decade, Hewitt continued as a solo star at the *Barn Dance*, eventually retiring to Florida. White returned to the Carolinas, where he remained semiactive until his death in 2005. Blanchard did comedy into the 1960s on the *WGN Barn Dance*.[31]

COWBOYS IN THE EAST AND SOUTH

New York has seldom been thought of as a country or western music center. Yet a surprising number of artists thrived there in the 1930s, including those normally based in Chicago who spent some time there. Tex Ritter had been there prior to his 1936 move to Hollywood, as had Ray Whitley. Carson Robison, although not really a western singer, cultivated a cowboy image along with his band, the Buckaroos. John White (1902–1992), known on radio as the Lonesome Cowboy, who worked there for several years as a part-time performer, wrote an authoritative book on cowboy songs in retirement. Tex Fletcher (1909–1987), known as the "Lonely Cowboy," had a lengthy radio career in New York. Wilf Carter (1904–1996), the Canadian cowboy singer and yodeler, had a CBS Radio Network program based there from 1936 to 1940, where he adopted the name "Montana Slim" for American audiences. After being sidelined by an auto crash in 1940, Carter never quite regained his momentum in the United States, but his lengthy recording career—much of it doing western songs—for Bluebird, R.C.A. Victor, and Apex make him one of the all-time great western singers.[32]

There were others in the American metropolis. Buck and Tex Ann Nation played radio there. Denver Darling (1909–1981), nicknamed "the Illinois Cowboy" by his biographer, W. K. McNeil, had radio programs on WOR and WNEW, sometimes with unrecorded radio veteran from WWVA Wheeling Silver Yodelin' Bill Jones. Darling recorded over the years with Decca, DeLuxe (as Tex Grande), and M-G-M. Tiring of New York and experiencing voice problems, he eventually returned to his Illinois homeland, with his principal legacy being the song "Silver Sage, Purple Skies, Eyes of Blue." In later years, Bobby Gregory and his Cactus Cowboys ranked among the leading purveyors of western music in the Big Apple.[33]

Several notable musical figures made New York their headquarters for at least a substantial portion of their careers. Elton Britt (1913–1972), the Arkansas-born yodeling champion and former Beverly Hillbilly, had some of his biggest hits while there, including the World War II patriotic classic "There's a Star-Spangled Banner Waving Somewhere" and his duets with Rosalie Allen (1924–2003). The latter also made solo recordings, had a local deejay show from 1949 until 1956, and was billed as "Queen of the Yodelers." Most of the songs of North Carolina–born Texas Jim Robertson (1909–1966) were standard country, but he emphasized a western image. David McEnery (1914–2002), known as "Red River Dave," based himself at several locales over the years, including New York (as well as Hollywood and San Antonio) and in spite of recording a considerable volume of western material is probably best remembered for his topical songs, such as "Amelia Earhart's Last Flight."[34]

The border radio stations also made significant contributions to cowboy and western music. By most accounts, the most popular vocalist on the stations was Nolan "Cowboy Slim" Rinehart (1911–1948), a true Texan who sang on the stations and sold thousands of songbooks. Unfortunately, Rinehart left no recordings as a legacy, but the few transcriptions available suggest that he showed a Jimmie Rodgers influence and did more country than western. A later border radio cowboy was Dallas Turner (b. 1927), usually known as "Nevada Slim." Unlike Rinehart, Turner made a number of long-play albums during the 1960s for Rural Rhythm Records.[35]

In fact, western music made an impact on major country radio jamborees all over the country. Kansas City's KMBC *Brush Creek Follies* boasted the talents of Cowboy Tex Owens (1892–1962), who wrote, introduced, and recorded on Decca the celebrated song "Cattle Call" long before Eddy Arnold ever heard of it. At the *Grand Ole Opry*, Tex's younger sister, Texas Ruby (1910–1963), worked for several years (1937–1939 and 1944–1948) as a vocalist, both before and after her marriage to Tennessee fiddler "Curly" Fox. Most of her recordings were honky-tonk, but her image was that of the yodeling cowgirl. Earlier, she had worked with Zeke Clements (1911–1994), who with his Bronco Busters also personified the cowboy image at the *Opry* for a number of years, although his only song to have a western theme was "Blue Mexico Skies."

At WWVA Wheeling, Doc Williams and the Border Riders readapted "Ridin' Down That Old Texas Trail" to "Ridin' Down That Old Border Trail" as a theme song and wore western outfits, but most of their music remained hard country. So, too, did Harry C. McAuliffe (c. 1903–1966), who as Big Slim, the Lone Cowboy, had a lengthy musical career. Slim did maintain some cowboy songs throughout, such as "Patanio, the Pride of the Plains," "Billy Venero," and "Cowboy's High-Toned Dance." He also had a trained horse. During World War II, the Radio Rangerettes (Millie Wayne and Bonnie Baldwin) proved to be one the station's more popular acts, with a style and song not unlike that of the Girls of the Golden West.

Downriver at WSAZ Huntington, Margie Shannon (b. 1922) delighted listeners as the Lone Star Yodeler. In New England, Yodeling Slim Clark (1917–2000) sustained a long career on radio and TV with a style and song repertoire faintly resembling Wilf Carter. In Charlotte, Fred Kirby (1910–1996) always favored cowboy styles, although he was essentially a country singer. During World War II, Kirby, the man formerly known as the "Carolina Cowboy" became known as the "Victory Cowboy" and hosted a kids' TV program until he was past eighty. Across the Appalachian Mountains, Homer Harris, known as the "Seven Foot Cowboy," sang and had a trained horse named Stardust who could, among other talents, climb up and down stairways. Well into the 1950s, it seemed that singing cowboys were everywhere.[36]

In fact, the phenomenon reached beyond the U.S. borders. In addition to Wilf Carter, Canada had Tex Cochrane, Allen Erwin (the Calgary Kid), and, for many years, Hank Snow (1914–1999), who later became a major figure in the United States but was known in his homeland for years as "Hank, the Yodeling Ranger" and then as "the Singing Ranger." In faraway Australia, Tex Morton, Buddy Williams, Smoky Dawson, and Slim Dusty (Gordon Kirkpatrick) all based their image on American cowboys to varying degrees. Australia even had yodeling cowgirls, typified by Shirley Thom and June Holm.[37]

However, with the demise of the musical western films, the days of the radio and television singing cowboys were numbered. Many went into other forms of livelihood, survived on children's TV programs, or, more likely, were absorbed into the country music mainstream. In some cases, about the only residue that remained was the western-styled stage clothing that most country singers favored for years, many of them designed and custom-made by Nudie, the Rodeo Tailor.

Still the music and songs did not die. The Sons of the Pioneers continued on even after the death of Lloyd Perryman, under the leadership of Dale Warren. Ritter, Wakely, Dean, and Allen continued even if more of their songs were country rather than western. Now and then, country singers had hit songs with western themes. Chief among them was Arizona-born *Grand Ole Opry* star Marty Robbins (1925–1982), who between 1959 and 1964 had several hit songs that were clearly western in theme and arrangement, beginning with "The Hanging Tree," peaking with the Latin-flavored "El Paso," and continuing with "Running Gun," "Big Iron," "Five Brothers," and "The Cowboy in the Continental Suit." He also had three high-ranking albums in this period that were all laden with western themes and, while mostly containing new songs, included a few traditional ones like "Utah Carroll" and "Little Joe, the Wrangler." Johnny Cash (1932–2003) had a big hit with "Don't Take Your Guns to Town" in 1959 and a lesser one with "The Rebel—Johnny Yuma" in 1961. The latter was the theme for a television "adult western." While the adult westerns had no singing cowboys, they did have popular theme songs, beginning with that of *The Life and Legend of Wyatt Earp* in 1955.[38]

The most popular of the adult western themes may well have been the "Ballad of Paladin" by Johnny Western (b. 1934) from *Have Gun, Will Travel*. However, other programs also had resonating themes, often sung by pop singers or vocal groups, such as *Cheyenne*, *Rawhide*, and *Bat Masterson*. An occasional western-flavored song ranked high on the country charts from time to time as well. These included two by Billy Walker, "Cross and Brazos at Waco" and "Matamoros"; two by Stu Phillips, "The Great *El Tigre*" and "Juanita Jones"; and "The Man Who Robbed the Bank at Santa Fe" by Hank Snow.[39]

THE COWBOY MUSIC REVIVAL

Eventually a renaissance of cowboy music developed among both groups and individuals, but in the early 1970s, it could hardly have been predicted. Until then, such groups as the Wagon Masters, who entertained at California's Knott's Berry Farm for thirteen years, or local groups, such as The Flying W Wranglers, who entertained at spots like the Flying W Chuck Wagon in Colorado Springs, kept live performances of the music alive. The Reinsmen, a part-time group, also gave quality, if infrequent, concerts, spawning imitators at a half-dozen other locales throughout the West. Nostalgic fans of the old movies began to organize western film fairs, where they watched the old motion pictures and listened to those old timers, like Eddie Dean and Carolina Cotton, who remained in good voice. As time passed on, the movie originals did the same, and the entertainment shifted to people like Johnny Western, Australian immigrants the LeGarde Twins (b. 1930); or Roberta Shore (b. 1943) and Randy Boone (b. 1942) from *The Virginian* TV series.[40]

Perhaps a leading factor in the rekindling of interest in western song came from the formation of the Riders in the Sky in the latter part of 1977. Douglas B. Green (b. 1946), a former oral historian at the Country Music Foundation with some writing credentials, formed the group with Fred LaBour (b. 1948) and Bill Collins (b. 1948) at first to play on the Nashville club scene. Styling themselves as "Ranger Doug, the Idol of American Youth" on guitar, "Too Slim" on bass, and Collins on fiddle—who soon gave way to Paul "Woody Paul" Chrisman, "the King of Cowboy Fiddlers"—Riders in the Sky combined quality harmony on vocals, yodeling, and more than a touch of satirical humor. Beginning in 1980, they turned out a series of albums on Rounder, MCA, and Columbia and joined the *Grand Ole Opry* in 1982. Their songs tended to be a combination of older items from B western film days and newer originals. Their best-known song was probably a number by Green called "That's How the Yodel Was Born," which offers the theory that the first yodel came from a cowboy who was being bounced up in the air by a bucking horse and came down with his posterior landing on the saddle horn. The yodel was the sound he made in reaction to this accident. While the theory may be of dubious authenticity, there can be little doubt that Riders in the Sky attracted a great deal of attention.

The Riders managed to get themselves seen and heard. In the early days of the Nashville Network on cable TV, they hosted a program called *Tumbleweed Theater*, which showed old B westerns interspersed with their songs, some factual history, and their humorous skits during breaks. From 1988 until 1996, they had a Saturday-morning program on National Public Radio titled *Riders Radio Theater* and during the 1991–1992 season had a CBS Saturday-morning TV program aimed at the children's market. By the end of the 1980s, they had added a fourth member, Joey "The Cowpolka King" Miskulin (b. 1949) on accordion. Through touring widely and offering quality music and entertainment ("the Cowboy Way"), Riders in the Sky have led the way in a rebirth of western music, even without the benefit of a charted hit record. Whether or not Ranger Doug (or his alter ego, Sgt. Dudley of the Royal Canadian Mounted Police) is really the "Idol of American Youth," may be hard to determine, but Douglas B. Green's recent book, *Singing in the Saddle: The History of the Singing Cowboy*, seems likely to endure as the definitive work on the subject.[41]

Other evidence of a renewal of interest in cowboy songs and music came with the creation of the Warner Western label in 1992 as a subdivision of Warner Brothers. The principal force behind this action was the success of one-time country singer Michael Martin Murphey (b. 1945), whose songs "Cowboy Logic" in 1990 and "Let the Cowboy Dance" in 1991 placed on the charts. Doing an entire album of traditional and newer *Cowboy Songs*, Murphey brought in a recently discovered trio from California, the Sons of the San Joaquin, for support. The trio, composed of Joe (b. 1932) and Jack Hannah (b. 1933) together with Joe's son Lon (b. 1956), had first gained an appreciative audience at the Cowboy Poetry Gathering in Elko, Nevada. They subsequently did two albums of their own for Warner Western. That label also signed Oregon ranch country born-and-reared Joni Harms (b. 1959), who cut a fine album, *Cowgirl Dreams*, containing songs like "Two-Steppin' Texas Blue" and "Blue Montana Moon." Another interpreter of the modern cowboy has been former rodeo rider Chris LeDoux (1948–2005), who experienced several mid-level hits for Liberty with newly composed songs, many of which touched on his own life on the circuit. His biggest number, "Whatcha Gonna Do with a Cowboy," reached number seven on the *Billboard* listings in 1992. A more traditional singer of western material, Don Edwards (b. 1939) has gained prominence in recent years. His double compact disc, *Saddle Songs*, released by Shanachie in 1997, is a tasteful tribute to tradition with a few respectful originals.[42]

So while western music generally surfaces around the outside edge of the contemporary country mainstream, somewhat like bluegrass and Cajun, it appears to be alive and well. The golden age of the singing cowboy, which thrived for about two decades from 1935, is gone forever, and the culture that produced it has changed with the times. Yet the myth of the singing cowboy, part based on truth but mostly a product of an image created by Hollywood, live radio, and television, survives and continues to fascinate the American imagination.

NOTES

1. For a brief account of the myth of cowboys and their music, see the first two chapters of Douglas B. Green, *Singing in the Saddle: The History of the Singing Cowboy* (Nashville: Country Music Foundation Press and Vanderbilt University Press, 2002), 1–19. In fact, Green's book is the indispensable source for this entire chapter, as many otherwise uncited small items have been gleaned from it.

2. Bill C. Malone, *Country Music, U.S.A.*, 2nd rev. ed. (Austin: University of Texas Press, 2002), 139; Green, *Singing in the Saddle*, 28–30.

3. John I. White, *Git Along Little Doggies: Songs and Songmakers of the American West* (Urbana: University of Illinois Press, 1975), 189–195.

4. Malone, *Country Music, U.S.A.*, 139; Henry Young, *"Haywire Mac" and the "Big Rock Candy Mountain"* (n.p.: Stillhouse Hollow Publishing, 1981); Charlie Seeman, "Cowboy Singers," *The Journal of the American Academy for the Preservation of Old-Time Country Music* 25 (hereafter cited as *The Journal*) (February 1995), 12–15.

5. Fred Hoeptner, "Goebel Reeves: The Texas Drifter," *Old Time Music* 18 (Autumn 1975), 10–18; Seemann, "Cowboy Singers," 12–15.

6. Green, *Singing in the Saddle*, 35–36.

7. Ibid., 49–50.

8. Ken Griffis, *Hear My Song: The Story of the Celebrated Sons of the Pioneers* (Los Angeles: John Edwards Memorial Foundation, 1974); Green, *Singing in the Saddle*, 69.

9. Green, *Singing in the Saddle*, 247–255.

10. Ibid., 94–112.

11. The Autry autobiography, Gene Autry, *Back in the Saddle Again* (Garden City, NY: Doubleday, 1978), is of limited value. It can be supplemented with David Rothel, *The Gene Autry Book* (Waynesville, NC: World of Yesterday Publications, 1986), and Douglas B. Green, "Gene Autry," in Bill C. Malone and Judith McCulloh, eds., *Stars of Country Music* (Urbana: University of Illinois Press, 1975), 142–156. A concise view is offered in Charlie Seemann, "Gene Autry: America's Singing Cowboy," *The Journal* 22 (August 1994), 8–11.

12. David Rothel, *The Singing Cowboys* (San Diego, CA: A. S. Barnes & Company, 1978), 103–107.

13. Johnny Bond, *The Tex Ritter Story* (New York: Chappell Music Company, 1976); Bill O'Neal, *Tex Ritter: America's Most Beloved Cowboy* (Austin, TX: Eakin Press, 1998); Green, *Singing in the Saddle*, 169.

14. Bobby J. Copeland, *The Bob Baker Story* (Oak Ridge, TN: BoJo Enterprises, 1997).

15. Rothel, *The Singing Cowboys*, 111–192; David Rothel, *The Roy Rogers Book* (Madison, NC: Empire Publishing, 1987). A concise survey is Lawrence Zwisohn, "Roy Rogers: King of the Cowboys," *The Journal* 2 (December 1992), 8–11.

16. Linda Lee Wakely, *See Ya up There, Daddy: The Jimmy Wakely Story* (Canoga Park, CA: Shasta Records, 1992); Rothel, *The Singing Cowboys*, 209–229. A good brief survey is Charlie Seeman, "Jimmy Wakely: Oklahoma Boy Goes West," *The Journal* 27 (June 1995), 16–17.

17. Rothel, *The Singing Cowboys*, 193–208; Boyd Magers, *Top 100 Cowboys of the Century* (Albuquerque, NM: Western Clippings, 1999), 29–30.

18. Rothel, *The Singing Cowboys*, 230–244; Green, *Singing in the Saddle*, 239–241.

19. Rex Allen, *The Arizona Cowboy: My Life, Sunrise to Sunset* (Scottsdale, AZ: RexGarRus Press, 1989); Green, *Singing in the Saddle*, 268; Charlie Seemann, "Rex Allen: The Arizona Cowboy," *The Journal* 24 (December 1994), 16–17.

20. Ken Griffis, "The Ray Whitley Story," *JEMF Quarterly* 6:2 (Summer 1970), 65–68; Rich Kienzli, "Tex Williams: Talking His Way to Fame," *The Journal* 16 (August 1993), 18–19; Green, *Singing in the Saddle*, 177–180, 242–245.

21. Boyd Magers and Michael G. Fitzgerald, *Westerns Women* (Jefferson, NC: McFarland, 1999), 84–90; Ivan M. Tribe, "Carolina Cotton: Hollywood's Yodelin' Sweetheart," *Old Time Country* 7:3 (Summer 1991), 5–8.

22. David Rothel, *Those Great Cowboy Sidekicks* (Waynesville, NC: World of Yesterday Publications, 1984), 3–40, 158–159, 218; Green, *Singing in the Saddle*, 141.

23. For music in the Starrett films, see Green, *Singing the Saddle*, 198–200.

24. Ken Griffis, "I've Got So Many Million Years: The Story of Stuart Hamblen," *JEMF Quarterly* 14 (Spring 1978), 4–22; Lawrence Zwisohn, "Johnny Bond: From Oklahoma to the Hollywood Hills," *The Journal* 35 (October 1996), 12–15; Packy Smith, *Wesley Tuttle: Detour* (Hamburg, Germany: Bear Family Records BCD 16416, 2002).

25. Green, *Singing in the Saddle*, 280–281.

26. Patsy Montana with Jane Frost, *Patsy Montana: The Cowboy's Sweetheart* (Jefferson, NC: McFarland, 2002); Ronnie Pugh, "Patsy Montana: America's Cowgirl Sweetheart," *The Journal* 14 (April 1993), 16–17. A forthcoming article by Wayne W. Daniel will likely become the definitive work on Montana.

27. Dave Samuelson, "The Prairie Ramblers: The WLS Swinging String Band," *The Journal* 24 (December 1994), 18–19.

28. Tony Russell and Charles Wolfe, "Two Cow Girls on the Lone Prairie: The True Story of the Girls of the Golden West," *Old Time Music* 43 (Winter 1986/1987), 6–13; Charles Wolfe, "Girls of the Golden West: The First Singing Cowgirls," *The Journal* 2 (December 1992), 16–17.

29. Jim Bob Tinsley, *For a Cowboy Has to Sing* (Orlando: University of Central Florida Press, 1991), 98–99, 234–235.

30. Dave Samuelson, "Bob Atcher: Dean of the Cowboy Singers," *The Journal* 17 (October 1993), 16–17.

31. For the Sage Riders, see Ivan M. Tribe, *Don White: Star of the WLS National Barn Dance* (Cattle Records LP 65, 1984), liner notes; Edward C. Allmon, *Dolph Hewitt: King of the Barn Dance* (Cattle Records LP 111, 1987), liner notes.

32. Green, *Singing in the Saddle*, 26–27, 46, 47, 66–68.

33. W. K. McNeil, "Denver Darling: Illinois Cowboy," *Old Time Country* 7 (Fall 1991), 4–12.

34. Green, *Singing in the Saddle*, 288; Charles Wolfe, "Red River Dave: The Legendary Old Cowboy Singer," *The Journal* 15 (June 1993), 16–17; W. K. McNeil and Louis Hatchett, *Elton Britt: The RCA Years* (Collectors' Choice Music CD031-2, 1997), liner notes; Robert K. Oermann, "Rosalie Allen: Queen of the Yodelers," *The Journal* 51 (October 1999), 3–5.

35. Gene Fowler and Bill Crawford, *Border Radio* (Austin: Texas Monthly Press, 1987), 82–86, 182–187; Guy Logsdon, *"The Whorehouse Bells Were Ringing" and Other Songs Cowboys Sing* (Urbana: University of Illinois Press, 1989), 18–21.

36. Guy Logsdon, *Tex Owens: Cattle Call* (Hamburg, Germany: Bear Family Records, 1994), liner notes; Charles Wolfe, *A Good Natured Riot: The Birth of the Grand Ole Opry* (Nashville: Country Music Foundation Press and Vanderbilt University Press, 1999), 254; Charles Wolfe, "Curly Fox & Texas Ruby: The Cowgirl & the Fiddler," *The Journal* 13 (February 1993), 18–19; Ivan M. Tribe, *Mountaineer Jamboree: Country Music in West Virginia* (Lexington: University Press of Kentucky, 1984), 47–49, 54, 77; Kevin Coffey, "Slim Clark: New England's Yodeling Cowboy," *The Journal* 33 (June 1996), 18–19; Homer Harris, *Life Story* (n.p.: c. 1991).

37. Fred Roy, "A Pictorial Review of Country Music in Canada," in Thurston Moore, ed., *The Country Music Who's Who*, Part 8 (Denver, CO: Heather Publications, 1966), 1–8; Eric Watson, *Country Music in Australia*, Volume 1 (Sydney, Australia: Cornstalk Publishing, 1983).

38. "Alias Marty Robbins," *Hoedown* 1 (June 1966), 8–12; Green, *Singing in the Saddle*, 308–311; Joel Whitburn, *Top Country Hits*, 4th ed. (Menomonee Fall, WI: Record Research, 1998), 294.

39. Whitburn, *Top Country Hits*, 268, 325, 366.

40. Green, *Singing in the Saddle*, 312–315.

41. *Grand Ole Opry Picture History Book* (Nashville, TN: Gaylord Entertainment, 2001), 106–107.

42. Green, *Singing in the Saddle*, 321–324.

4

Western Swing

The decade of the 1930s is mostly remembered as the era of the Great Depression and of those efforts after 1933, known as the New Deal, to combat this major economic downturn. Yet within the realm of American musical culture it was a time of innovation. The popular music mainstream saw the rise of what became known as the big band sound, in which jazz-influenced orchestras led by such men as Benny Goodman, Glenn Miller, and Sammy Kaye became prominent. Vocalists like Bing Crosby and later Frank Sinatra and Doris Day became popular, eventually becoming bigger names than their original employers. The world of country music had its equivalent of this jazz infusion in music. At first it went by such names as "Texas Swing," "Okie Jazz," and "Hot String Bands." Only during World War II did the term "western swing" emerge. By that time, it had spread to California, and even in the eastern states, bands were playing the music. The fiddle ranked as the dominant instrument in western swing, but the stylings were quite different from the fiddle as played by Clark Kessinger, Eck Robertson, and Doc Roberts. The smooth jazzy approach seemed more like that of pop music, and the vocals exemplified by singers like Tommy Duncan or Milton Brown bore little resemblance to those of Charlie Poole, Uncle Dave Macon, or Ernest Stoneman. Since the music had been essentially created for the dance halls of Texas and adjacent states, western swing bands also pioneered the use of amplified electric instruments that produced more volume in order to be heard above the crowds. Furthermore, band members might indulge in what became known as improvised "take off" instrumental solos. Some swing bands even had trumpets and clarinets at times. The rise of the coin-operated jukebox trade also called for more volume and ranks as another major factor in the growth of western swing. Some swing groups might have as few as four or five members while others might have ten or more. Many swing numbers were instrumentals with no vocals at all.

TEXAS AND THE BIRTH OF A NEW MUSIC

Historians searching for the roots of western swing invariably find it in Texas. The two persons cited by most scholars as its creators are the fiddler Bob Wills (1905–1975) and the singer Milton Brown (1903–1936). Scholars also find antecedents in an otherwise obscure fiddler, known as "Prince Albert" Hunt, who made a few OKeh recordings in 1928 and 1929 before he became a homicide victim in 1931. Others see elements of western swing in the East Texas Serenaders, while some do not. One recent work sees elements of Texas swing in the efforts of even more obscure combinations as the Paradise Joy Boys and the Three Virginians, each of which made a few recordings for Brunswick and OKeh in 1928 and 1929, respectively.

Some consensus, however, can be found that the elements of Texas swing came together in 1931–1932 through the efforts of the aforementioned Milton Brown and Bob Wills, who came together as a team in the employment of Burris Mills, the manufacturer of Light Crust Flour. A commercial-minded company manager nonmusician named W. Lee O'Daniel (1890–1969) hired Brown and Wills as a radio act to promote Light Crust Flour under the name of Light Crust Doughboys. A third musician, initially Herman Arnspiger (1904–1984) but later Sleepy Johnson (1909–1976), played guitar. On February 9, 1932, Brown, Wills, Johnson, and Brown's kid brother Derwood recorded two songs—"Nancy Jane" and "Sunbonnet Sue"—for Victor under the name Fort Worth Doughboys. While this foursome were hardly a full band at this point, it can be said to have been the birth date of western swing.[1]

In September 1932, Brown and then Wills (the following August) left Burris Mills to each create their own bands. O'Daniel hired more musicians and headed the band himself, although he still was a nonperformer. Later he would also leave and start his own company, "Hillbilly Flour," and create still another band. Meanwhile, the Light Crust Doughboys still continued on under Burris Mill sponsorship. Journeyman musicians moved from one band to another and helped each other on recording sessions. As western swing became more popular, it seemed that every major city in Texas and Oklahoma had at least one band. So, too, did the three major recording firms Decca, Victor, and that conglomeration known as the American Record Corporation, all of which preserved a large volume of the music. Those who would not classify western swing as being country ignore the fact that these record companies all classified it as part of their "hillbilly" or country releases at the time.[2]

After Brown and Wills departed from O'Daniel and formed their own bands, the former achieved success first. Milton Brown was born and reared at Stephensville, Texas, some sixty miles south of Fort Worth. As he grew up, Brown developed a pleasant singing style that was compatible with popular, country, and jazz vocals. His family had moved to the city during World War I, and Milton worked as a salesman until 1930, when he lost his job and a chance meeting with fiddler Bob Wills changed his life. With Herman Arnspiger, the two formed a trio that soon landed a radio spot at WBAP under the sponsorship of the Aladdin Lamp Company. They also began to play dances at a place on the edge of town called Crystal Springs. Within a few months, they gained Burris Mills as a sponsor and became the Light Crust Doughboys. Seven months after they had recorded the two songs for Victor as the Fort Worth Doughboys, Brown went on his own in September 1932 and formed the Musical Brownies and did a radio program at KTAT. Brown did the vocals, his brother Derwood Brown (1915–1978) played guitar, Jesse Ashlock (1915–1976) did the fiddling, Ocie Stockard (1909–1988) played tenor banjo, and Wanna Coffman (1911–1991) played bass. A little later they added Fred Calhoun (1904–1987) on piano and Cecil Brower (1914–1965) as a second fiddler. Ashlock dropped before the Brownies made their first recordings for Bluebird in April 1934. For their second Bluebird session four months later, Ted Grant was added as a second fiddler. With their regular radio programs at KTAT, dances at Crystal Springs, and dances in other area communities on the other nights, the Musical Brownies were in constant demand while simultaneously creating a new musical form.

By January 1935, the Brownies had signed with the new Decca label, and although Grant had left, Bob Dunn (1908–1971) had been with the group for a few months on steel guitar. Dunn is usually credited with introducing the electric steel guitar to the world of country music. The thirty-six numbers the Brownies recorded in Chicago over a two-day period pretty much solidified the western swing sound and included such standards as "Beautiful Texas," "My Mary," and "Who's Sorry Now." A few months later, the band moved to WBAP—the city's biggest station—and added a second fiddler in the person of twenty-year-old Cliff Bruner (1915–2000).

The next Decca sessions, over three days in March 1936 in New Orleans, resulted in some forty-nine masters, which proved fortunate because some six weeks later Brown died in a fatal automobile crash. The songs included "Right or Wrong," "The Eyes of Texas," and a clever set of double-entendre lyrics entitled "If You Can't Get Five Take Two," which taken literally tells of the survival of a grocery store during a time of economic hardship, but it could also be about a prostitute who reduces her service fee. Brown's death hit the band hard, and Derwood tried to keep them together with slight personnel changes, but it was not to be. After a final session for Decca in February 1937 that yielded a dozen more numbers, the Musical Brownies dissolved. Milton Brown not only had been a strong leader and fine vocalist, but his charisma had kept

Bob Wills and his Texas Playboys dominated western swing music in the 1930s and 1940s. Shown here with his favorite saddle, Bob had a great love for horses. *Copyright © Corbis.*

the band on an even keel; and he was the irreplaceable man. As Cliff Bruner, who went on to lead a quality western swing band himself, told Cary Ginell in 1995, Milton Brown "was the greatest bandleader who ever lived and . . . if he was still living, I'd still be working for him."[3]

During the time Milton Brown led the Musical Brownies successfully in Fort Worth, his one-time companion in the Doughboys, Bob Wills, also started his own band. Tommy Duncan (1911–1967) was hired to replace Brown as vocalist. In August 1933, O'Daniel and Wills parted ways, and Wills went to Waco. There Wills formed the Texas Playboys, with Duncan as lead vocalist, Kermit Whalin (1905–1978) on bass, June Whalin (1907–1991) on guitar, younger brother Johnny Lee Wills (1912–1984) on tenor banjo, and himself on fiddle. The Texas Playboys had a program on WACO radio from September 1933 until January 1934. Legal battles with O'Daniel continued for a time, but while Wills triumphed in the courts, O'Daniel used his influence to get Wills removed from radio programs in Waco and at WKY in Oklahoma City, where the group played for only about a week. Beginning on February 9, 1934, the Texas Playboys found a radio home at KVOO Tulsa.

Over the next several months, Wills added more musicians to the Texas Playboys, and like in all bands, personnel changes took place, The Whalins departed and new musicians joined—most notably, Arnspiger and Cliff "Sleepy" Johnson, who had left O'Daniel's employ. The most notable former Doughboy was a teenage steel guitar player, Leon McAuliffe (1917–1988), who came on board in March 1935. McAuliffe soon equaled or surpassed the Brownies' Bob Dunn as an innovator, and the phrase "Take it away Leon" became almost as famous as Will's trademark "Ah-haa." Leon's "Steel Guitar Rag," an adaptation of blues musician Sylvester Weaver's "Guitar Rag," went on to become the most famous tune in that instrument's history.

By the time the Playboys did their first session for the American Record Corporation in September 1935, Wills had added some additional band members, including Jesse Ashlock on fiddle, Smokey Dacus (b. 1911) on drums, Zeb McNally (1914–1964) on alto saxophone, and Al Stricklin (1908–1986) on piano. The twenty numbers they recorded exemplified the diverse nature of their music. Such pop classics as "I Can't Give You Anything but Love" competed with Jimmie Rodgers's "Never No More Blues." Wills included two of his longtime favorite originals, "Spanish Two-Step" and "Maiden's Prayer," along with blues songs like W. C. Handy's "St. Louis Blues" and the Mississippi Sheiks' "Sittin' on Top of the World." Other instrumentals included numbers that they performed at dances, like "Osage Stomp" and "Oklahoma Rag," while Duncan vocalized to advantage on songs typified by "I Ain't Got Nobody" and "I Can't Be Satisfied."

With two nights a week playing regular dances at the large dance hall known as Cain's Dancing Academy in Tulsa, four nights on the road usually at dances within driving distances, and six radio programs per week at KVOO, the Texas Playboys soon had all the work they could handle. Their recordings were selling nationwide but most heavily in the southwestern states. While musicians came and went from the band, the changes tended to be minimal, with not much turnover in the nucleus of the group. One especially significant addition in November 1937 was Eldon Shamblin (1916–1998), who would play electric lead guitar for the Playboys off and on for many years. Several of the songs recorded in the later 1930s would enter the list of Wills classics, such as "Trouble in Mind," "Time Changes Everything," "I Wonder If You Feel the Way I Do," and "San Antonio Rose" in 1938.

The latter song had been so popular as an instrumental that it was redone in 1940 with added lyrics as "New San Antonio Rose." This was the arrangement with two fiddles and a full horn section that would become the signature song for Bob Wills and the Texas Playboys. Bing Crosby soon covered it for the popular music market, where it became a top ten hit, and in the early 1970s, two astronauts actually sang it on prime-time television in outer space. As Charles Townsend puts it, "New San Antonio Rose" transformed Bob Wills from a regional to a national figure.[4]

Even before "New San Antonio Rose" was released, Bob Wills and five band members had journeyed to Hollywood and made their first of several motion picture appearances. Their first movie was Take Me Back to Oklahoma in the summer of 1940 with Tex Ritter. The following year, the next film for Columbia, Go West Young Lady, was a more elaborate affair and starred Penny Singleton, Ann Miller, and Glenn Ford. The remaining films generally starred Russell Hayden and bore such titles as A Tornado in the Saddle, Saddles and Sagebrush, and Wyoming Hurricane. While most ranked as otherwise undistinguished B westerns, they did give moviegoers all over the nation a chance to see the man that most knew only from his records.

The coming of World War II saw the end of the golden era of the Texas Playboys. Tommy Duncan enlisted shortly after Pearl Harbor, and others were either conscripted or placed in defense plants. When the band did record sessions in 1942, only Bob Wills and Leon McAuliffe remained of the old band members. The others were new, although some like Joe Holley (1917–1987) and Leon Huff (1912–1952) had been accomplished veterans of other western swing bands. Wills himself entered the army in December 1942 for an eight-month stretch, which above all else demonstrated that he was too old and not really cut out to be a soldier.

Wills and the musicians he could keep together survived the rest of the war, mostly in California. The Golden State had become a hot locale for Texas swing music because of wartime conditions and the large concentration of defense workers and military personnel on the West Coast. As former band members got released from military duties, many reassembled in a revamped version of the Texas Playboys, including Duncan, Holley, and Shamblin, along with several newcomers. They resumed recording for Columbia (previously known as the American Record Corporation) in late January 1945. Many of their new songs from 1945 reflected the not yet ended war, such as "Smoke on the Water," "Stars and Stripes on Iwo Jima," "Silver Dew on the Bluegrass Tonight," "White Cross on Okinawa," and "Empty Chair at the Christmas Table." Other new songs made a more lasting impression on Wills fans, including "Roly Poly," "Hang Your Head in Shame," and "There's a Big Rock in the Road." On October 16, 1947, Wills did his last recording for Columbia and on October 30 began a seven-year association with M-G-M. The hundred numbers he made in those years did not yield the numbers he had made famous over the previous twelve but did include one giant, "Faded Love," in 1950, which probably ranks second only to "San Antonio Rose" as his most famous song. In September 1948, Tommy Duncan had left and formed his own band, and Rusty McDonald did the vocal lead. Ironically, those April 1950 sessions would be the only ones the latter ever did as a Texas Playboy, and Duncan would return again in the early 1960s. During the M-G-M years, Wills also experimented with adding female vocalists to the line-up, including Laura Lee Owens (1920–1989), the daughter of Tex Owens and, in the early 1950s, Hollywood yodeling cowgirl Carolina Cotton.

The popularity of western swing went into decline during the course of the 1950s, especially after the rise of rock and roll in mid-decade, although Wills remained sufficiently popular to earn a comfortable living. Shifts of location and some bad business decisions left him in debt much of the time, and his periodic drinking bouts caused occasional problems. He left California for Oklahoma City in 1949 and a year later shifted to Dallas, where he built a dance hall almost twice the size of Cain's in Tulsa but found it challenging to be both a businessman and a musician. He had to work on the road to keep the hall open because of a dishonest accountant. After two years, he sold it to Jack Ruby, who eventually achieved a different kind of fame. Over the next several years, Wills moved from time to time, looking for another home like he had in Tulsa between 1934 and 1942 while continuing to be away on tours much of the time. Sacramento, Amarillo, Houston, Fort Worth, and Abilene were all residences at one time or another. In 1955, he began recording for Decca and in 1960 for Liberty. Many of the latter efforts brought Tommy Duncan back on the lead vocals again, and they also did some touring. After 1964, Wills no longer kept a band together but had made some recordings both before and after for the Texas-based Longhorn company and then made some albums for Kapp with studio musicians. The 1960s also saw health problems giving him troubles. In 1968, the Country Music Association elected him to its Hall of Fame. In 1971, reigning country star Merle Haggard made a tribute album on Capitol with Wills present and leading a band that included several of the older Playboys. In December 1973, United Artists assembled another group of former band members for two days of sessions. By this time, Bob Wills was in a wheelchair but made token efforts at leading the first day. Overnight he suffered a stroke and slipped into a coma that lasted for eighteen months until his death on May 13, 1975. The man had died, but his music lived on in one form or another.

Even after Milton Brown and then Bob Wills departed from the Light Crust Doughboys, and despite O'Daniel's initial personal distaste for the music he had earlier derided, "Pappy" O'Daniel was an astute businessman who realized that the sponsorship could sell flour. Unlike the Brown and Wills aggregations, the Doughboys did not play dances but concentrated on radio and promotional tours for Burris Mills. Therefore, O'Daniel hired more musicians to augment the remaining Arnspiger and Johnson. Clifford Gross replaced Wills on fiddle, Leon Huff became their vocalist, teenage guitarist Leon McAuliffe played steel, and Ramon DeArman (1911–1940) handled the bass fiddle rhythm. In October 1933, O'Daniel took them to the World's Fair at Chicago and sessions for the American Record Corporation (which beat either the Musical Brownies or the Texas Playboys into the studios), where they cut their own version of his composition "Beautiful Texas" and such topical numbers as "On to Victory, Mr. Roosevelt" and "Memories of Jimmie Rodgers." In 1934, they had additional sessions for the same company at San Antonio in April and Fort Worth in October.

After one session in 1935, W. Lee O'Daniel left Burris Mills to start his own company, Hillbilly Flour, taking Leon Huff as the centerpiece of a new band called, not surprisingly, the Hillbilly Boys. Burris Mills continued a Doughboy band, with Kenneth Pitts joining Gross on fiddle and bringing in Dick Reinhart as a vocalist with other musicians. Personnel changed, but the Light Crust Doughboys remained an active radio and recording group until they temporarily disbanded during World War II. Prominent members over the next three or four years included Marvin Montgomery (1913–2001) on tenor banjo, Zeke Campbell (1914–1997) on electric lead guitar, and John "Knocky" Parker (1918–1986) on piano. Through 1941, the band had some 128 sides released by the American Record Corporation.

Some band members took the name Coffee Grinders for a time during the war, when they had a sponsorship from the Duncan Coffee Company. After World War II, the band reformed and recorded two sessions for King in 1947. For a time, they were also known as the Flying X Ranch Boys but ultimately resumed with their old name. After that, they did not record again until 1989, and their radio programs were phased out in the early 1950s, but they continued to exist as a group, often doing promotional appearances for Burris Mills even after Burris was bought out by Cargill in 1971. Veteran swing musicians Marvin Montgomery and Jim Boyd usually led them during this period, and since Montgomery's demise, Art Greenhaw has served as leader in recent times.[5]

W. Lee O'Daniel remained serious in the flour business for three years before turning his attention to politics. During that time, his Hillbilly Boys played radio programs on border radio, multi-station "Texas Quality Network," and made some sixty-six sides for the American Record Corporation. Huff, who Pappy nicknamed the "Texas Songbird," did most of the vocals, and at times, the Hillbilly Boys had some other quality musicians in the group, including Kermit and June Whalin, a young fiddler named Carroll Hubbard (b. 1918), and Lefty Perkins (1917–1984) on steel guitar, who would go on work with several groups. Their most famous number was "Please Pass the Biscuits, Pappy." Increasingly, Pappy's sons, Pat and Mike O'Daniel, took prominent roles in the group, on tenor banjo and fiddle, respectively. In 1938, Pappy threw his hat into the race for governor, and the Hillbilly Boys did their part in getting the flour executive into the governor's office. In spite of breaking with Leon Huff, who quit in a huff, O'Daniel got a second term in 1940 and was elected to fill an unexpired term in the Senate the next year, where he remained until January 3, 1949. Leon Huff eventually joined the Texas Playboys in California and then went to Tulsa, where he spent the rest of his short life as vocalist with Johnnie Lee Wills and his Boys at KVOO Tulsa, recording with them on Decca, Bullet, and RCA Victor.[6] Although W. Lee O'Daniel's political career is beyond the scope of this study, one can say in retrospect that while his achievements were minimal, his skill at combining music, radio personality, and show business with politics set something of a precedent that paved the way for the later success of Jimmie Davis, and one might even add such figures as George Murphy and Ronald Reagan to the list.

Fort Worth may have been the birthplace of Texas or western swing, but the style soon made an impact on other Texas cities as well, including nearby Dallas. In that city, there were radio bands at stations like WRR and WFAA but no dance bands per se. The two key figures in recording were a western-styled singer, Bill Boyd (1910–1977), and a staff pianist, Roy Newman (1899–1981), with a jazz preference. Both entered the record studios in 1934, Boyd a few months earlier than Newman. Boyd had come to the city from rural Fannin County, began singing at WFAA in 1930, and moved over to WRR two years later. In August 1934, Boyd with three band members from WRR, styled the "Cowboy Ramblers," began what would be a seventeen-year career with Bluebird/RCA Victor that resulted in 229 masters, of which 227 were issued, a figure that would place him second only to Wills in recorded output. While the Cowboy Ramblers had a swing sound, after their first session they did not tour as such or play dances. Boyd played theaters and fairs as a vocalist, sometimes with a small band, but did not do dances, although his records did very well on jukeboxes. In a sense, he was Victor's answer to the Texas Playboys. According to one estimate, the Cowboy Ramblers' instrumental rendition of "Under the Double Eagle" may have ranked second only to "Steel Guitar Rag" as a Texas swing instrumental. Many of Boyd's musicians were staff band musicians from WRR, with a few pickers borrowed from the Light Crust Doughboys or other bands. His most often used musicians included his brother, Jim Boyd (1914–1993), who worked often with both Roy Newman and especially the Light Crust Doughboys; Walter Kirkes (1918–1996), a staff band member from WRR on tenor banjo; and fiddler Art Davis (1913–1987). Others who spent time in the studios as a Cowboy Rambler included Cecil Brower, Kenneth Pitts, Carroll Hubbard, and Marvin Montgomery. After his career as a musician with RCA Victor ended in 1951, Bill Boyd made a few recordings for Starday and TNT and then worked as a deejay until he retired in 1973.[7]

Roy Newman and his Boys started their recording careers for the American Record Corporation only a few weeks after the Cowboy Ramblers debuted on disc. In this case, the "Boys" included the same Art Davis, Jim Boyd, and Walter Kirkes, along with three additional musicians, one being Holly Horton (1892–1944), a veteran Dixieland clarinetist. While Newman's sessions usually included Horton's clarinet, they seldom used a steel guitar, except in 1937 when they used the services of Bob Dunn. Through June 1939, Roy Newman and his Boys amassed a recorded legacy of seventy-two sides, but they disbanded soon afterward.[8]

Straddling a fence somewhere between western swing and the more traditional country duet were the Shelton Brothers, who divided their time between WWL New Orleans, KWKH Shreveport, and WFAA Dallas. They originally recorded as a mandolin-guitar duo, but at their second Decca session in December 1935, they added traditional fiddler Curley Fox to their recording and, in 1937, a swing fiddler, Lonnie Hall, from Leon's Lone Star Cowboys; an accordion played by Harry Sorenson; and Slim Harbart on bass. Later Shelton recordings had a tenor banjo and an electric mandolin. In addition, some of the Shelton band had separate recording sessions as the Sunshine Boys, one of which was augmented by legendary Houston piano player Moon Mullican singing a rendition of his oft-recorded "Pipeliner's Blues."[9]

Western swing bands were soon flourishing in other urban centers within the Lone Star State. Far South of Dallas–Fort Worth, where strong Hispanic influences mingled with the Anglo-Celtic culture, three groups made a regional impact. The first to make it into the recording studio, the Tune Wranglers, had been organized in 1935 by Edwin "Buster" Coward (1903–1975), an area ranch hand and guitar player. He assembled four friends: fiddler Tom Dickey (1900–1956), tenor banjoist Joe Barnes (1910–1981), pianist Eddie Whitley, and bassist Charlie Gregg (1909–1977). The Wranglers played on KTSA and WOAI, assembling for their first Bluebird session in February 1936, where they put sixteen numbers on disc, including what would become their best-known original song: "Texas Sand." Over the next two years, the Wranglers placed a total of seventy-nine songs and tunes on disc. Among their more notable later efforts were the song "Hawaiian Honeymoon" and a musical adaptation of a cowboy poem about a heroic horse named "Chopo." Personnel shifted somewhat, and two sessions had a steel guitar played by Eddie Duncan. Dickey left the band after their second session, was replaced by Ben McKay and later by twin fiddlers Leonard Seago (d. 1949) and Noah Hatley. Despite the quality and spirit of their music, the Tune Wranglers never had much impact outside of the San Antonio area and disbanded around 1940.[10]

Some members of the Wranglers also worked in San Antonio's second swing band: Jimmie Revard (1909–1991) and the Oklahoma Playboys. Revard was an Oklahoman who moved to San Antonio as a child and put his Oklahoma Playboys together about the same time or slightly later than the Coward band. The Oklahoma Playboys also played on different local radio stations and began recording for Bluebird in October 1936. Two stalwart members of the Oklahoma Playboys throughout the band's existence were two brothers from the Czech-German community in south Texas, Adolph and Emil Hofner, who would eventually have their own band. Another was John H. "Curley" Williams (1914–1993), a former Tune Wrangler, who shared the lead vocals with Adolph Hofner. The Playboys obviously based much of their style on that of the increasingly well-known Texas Playboys and would eventually place eighty-one numbers on disc. However, Revard made a mistake when on poor advice he moved the band to fresh territory at KOAM in Pittsburg, Kansas. Their dance opportunities there were almost nonexistent, and things fell apart. They made it back to San Antonio, where the band broke up after its October 1938 session. Revard made a final appearance on Bluebird in 1940 with a studio group that included Leonard Seago and the Hofners. By that time, Revard had joined the San Antonio police force and thereafter played music only on a part-time basis.[11]

The swing band that ultimately endured in San Antonio was that of Adolph Hofner (1916–2000). A native of Moulton, Texas, Hofner also made forays into the Czech music of his home community. In fact, Hofner's band, initially known as the Texans but then as the San Antonians and eventually as the Pearl Wranglers (from its Pearl Beer sponsor), eventually outlived any western swing band other than the Light Crust Doughboys. Adolph had initially learned singing from recordings as diverse as those of Bing Crosby and Jimmie Rodgers, but after he heard Milton Brown and the Brownies, he became a swing convert. Emil or "Bash" (b. 1918) played steel guitar for his brother's band throughout its existence, as he did for the Oklahoma Playboys and the short-lived Tom Dickey Show Boys. Adolph Hofner began recording for Bluebird under his own name in April 1938, when he and Emil were still affiliated with Revard. He did not really have a hit record until 1940 with the Spanish-flavored slow-ballad "Maria Elena." The next year, Hofner went to the American Record Corporation and scored again with instrumentals "South

Texas Swing"/"Jessie Polka" both co-composed with his new and already accomplished fiddler, J. R. Chatwell (1915–1983), who had already displayed his skills with Bill Boyd's Cowboy Ramblers and the Modern Mountaineers, among others.

Following these successes, Hofner took his band to California for a time to cash in on the growing popularity of swing on the West Coast. Wartime attitudes led Adolph to become known as "Dub" Hofner until the conflict ended. Returning to San Antonio in 1946, he became a fixture in south Texas and from 1950 was sponsored by Pearl Beer, another long-time Texas institution. In later years, he recorded for Columbia, Decca, Imperial, and Sarg. In 1994, he celebrated his fifty-fifth anniversary as a full-time musician at his favorite San Antonio dance hall, the Farmer's Daughter. In succeeding years, however, old age and health problems began to slow him down.[12]

The largest population center in Texas—Houston—also emerged as a center of swing music in 1936. The first person to lead a swing band from Houston to the recording studio was a younger fiddler, Leon "Pappy" Selph (1914–1999), who took his Blue Ridge Playboys to a makeshift session for the American Record Corporation in November 1936. That band included two key persons on the Houston swing scene who would eventually attain some fame on their own: singer-pianist Aubrey "Moon" Mullican (1909–1967) and singer-songwriter Floyd Tillman (1914–2003). Selph took the name of his band from a Blue Ridge land project of Houston developer Jesse Jones, who owned radio KXYZ, where they had a regular program. He got his nickname from the fact that he had just become a father. Selph's band was quite active in the area until the onset of World War II. Selph recorded thirty issued sides for American Record Corporation and eight for Decca but in later years worked as a fireman and played music only part-time.[13]

In theory, the leading western swing figure in prewar Houston should have been Cliff Bruner. This innovative fiddler with his bands, first the Texas Wanderers and then simply the Boys, ranked right behind Wills, Boyd, Brown, and the Light Crust Doughboys among the giants of the music's first decade. However, for a complexity of reasons, Bruner found himself in and out of the city more than once with side junkets to such spots as Beaumont, Austin, and Shreveport. As a twenty-year-old, Bruner had recorded forty-nine numbers with Milton Brown's Musical Brownies in that marathon session that took place in New Orleans only weeks before the leader's fatal crash. He left the band shortly after the wreck, after concluding that Derwood Brown was no leader. Not long afterward, he came to Houston, organized the Texas Wanderers, got a radio spot at KXYZ, and secured a contract with Decca on the strength of his prior work with the Brownies. With all this going his way, he soon aroused the ire of *Houston Chronicle*-KXYZ owner Jesse Jones, who if anything caused him more problems than Pappy O'Daniel created for Bob Wills. It all began when Jones demanded that Bruner's band play all its dances at the Jones-owned Aragon Ballroom for less money than Bruner was already being paid for playing dances. Bruner refused and immediately found himself fired and unable to get a job at the other stations in Houston that were also Jones properties. Put plainly, Jesse Jones almost literally ran Bruner and the Texas Wanderers out of town.

However, with his band intact, including both Moon Mullican and Bob Dunn, Bruner went to KFDM in Beaumont, where he not only survived but thrived. About the time of his move, he also did his first session for Decca on February 5, 1937. Over the next five years, Bruner formed and re-formed his band more than once, had brief associations with the campaigns of Jimmie Davis, Jerry Sadler, and W. Lee O'Daniel (very short), and hoped to find a job out of music that would bring about a more settled home life. Meanwhile, his band returned to the studio several times and placed ninety-seven masters in the Decca vaults, all of which would eventually be released. After the war, Bruner had a session for Mercury and two for the regional Ayo label, but by the end of 1950, he had gone into insurance sales full-time. Thereafter, he played sporadically and part-time.

Two offshoots of the Bruner band made something of a splash in Houston circles. Steel guitarist par excellence Bob Dunn had three Decca sessions. Dunn's band, styled the Vagabonds, has been described as Bruner's band without its normal leader. Another Bruner alumnus, Dickie McBride (1913–1971), a quality vocalist, had been the singer on Bruner's Decca rendition of Floyd Tillman's classic composition, "It Makes No Difference Now." McBride had two sessions with the Village Boys in 1939 and 1941 on Decca. The band did three additional sessions on Bluebird, two without McBride. After the war, McBride and his wife, Laura Lee, remained active on the Houston scene.[14]

Shelley Lee Alley (1894–1964) and his Alley Cats constituted another Houston-based swing band. Alley had written two songs—"Traveling Blues" and "Gambling Barroom Blues"—for Jimmie Rodgers and had a record session with him in January 1931. Shelley Lee and his brother Alvin had backgrounds in pop and Dixieland but switched to string music in the mid-1930s, placing over fifty released sides on disc for the American Record Corporation and Bluebird between 1937 and 1941. Shelley Lee's Alley Cats included Ted Daffan (1912–1996), who later led his own band, on steel guitar and sometimes borrowed Leon Selph and Cliff Bruner for recording sessions.[15]

A short-lived but exciting Houston group, the Modern Mountaineers, played at KTRH and were led by John (1913–1960) and Roy Thames (1915–1939) and paced by "hot jazz" fiddler J. R. Chatwell, who later spent many years in San Antonio with Hofner's bands. On the first of two 1937 Bluebird sessions, the Mountaineers had the services of John B. "Smokey" Wood (1918–1975), a piano-playing marijuana user who soon formed an even more short-lived band called the Wood Chips that had a single session on Bluebird in September 1937. After an unsuccessful move to KWKH Shreveport, the group returned to Texas and disbanded. In 1940, the Texas Wanderers, of which the Thames boys were members, revived the name Modern Mountaineers and did three more sessions, one of which had Moon Mullican on piano and vocal and another with Bob Dunn on steel.[16]

Ironically, what had been the oldest established band in Houston—the Bar X Cowboys—never entered a recording studio until Selph's, Bruner's, and Alley's bands had already been there. Led first by fiddler Ben Christian (1885–1956) and then by his brother Elwood (1892–1970), the Cowboys played from 1932 until the early 1950s and were, according to Kevin Coffey, "more musically conservative than most western swing bands." They recorded for Decca in 1937 and for Bluebird in 1940 and 1941. Ted Daffan played steel on two of their sessions, and on their last recording trip in 1941, Jerry Irby (1917–1983), who would emerge as a major figure in postwar Houston, did the vocals on their final prewar discs. After World War II, their discs appeared on small local labels, such as Globe and Macy's.[17]

By the time the Alley Cats had dissolved, Ted Daffan and his Texans had become a major force on the Houston scene. In 1939, he began to develop a reputation as a songwriter when Cliff Bruner cut his song "Truck Driver's Blues." Daffan had previously recorded with other Houston groups but not under his own name until he stepped in front of the microphone as leader of Ted Daffan's Texans on April 25, 1940, and cut a dozen titles, including his first real hit, "Worried Mind," and his first original instrumental, "Blue Steel Blues." Continuing with two sessions in 1941 and then in February 1942, he came up with a two-sided hit "No Letter Today"/"Born to Lose." Guitarist Chuck Keeshan handled most of the vocals on Texans discs, with fiddler Leonard Seago and occasionally Daffan himself singing a bit on some numbers. On the strength of these numbers, the band shifted operations to southern California, where they worked on the circuits and appeared on a regular basis at the Venice Pier Ballroom. Daffan scored another hit with "Headin' down the Wrong Highway." In 1946, Daffan returned to Texas and continued to record on Columbia, where with a new band he experienced another hit with "Shut That Gate," featuring George Strange on vocal. His hits slowed down thereafter, but one of his 1950 efforts, "I've Got Five Dollars and It's Saturday Night," became a major hit for Faron Young in 1956. Daffan in later years concentrated on songwriting and in 1955 started a record company called Daffan, which cut some records by newer local artists, including Jerry Jerico, as well as some older ones.[18]

In addition to Daffan, the music scene in postwar Houston included Dick and Laura Lee McBride; Floyd Tillman, who was becoming more of a honky-tonk singer; and the Bar X Cowboys. However, the artist who may have made the biggest impression—other than Tillman, who had major hits—was former Bar X Cowboy vocalist Jerry Irby (1917–1983). He formed a band, the Texas Ranchers, and opened his own dance hall, the Texas Corral, in 1948. He also had a signature song in "Drivin' Nails in My Coffin" and recorded for both Imperial and M-G-M in the later 1940s. In spite of a couple of chart appearances in 1948, he never became more than a regional performer and ultimately turned to gospel music in the 1970s.[19]

Smaller Texas urban centers also had some worthwhile bands. Amarillo, the Texas Panhandle city, although much smaller (population 51,000 in 1940), boasted a quality swing band in the Sons of the West. This aggregation included bass player-vocalist Jimmie Meek (b. 1911); a steel guitarist of quality in Billy Briggs (1919–1984), a Bob Dunn protégé who had once worked with the Hi-Flyers; and pianist Loren Mitchell (1912–1992), a veteran of the Crystal Springs Ramblers (the band that played at Crystal Springs when the Brownies were absent). The Sons of the West recorded a total of sixteen sides for Decca in 1938 and for the American Record Corporation in 1941. However, the band became a casualty of World War II, although some members worked in a postwar group called the XIT Boys. Briggs later recorded solo for Imperial and had a 1951 novelty hit with "Chew Tobacco Rag." Bob Skyles (1910–1998) and his Sky-rockets rank somewhere between a novelty group and a swing band. Working out of Brady, San Angelo, and El Paso at various times they recorded for Bluebird and Decca during their seven-year existence. Finally, like Floyd Tillman, Al Dexter (1905–1984) and His Troopers, who worked out of Longview, fall into a category somewhere between western swing and honky-tonk. They are best remembered for their giant 1942–1943 hit, "Pistol Packin' Mama."[20]

THE EXPORT OF TEXAS SWING

Texas swing music had major centers outside the Lone Star State. After all, Bob Wills and the Texas Playboys had found their first true success at KVOO and Cain's in Tulsa. After Bob moved to California, Johnnie Lee Wills and His Boys continued on in Tulsa with a quality dance group that lasted until 1964. Johnnie Lee began recording for Decca in April 1941 and, with fiddler Guy "Cotton" Thompson, virtually made the Kokomo Arnold blues number "Milk Cow Blues" his own. Later the band had hits with "Rag Mop" and the kiddie Easter classic "Peter Cottontail" on Bullet and cut some good numbers on RCA Victor that featured Leon Huff on vocals. Earlier the Texas Playboys had a rival in Tulsa at KTUL radio: Dave Edwards and his Alabama Boys. However, this band broke up soon after their only record session for Decca in December 1937, although some of its members later played in both Wills groups, including Eldon Shamblin and the aforementioned Cotton Thompson.[21]

Oklahoma City, perhaps because Bob Wills had only a short stay there, never really had a top quality band until the advent of Hank Thompson (b. 1925) and his Brazos Valley Boys after World War II. However, the prewar period was not exactly barren either. The Hi-Flyers had been based in Fort Worth at KFJZ, where they were initially an old-time group and moved with the times toward swing. Finding the field crowded in Fort Worth, the band relocated to a border station across the river from Eagle Pass, and then in 1939 to KOMA in Oklahoma City. Recording over fifty sides for the American Record Corporation between 1937 and 1941, their most notable recording was probably the original of steel guitarist Andy Schroeder (1916–1977),

"Roadside Rag." Like many other swing bands, the Hi-Flyers became a casualty of World War II.[22]

Although not a swing band, the duo of Wiley Walker (1911–1966) and Gene Sullivan (1914–1984) at Oklahoma City's largest station, WKY, used swing band accompaniment on most of their recordings beginning in 1939 (not unlike the Shelton Brothers). Sullivan was a veteran of such Dallas recording groups as Roy Newman's Boys and Leon's Lone Star Cowboys. Wiley and Gene had a major two-sided hit in 1942 with "When My Blue Moon Turns to Gold"/ "Live and Let Live" and continued into the early 1950s. Hank Thompson in many respects was more of a honky-tonk singer, but he also had a top flight western dance band that had first made its name in Oklahoma City, especially between 1954 and 1957.[23]

Another place outside of Texas where a degree of swing music flourished was at KWKH Shreveport, although in some respects it was more of a place where vocalists used swing music on their records. The best example of this was Jimmie Davis, and as Davis moved toward more acceptable mainstream song material, the more rowdy subject matter was taken up by his protégé, Shreveport police officer Buddy Jones (1906–1956), who continued to favor material from the low-down white blues material that Davis had favored in the earlier days—typified by "Mean Hangover Blues" and "She's Selling What She Used to Give Away"—and was far removed from his own straight lifestyle. Jones used swing musicians on his forty-plus Decca recordings, many of these musicians associated with Cliff Bruner bands, including Bob Dunn, Johnny Thames, and Leo and Randall Raley, in addition to Bruner himself. Another Louisiana group who leaned toward swing was Bill Nettles (1903–1967) and his Dixie Blue Boys. Nettles spent many years in radio, mostly in the Pelican State. Shreveport and the smaller city of Monroe seem to have been his favored spots. The Dixie Blue Boys had sessions with the American Record Corporation, Bluebird/RCA Victor, and Bullet over a number of years beginning in 1937, but their only major hit came in 1949 on Mercury with a song about the patent medicine that temporarily took the nation by storm, "Hadacol Boogie." In addition, rumor has it that Nettles had earlier composed "Nobody's Darling but Mine" and sold it to Jimmie Davis.[24]

Perhaps the most swing-oriented Shreveport band was the Rice Brothers Gang, led by two Georgia Boys, Hoke (1909–1974) and Paul Rice (1913–1988). As Paul Rice later told historian Wayne Daniel, "We was hillbillies, but we didn't play hillbilly." Hoke made some early recordings on the Brunswick label in 1930, but the brothers formed their act in 1934. Dividing their time between Atlanta and other eastern locales, the Rices first came to Shreveport in 1935–1936 and then returned again in 1939 and remained there until the war broke up their act in 1942. Meanwhile, they made the first of their fifty-six issued sides for Decca in 1937 with a band that included their own guitars, steel guitar, harmonica clarinet, and bass. Later, after they returned to Shreveport, the Rices added a fiddle to their sessions in 1940 and 1941. Their efforts to avoid sounding corny, or excessively hillbilly, largely succeeded, although Decca still issued their recordings of such numbers as "Japanese Sandman" and Jimmy McHugh's pop classic, "On the Sunny Side of the Street," in its "hillbilly" series. In retrospect, their most interesting effort was a rendition of "You Are My Sunshine" made nearly a year before the Jimmie Davis version but after the first effort by Atlanta's Pine Ridge Boys on Bluebird. After World War II military service, the Rice Brothers Gang never reformed. Hoke remained in Shreveport outside of music, while Paul eventually returned to Atlanta and worked in daily television with the T.V. Wranglers, who also consisted of Cotton Carrier, Boots Woodall, and the Smith Brothers.[25]

WESTERN SWING MOVES EASTWARD

Not all the western swing sounds were even remotely of Texas origin or even in the West, although those in the East certainly had the Texas influence. One of the first to favor that kind of music in a big way was Alabama-born, Atlanta-based Herbert "Hank" Penny (1918–1992) and his Radio Cowboys. Penny's band included Noel Boggs (1917–1974), who quickly developed into one of the best steel guitarists anywhere, and classically trained Boudleaux Bryant (1920–1987), who ultimately became one of the greatest songwriters in the history of country music. The Radio Cowboys made some forty-seven issued sides for the American Record Corporation through 1941. When the war broke up his band, Penny moved to WLW Cincinnati, where he began recording for the new King label just before moving to California. However, he continued through the rest of the decade with King, where his repertoire included both vocal numbers, such as "Bloodshot Eyes," "Get Yourself a Redhead," and "The Freckle Song," and swinging instrumentals of quality, typified by "Steel Guitar Stomp" and "Penny Blows His Top." By the time, Penny signed with RCA Victor in 1951, he called his band the California Cowhands, and with Boggs back on steel, they turned out quality material—some with a touch of humor, like "White Shotgun" and "The Mink on Her Back"—but western swing was not doing so well on disc by that time. Penny went on to Decca in the mid-1950s, but the golden age of western swing was pretty much over, although he continued to earn a living with his music and comedy in Las Vegas and elsewhere.[26]

There was no "King of Swing" in the Carolinas, but the music had its proponents. The first band to reflect the swing influence, Dick Hartman's Tennessee Ramblers, began recording for Bluebird in January 1935, but the amount of swing infusion increased with the passage of time. The swing sound showed even more prominence on the risqué numbers made by Hartman's Heartbreakers with Betty Lou DeMorrow on vocals and those of the Washboard Wonders that featured Kenneth Wolfe on washboard. The principal sounds came from Garnett "Elmer" Warren (1909–1997) on fiddle and Cecil

Campbell (1911–1989) on tenor banjo and later electric steel guitar. By 1939, they had gone swing in total with Campbell on steel, Jack Gillette on fiddle, and Harry Blair and Tex Martin on guitars. After the war, the Tennessee Ramblers were led by Cecil Campbell, who contributed numerous original steel numbers to their RCA Victor recordings. By the mid-1950s, they had moved to M-G-M and were experimenting with rockabilly. In the early 1960s, they ceased to be a major force, although Campbell remained semi-active into the 1980s. Ironically, the Ramblers never had a Tennessean in their aggregation.[27]

In some respects, the best—although short-lived—swing band in the Carolinas was the group led by sometime-Tennessee Rambler Claude Casey (1912–1999), with his Pine State Playboys. The instrumental stars of this band included Willie Coates on piano and Jimmy Rouse on fiddle. Carl (1912–1992) and Lawrence Boling (1910–1986) filled out the group, and they cut eighteen numbers for Bluebird at two separate sessions in 1938. Later line-ups included Clinton Collins on fiddle, Jimmy Colvard on steel, Kelland "Kid" Clark on accordion, and Gilbert Young on electric lead guitar. In all, the Pine State Playboys placed thirty numbers on Bluebird, including such spirited instrumentals as "Pine State Honky Tonk," "Kinston Blues," and "Swinging with Gilbert." During World War II, Casey worked with both the Tennessee Ramblers and Briarhoppers, revived a solo career, and eventually went into radio station management.[28]

A few other swing groups graced the Carolinas with a brief presence, all making recordings for Bluebird. The Swing Billies probably ranked as the most notable of these. Led by Charlie Poole Jr. (1912–1968) as vocalist, this group made ten sides that ranged from their rendition of the pop classic "I Can't Give You Anything but Love" to an updated rendition of the old North Carolina Rambler song "Leavin' Home." Carl Boling (1912–1992) and his Four Aces were a spin-off of Claude Casey's band. The Asheville-based Slim Johnson and the Singing Cowboys furnished backing for vocalist Walter Hurdt (1910–1966) in addition to recording some under their own name. Finally, the Tobacco Tags were essentially a country version of the old-fashioned mandolin orchestra but after adding young fiddler Harold Hensley (b. 1922) to their number in 1941 had pretty much of a swing sound. The American Record Corporation boasted one swinging Carolina group, the Hi-Neighbor Boys, a four-man team led by Zeb Turner that boasted the services of a real Texas fiddler in Cecil "Tex" Wilson.[29]

Over in the Virginia Tidewater region, the three Phelps Brothers and their Virginia Rounders demonstrated a strong swing influence on their numerous 1936 Decca offerings. Earl Phelps (1916–1971) played a hot fiddle and Norman (1912–1981) played bass, while guitar-picking brother Willie (b. 1914) had an excellent singing voice. Ken Card's (1912–1990) tenor banjo gave them a fuller sound. As the Six Bar Cowboys, they also provided a band sound to Ray Whitley's vocal offerings on the same label in 1936 and 1938. Journeying to

California, they even appeared in some of his RKO radio films. In the 1950s, they owned and operated a dance hall at Fernwood Farm, reputedly the largest dance floor on the East Coast.[30]

Even the northeastern states had a few bands. Mention has already been made of the Prairie Ramblers and Massey's Westerners, each of whom left their Chicago base to do radio in New York for a year. Pennsylvania had Jack Pierce (1908–1950) and his Oklahoma Cowboys, whose leader had once been a member of the old-time string band the Tenneva Ramblers. In 1936, they recorded eight sides for the American Record Corporation and then thirty in one day for Bluebird. A little later, the Keystone state was home base for George Long and his 101 Ranch Boys. New Jersey in the 1940s and 1950s was home for singer Smokey Warren (b. 1916) and bandleader Shorty Warren, who with his Western Rangers had become known as the Eastern King of Western Swing. The Warrens hosted a TV program in the 1950s known as *The Garden State Jamboree*.[31]

In the upper South, Knoxville has long been known as radio base for early bluegrass, but in addition to "Seven-Foot Cowboy" Homer Harris, that Appalachian city's WNOX also served as a longtime home for the station's staff musicians, who cut numerous sides for Bluebird in the late 1930s as the Dixieland Swingsters. Their principal leader, David Durham, was equally adept as a hot fiddler and trumpet player. Memphis radio had a swing band in the Swift Jewel Cowboys, so called from their sponsor, Swift's Jewel Shortening. The Cowboys originated in Houston but soon moved to Memphis, where they were heard first on WMC and then WREC. They made twenty sides for the American Record Corporation in 1939. Until they disbanded in July 1942, the Cowboys, who also did horse tricks on their live shows, advertised themselves as the "only mounted cowboy band in America." The first swing-oriented group at WSM, Herald Goodman (1900–1974) and the Tennessee Valley Boys, was led by a former Vagabond and had two teen-age musicians in the band who went on to become legendary sidemen: guitarist Billy Byrd and fiddler Howdy Forrester. They made eight sides for Bluebird in 1938 before going to Texas, where they disbanded. During the 1940s, the *Grand Ole Opry* served as home for Paul Howard (1908–1984) and his Arkansas Cotton Pickers, who also recorded for both King and Columbia. Howard is credited with such things as introducing drums to the *Opry* stage as well as guitarists who later became renowned session musicians, such as Hank Garland and Grady Martin. Realizing that swing sounds did not attain as much popularity in Nashville as farther west, Howard left there in 1949 for a friendlier home in Shreveport, where he remained active until the advent of rock and roll. In 1951, longtime western swing pianist Aubrey "Moon" Mullican joined the *Opry* but by this time was less of a swing musician and more of the "King of the Hillbilly Piano Players," his new nickname. He also enjoyed seven top ten hit records on King between 1947 and 1951, most notably, "I'll Sail My Ship Alone" in 1950.[32]

Actually, one western band did win wide acceptance in Nashville, but it was that of Pee Wee King (1914–2000), who perhaps did better because he had one of the great managers in country music history behind him, his father-in-law, J. L. Frank (1900–1952). King had been born Francis Kuczynski in Milwaukee and had been an accordion player for polka bands until hired to back Gene Autry on tours through the Midwest. This led to his organizing the Golden West Cowboys in 1936, and within a year, they had moved to WSM and the *Grand Ole Opry*, where they remained for a decade. During that period, the Golden West Cowboys introduced electric instruments to the program and also used drums, wore high-quality western outfits, and played dance music in addition to songs for listening. They also put together a fine touring group. Since King was not generally a singer, his wartime band included later solo singing stars like Eddy Arnold and Lloyd "Cowboy" Copas. However, their best-known vocalist was a fiddler who cowrote many songs with King named Redd Stewart (1921–2003).

Despite the acclaim that the Golden West Cowboys attained from their *Opry* appearances and with the wartime touring group known as the Camel Caravan, they did not record until the end of World War II, when after one single on Bullet they signed with RCA Victor. Over the next several years, they turned out an impressive string of hits, many of them with crossover appeal in the pop market. These included "Tennessee Waltz," which has been covered by a range of singers, from pop vocalist Patti Page to the wife of British Prime Minster Tony Blair; "Tennessee Polka"; "Bonaparte's Retreat"; "Silver and Gold"; "Changing Partners"; and "Slow Poke," which stayed on top of the *Billboard* country charts for fifteen weeks and the pop charts for three. Ironically, by the time King began to have hit records, he had left Nashville for Louisville, where he had a regionally popular TV program. His hits slowed up after 1954, and he dropped the TV shows in 1962 but continued to remain popular on the Midwestern county fair circuit into the 1970s. Success has a way of bringing respect, and Pee Wee King kept it for the rest of his life.[33]

Elsewhere, the upper Midwest and Ohio contributed some swing groups to the field. Prior to Pee Wee King's arrival in Louisville, the Falls City had been headquarters for former Skillet Licker old-time fiddler Clayton McMichen (1900–1970), who adopted more uptown sounds with his Georgia Wildcats beginning in 1931. After recording briefly on Columbia in 1931 and on Crown in 1932, the Georgia Wildcats concentrated on radio for some years, mostly in Louisville but also in Chicago, Cincinnati, St. Louis, and Pittsburgh. From 1937 to 1939, the Georgia Wildcats recorded a number of sides for Decca. When McMichen finally broke up the band, longtime guitarist Hoyt "Slim" Bryant renamed them the Wildcats, and they settled down as longtime fixtures in Pittsburgh.[34]

There were other swing-oriented groups scattered throughout the Midwest. Hugh and Shug's Radio Pals worked out of WWVA Wheeling from 1933 to 1937 and then moved to WLW Cincinnati for the rest of the decade, cutting

fourteen sides for Decca in 1937. At WLW they shared honors with Eldon
Baker (1898–1973) and his Brown County Revelers. Ambrose Haley (1898–
1977) and his Ozark Ramblers worked mostly out of St. Louis and boasted of a
young Wade Ray (1918–1988) on fiddle. Both the Baker and Haley groups cut
discs for the American Record Corporation. The Sons of the Ozarks, formed in
Quincy, Illinois, featured a young Rusty Draper on vocal and recorded on
Bluebird in 1939. Somewhere in this mix was Cody Fox and his Yellow Jackets,
who also labored in the studios of the American Record Corporation.[35]

THE CALIFORNIA CONNECTION

However, the advent of World War II saw a major shift of much western
swing activity to California. With thousands of young soldiers, sailors, and
airmen stationed there, as well as thousands of defense workers, many of them
transplanted from Texas, Oklahoma, and Arkansas and having a little more
spending money than they had possessed in years, there were unlimited opportunities for those swing musicians not called to military service. Bob Wills
and the Texas Playboys led the pack of those who relocated to the Golden
State, although military service and defense work cut into the band, eventually
taking the leader himself for a few months. However, the Playboys drew record
crowds when they managed to assemble. In the immediate postwar years,
younger brothers Luke (1920–2000) and Billy Jack Wills (1926–1991) each led
their own bands for a time. Other Texas swing outfits that took in the California scene for a time included those of Adolph Hofner and Ted Daffan.
However, the main rival of the Texas Playboys came from a new group put
together by a fiddler of Oklahoma birth.

Donnell "Spade" Cooley (1910–1969) grew up in Oregon after his parents
had migrated westward in his youth, won his nickname as a skilled poker
player, and became a highly skilled fiddler. He found some work around the
Republic studios, where he doubled for Roy Rogers and also toured with him as
a fiddler, and did session work on Decca with the King of the Cowboys. In 1942,
promoter Foreman Phillips began holding dances at the Venice Pier Ballroom
in Santa Monica. Cooley soon emerged as the leader and became phenome-
nally successful with a somewhat more orchestral approach to the music than
that of Wills, whose band he once bested in a contest at the Pier and took the
title "King of Western Swing" for himself. His band included such stellar
musicians as Joaquin Murphey on steel and Smokey Rodgers on lead guitar,
along with such vocalists as Rogers, bass man Deuce Spriggins, and vocalist
Tex Williams. Once the first Petrillo Recording ban ended, in September 1943,
Cooley signed with OKeh (formerly the American Record Corporation and
soon to be Columbia). His first record to hit the charts, "Shame on You," with
vocals by Williams, stayed there for thirty-one weeks and spent three months
in the number one position. Five more hit records followed. Cooley and his
Orchestra, as it was termed, had reached the pinnacle of musical success.

However, the Oklahoma boy-made-good soon became the personification of a country song he never recorded, titled "It's a Long, Long Way to the Top of the World (but Only a Short Fall Back Down)." However, it did take Cooley some time to hit bottom. He became increasingly egotistical and abrasive when drinking. In mid-1946, Tex Williams and about half of the band either quit or were fired. In 1947, Cooley switched labels to RCA Victor and with a partly different band managed to turn out a product, but of uneven quality and with no certified hits. His popularity seemed unabated, and he had a top-ranked southern California KTLA-TV program, *The Hoffman Hayride*. In 1951, he went with Decca, and although the music was fine, again there were no hits. Western swing was on the decline, and even the big pop bands that Cooley emulated were in big trouble. The popularity of Lawrence Welk on network television took much of his audience, and by 1958, his show had been canceled. He still had income from various investments, but his health, drinking, and domestic situation worsened. On April 3, 1961, he beat his wife, Ella May, a former vocalist with his band, to death. Convicted of first-degree murder, he received a life sentence. He soon became a model prisoner and was scheduled for parole in February 1970. However, given a temporary furlough to perform at a function for law officers, Spade Cooley suffered a massive and fatal heart attack on November 23, 1969, shortly after receiving a standing ovation.[36]

Cooley's former vocalist, Sollie "Tex" Williams (1917–1985), soon formed his own Western Caravan swing band and almost immediately began to record for Capitol. His first release, "Rose of Alamo"/"The California Polka" proved to be a hit, with the latter reaching number four in December 1946. In mid-1947, his "Smoke! Smoke! Smoke! (That Cigarette)"/"Roundup Polka" stayed on top of the country charts for sixteen weeks and the pop charts for six, giving Capitol its first million-selling disc. By the end of the 1940s, Williams had placed thirteen numbers on the *Billboard* charts, compared with six for Cooley (all made while Tex was still in his band). True, some of his biggest hits were novelty-narration numbers, such as "Smoke! Smoke! Smoke!" and a cover of Carson Robison's "Life Gits Tee-Jus Don't It?," but many of them were backed by traditional swing numbers. The novelty successes did have a tendency to obscure Williams's considerable vocal talents.

By 1951, Williams decided on a label switch and went to RCA Victor, but despite continued good material he had no hits, neither did any of his Decca sides click between 1953 and 1958. The golden era of western swing had ended, and Williams disbanded his Western Caravan and thereafter worked as either a solo country singer or with a small band. He later returned to Capitol and recorded with Liberty and a variety of other labels into the 1970s, having a number of mid and lower level hits, most notably, the clever tongue-in-cheek "The Night Miss Nancy Ann's Hotel for Single Girls Burned Down" on Monument in 1971. Unlike Spade Cooley, Tex Williams had a character and personality that resonated with people in a positive manner. Roberta Shore, who had worked part-time with the Western Caravan in the early 1950s as a

Tommy Duncan (far right) joined the Texas Playboys as lead vocalist in 1933. He is shown here with Joe Ferguson on fiddle, the band's founder Bob Wills, and Laura Lee McBride (behind microphone).
Copyright © Corbis.

child yodeling cowgirl (prior to becoming a teenage heartthrob with Disney and leading lady in *The Virginian* series), recalled in July 2003 that Tex was "truly a wonderful man." Unfortunately, Williams also personified the lyrics of his most famous song and died of lung cancer. But as Rich Kienzle, reflecting on Williams and the Western Caravan, said, "not only were they on the cutting edge of western swing, they remain one of the most innovative country acts of any era."[37]

Another vocalist gone on his own, former Texas Playboy Tommy Duncan (1911–1967) experienced less success than Williams, despite putting a quality band together. Williams having more time to establish himself may have been a factor. Duncan put together a band called the Western All-Stars that included some former Texas Playboys, such as Noel Boggs, Millard Kelso, Joe Holley, and former Musical Brownie Ocie Stockard, that opened at the 97th Street Corral on October 11, 1948. In January 1949, they began recording for Capitol but turned out only one hit, a cover of the old Jimmie Rodgers favorite, "Gamblin' Polka Dot Blues." Critics thought that while Duncan's vocal was strong and the musicians competent, the instrumental support was more subdued than that of the Texas Playboys. Capitol dropped him after a dozen sides, and Duncan broke up his band before the end of 1950. He spent the first part of the 1950s with the independent label Intro and mid-decade with Coral. Some of the material was good—especially with borrowed musicians from Ole Rasmussen's Nebraska Cornhuskers—but again there were no hits. Swing bands were no longer in vogue, and Duncan generally worked as a solo vocalist with local musicians. He reunited with Wills for a couple of years and recaptured some of the old magic but then went back to solo work. Heart trouble ended both his life and career in 1967.[38]

Other split-offs from the Texas Playboys also met with mixed success. In 1946–1947, bass player Luke Wills headed what might have been termed a Texas Playboys second unit to cover the demands that Bob himself could not handle. Early in 1947, they cut four numbers on King and in four sessions for RCA Victor later that year made twenty masters as Luke Wills' Rhythm Busters. Later Luke had a band in Oklahoma City for several months at the

Trianon Ballrom while Bob was working at his Ranch House in Dallas. Later he returned to the Texas Playboys. Billy Jack Wills had joined the Texas Playboys in 1947 as a drummer. When Bob purchased the Aragon Ballroom in Sacramento and renamed it Wills Point, he hired Texas Playboy Tiny Moore to lead the house band while the Texas Playboys were on tour and when Bob returned to Oklahoma and Texas. Moore thought the band needed a Wills out front, so Billy Jack also became the bandleader at Wills Point and on KFBK radio in Sacramento. Billy Jack made solo recordings for M-G-M from 1954 to 1956 and with swing in decline moved the sound somewhat in the direction of rock and roll, but eventually Bob returned and reintegrated Billy Jack's band back into his own Texas Playboys.[39]

The one band totally independent of either Cooley or Wills nonetheless owed a great deal to the latter in style and influence. Ole Rasmussen (1914–1978) and his Nebraska Cornhuskers took a decidedly Farm Belt sounding name. The band boasted a quality lead vocalist in Ted Wilds and counted ex-Prairie Rambler fiddler Tex Atchison in its number. The band had a radio program for KXLA and cut twenty-eight fine sides for Capitol between 1950 and 1952—most notably, Atchison's "Sleepy Eyed John" and "Somewhere in San Antone." The Cornhuskers were a popular attraction on the southern California dance hall circuit for two or three years but came on the scene a little too late to make a lasting impression.[40]

Another band that had been around the Golden State since 1940 combined swing and novelty sounds. Texas Jim Lewis (1909–1990) and his Lone Star Cowboys, had been on radio from 1933, in a variety of locales, before coming to California in 1940. The Lone Star Cowboys worked on radio, did a few movies, and, after having done a session for the American Record Corporation in 1937, began a longer stay with Decca in 1940. Andrew "Cactus" Soldi, who later became an important fiddler in Spade Cooley's band, got his start with Lewis, as did Jim's brother Rivers, who worked both with the Lone Star Cowboys and by himself under the name "Jack Rivers." The Lone Star Cowboys had the first recordings of "The Covered Wagon Rolled Right Along" and "Squaws Along the Yukon," the latter of which later also became a hit for Hank Thompson. The band eventually made its base in Seattle, Washington, and after western swing faded, Texas Jim Lewis became "Sheriff Jim" in local children's television.[41]

DECLINE, SURVIVAL, AND REVIVAL

While western swing music lost much of its luster in California during the first half of the 1950s, it managed to survive in other locales. Both Bob and Johnnie Lee Wills maintained bands until about 1964. Tulsa also had room for former Texas Playboys steel guitarist Leon McAuliffe, who organized his Cimarron Boys after World War II. The latter opened his Cimarron Ballroom in 1950, giving the Tulsa area a second major outlet for dance music (in addition to Cain's). He also recorded profusely on Majestic, Columbia (where his "Panhandle Rag" was a 1949 hit), Dot, Capitol, Starday, and his own Cimarron label. He eventually broke up his band and concentrated on business activities, especially his radio station in Rogers, Arkansas, but did participate in many later Texas Playboy reunion activities. Meanwhile, the Sooner State capital had a second band, Merle Lindsey and the Oklahoma Night Riders, which did well in the early and mid-1950s, furnishing a place of apprenticeship for country girl Norma Jean Beasler (b. 1938), who as "Pretty Miss Norma Jean" became one of the new breed of female country stars in the 1960s.[42]

The music also survived in the Lone Star State. Adolph Hofner's band remained active into the 1990s. Younger practitioners of swing music included Jimmy Heap, Clyde Brewer, Dewey Groom, Leon Rausch (who took over the Texas Playboys for a time), and the lesser-known but devoted-to-the-cause Hoyle Nix (1918–1985). Nix not only maintained a band for some thirty years from 1950, but also operated a large dance hall at Big Spring, Texas. Johnny Gimble (b. 1926) worked with a variety of bands, including the Texas Playboys (1949–1951), and ultimately became a top session fiddler in Nashville, playing a role in the western swing revival that evolved in the 1970s. In a sense, another factor in western swing revival was the election of Bob Wills to the Country Music Hall of Fame in 1968. The renewed interest in Wills's music was also reflected in reigning country superstar Merle Haggard's decision to make a Bob Wills tribute album in 1970. Shortly after Wills's death, Waylon Jennings had a hit with his tribute song "Bob Wills Is Still the King."[43]

Other than Gimble and Texas Playboy reunions, a leading new factor in the western swing revival was the rise of a band that called itself Asleep at the Wheel. Founded in Paw Paw, West Virginia, around 1969 by Ray Benson Siefert and Reuben Gosfield, the group knocked around in several locales, but moved to Austin, Texas, about the time that the Texas capital was gaining musical significance. Although they could not be termed exclusively a western swing group, that sound was dominant, and they combined a repertoire of old rhythm and blues, western swing, and honky-tonk country. While they recorded older songs from all those styles, their newer swing songs, such as "Miles and Miles of Texas" and "Boot-Scootin' Boogie," certainly had a swing feel. They also used recognized swing greats, such as Johnny Gimble, Leon Rausch, and Eldon Shamblin, on their recordings. While finding new audiences for the music, they also won nods of approval from older lovers of the music. Personnel changed frequently until eventually only Benson (he dropped use of his last name for stage purposes) remained, yet the swing influence remained strong.[44]

The decline of western swing and hot string bands coincided in large part with the erosion of the big bands in the popular music mainstream. Television received much of the blame for the decline in the dance crowds, but one can almost as easily conclude that the styles and trends would have changed anyway. At any rate, the expense of maintaining larger bands had become increasingly prohibitive. With few exceptions, western swing came to an end about the time that rock and roll appeared on the musical horizon. Yet, just as Bing Crosby, Frank Sinatra, and Doris Day became more popular than Paul Whiteman, Tommy Dorsey, and Les Brown, who had once employed them, country music came to be increasingly dominated by solo stars. However, unlike the pop stars, the country solo stars had not been vocalists with the swing groups. Ernest Tubb, Hank Williams, and Hank Snow had never been with the dance bands, although Eddy Arnold had been briefly with Pee Wee King's Golden West Cowboys. The electric lead and steel guitars that vied with fiddle in their instrumental backing owed prominence to the swing bands, but the musical support they provided had not been designed for the dance halls. Yet swing influence remained and continues to remain. Strains of it can be heard in the music of those as diverse as Ricky Skaggs and George Strait.

NOTES

1. Both Brown and Wills have their scholarly advocates. Definitive biographies are Charles Townsend, *San Antonio Rose: The Life and Music of Bob Wills* (Urbana: University of Illinois Press, 1976), and Cary Ginell, *Milton Brown and the Founding of Western Swing* (Urbana: University of Illinois Press, 1994). While scholarly and excellent in most respects, both have drawbacks. Townsend takes the view that Wills and his music should be classified with jazz and writes as though Wills worked in a vacuum. For instance, he never mentions other significant swing groups, such as those of Bill Boyd and Cliff Bruner. Ginell displays better balance but overstates his advocacy for Brown primarily as a refutation of the excessive attention given to Wills by earlier scholars. Certainly Brown came to prominence first, but since Wills lived longer, he displayed greater influence in the long run. I choose to follow Bob Pinson, whose knowledge of the music may have exceeded those of the others and who quotes Wills in giving equal credit to both.

2. Some idea of the large volume of western swing recordings can be ascertained from Cary Ginell and Kevin Coffey, *Discography of Western Swing and Hot String Bands, 1928–1942* (Westport, CT: Greenwood Press, 2002). One might note that neither of these writers include the East Texas Serenaders as prewestern swing but do include Hunt, the Paradise Joy Boys, and the Three Virginians.

3. Ginell, *Milton Brown and the Founding of Western Swing*; Bruner quoted in Cary Ginell, *The Complete Recordings of Milton Brown and the Musical Brownies* (Santa Monica, CA: Texas Rose Records, 1995), 34.

4. Townsend, *San Antonio Rose*.

5. John Mark Dempsey's *The Light Crust Doughboys Are on the Air* (Denton: University of North Texas Press, 2002) is more of an anecdotal than a formal history, with an emphasis on more recent years, but is nonetheless useful. A brief but better perspective is Kevin Coffey, "The Light Crust Doughboys: Western Swing Training Ground," *The Journal* 27 (June 1995), 12–15; see also Ginell and Coffey, *Discography of Western Swing*, 73–82.

6. Cary Ginell, *W. Lee O'Daniel and His Hillbilly Boys* (Texas Rose TXR-2702, 1982), liner notes; Ginell and Coffey, *Discography of Western Swing*, 98–101. For a brief sketch of Leon Huff, see Kevin Coffey, "Leon Huff: From Rodgers Disciple to Master Western Swing Vocalist," *The Journal* 38 (April 1997), 24–25.

7. Bob Pinson, *Bill Boyd's Cowboy Ramblers* (Bluebird AXM2 5503, 1975), liner notes; Ginell and Coffey, *Discography of Western Swing*, 8–16.

8. Cary Ginell, *Roy Newman & His Boys, 1934–8: Western Swing Classics* (Origin Jazz OJL 8102, 1981), liner notes; Ginell and Coffey, *Discography of Western Swing*, 92–96.

9. Ginell and Coffey, *Discography of Western Swing*, 140–146, 152–153.

10. Kevin Coffey, "The Tune Wranglers: Texas Swing in the 1930's," *The Journal* 40 (December 1997), 6–7; see also Ginell and Coffey, *Discography of Western Swing*, 159–162.

11. Marty Pahls and Jeff Richardson, *Jimmie Revard and His Oklahoma Playboys, Oh! Swing It, 1936–38* (Rambler 108, 1982), liner notes; see also Ginell and Coffey, *Discography of Western Swing*, 130–133.

12. Tony Russell, *Adolph Hofner & His Texans: South Texas Swing* (Arhoolie CD 7029, 1994), liner notes; Kevin Coffey, "Adolph Hofner: Texas Legend, Western Swing Proponent," *The Journal* 32 (April 1996), 12–15; Ginell and Coffey, *Discography of Western Swing*, 60–62; Adam Komorowski, "That Honky Tonk Rhythm: The Adolph Hofner Story," *The Hillbilly Researcher* 20 (c. December 1995), 22–31.

13. Kevin Coffey, "Leon 'Pappy' Selph: First Generation Western Swing Legend," *The Journal* 37 (February 1997), 18–19; Ginell and Coffey, *Discography of Western Swing*, 138–139.

14. Kevin Coffey, *Cliff Bruner and His Texas Wanderers* (Hamburg, Germany: Bear Family Records, 1997).

15. Bob Healy et al., "Shelley Lee Alley: A Discography," *JEMF Quarterly* 9 (Spring 1973), 33–34; Ginell and Coffey, *Discography of Western Swing*, 3–5.

16. Kevin Coffey, "Modern Mountaineers," in Paul Kingsbury, ed., *The Encyclopedia of Country Music* (New York: Oxford University Press, 1998), 349–350; Tony Russell, "A Modern Mountaineer: J. R. Chatwell, Western Swing Fiddle Ace," *Old Time Music* 31 (Winter 1978/1979), 15–20; Ginell and Coffey, *Discography of Western Swing*, 87–88, 188–189.

17. Kevin Coffey, "Bar X Cowboys," in Kingsbury, *Encyclopedia of Country Music*, 28, 255; Ginell and Coffey, *Discography of Western Swing*, 6–7.

18. Daffan's entire career is best summarized by Kevin Coffey, *The Daffan Records Story* (Hamburg, Germany: Bear Family Records, 1995).

19. Ray Topping, "Jerry Irby: Uptown Swing," *The Hillbilly Researcher* 8 (c. 1990), 19–23; Kevin Coffey, "Jerry Irby: The Texas Gulf Coast Music Scene," *The Journal* 36 (December 1996), 18–19.

20. Cary Ginell, *Sons of the West, 1938–1941* (Texas Rose TXR-2708, 1982), liner notes.

21. Charles K. Wolfe, "Making Western Swing: An Interview with Johnnie Lee Wills," *Old Time Music* 15 (1975), 15–17; Rich Kuenzle, *Johnnie Lee Wills & His Boys* (Bear Family BFX 15103, 1983), liner notes; Cary Ginell, *Dave Edwards and His Alabama Boys* (Texas Rose TXR-2707, 1982), liner notes.

22. Cary Ginell, *The Hi-Flyers, 1937–41* (Texas Rose TXR-2705, 1982), liner notes; Ginell and Coffey, *Discography of Western Swing*, 57–59.

23. Bill C. Malone, *Wiley Walker and Gene Sullivan: Radio Favorites* (Old Homestead OHCD 4188, 2000), liner notes; Ginell and Coffey, *Discography of Western Swing*, 164–165; Rich Kienzle, "Hank Thompson: Brazos Valley Boy," *The Journal* 21 (June 1994), 8–11.

24. Donald Lee Nelson, *Buddy Jones: Louisiana's Honky Tonk Man* (Texas Rose TXR-2711, 1984), liner notes; Ronnie Pugh, "Bill Nettles," in Kingsbury, *Encyclopedia of Country Music*, 376; Ginell and Coffey, *Discography of Western Swing*, 65–68, 90–92.

25. Wayne W. Daniel, "The Rice Brothers: Hillbillies with Uptown Ambitions," *The Journal* 35 (October 1996), 18–19; Ginell and Coffey, *Discography of Western Swing*, 133–135.

26. Rich Kienzle, "Hank Penny: Peerless Bandleader, Pioneer Comic," *The Journal* 2:4 (August 1992), 18–19; Rich Kienzle, *Hank Penny: Hillbilly Be-Bop, the King Anthology, 1944–1950* (Westside WESA 914, 2001), liner notes; Ginell and Coffey, *Discography of Western Swing*, 102–103.

27. Ginell and Coffey, *Discography of Western Swing*, 54–56, 154–156, 165–166.

28. Ivan M. Tribe, *Claude Casey and the Pine State Playboys* (Old Homestead OHCS 182, 1987), liner notes; Ginell and Coffey, *Discography of Western Swing*, 25–26.

29. Kevin Coffey, *Farewell Blues: Hot String Bands, 1936–1941* (Bexhill-on-Sea, England, 2003), liner notes, 6–8, 19–22; Ginell and Coffey, *Discography of Western Swing*, 59–60, 64–65, 153–154.

30. Dagmar Anita Binge, *Two Decades of Country Music by the Phelps Brothers* (Bronco Buster CD 9043, c. 1998), liner notes; Ginell and Coffey, *Discography of Western Swing*, 103–104.

31. Coffey, *Farewell Blues*, 22–23; Billy Wilson, *Smokey Warren: The Eastern King of Western Swing* (Cattle LP 50, 1983), liner notes.

32. Kevin Coffey, *Farewell Blues*, 5, 14–15; Ginell and Coffey, *Discography of Western Swing*, 46–47, 153; Tony Russell, "Chuck Wagon Swing: The Story of the Swift Jewel Cowboys," *Old Time Music* 32 (Spring 1979), 5–16; Max M. Cole, *Paul Howard and His Arkansas Cotton Pickers: Western Swing at Its Best* (Cattle LP 57, 1984), liner notes.

33. Wade Hall, *Hell-Bent for Music: The Life of Pee Wee King* (Lexington: University Press of Kentucky, 1996). This work is actually more of an autobiography despite Hall's name as author. A brief but more analytical piece is Charles Wolfe, "Pee Wee King: Golden Touch," *The Journal* 2 (August 1992), 9–11.

34. Coffey, *Farewell Blues*, 3–4; Charles Wolfe, "Clayton McMichen: Taking Country Music Uptown," *The Journal* 15 (June 1993), 12–15; W. K. McNeil, "Hoyt 'Slim' Bryant," *Old Time Country*, 22–25; Ginell and Coffey, *Discography of Western Swing*, 84–86.

35. Coffey, *Farewell Blues*, 8–9, 10–12, 15; Ginell and Coffey, *Discography of Western Swing*, 45–46, 51.

36. Rich Kienzle, "Spade Cooley: Western Swing Goes Hollywood," *The Journal* 2:2 (April 1992), 18–19; Al Quaglieri, *The Essential Spade Cooley: Spadella* (Columbia Legacy CK 57392, 1994), liner notes; for the more bizarre portion of the Cooley saga,

see Rich Kienzle, "When a Country Star Turns Murderer: The Strange, Tragic Case of Spade Cooley," *Country Music* 5 (July 1977), 34, 36, 38, 64.

37. Ken Griffis, "The Tex Williams Story," *JEMF Quarterly* 15:1 (Spring 1979), 5–19; Rich Kienzle, *Tex Williams & His Western Caravan: Vintage Collections* (Capitol 7 2438 36184, 1996), liner notes. Roberta Shore's comments regarding Tex Williams come from a conversation with Shore by Deanna and Ivan Tribe, Charlotte, NC, July 11, 2003. These remarks are similar to those quoted in Boyd Magers and Michael G. Fitzgerald, *Westerns Women* (Jefferson, NC: McFarland, 1999), 204–205.

38. Rich Kienzle, "Tommy Duncan: Bob Wills' Right Hand and More," *The Journal* 46 (December 1998), 12–13; Rich Kienzle, *Tommy Duncan: Texas Moon* (Bear Family BCD 15907, 1996), liner notes.

39. Rich Kienzle, *Luke Wills: High Voltage Gal* (Bear Family BFX 15333, 1988), liner notes; Rich Kienzle, "Billy Jack Wills: Western Swing with a Modern Twist," *The Journal* 36 (December 1996), 16–17.

40. Kevin Coffey, *Ole Rasmussen: Sleepy Eyed John* (Bear Family BCD 16255, 1999), liner notes.

41. Dennis Flannigan, *Texas Jim Lewis* (Cattle LP 81, 82, 83, 1985), liner notes; Ginell and Coffey, *Discography of Western Swing*, 71–72.

42. Bob Pinson, *Leon McAuliffe: Columbia Historic Edition* (Columbia FC 38908, 1984), liner notes. See also Ivan M. Tribe, "Norma Jean: Country Sweetheart of the Sixties," *The Journal* 31 (February 1996), 16–17.

43. For Hoyle Nix, see Joe W. Specht, "An Interview with Hoyle Nix: The West Texas Cowboy," *Old Time Music* 34 and 35 (Summer/Autumn 1980), 7–13; (Winter 1980/Spring 1981), 15–18; Joel Whitburn, *Top Country Singles, 1944–1993* (Menomonee Falls, WI: Record Research, 1994), 180.

44. Rich Kienzle, "Asleep at the Wheel," in Kingsbury, *Encyclopedia of Country Music*, 19.

5

Hillbilly Music II:
Honky-Tonkin' around This
Town, 1941–1955

During the 1940s and first half of the 1950s, the dominant style in country music had come to be known as honky-tonk. This form featured electric instrumentation dominated by lead and steel guitars, fiddle, and rhythm supplied by a stand-up bass and sometimes another guitar. Subject matter often concentrated on romantic breakups, fast living, and sometimes marital infidelity but could also include some nostalgia for a vanishing rural lifestyle or personal mistakes. Some even painted a more pleasant view of romance and love of family, but the pitfalls of love tended to be most common. Music for the jukebox trade continued to play a significant role in determining the commercial market—thus the use of electric instruments to give the music more volume.

Several significant new record labels sprang up during or right after World War II. The most important was the California-based Capitol in 1942 and M-G-M in 1946, but there was also Coast, Intro, and Black & White. Chicago boasted Mercury from 1945, and Cincinnati had King Records from 1944, while Starday started in Texas in 1952 but relocated to Nashville later in the decade. Many, although not all, of the great honky-tonk singers tended to gravitate toward Nashville and station WSM and the *Grand Ole Opry*.

If the country music scene had a trendsetter during the World War II era and the decade immediately following, that individual would have to be Ernest Tubb (1914–1984), who came to be known as the "Texas Troubadour."

Ernest Tubb's talent epitomized the honky-tonk style of country music.
Courtesy of Photofest.

The youngest child in a farming family, Tubb grew to adolescence in Ellis and Knox Counties (Texas), working hard at chopping cotton. His family life was not a pleasant one. His parents separated when he was ten, and his mother remarried. He found some solace in music, especially that of Jimmie Rodgers, whose recordings he first heard when he was about fourteen. From then on he idolized the Mississippi Blue Yodeler. After Rodgers died, Ernest sought out his widow to console her. Later, Mrs. Rodgers helped him get his first recording contract. Although Texas swing was rising in popularity in the mid-1930s, Tubb remained a solo performer in the Rodgers style. However, when he began to hit his stride, he did add additional instrumentation to his sound, beginning with an electric lead guitar. His backup support also came to include a prominent fiddle and steel guitar and, in essence, was a small western swing combo. The added instrumentation resulted in large part from the demands of the jukebox trade, as his recordings needed more volume in order to be heard in the bars and honky-tonks where listeners congregated.

Ernest Tubb's career began in modest fashion. After his mother remarried in 1930, he often lived with older siblings until his own marriage at age twenty. By that time, he was playing on small radio stations in San Antonio and singing with friends for tips at local drive-ins. In 1936, Mrs. Rodgers helped him get a contract with Bluebird Records, and the two made a brief tour of theaters in south Texas, but the yields remained small. Over the next couple of years, he knocked around some other Texas towns working as a beer salesman and trying to make a go of it at small radio stations, doing somewhat better at KGKL San Angelo than elsewhere. He also had his tonsils removed there, which proved to be a godsend because he could no longer yodel and was forced to develop a more original style. This newer approach could be heard on his first Decca recording in April 1940 of "Blue-Eyed Elaine" and "I'll Get Along Somehow."

Not long afterward, Ernest Tubb secured a better radio job for Gold Chain Flour as the Gold Chain Troubadour for $25.00 weekly (later increased to $75.00) at station KGKO in Fort Worth and went in October 1940 to Hollywood, where he recorded a dozen more songs. However, true stardom followed in the wake of his third session in April 1941, which saw the release of

"Walking the Floor over You." This became his signature song and propelled him into a pair of Charles Starrett films in 1942 and a regular spot at WSM Nashville and the *Grand Ole Opry* in January 1943. By the end of World War II, Ernest Tubb had become one of the biggest stars in the country field and, perhaps even more important, the one whose style seemed to be the trendsetter. Roy Acuff and Gene Autry may have been bigger, but the honky-tonk style associated with Tubb, the electric lead guitar with an amplified steel, and fiddle was the format most emulated.

Tubb would remain a major force for another decade, touring and starring on the *Opry* into the early 1980s. He continued to turn out a string of hits on Decca. Some of the more memorable included the World War II classics "Soldier's Last Letter," "Rainbow at Midnight," "It's Been So Long Darling," "Have You Ever Been Lonely," "Letters Have No Arms," "Careless Darlin'," "Are You Waiting Just for Me," "Blue Christmas," and "Fortunes in Memories." In 1949, Decca paired him with its pop music trio the Andrews Sisters and produced a minor crossover hit, "I'm Bitin' My Fingernails and Thinking of You." He and fellow *Opry* star Red Foley did several novelty numbers that reached hit status, such as "Tennessee Border No. 2," "Goodnight Irene," and "Hillbilly Fever No. 2." As late as 1963 and 1965, he produced such favorites as "Waltz across Texas" and "Thanks a Lot." Through 1979, he appeared on the *Billboard* country charts a total of ninety-one times. He also gained a name as one who was more than willing to provide encouragement to younger performers and through the Ernest Tubb Record Shop started a major retail outlet for country music record buyers and fans.[1]

In the early years as a purveyor of the honky-tonk style, Tubb received some notable aid from a pair of fellow Texans who had emerged from the western swing scene: Al Dexter and Floyd Tillman. Al Dexter (1902–1984) had been recording since 1936 with swing support provided by members of the Nite Owls. A onetime handyman and house painter, Dexter had first sung in a club at Longview and later bought his own establishment. One of Dexter's early songs, "Honky-Tonk Blues," helped give the style its name. However, Dexter enjoyed only moderate success until 1942, when he found himself with a monumental hit, "Pistol Packin' Mama," about a rowdy woman in a cabaret. It became one of the biggest songs of the war years. Dexter had some good follow-up songs typified by "Too Late to Worry" and "Guitar Polka," but by the end of the 1940s, his popularity began to fade.[2]

Floyd Tillman (1914–2003) had been born in Oklahoma but achieved his greatest fame in the Texas metropolis of Houston. Tillman had been a member of such Houston swing bands as Leon Selph's Blue Ridge Playboys, Shelley Lee Alley's Alley Cats, and Dickie McBride's Village Boys and cut his first session under his own name for Decca in August 1939, eight months prior to Tubb's initial Decca offerings. As a writer, many of his songs had already been recorded by the above bands as well as by Cliff Bruner, who had hits with his 1938 compositions "It Makes No Difference Now" and "I'll Keep on Loving You."

His own best Decca efforts included "They Took the Stars out of Heaven" and a war-flavored ballad, "Each Night at Nine." Tillman's immediate postwar offerings on Columbia included "I Love You So Much It Hurts"; "This Cold War with You"; and his masterpiece, "Slipping Around." The latter became one of the first major hits to deal directly with marital infidelity, a subject that would soon become a staple in the trade. While Tillman had a distinct style as a vocalist, his lyrics were often bigger hits for other singers, such as Jimmy Wakely. While Tillman had no hit records himself after 1949 (with the exception of a brief chart appearance in 1960), he continued to be active through the 1950s and sometimes thereafter. However, he became more and more of a regional performer from the 1960s onward, although he did make the Country Music Hall of Fame in 1984.[3]

Dexter, Tillman, and the continuing efforts of Ernest Tubb notwithstanding, most of the other great practitioners of honky-tonk country won their greatest acclaim in the years immediately following World War II. This coincided with a period of economic prosperity when tens of thousands of rural folk, southern and otherwise, were moving to the city and had more money to attend shows, buy records, listen to their radios, and watch the increasingly popular medium of television. In essence, the dark days of the Great Depression faded, and what one might term "hillbilly culture" entered in to a new golden era. Tubb's movement to Nashville also helped to nationalize the honky-tonk sound and make the Tennessee city and the *Grand Ole Opry* the major focal point for this brand of country.

THE HONKY-TONK SOUND DOMINATES NASHVILLE

One of the first new stars to gain widespread acclaim was Eddy Arnold (b. 1918), who had first come to Nashville as a vocalist with Pee Wee King's Golden West Cowboys. A native of Chester County, Tennessee, Arnold grew up poor and gained his first radio experience in nearby Jackson in 1934, but soon moved on to larger stations in Memphis, St. Louis, and Louisville before arriving at WSM in 1942 with the Golden West Cowboys. By 1944, he had gained a solo recording contract with his first releases on the Bluebird label, but he soon moved to the more prestigious RCA Victor (with postwar prosperity, the Depression-era Bluebird label was soon discontinued). Arnold's first number was a western song, "Cattle Call," that had initially been composed and popularized a decade earlier by Tex Owens. Most of his songs were in a honky-tonk vein, although they did not display quite the hard-edged themes of the Texas vocalists. Like Ernest Tubb, he gained a nickname, "the Tennessee Plowboy," and built a distinctive sound that included the steel guitar of Little Roy Wiggins (b. 1926), the fiddle of Howard "Speedy" McNatt, and the lead guitar of Herbert "Butterball" Paige (who also made his share of contributions to the Tubb sound).

Through his 1950 recordings, Arnold made a total of thirteen number one hits. Six of these—"I'll Hold You in My Heart," "Anytime," "Bouquet of

Roses," "Just a Little Lovin'," "Don't Rob Another Man's Castle," and "There's Been a Change in Me"—remained at the top spot for a minimum of eight weeks. Twenty-six more of his efforts made the top ten. Several of them registered on the *Billboard* pop listings as well. He remained with the *Opry* until September 1948, when he left to pursue a more independent career, having felt with considerable justification that he had outgrown the program. Since Arnold had five songs on the top ten at *Billboard* the week of his departure, his judgment seemed sound. In addition, the Tennessee Plowboy starred in a pair of low-budget Columbia pictures, *Hoedown* and *Feudin' Rhythm*, both in 1949.

Through the 1950s and 1960s, Eddy Arnold toned down his honky-tonk and hillbilly image and moved toward a softer middle-of-the-road image to make himself more acceptable to a popular audience. Eschewing his Tennessee Plowboy nickname, he preferred to be known as a singer of love songs and eventually as the "Last of the Love Song Singers." He continued to make the charts with regularity. The mid-1960s were especially good years for Arnold, as his song "Make the World Go Away"

topped the country charts and reached number six on the pop listings. He continued to have mid- and lower level hits through 1983, by which time he had appeared on the *Billboard* charts a total of 145 times. While hillbilly purists might decry Arnold's abandonment of his roots, few could fault his commercial success.[4]

Eddy Arnold's movement away from the hard honky-tonk sound did not in any way diminish the overall dominance or popularity of the style with the rural audience. Other figures simply moved in to occupy the spot. Nine months after the Tennessee Plowboy made his last *Opry* appearance, Hank Williams (1923–1953) made his debut on the stage at the Ryman. Like Tennessee Plowboy Arnold, Williams grew up poor but in south central Alabama. Unlike Arnold, who was always a man of steady habits and came to symbolize middle-class values and respectability, Williams was a troubled soul addicted to alcohol and painkillers that resulted in a short life that grew to legendary proportions within a few months of his untimely death. When he came to Nashville, Hank had a decade of radio experience behind

Hank Williams's fame as a songwriter reached legendary heights, even though he was only thirty years old at the time of his death.
Courtesy of Photofest.

him in Montgomery and Shreveport and a flair for writing original songs that by the early 1940s attracted the attention of insiders. His own recording career began in 1946, and he had his first hit in the late summer of 1947. He spent the last half of 1948 on the *Louisiana Hayride* at KWKH, where he quickly became the principal star. Ironically, the song that elevated Williams to major stardom, "Lovesick Blues," was one of his few major offerings that he did not compose but was an old pop song that dated back to 1920s minstrel man Emmett Miller. Regardless, it remained at the top if the *Billboard* charts from May through July and rivaled "Slipping Around" as the premier country song of 1949.

Hank Williams went on to enjoy five more number one songs in his lifetime, including "Cold Cold Heart," which some critics considered his masterpiece. He had four more in the six months that followed his death. Another thirty reached high chart positions. Popular artists such as Tony Bennett and Jo Stafford began recording his compositions. However, he also became the personification of an old country saying that "some people can't stand prosperity." He spent lavishly and irresponsibly, and his stormy relationship with his wife Audrey ended in separation in January 1952 and divorce in late May. *Opry* management dismissed him from the program in August for missing shows and excessive drinking, and he returned to KWKH and the *Hayride*, where he remarried in October. Oddly enough, his Cajun-flavored song "Jambalaya" held the number one position during his declining months. Whether he was getting his life in order at the end of the year will never be known since he died en route to a show date and was pronounced dead on the morning of January 1, 1953. Legal wrangling over his estate continued intermittently for years. However, his songs continue to be heard, and he has become the most legendary figure in country music history.[5]

A fourth major figure to emerge as an *Opry* star in Nashville was Nova Scotia–born Clarence "Hank" Snow (1914–1999), who had been around on the Canadian country music scene for more than a decade, where he was first known as "Hank, the Yodeling Ranger" and then as "Hank, the Singing Ranger." Like the others, Snow had survived a poverty-stricken youth but, unlike them, did so in the Atlantic-coastal fishing village of Liverpool. Like Ernest Tubb, he had idolized Jimmie Rodgers and emulated his style in the early years. He began recording for the Canadian Bluebird label in 1936 and slowly built up an audience in Canada, where he toured extensively with his trained horse, Shawnee. However, Snow aspired to make it in the United States. He finally succeeded on his third try in 1949, when Ernest Tubb helped him get a spot on the *Opry*.

Hank Snow's success was hardly assured, and WSM was about to drop him from the roster when his song "I'm Movin' On," a broken romance lyric with a railroad flavor, skyrocketed to the top, spending forty-four weeks on the charts, twenty-one of them at number one. He followed with two other top hits: "The Golden Rocket" and "The Rhumba Boogie." From then on, he ranked among the top country stars. Although he never had another hit as big as "I'm Movin'

On," the Singing Ranger compiled an impressive list of winners, with "I Don't Hurt Anymore" hitting the top for twenty weeks in 1954. Somewhat more versatile than his contemporaries, Snow found success with songs that had a foreign flavor, such as "Spanish Fireball," "My Arabian Baby," and "When Mexican Joe Met Jole Blon." He also made successful country versions of pop hits, such as "Let Me Go Lover." Well rooted in country tradition, he also kept railroad and hobo songs in his repertoire, not only Jimmie Rodgers numbers but such obscurities as "The Last Ride," a reworking of an old Goebel Reeves song. Although he had no more education than many of the poor southerners who came to Nashville, his immaculate English phrasing made him a favorite among foreign fans of American country music. His last number one hit, "Hello Love," came out in 1974, and he still made the charts through 1980. In later years, he still played the *Opry* regularly, but his career slowed down considerably.[6]

Hank Williams ranked as only the first of a series of a string of country singers that gave the *Louisiana Hayride* the sobriquet "Cradle of the Stars." Webb Pierce (1921–1991) had more experience when he burst on the national country scene in early 1952. A native of West Monroe, Louisiana, Pierce had some early radio experience in his home locale but became more serious about a musical career when he moved to Shreveport. He initially had some programs on smaller stations while working a regular job for Sears, Roebuck and Company. Around 1949, he began making appearances on the *Hayride* at KWKH and recording for the smaller Four Star and Pacemaker labels.

In 1951, Webb Pierce signed a contract with Decca. His third release, "Wondering," a revival of a Cajun-flavored song from 1937 by Joe Werner and his Riverside Ramblers, took off slowly but eventually spent four weeks at the top. Afterward, for the next five years, every one of his single releases—with two exceptions—achieved hit status, a dozen reaching number one. Although considered a honky-tonk singer, the late researcher Otto Kitsinger points out that only one of Pierce's major efforts, "Back Street Affair," dealt with cheating, and only "There Stands the Glass" concerned drinking. His other biggest hits were mostly songs of romance ("Slowly," "More and More," "I Don't Care," and "Love, Love, Love") or broken romance ("That's Me without You," "I'm Walking the Dog," "Even Tho," and "The Last Waltz"). A few songs did deal with a honky-tonk lifestyle, such as "I'm Tired"; "Honky-Tonk Song"; and his biggest hit, "In the Jailhouse Now" (a revival of a Jimmie Rodgers standard). In addition, his 1954 hit, "Slowly," has been widely credited with introducing the pedal steel guitar to country music. When rock-and-roll influences crept into country music in the middle of the decade, Pierce adapted to the changes better than most of his rivals with such songs as "Teenage Boogie," "I Ain't Never," and a cover of the Everly Brothers' "Bye Bye Love."

Webb Pierce also helped define the image of the country singer during the 1950s. Although neither the first nor the only hillbilly star to be associated with tailored, rhinestone western suits, he did possess a custom-made silver dollar-studded Cadillac and guitar-shaped swimming pool. Such trappings constituted examples of what intellectual elites considered tackiness and conspicuous consumption, but to Webb and his fans they symbolized success and that the American dream could become reality for southern boys from modest circumstances. Showiness notwithstanding, Pierce invested well in radio stations and music publishing, among other things. As his career wound down, his recordings generally dropped to the lower echelons of the charts as the 1960s progressed and they virtually vanished in the mid-1970s, but he continued to live comfortably. Still, as the compilations by Joel Whitburn from *Billboard* listings demonstrate, Pierce's achievements were real, and he led the pack during the all-important decade of the 1950s.[7]

The aforementioned vocalists perhaps did the most to personify the honky-tonk brand of country music that dominated the decade after World War II. Yet there were others. Faron Young (1932–1996) followed Williams and Pierce in the route from Shreveport to Nashville. Beginning with "Goin' Steady" in January 1953, Young had at least one song on the *Billboard* charts every year until 1981. After a decade with Capitol, he signed with Mercury and continued to have hit songs. He carried honky-tonk music into the 1960s and 1970s.[8]

Other honky-tonk singers with a degree of radio experience behind them made their way to Nashville from a variety of Appalachian locales. Carl Smith (b. 1927), an east Tennessee native who cut his teeth on Knoxville radio, sang in a crooning style that combined wholesomeness and a thinly veiled suggestiveness typified by songs heard on Columbia Records and the *Grand Ole Opry*, such as "Let Old Mother Nature Have Her Way," "Hey Joe!," and "Don't Just Stand There." Another east Tennesseean, Carl Butler (1927–1994), had a hard country voice not unlike that of Roy Acuff, but his best-known songs typified by "Honky-Tonkitis" and the duet with wife Pearl "Don't Let Me Cross Over" were as honky-tonk as you could get. Lloyd "Cowboy" Copas (1913–1963), from hilly southern Ohio, became a mainstay at the *Opry* and King Records with such hits as "Filipino Baby," "Signed, Sealed and Delivered," and "Down in Nashville, Tennessee." West Virginia native Little Jimmy Dickens (b. 1920) often combined humorous novelty numbers with honky-tonk material, but his style clearly fit into the latter mode. His songs that became hits, such as "Take an Old Cold Tater (and Wait)," "Sleepin' at the Foot of the Bed," and "Hillbilly Fever," nearly all fit into the comical category. Another Mountain State vocalist, Hawkshaw Hawkins (1921–1963), who first made his name at the WWVA Jamboree in Wheeling before coming to Nashville by way of the *Ozark Jubilee*, was strongly influenced by Ernest Tubb and could interpret a song in virtually any style but was most at home with honky-tonk material.[9]

The first female country music vocalist to achieve star status—Kitty Wells (b. 1919)—also came out of the honky-tonk era. However, the content of her lyrics might more correctly be termed "anti-honky-tonk," although her style ranked in the mainstream of the genre. Born Muriel Deason in Nashville, Kitty Wells was the stage name of Mrs. Johnnie Wright, who worked as a girl vocalist with the brother-in-law duet of Johnnie (Wright) and Jack (Anglin). Her earliest recordings on RCA Victor in 1949 and 1950 attracted minimal attention, but her 1952 "It Wasn't God Who Made Honky-Tonk Angels," an "answer" to Hank Thompson's "The Wild Side of Life," became one of the most successful numbers of its type, spending six weeks at number one. Her follow-up hits, like "Paying for that Back Street Affair" and "Hey Joe," also were answer songs, but she soon emerged from the shadow of others with independent lyrics, such as "Cheatin's a Sin," "Who's Shoulder Will You Cry On," "Making Believe," and "Heartbreak, U.S.A." While women were usually portrayed as victims of cheating spouses and unfaithful lovers in the Wells songs, they also manifested a certain degree of a survivor's strength.[10] Like Webb Pierce, with whom she was sometimes paired in duets, Kitty Wells exemplified what came to be described as unabashed "hard country with a strong nasal twang." Her impact lessened in the 1960s as a younger breed of female vocalists typified by Wanda Jackson and Norma Jean (Beasler) took stronger positions in their attitude toward erring men.

WEST COAST HONKY-TONK

Merle Travis (1917–1983) probably ranked as the leading purveyor of honky-tonk sounds on the West Coast, although he became better remembered in later years for his guitar stylings and songwriting. A native of the same area of western Kentucky that produced such musical luminaries as the Monroe Brothers and the Everly Brothers, Travis came to California in 1945 after serving briefly as a member of Clayton McMichen's Georgia Wildcats and longer with a WLW Cincinnati radio group, the Drifting Pioneers. Signed to Capitol Records, he scored such hits as "Cincinnati Lou," "So Round, So Firm, So Fully Packed," and "Divorce Me, C.O.D." In addition to his own work, he did studio session work for most country and western artists on Capitol. As a composer, he became best known for his songs about coal mining, especially "Dark as a Dungeon" and "Sixteen Tons."[11]

No other West Coast honky-tonk singers of the early years ever came close to matching the success of Travis, although there were a number of them on the scene. They included Ramblin' Jimmie Dolan (1924–1994), a transplanted Missourian who recorded for Capitol, making the charts with his cover of "Hot Rod Race"; Jess Willard (1916–1959), who had the first recording of Tex Achison's "Honky-Tonk Hardwood Floor"; West Virginia-migrant Jimmy Walker (1915–1990), who had the first recording of "Detour"; Arkansas-born Rog Hogsed (1919–1978), who revived "Cocaine Blues"; and the tragic tubercular Jack Guthrie (1915–1948). The latter, a cousin of folksong legend Woody Guthrie, had a major hit with "Oklahoma Hills" and might have had a lengthy career had not illness and an early death intervened.[12]

During the 1950s, Bakersfield, California, began to emerge as a secondary country music center and would really come into major prominence in the mid-1960s. Bakersfield grew from a city of 34,000 to more than 56,000 during the 1950s. A working-class population made up of people with southern roots made Bakersfield a popular stopping place for big-name artists. Live music played by bands of such artists as Billy Mize and Bill Woods flourished in this town where the economy was partly based on oil fields, in much the same fashion as numerous towns in Texas. Ferlin Husky (a.k.a. Terry Preston; b. 1925) headquartered there for a time in the early 1950s but had moved on to Nashville as he began to experience real stardom—stimulated by his shared hit with Jean Shepard, "A Dear John Letter"—and progress toward a style that was more acceptable to middle-of-the-road audiences and gave him such crossover hits as "Gone" and "Wings of a Dove." Husky also starred in several low-budget motion pictures in which he invariably played a country bumpkin who got out of military service and tried to start either a musical career or night club, where he encountered a series of country music guest stars who augmented his business or career.

Meanwhile, the honky-tonk scene in Bakersfield soon produced another star in a transplanted Oklahoman, Tommy Collins (born Leonard Sipes; 1930–2000), who began recording for Capitol in 1953. Collins turned out hits with a novelty bent and a hint of suggestiveness typified by "You Better Not Do That," "Whatcha Gonna Do Now," and "It Tickles," which were often coupled with more serious honky-tonk songs, such as "High on a Hilltop." Uncomfortable with his success, Collins dropped out of music for a time and entered the ministry. When he re-entered the business in 1964, Collins found it difficult to recover his momentum, despite the patronage of Buck Owens and Merle Haggard, who had become the Bakersfield superstars of the late 1960s. Nonetheless, he continued to be a notable songwriter.[13]

MEANWHILE, BACK IN TEXAS

Texas, which to a large degree had originated the honky-tonk style (or as Columbia producer Don Law called it, "Texas Dance Hall Music"), turned out several younger honky-tonk vocalists, although some did not really hit their stride until the 1960s but still remained true to the older styles. One of the first was Charlie Adams (b. 1920), who emerged from a swing outfit called the Lone Star Playboys to record for Imperial, Decca, and Columbia. Adams was popular and toured extensively in Texas and states to the west but never really enjoyed a major hit, despite such catchy songs as "If a Beer Bottle Had a Nipple on It." As rock-and-roll influences became paramount, Adams retired from music to an insurance business in Scottsdale, Arizona. Victoria, Texas, native Frankie Miller (b. 1930) recorded some great material for Gilt Edge and Columbia in the early and mid-1950s but did not really have a major hit until the end of the decade when his Starday single, "Blackland Farmer," reached number five.

As Hank Davis and Colin Escott wrote, Miller had his biggest success at a time when his style was becoming a virtual anachronism.[14]

The most notable of the Texas honky-tonkers who would prove almost as influential as Ernest Tubb, although ultimately shorter lived and less successful, William Orville "Lefty" Frizzell (1928–1975) came out of the east Texas oil-field country with a strong appreciation for the music of Jimmie Rodgers and, to a lesser degree, Ernest Tubb and Ted Daffan. Through the 1940s, he worked in clubs and local radio in New Mexico and Texas with minimal success, experiencing marriage, fatherhood, and a six-month jail term while still a teenager. In mid-1950, he made some demo recordings at the Jim Beck studio in Dallas, which soon resulted in a contract with Columbia. His vocal style, which combined slurring some words and drawing out others, gave him a certain uniqueness. His first release, "If You've Got the Money, I've Got the Time"/"I Love You a Thousand Ways," became a hit, and Frizzell became a hot property. In 1951, he had two even larger hits with "I Want to Be With You Always" and "Always Late." "Mom and Dad's Waltz" spent eight weeks at number two, and for a three-week period in October, he found himself with four songs in the top ten at once.

However, after "Give Me More, More (of Your Kisses)," in early 1952, Lefty Frizzell's hit production slowed because of a combination of his rowdy lifestyle and poor management decisions. He did not record in Nashville until 1956 and did not live in Tennessee for more than a few months until 1962. Still he remained with Columbia through 1972, although his only major hits in the last fifteen years were "The Long Black Veil," "Saginaw, Michigan," and "Gone, Gone, Gone," the two former songs fitting more into the category of "saga" songs than honky-tonk. He spent the early 1970s with ABC records, and while his efforts were artistically strong, they never matched his early years with Columbia. Frizzell's years of hard living eventually caught up with him, and he died of a stroke at age forty-seven.[15]

Hank Thompson (b. 1925) carried a swing band—the Brazos Valley Boys—through the 1950s and 1960s, creating some of the best honky-tonk songs of the era. Starting in Waco, Thompson shifted his base of operations from time to time, going to both Tulsa and Oklahoma City, operating the Trianon Ballroom in the latter place. He turned out a steady stream of hits on Capitol beginning with "Humpty-Dumpty Heart" in 1947 and ending with "Then I'll Start Believing in You" in 1965. In between in 1951–1952, "The Wild Side of Life," probably represented his masterpiece, being number one for fifteen weeks. But other defining numbers included "Wake Up, Irene," "Rub-a-Dub-Dub," "Honky-Tonk Girl," and "A Six Pack to Go." Switching to Warner in 1966 and then to Dot in 1968, Thompson adapted to the Nashville sound and continued to make the charts for another fifteen years, but much of his material continued to reflect the tried and true formula with songs ranging from "On Tap, in the Can, or in the Bottle" to "Tony's Tank-Up, Drive-In Cafe."[16]

A pair of unrelated Texans bearing the surname Walker had little more than a regional impact through most of the 1950s, but ultimately had major hits and enjoyed long careers at the *Grand Ole Opry*. Billy Walker (b. 1929), although younger, gained prominence first. A native of the Texas Panhandle, he spent some of his childhood years in an orphanage but, inspired by Gene Autry, desired and got a singing career. It began in Clovis, New Mexico, in the mid-1940s, and by 1949, he reached the *Big D Jamboree* in Dallas and Capitol Records. He actually used a gimmick of singing on stage with a mask for a few months until his first record, "Headin' for Heartaches," came out, at which time he reverted to using his real name. A modest success, he moved on to Columbia in 1951 and remained with the label through 1965 while cutting over 140 songs. He spent time at the *Louisiana Hayride* and the *Ozark Jubilee* in the 1950s, but with the exception of "Thank You for Calling" in 1954 and "On My Mind Again" in 1957, real hits eluded him. As Walker later told Colin Escott, he still managed to sell enough records to stay on the label. He guested on the *Grand Ole Opry* in November 1959 and became a regular as of January 1960, where he has remained for more than four decades. By 1960, the "Nashville Sound," was becoming dominant in Music City, but Walker's major hits, such as "Charlie's Shoes" and "Willy the Weeper," were classic cheating songs. A little later, he scored big with western themes, such as "Cross the Brazos at Waco" and "Matamoros." Billy Walker moved on to other labels, including Monument, M-G-M, and RCA Victor in the next decade, remaining consistently on the charts and occasionally ranking in the top ten.[17]

Charlie Walker (b. 1926) first made a name for himself as a disc jockey at KMAC in San Antonio from 1951, but he also played music during the 1950s. In fact, prior to World War II service, he even served a stint with Bill Boyd's Cowboy Ramblers. Active as a musician and deejay in Corpus Christi from 1947, Walker moved to KMAC in 1951. He recorded ten sides for Imperial in 1952 and through the help of Ernest Tubb landed a contract with Decca beginning in 1954. Two years later, "Only You, Only You" briefly crashed the top ten. None of his Mercury sides did anything, but one side of his first Columbia release, "Pick Me up on Your Way down," stayed on the charts for twenty-two weeks, peaking at number two for four weeks (unable to dislodge Ray Price's "City Lights") and provided Walker with a signature song. Even though infused with the Nashville Sound, he continued to favor honky-tonk subject matter, including "Who Will Buy the Wine," "Wild as a Wildcat," "A Honky-Tonk in Dallas," "Don't Squeeze My Sharmon," and "Honky-Tonk Season." Although not as consistent on the charts as Billy Walker, Charlie Walker remained on the listings through the mid-1970s, cutting among other things a live album in 1969 at the Longhorn Ballroom in Dallas and remaining a true champion of Texas dance hall music.[18]

Neither Walker, however, could match either the success or the musical longevity of an east Texas honky-tonker who also personified the lifestyle much more than any contemporary except the short-lived Hank Williams. He also would place more songs on the country charts (some with duet partners) than anyone in country music history. George Jones (b. 1931) hailed from Beaumont, Texas, where he grew up hard with a heavy-drinking father and Pentecostal mother. His musical career really started after he got out of the Marine Corps in November 1953. Jack Starnes and Harold "Pappy" Daily had recently started Starday Records in 1951. George cut five numbers for them in January 1954, including "No Money in this Deal," and his career was off and running. However, it was his seventh release, "Why Baby Why," that elevated him to star status. After several more singles, five of them on the charts, Jones moved to Mercury in 1957, where he had several more hits, with the rockabilly-flavored "White Lightning" hitting number one in 1959. Through this period, Pappy Daily continued producing Jones's records (until 1971). Although he did a few rockabilly numbers (sometimes as "Thumper" Jones) and accommodated to the Nashville Sound, George Jones always remained essentially a honky-tonk or Texas dance hall singer of the hard country variety.

Living legend George Jones has had 165 *Billboard* Country chart appearances, 142 of those in the Top Forty. *Copyright © Corbis.*

Although George Jones had only two number one hits during the 1960s, he had a total of fifty-seven songs on the *Billboard* listings. These included not only some of his best known numbers typified by "The Window up Above," "Tender Years," "She Thinks I Still Care," and "The Race Is On," but also songs with such duet partners as Melba Mongomery ("We Must Have Been out of Our Minds"), Brenda Carter ("Milwaukee, Here I Come"), and pop rocker Gene Pitney ("I've Got Five Dollars and It's Saturday Night"). All this time his reputation as an erratic hard drinker continued to grow, while his popularity held steady if not actually increasing. After his break with Pappy Daily and marriage to Tammy Wynette in 1969, Jones moved to Epic Records, acquired a new producer in Billy Sherrill, and moved closer to the Nashville Sound.[19]

Other figures who began their careers as honky-tonk singers would make their major mark in the country field in later styles. These included the Texans Ray Price and Jim Reeves. Not a Texan but very much a product of the West, Arizonan Marty Robbins also hit his prime somewhat later.

OTHER COUNTRY SINGERS

Some country singers encountered success in this era while only marginally associated with honky-tonk styles. Perhaps the most notable, Clyde "Red" Foley (1910–1968) had long experience with such radio venues as *National Barn Dance*, *Renfro Valley Barn Dance*, and *Grand Ole Opry*, where he hosted the network portion for a number of years. In spite of his popularity with the nostalgic boy-and-his-dog song "Old Shep," Foley's first real hit came in 1944 with his patriotic anti-Axis lyric, "Smoke on the Water." His other gigantic hit, "Chattanoogie Shoe Shine Boy" in 1950, topped the country charts for thirteen weeks and the pop listings for eight. Of his other major hits, only "Tennessee Saturday Night" fit into the honky-tonk category. Despite a well-concealed problem with alcohol, Foley also possessed a convincing manner for sacred material, and his 1951 rendition of the African American composer Thomas Dorsey's "Peace in the Valley" became the first religious song to earn a gold record. Foley left the *Opry* in 1954 for Springfield, Missouri, where he served as host of *Ozark Jubilee*, the first country music show to survive more than a season on prime-time network television. Foley's achievements and reputation have not endured the test of time as much as that of Hank Williams or Lefty Frizzell, but in his time his popularity equaled and surpassed that of many of his contemporaries. In retrospect, much of his success probably derived as much from his warm personality and winning manner as it did from his music.[20]

George Morgan (1924–1975) fit more into the mold of a "country crooner" than a honky-tonk singer. He emerged in 1949 as Columbia Record's answer to Eddy Arnold. A Tennesseean who grew up in suburban Akron, Ohio, his major songs, "Candy Kisses," "Almost," "I'm in Love Again," and "Room Full of Roses," were the type of love songs that had potential crossover appeal, although only "Room Full of Roses" ever made the pop charts. Except for a brief period in the later 1950s when he had a local program on WLAC television, Morgan remained with the *Opry* until his death.[21]

On the West Coast scene, Tennessee Ernie Ford (1919–1991) bridged the gap between country and pop music with a rich baritone voice and a variety of songs, none of which could be classified as honky-tonk. A former deejay from Bristol, Tennessee, who relocated to the West after World War II, Ford exhibited success with such novelty songs as "Mule Train" and "Cry of the Wild Goose." Otherwise, his other hits were often hillbilly boogie numbers, such as "Smoky Mountain Boogie," "Blackberry Boogie," and "Shotgun Boogie." Ford also landed a daytime television network program with NBC and capitalized on the national Davy Crockett fad with his "Ballad of Davy Crockett" and even more so with "Sixteen Tons," a Merle Travis coal-mining song that topped both the country and pop charts. This led to a prime-time network variety show that lasted for five years (1956–1961). Ford also capitalized on a winning personality and won fans with such down-home phrases as "bless your little pea-pickin' hearts" and metaphors like "nervous as a long-tailed cat in a room full of rocking chairs." From the later 1950s on, Ford concentrated on the album market, particularly of sacred songs that appealed to both pop and country audiences. His Capitol album simply titled *Hymns* ranked for years as one of the all-time best-sellers. Although he made a few appearances on the country charts in later years, his fame still rested largely on his efforts from the mid-1950s.[22]

Other country music locales back in the Eastern states produced some country singers of note. At Wheeling's WWVA and the *World's Original Jamboree*, a more traditional approach dominated. Doc Williams (b. 1914) and his Border Riders developed a unique sound that blended old-time and mainstream country with a touch of East European polka music furnished primarily by blind accordionist Marion Martin and Doc himself, whose parents were Slovak immigrants. His wife Chickie (b. 1919), who sang in the band, favored more traditional songs performed in what folklorist D. K. Wilgus termed a "sweet" voice. Harry C. McAuliffe (1903–1966), known as Big Slim, the Lone Cowboy, combined cowboy and honky-tonk material, with his main contribution to the industry being the song "Sunny Side of the Mountain," which eventually became a bluegrass favorite. Lee Moore (1914–1997) favored similar material, sometimes performing as a duet (until 1960) with his wife Juanita. The husband-wife duo of Wilma Lee (b. 1921) and Stoney Cooper (1918–1977) also favored a more traditional sound in their decade at WWVA before moving to the *Grand Ole Opry* in 1957. Closer to honky-tonk was another married duo, the Maine New Englanders of French extraction Lone Pine (Harold Breau) and Betty Cody, who performed both individual solo and harmony numbers. Bob Gallion (1929–1999) spent several years at WWVA, among other locales, and cut some good honky-tonk songs as well, dabbling in rockabilly and more modern country.[23]

The one true major WWVA honky-tonk exponent, Huntington, West Virginia-native Harold "Hawkshaw" Hawkins (1921–1963), began his recording career doing creditable covers of Ernest Tubb songs for the Cincinnati-based King label. After several years at King and Wheeling, the "Hawk of the West Virginia Hills" moved on to the *Ozark Jubilee* and in 1955 to the *Grand Ole Opry*. After leaving King, he made excellent (but no hit) recordings for RCA Victor and Columbia before returning to his original label in 1962. His one big hit, "Lonesome 7-7203," hit the top of the charts in the spring of 1963 after his tragic death in a plane crash.[24]

With two radio stations providing live programming—WNOX and WROL—Knoxville, even more than Wheeling, proved something of a haven for more traditional music and the merging neotraditional sounds that would become bluegrass. However, in addition to Carl Smith, the radio stations did come up with a couple of significant honky-tonk stylists. Red Kirk (b. 1925), who became known as "the Voice of the Country," had a couple of chart makers for Mercury, one of them a cover of Hank Williiams's "Lovesick Blues." Carl Butler (1927–1992) made a much bigger impact, although it took several years for him to find a signature song. Butler's first recordings on Capitol used bluegrass instrumentation, but by October 1951, he had switched to electric instruments. In spite of writing songs that became hits for others, such as "If Teardrops Were Pennies" and "My Tears Don't Show," Butler could not seem to score one himself on either Capitol or Columbia until 1961, when he came out with "Honk-Tonkitis," and followed it in 1962 with "Don't Let Me Cross Over." The latter song, a duet with wife Pearl (1927–1988), spent eleven weeks at number one and was considered the song of the year. Ironically, the Butlers hit their stride at a time when the smoother Nashville Sound was displacing the hard country approach favored by Carl and Pearl. They made the *Billboard* charts a dozen more times during the decade, but nothing ever approached the popularity of "Don't Let Me Cross Over."[25]

THE PERSISTENCE OF PRE–HONKY-TONK STYLES

In spite of the dominance of honky-tonk songs, electric instruments, charismatic young performers, jukebox, and radio deejay air play, popularity polls conducted by emerging fanzines, such as *Country Song Roundup*, and by the *Billboard* and *Cashbox* charts, there was a great deal more to the country music scene in this era. Some popular performers and artists seldom, if ever, had charted records. Others endeared themselves through their rustic comedy. Holdovers from an earlier era, such as Roy Acuff at the *Opry* or Lulubelle and Scotty at the *Barn Dance*, continued to warm the hearts of their fans.

Among the most enduring and endearing nonsuperstar performers were the banjo-playing singers who also did a bit of comedy in the tradition of Uncle Dave Macon, who continued to work the *Opry* until a few weeks before his death in 1952. They included Manuel "Old Joe" Clark (1922–1999), who usually worked at the *Renfro Valley Barn Dance*. Clark (as well as the others) specialized in such perennial favorites as "Good Old Mountain Dew" and originals like "Old Age Won't Kill You, But Will Slow You Down." David "Stringbean" Akemon (1915–1973), who wore short pants and a shirt that both reached to his knees to emphasize his lanky nature, interspersed his banjo songs with such trademark phrases as "Lord, I feel so unnecessary." Akemon eventually gained a wider audience through his work on the country variety TV show *Hee Haw*, but he and his wife were tragically murdered in 1973. Beecher "Bashful Brother Oswald" Kirby (1911–2002) spent most of his career as a resonator guitar player and tenor singer with Roy Acuff, but he also did banjo work and comedy frequently accompanied by his catch phrase, "can everybody hear me alright?" followed by his unique laugh. "Lazy Jim" Day (1911–1959) made a career out of comedy numbers—most notably, "The Singing News," which offered a humorous look at current events, usually of a human interest nature, and utilized the chorus of a 1925 Macon song, "I Don't Reckon That'll Happen Again." Day changed the news event verses every week to keep the song up to date.[26]

However, the dominant figure in this category was Louis Marshall "Grandpa" Jones (1913–1998). A native of western Kentucky who grew up in Akron, Ohio, Jones got his start on local radio with Warren Caplinger's Pine Ridge Band and then went to work with Bradley Kincaid until going on his own at WWVA Wheeling, WMMN Fairmont, and other places, finally reaching a 50,000-watt station at WLW Cincinnati and WSM Nashville by the end of World War II. Jones acquired a large song repertoire and recorded frequently from 1944 on, but while his discs sold reasonably well, none classified as hits. He had trademark banjo songs, like "Good Old Mountain Dew" and the dog tribute "Old Rattler," but could also perform more serious material, such as "Are There Tears Behind Your Smile," "Send Me Your Address from Heaven," and the nostalgic salute to the Kentucky metropolis "Eight More Miles to Louisville." With his wife Ramona, who played fiddle and mandolin, the pair did excellent traditional duets. He mixed a degree of comedy in his programs and remained a stable figure on the country scene for decades without being a top star. Like Stringbean, he gained a higher profile as a *Hee Haw* regular from 1969, and in 1978 was inducted into the Country Music Hall of Fame despite only two chart makers in a sixty-five-year career.[27]

Alabama native Lew Childre (1901–1961) preserved some of the characteristics of the old medicine show in a three-decade career that included a large repertoire of songs and an informal down-home style while puttering around on an acoustic guitar played in the Hawaiian style. Childre worked for years at WSM and other radio locales, recorded sparingly from 1930, made numerous transcriptions, and preserved such old songs as "Riding on the Elevated Railway" (from 1879) and "Hang Out the Front Door Key" (from 1908).[28]

A few persons emphasized comedy and sang sparingly or not at all. The blackface comedy team of Lasses and Honey (Lasses White and Honey Wilds) was popular for many years. After White went to Hollywood to become a western movie sidekick, Wilds took on as a partner Bunny Biggs, who took the name "Jamup," and the new duo became Jamup and Honey until the early 1950s, when their brand of humor reached the status of an anachronism. Benjamin "Whitey" Ford (1901–1986), known on stage as the "Duke of Paducah," hailed from Missouri and had a Dixieland jazz tenor banjo-playing background. He turned to radio comedy in the mid-1930s, working at WLS Chicago and WLW Cincinnati before coming to WSM in 1942. Many of his jokes centered around his "big fat wife," and he always closed his routines with "I'm going back to the wagon, these shoes are killing me." Rod Brasfield (1910–1958), a native of the Mississippi hill country, worked on tent show dramas throughout the South in early adulthood before settling in at the NBC Network portion of the *Opry* in 1944. While urban sophisticates must have thought that Brasfield's brand of humor was dated and rustic, rural audiences loved it. He developed a line of jokes about some fictional bucolic characters who inhabited his adopted hometown of Hohenwald, Tennessee, including his "gal Suzie" and his "Uncle Cyp," and nagging wife "Aunt Sap." Eventually,

Brasfield's older brother Lawrence "Boob" (1898–1966) and his wife Neva (1889–1980), also tent show veterans, developed a series of Uncle Cyp and Aunt Sap skits, which they performed on ABC television's *Ozark Jubilee*.[29]

Brasfield however was outstripped in both popularity and longevity by Sarah Ophelia Colley Cannon (1912–1996), who developed the character of "Minnie Pearl," the man-chasing old maid from Grinder's Switch who was a favorite with *Opry* fans for half a century. The real person behind Minnie had two years of college education and a middle-class Southern background, but Minnie's stories from Grinder's Switch concerning her "feller Hezzie," her unnamed boozing brother, "Uncle Nabob," "Aunt Ambrosia," and other assorted characters, along with occasional discussions with Rod Brasfield, made her one of country music's enduring individuals. Minnie sang a song now and then, usually in an outlandish comedic vein, such as "How to Catch a Man (on the Minnie Pearl Plan)," and even made the charts once with her 1966 recitation "Giddyup Go-Answer." Among female performers, only the deceased Patsy Cline preceded Minnie into the Country Music Hall of Fame.[30]

After the death of Rod Brasfield, Archie Campbell (1914–1987) continued the *Opry* comedy tradition. Known as the "Mayor of Bull's Gap," Campbell had twenty years of experience on Knoxville, Bristol, and Chattanooga radio and television behind him. While his *Opry* comedy was augmented by some occasional singing and spoonerism renditions of standard fairy tales, such as "Rindercella," "The Pee Little Thrigs," and "Beeping Sleuty," Campbell really came into his own on the *Hee Haw* TV series beginning in 1969. He adapted some of the skits he first developed in Knoxville to television, playing a country doctor and a barber, among others.[31]

Duet acts continued to render some memorable music, although they had many fewer hits than the honky-tonk vocalists. The first to gain prominence, Johnnie (b. 1914) and Jack (1916–1963) (Johnnie Wright and Jack Anglin), were brother-in-laws who had several years of radio in Knoxville, Shreveport, Charleston, and Raleigh behind them before settling in Nashville. While the content of many of their numerous recordings for RCA Victor, such as "Poison Love" and "Ashes of Love," resembled the kind of songs favored by honky-tonk vocalists, their instrumentation remained primarily acoustical, with a Dobro guitar played by Shot Jackson, a fiddle by Paul Warren, and mandolin played by various pickers, including Paul Buskirk, Clyde Baum, and Ernest Ferguson at one time or another. As the 1950s progressed, the team came closer to mainstream country, but their work ended in 1963 with Jack's demise in an auto crash.[32]

The Louvin Brothers probably reached the ultimate harmony duet sound in the late 1940s and the 1950s. Ira Louvin (1924–1965) played mandolin, sang in a high tenor voice, and exhibited a flair for writing all kinds of songs, including sacred, comedy, romantic, and honky-tonk. Charlie Louvin (b. 1927) played rhythm guitar, sang lead, wrote a little, and provided emotional stability. Beginning in the mid-1940s, the Louvins played at various radio locales before settling in at the *Opry* in 1955. They had brief experiences with Apollo, Decca, and M-G-M before beginning a long association with Capitol in 1962. Most of their earlier efforts were sacred songs, such as "The Great Atomic Power" and "The Family Who Prays," but they finally persuaded their producer to let them do secular material and began turning out such major hits as "When I Stopped Dreaming," "I Don't Believe You Met My Baby," and "Cash on the Barrel-head." Unfortunately, the advent of rock-and-roll influences damaged the Louvin's commercial appeal, and they experienced difficulty, finally dissolving in 1963. Ira's death ended any possibility of a reunion, but Charlie enjoyed a significant solo career, placing over twenty songs on the charts during the 1960s and early 1970s, most notably, "I Don't Love You Any More" in 1964.[33]

Some other family acts had members of both sexes in their entourages. Lynn Davis (1914–1999) and Molly O'Day (1923–1987), from the mountains of eastern Kentucky, remained closer to traditional music with both duets and Molly's solo voice heard on their Columbia recordings. The numbers "Tramp on the Street," "Matthew Twenty-Four," and the traditional "Poor Ellen Smith" rank among Molly's best. But the duo sometimes dabbled in honky-tonk songs typified by "This Is the End" and "With You on My Mind." In 1950, they dropped out of show business and pursued evangelistic work for the remainder of their lives. The aforementioned West Virginians Wilma Lee and Stoney Cooper followed a somewhat similar path but remained in music, spending a decade at WWVA and another twenty years at the *Opry* and retained an old-time flavor to their music.[34]

In California, the depression-displaced Alabama-born Maddox Brothers and Rose displayed an eclecticism that was almost unique. Their repertoire varied from old-time and hillbilly hymns to raucous honky-tonk, comedy, and ultimately even rockabilly songs. After a decade of touring, of colorful entertainment, and of numerous recordings on the Four Star and Columbia labels, the Brothers switched to other careers, but Rose Maddox (1925–1998) continued on for several more decades, recording in essentially a honky-tonk style for Capitol in the late 1950s and early 1960s and having hits with such numbers as "Sing a Little Song of Heartache," "Loose Talk," and the duet "Mental Cruelty" with Buck Owens. In later years, she often recorded with bluegrass accompaniment.[35]

The changes in country music that made continuing success a challenge for hard country acts like the Louvin Brothers in a sense signaled the approaching end of one era of country music and the ushering in of a new one. The honky-tonk sounds that had dominated the music since the early months of World War II would be impacted by new styles that contained a considerable African American influence and would be geared largely to teenagers. Charlie Adams may have unwittingly begun to pull down the curtain on the type of music that had brought stardom to Ernest Tubb and Hank Williams in 1955 when he recorded a song titled "Pistol Packin' Mama Has Laid Her Pistol Down." A few months later, another honky-tonk singer, Bob Gallion, at his first session cut a number titled "My Square Dancin' Mama (She's Done Learned to Rock 'n' Roll)."[36] Together, the two songs symbolized an "out with the old" and an "in with the new" attitude. The new music would be termed "rockabilly."

NOTES

1. For a thorough biography of this key individual, see Ronnie Pugh, *Ernest Tubb: The Texas Troubadour* (Durham, NC: Duke University Press, 1996).

2. Nick Tosches, "Al Dexter," *Old Time Music* 22 (Autumn 1976), 4–8.

3. Kevin Coffey, *Floyd Tillman: I Love You So Much It Hurts* (Hamburg, Germany: Bear Family Records, 2004).

4. The Tennessee Plowboy has been the subject of two biographies: Don Cusic, *Eddy Arnold: I'll Hold You in My Heart* (Nashville, TN: Rutledge Hill Press, 1997), and Michael Streissguth, *Eddy Arnold: Pioneer of the Nashville Sound* (New York: Schirmer Books, 1997).

5. Hanks Williams has unsurprisingly drawn more biographers than any figure in country music, each of which makes some contribution to his complex story. The most thorough is probably Colin Escott, *Hank Williams: The Biography* (Boston: Little, Brown, 1994). Others are Roger M. Williams, *Sing a Sad Song: The Life of Hank Williams* (Urbana: University of Illinois Press, 1981); Jay Caress, *Hank Williams: Country Music's Tragic King* (New York: Stein & Day, 1979); and George William Koon, *Hank Williams: A Bio-Bibliography* (Westport, CT: Greenwood Press, 1983). The latter work, revised as Bill Koon, *Hank Williams: So Lonesome* (Jackson: University Press of Mississippi, 2001), 119–134, contains an excellent bibliographic essay on Williams literature. Colin Escott and Kira Florita, *Hank Williams: Snapshots from the Lost Highway* (Cambridge, MA: Da Capo Press, 2001), includes numerous previously unpublished photos and documents.

6. Hank Snow's autobiography, *The Hank Snow Story* (Urbana: University of Illinois Press, 1994), provides a good account of Snow's life.

7. Webb Pierce has received inadequate attention from biographers, but Otto Kitsinger, *Webb Pierce: The Wondering "Boy," 1951–1958* (Vollersode, Germany: Bear Family Records, 1990), provides a good starting point. A good brief evaluation is Rich Kienzle, "Webb Pierce: Honky Tonk Hitmaker," *The Journal* 1 (June 1991), 14–18.

8. Young has been understudied, but the detailed liner note booklet by Daniel Cooper, *Faron Young: Live Fast, Love Hard, 1952–1962* (Nashville, TN: Country Music Foundation Records, CMF D20, 1995), contains a good sketch and evaluation. See Rich Kienzle, "Faron Young: The Singing Sheriff," *The Journal* 2 (February 1992), 14–15.

9. Charles Wolfe, *Carl Smith: Satisfaction Guaranteed* (Hamburg, Germany: Bear Family Records, 1996). See also Ivan M. Tribe, "The Long Road from West Virginia to the Country Music Hall of Fame: The Career of Little Jimmy Dickens," *JEMF Quarterly* 19 (Winter 1983), 207–218; Rich Kienzle, "Cowboy Copas: The Ohio Ridge Runner," *The Journal* 30 (December 1995), 12–15.

10. Walt Trott, *The Honky Tonk Angels: A Dual Biography* (Nashville, TN: Nova Books, 1993). See also Charles Wolfe, "Kitty Wells: The Woman's Point of View," *The Journal* 1 (October 1991), 16–19.

11. Rich Kienzle, *Merle Travis* (Vollersode, Germany: Bear Family Records, 1994). See also Pat Travis Eatherly, *In Search of My Father* (Nashville, TN: Boardman Press, 1987), for a memoir from a daughter's viewpoint.

12. Bear Family Records has issued a series of compact discs of California honky-tonk singers associated with Capitol Records with accompanying biographical data, including *Rambling Jimmie Dolan: Juke Box Boogie* (BCD 16192, 2000), *Jack Guthrie: Oklahoma Hills* (BCD 15580, 1991), *Roy Hogsed: Cocaine Blues* (BCD 16191, 2000), and *Jess Willard: Honky-Tonk Hardwood Floor* (BCD 16256, 2000). Most of Ernest E. "Jimmy" Walker's recordings for Coast, M-G-M, and Intro were reissued on two Old Homestead albums (OH 310 and OH 311) in the late 1980s.

13. Ivan M. Tribe, "Tommy Collins, The Man Called Leonard" *The Journal* 2 (October 1992), 18–19. See also Dale Vinicur, *Tommy Collins: Leonard* (Vollersode, Germany: Bear Family Records, 1994).

14. See Kevin Coffey, *Charlie Adams & the Lone Star Playboys: Cattin' Around* (Bear Family BCD 16312, 2000), liner notes; Kevin Coffey, "Frankie Miller: Pure Country in the Days of Rock 'n' Roll," *The Journal* 28 (August 1995), 16–17; Hank Davis and Colin Escott, *Rockin' Rollin' Frankie Miller* (Bear Family BFX 15128, 1983), liner notes.

15. Daniel Cooper's *Lefty Frizzell: The Honky-Tonk Life of Country Music's Greatest Singer* (Boston: Little, Brown, 1995) is a credible biography in spite of a subtitle many would consider overstated. One should also consult Charles Wolfe, *Lefty Frizzell: His Life, His Music* (Vollersode, Germany: Bear Family Records, 1984), which is more focused on Frizzell's recordings.

16. Rich Kienzle, Hank Thompson: Brazos Valley Boy," *The Journal* 21 (July 1994), 8–11. See also Rich Kienzle, *Hank Thompson* (Vollersode, Germany: Bear Family Records, 1996).

17. Colin Escott, *Billy Walker: Cross the Brazos at Waco* (Hamburg, Germany: Bear Family Records, 1993).

18. Chris Skinker, *Charlie Walker: Pick Me up on Your Way Down* (Hamburg, Germany: Bear Family Records, 1998).

19. George Jones has attracted two biographers: Dolly Carlisle, *Ragged but Right: The Life & Times of George Jones* (Chicago: Contemporary Books, 1984), and Bob Allen, *George Jones: The Life and Times of a Honky Tonk Legend* (New York: Birch Lane Press, 1994). Jones covers his own life in George Jones, *I Live to Tell It All* (New York: Villard, 1996).

20. Foley has generated relatively little scholarly or reissue attention, but a good albeit brief sketch is Adam Komorowski, *Red Foley: Tennessee Saturday Night* (Kent, England: Proper PVCD 105, 2002), liner notes. See also Charles K. Wolfe, *Kentucky Country: Folk and Country Music of Kentucky* (Lexington: University Press of Kentucky, 1982), 130–136.

21. Morgan has not been adequately studied, but Ivan M. Tribe, "George Morgan" in Barry McCloud, ed., *Definitive Country: The Ultimate Encyclopedia of Country Music and Its Performers* (New York: Perigee Books, 1995), 563, offers a thorough sketch.

22. The autobiographical Tennessee Ernie Ford, *This Is My Story, This Is My Song* (Englewood Cliffs, NJ: Prentice-Hall, 1963), is anecdotal and of limited value; more useful is Charles K. Wolfe, *Tennessee Strings: Country Music in Tennessee* (Knoxville: University of Tennessee Press, 1977), 80–82; and Gerald W. Haslam, *Workin' Man Blues: Country Music in California* (Berkeley: University of California Press, 1999), 161–164.

23. For the Wheeling Jamboree, see Ivan M. Tribe, *Mountaineer Jamboree: Country Music in West Virginia* (Lexington: University Press of Kentucky, 1984), 43–72.

24. Ibid., 55–58. A good view of Hawkins is offered by Rich Kienzle, "Hawkshaw Hawkins: Easygoing Nature: Unpretentious Career," *The Journal* 28 (August 1995), 12–15.

25. The country scene in Knoxville is briefly covered in two works of Charles Wolfe, "Country Music," in Jim Stokely and Jeff D. Johnson, eds., *An Encyclopedia of East Tennessee* (Oak Ridge, TN: Children's Museum, 1981), 132–140, and *Tennessee Strings*, 85–88. For Butler, see Ronnie Pugh, *Carl Butler: A Blue Million Tears* (Hamburg, Germany: Bear Family Records BCD 16118, 2003), liner notes.

26. All of these individuals are discussed in Wolfe, *Kentucky Country*, especially Stringbean on 124–129.

27. Jones tells his story accurately in Louis M. "Grandpa" Jones with Charles K. Wolfe, *Everybody's Grandpa: Fifty Years Behind the Mike* (Knoxville: University of Tennessee Press, 1984). See also Ramona Jones, *Make Music While You Can: My Story* (Madison, NC: Empire, 2000).

28. Charles K. Wolfe, "Doc Lew: The Life and Times of Lew Childre," *Bluegrass Unlimited* 13 (November 1978), 26–30.

29. A brief sketch of Ford is found in Tribe, "Duke of Paducah," in McCloud, *Definitive Country*, 253–254. Rod Brasfield's career is discussed in Minnie Pearl, *Minnie Pearl: An Autobiography* (New York: Pocket Books, 1980), 209–212. For Jamup and Honey, see Charles Wolfe, "Jamup and Honey (Lasses and Honey)" in Kingsbury, *The Encyclopedia of Country Music* (New York: Oxford University Press, 1998), 261.

30. Pearl, *Minnie Pearl: An Autobiography*.

31. See Archie Campbell, *Archie Campbell: An Autobiography* (Memphis, TN: Memphis State University Press, 1981).

32. Trott, *The Honky Tonk Angels*.

33. Charles Wolfe, *In Close Harmony: The Story of the Louvin Brothers* (Jackson: University Press of Mississippi, 1996).

34. Ivan M. Tribe and John W. Morris, *Molly O'Day, Lynn Davis and the Cumberland Mountain Folks: A Bio-Discography* (Los Angeles: John Edwards Memorial Foundation, 1975); Robert Cogswell, "We Made Our Name in the Days of Radio: A Look at the Careers of Wilma Lee and Stoney Cooper," *JEMF Quarterly* 11 (Summer 1975), 57–69; Ivan M. Tribe, "Wilma Lee and Stoney Cooper: The Singing Pals," *The Journal* 2 (February 1992), 12–13.

35. Jonny Whiteside, *Ramblin' Rose: The Life and Career of Rose Maddox* (Nashville, TN: Country Music Foundation Press and Vanderbilt University Press, 1997). See also Charlie Seemann, "The Maddox Brothers and Rose," *The Journal* 16 (August 1993), 12–15.

36. See Charlie Adams, "Pistol Packin' Mama Has Laid Her Pistol Down" (Columbia 21443, reissued on Bear Family BCD 16312, 2000); Bob Gallion, "My Square Dancin' Mama (She's Done Learned to Rock 'n' Roll)" (M-G-M 12195, reissued on Bear Family BCD 16439, 2000).

6

Rockin' in the Country, 1954–1960

The decade of the 1950s—especially the mid- to late segments of that era—are often thought of as a time of great ferment and change in American popular culture, particularly that of teens and young adults. Characteristic symbols include motorcycles, hot rod cars, drag racing, ducktail haircuts, rebellion, *American Bandstand*, James Dean, and the rise of Elvis Presley. In some respects, the changes were less deep than often imagined, but in other respects, they ring true. Among those in the latter category are the changes that occurred within the realm of country music.

The rise of what became known as "rockabilly" music resulted in large part from a mixture of African American rhythm and blues influences into country, which had a few years earlier been impacted by what was known as country or hillbilly "boogie." Those songs with boogie in the title and boogie beats in the music dated from 1945, when the hitherto traditionally oriented harmony duet the Delmore Brothers recorded a number called "Hillbilly Boogie." They followed with "Barn Yard Boogie," "Pan-American Boogie," and, in league with harmonica player Wayne Raney (1921–1993), "Jack and Jill Boogie" and "Lost John Boogie." Numerous other country artists did boogie numbers with various degrees of success—most notably, Tennessee Ernie Ford and the Maddox Brothers and Rose. Others may see the roots of rockabilly in the early Hank Williams hit of "Move It on Over," some of the songs of Moon Mullican, or certain songs of country singer Lattie Moore. Bill Haley (1925–1981), who had

Beautifully close harmonies, intricate guitar playing, and original compositions made the Delmore Brothers a tough act to follow.
Courtesy of Photofest.

the first certifiable rock-and-roll hit, had a modest country music background, although his hit records—most obviously, "Rock Around the Clock," cut in March 1954—had only an indirect influence on country.

African American prewar blues music had evolved into what became known as rhythm and blues in a manner that was somewhat similar to less complex pre-World War II country music moving toward the previously discussed honky-tonk styles. Migration of southerners to northern cities, increased use of electric instruments, and the importance of the jukebox trade ranked among the social and technical factors that accompanied these changes. In addition, the increased radio air play of programs that appealed to African American audiences—such as those heard on WLAC Nashville—were also heard by white youth and led some white country musicians to adopt techniques utilized by black musicians into their own sounds. Within the record industry, some companies, such as King, which specialized in black rhythm and blues on the one hand and white country on the other, urged their artists from one style to record songs in the other style. Thus, a rhythm and blues artist such as Bull Moose Jackson recorded the hillbilly hit by Wayne Raney, "Why Don't You Haul Off and Love Me," while country artist Hawkshaw Hawkins covered black rhythm and blues artist Lucky Millinder's recording of "I'm Waiting Just for You." Since rights to the songs were owned by King's publishing subsidiary—Lois Music—it would increase royalties for both publisher and writer. In its own way, corporate realities served as a catalyst for cultural interchange at a time when racial barriers were beginning to crumble.

MEMPHIS AND THE BIRTH OF ROCKABILLY

Various theories exist as to the first rockabilly artists, but there is no doubt that the development of the music as a fad and trend took place in Memphis, Tennessee, where a man named Sam Phillips had a small recording studio and the Sun Record label. Much of Phillips's income came from custom work for both black and white individuals and from making master recordings of rhythm and blues musicians, which he then turned over to other firms, such as the Chicago-based Chess label. He also recorded some local white country musicians.[1]

The situation at Sun changed dramatically in mid-1954 when Phillips recorded a young truck driver named Elvis Presley (1935–1977). Presley's style in essence fused white country with black rhythm and blues with overtones of both black and white gospel. Accompaniment consisted of two guitars and a bass. His initial record release illustrated the musical mixture. One side featured "That's All Right," a cover of an Arthur "Big Boy" Crudup "R and B" number, backed with a Bill Monroe song, "Blue Moon of Kentucky." His fourth release, "Baby, Let's Play House"/"I'm Left, You're Right, She's Gone," rose to the fifth spot on the *Billboard* country charts in July 1955. Several weeks later, another Sun single, "I Forgot to Remember to Forget"/"Mystery Train," also hit the charts with the first side hitting number one. In the meantime, Presley had made guest appearances in September 1954 on the *Grand Ole Opry* and in October 1954 on the *Louisiana Hayride*, where he was quickly contracted as a regular member. In November 1955, RCA Victor acquired Presley's contract and rereleased his five Sun singles and also acquired the unreleased material from the Sun vaults, which were subsequently released on either singles, albums, or both.

In mid-January 1956, Elvis Presley had his first RCA Victor session in Nashville;

Many people tend to forget that Elvis Presley, the "King of Rock and Roll," began his career in country music. Elvis's induction into the Country Music Hall of Fame in 1998 serves to confirm his success as a country music artist. *Courtesy of Photofest.*

the first release from that session, "Heartbreak Hotel," went to the top of the country charts for seventeen weeks and the pop charts for eight. During that year, "I Want You, I Need You, I Love You," "Don't Be Cruel," and "Hound Dog" all reached number one in both country and pop, while "Love Me Tender," the title song from his first motion picture, also reached the top of the pop charts. Songs like "All Shook Up," "Teddy Bear," and "Jailhouse Rock" hit number one on the country listings in 1957. Having altered both the country and pop music scene, Presley was increasingly viewed as a pop performer and in fact did not appear on the country charts at all between 1961 and 1968, although his songs continued with regularity on the pop listings, many of them from the series of popular—if lightweight—motion pictures he made during that decade. However, the trend that he initiated continued unabated in the country field for a few more years.[2]

One of the first to follow in the Presley footsteps was another west Tennessee resident and product of the cottonfields, Carl Lee Perkins (1932–1998), who had been performing—with his two brothers—a mixture of hillbilly and blues on the club scene in the general vicinity of his Jackson, Tennessee, home. Perkins made his first recordings in October 1954 for Sun (released on a subsidiary label, Flip). Another release on Sun came out in 1955, and his third single, "Blue Suede Shoes," climbed to number one (and number two in pop). Meanwhile on March 21, 1956, Perkins and his brothers suffered auto crash injuries on the way to a network television appearance in New York, which hurt his momentum. Nonetheless, he had two more hits that year with "Boppin' the Blues" and "Dixie Fried" but never managed to surpass or even equal "Blue Suede Shoes." He had a moderate success with "Pink Pedal Pushers" on Columbia in 1958 and went to work with Johnny Cash from 1965 to 1975, during which time he wrote one of Cash's big hits, "Daddy Sang Bass." Perkins continued recording into the 1990s and remained a major figure among rockabilly fans in Europe until his death.[3]

A third legendary rockabilly figure to be associated with Sun, Johnny Cash (1932–2003) remained closer to the country mainstream than did the others. Cash grew up in the Resettlement Administration community of Dyess, Arkansas, and got serious about music after military service in the U.S. Air Force. Settling in Memphis in 1954, he sang on local radio and made his first recording on Sun in mid-1955. His first single, "Cry, Cry, Cry," made a brief chart appearance on November 26, but the following year, he had five songs on the *Billboard* listings, of which "I Walk the Line" and "There You Go" reached the top, and the former number registered as a crossover hit as well. Cash hits often tended to be slower ballads, such as "Guess Things Happen That Way" and "Ballad of a Teenage Queen," while the more fast-paced rockabilly songs, such as "Get Rhythm" and "Luther Played the Boogie," attracted less attention. He moved to Columbia in 1958 and continued to rack up a string of high-level hits in the next dozen years and lesser ones through the 1980s. Those reaching number one included "Ring of Fire," "Understand Your Man," "Folsom Prison Blues," "Daddy Sang Bass," "A Boy Named Sue,"

"Sunday Morning Coming Down," "Flesh and Blood," and finally his last, "One Piece at a Time," in 1976.

To list all of Cash's achievements and hit songs would take considerable space, but a few are in order. Through 1990, he had placed 135 songs on the *Billboard* country charts and an additional thirteen on the pop top forty. From 1969 until 1971, he hosted an ABC prime-time network television show. In 1968, he married June Carter and thus gained a connection to one of the most legendary names in the business and helped to revive interest in the Carter heritage. Several of his albums explored various themes, ranging from *Bitter Tears*, which took a serious look at the plight of Native Americans, to *From Sea to Shining Sea*, which offered slices of American life from a variety of angles. On top of that, he gained a degree of wide respect for overcoming his personal problems with pills and drugs and identified widely with his renewed religious faith. Many mainstream journalist wrote positive editorials on the man following his death.[4]

Johnny Cash's consistent chart-topping songs have transcended both time and genre, making him a country music legend today.
Courtesy of Photofest.

A fourth major figure to emerge from the Sun Record stable of rockabilly legends was Jerry Lee Lewis (b. 1935), who played piano and generated controversy. Known as "the Killer," among other things, Lewis and his "pumping piano" scored initially with wild rockabilly songs like "Whole Lot of Shakin' Going On," "Great Balls of Fire," and "High School Confidential," but he also rendered credible versions of slower country hits ranging from Hank Williams's "Cold Cold Heart" to Ray Price's "Crazy Arms." On stage he pounded his piano like a wild man and sometimes set it afire for shock effect, and he created a sensation that nearly destroyed his career when he married his thirteen-year-old cousin, Myra Gail Brown, in 1958. He eventually regained stature from the late 1960s as he alternated between mainstream country and rockabilly. Nonetheless, his bizarre actions continued as he survived a number of unsuccessful marriages—one of his wives drowned in their swimming pool—and several serious bouts of near fatal health crises, many of them the result of his reckless lifestyle. Yet, Jerry Lee Lewis, for better or worse, ranks as a true American original.[5]

Roy Orbison (1936–1988) ranks as the fifth major product of Sun Records, although his most enduring songs came in the field of popular music. A native of west Texas, Orbison had country roots similar to the others and had a western band in high school. As a young collegian, he met Elvis Presley, who encouraged him to try a rockabilly style, which in 1956 landed him with Sun, where his recording of "Ooby Dooby" rose to number 59 on the *Billboard* pop charts. During the 1960s, he had several major hits, including "Only the Lonely" and "Oh Pretty Woman," which later enjoyed a revival when it became the theme of a classic Julia Roberts film. Ironically, Orbison never appeared on the country charts until 1980. A tragic figure in many respects, Orbison suffered from poor eyesight most of his life, his wife Claudette died in a motorcycle crash, two of his three children perished in a house fire, and he died at fifty-two at the height of a musical comeback.[6]

A string of other rockabilly performers graced the Sun Studios in the later 1950s, all hoping to be another Elvis Presley. Although no others really succeeded, they did produce some fine music in that style, and many of their recordings went on to become legendary as collector's items. Some of the more significant included Warren Smith (1932–1980) with "Rock and Roll Ruby" and "Ubangi Stomp"; Billy Lee Riley (b. 1933) with "Flyin' Saucer Rock 'n' Roll" and "Red Hot"; Ray Smith (1934–1979) with "Right Behind You Baby" and "Shake Around"; Charlie Feathers (1932–1999) with "Defrost Your Heart" and "Wedding Gown of White"; and an older man, Malcolm Yelvington (b. 1918) with "Rockin' with My Baby" and "Drinkin' Wine Spodee-O-Dee" (the latter an R & B favorite recorded by several rockabilly artists).[7]

ROCKABILLY GOES TO TEXAS

The birth of the Elvis phenomenon soon spread the interest in rocking types of country music to Nashville and other centers. Major record companies did not take long to capitalize on Presley's impact and to look for those who could repeat what had happened in Sam Phillips's little studio in Memphis. However, as Rich Kienzle points out, "since older producers rarely understood the music, they often tried too hard to control it, resulting in many failed recordings."[8] Not all such efforts failed the test. One of the first to even try was the Texas band that soon came to be known as Sid King and the Five Strings, led by two brothers, Sid (b. 1936) and Billy Erwin (b. 1938), from Denton, Texas. After a single on Starday, the Five Strings signed with Columbia in December 1954, moving from honky-tonk to rockabilly (or what Sid termed "hillbilly beebop") with relative ease. On latter sessions they even added a saxophone. The band put together some rocking material of their own, such as "Sag, Drag and Fall," "Gonna Shake This Shack Tonight," "Good Rockin' Baby," and "Booger Red," as well as credible covers of "Oobie Doobie [sic]" and "Blue Suede Shoes," but could never really break out of a regional mold in spite of its major label connection. The band broke up after it lost its Columbia contract, although Sid had another regional success with "Once Upon a Time" and "Hello There Rockin' Chair" in 1962. Other Texas rockabillies with fleeting careers included Sonny Fisher (b. 1931), Johnny Carroll (1937–1995), Mac Curtis (b. 1939), Andy Starr (b. 1932), and Wayne "Buddy" Knox (b. 1933) who managed a number one pop hit with "Party Doll" in 1958.

One Texas rockabilly gained a true legendary status. Charles "Buddy" Holly (1936–1959) grew up in Lubbock in more middle-class circumstances than most people identified with rock-and-roll music. While his own musical background was more country than anything else, he made little impact on that scene but had great impact and influence on popular music, which was where all his hits registered. He initially signed with Decca and recorded in Nashville early in 1956 but with little success. Holly had better luck with a February 1957 session at Norman Petty's studio in Clovis, New Mexico, where his first release (credited to his band, the Crickets) titled "That'll Be the Day" sold a million and hit number one on the pop charts. The follow-up, "Peggy Sue," did nearly as well, and six more songs ranked in the Top Forty. Unfortunately, Holly died in a plane crash prior to his twenty-third birthday. But his stature in the field ranked second only to Elvis Presley.[9]

CALIFORNIA ROCKS

Rockabilly also thrived on the West Coast. The aforementioned multifaceted Maddox Brothers and Rose dabbled in the style, and sister Rose continued to do so after her brothers dropped from the scene. The short-lived Eddie Cochran (1938–1960) had three pop hits with a rockabilly flavor—most notably, "Summertime Blues"—prior to his death in an automobile accident. Ricky Nelson (1940–1985), the son of Ozzie and Harriett Nelson of television fame, sang rocking songs on his family sitcom television program and began recording for Imperial in 1957. His acting and singing made him a true teenage idol in the 1957–1963 era. His "I'm Walking" came from the repertoire of Fats Domino, while "My Bucket's Got a Hole in It" was an old blues number that Hank Williams had first revitalized in 1949. Despite an obvious affection for country music and several listings on the country charts, Nelson remained a pop star who sang country-influenced soft rock-and-roll music. Nelson's status waned somewhat in the later 1960s, but he remained active until his death in a plane crash.[10]

The Collins Kids probably ranked as the best rockabilly act on the California scene. Oklahoma-born Lorrie (b. 1942) and Larry Collins (b. 1944) showed extraordinary musical skills at an early age, and their parents moved to the Golden State to give the children an opportunity to develop their talents to the fullest. Contests and guest shots on radio and television led them to a regular spot on *Town Hall Party* in 1954 and to a Columbia recording contract in 1955. Larry quickly apprenticed himself to guitar wizard Joe Maphis and became adept on the double-necked electric guitar, while Lorrie had excellent vocal power. Their songs varied from country novelty numbers, such as "Hush Money" and "Go

Away, Don't Bother Me," to rockers like "Whistle Bait" and "Beetle Bug Bop." Even nursery rhymes got a rockabilly treatment, such as "Shortnin' Bread Rock" and "Cuckoo Rock." With Lorrie as a wholesome but emerging teen beauty and Larry as the smark-aleck kid brother, the Collins Kids were a most impressive visual act. Although none of their moderate-selling records ever became major hits, they ranked as quite successful, but Lorrie's marriage in 1959 and motherhood in 1961 first curtailed and then virtually terminated their momentum.[11]

ROCKIN' IN SHREVEPORT AND NASHVILLE

The rockabilly fever also hit the older country radio musical centers. Mention has already been made of the KWKH *Louisiana Hayride* as a springboard for Elvis Presley. Johnny Cash also spent a year at the "Cradle of the Stars." Werly Fairborn (b. 1924), another older performer, did some rocking numbers as did the young Cajun duo of Rusty and Doug (Kershaw). However, one country performer who remained with the *Hayride* from 1955 was Johnny Horton (1925–1960). Unlike many country and rockabilly stars, Horton, who grew up in Texas, seemed to lack the hard desire and ambition to succeed and had more interest in hunting and fishing but eventually became a star in spite of himself. His early recordings for Cormac, Abbott, and Mercury made little impact, but when Tillman Franks began to manage him and he went with Columbia in 1956, things began to change. He had modest hits with rockabilly-flavored country songs, such as "Honky-Tonk Man," "I'm a One-Woman Man," and "Honky-Tonk Hardwood Floor."

However, what really put Horton on top was a series of "saga songs." This particular type of song was what one might term folk-flavored songs about real or fictional events. The trend toward such material seems to have been related to the popular success of "Tom Dooley," an old murder ballad (first recorded in 1927 by the old-time duo of Grayson and Whitter). "When It's Springtime in Alaska" with an imagery reminiscent of a Robert Service poem provided Horton with his first number one hit early in 1959. His follow-up "Battle of New Orleans" provided him with not only a gold record but also the song of the year for 1959 in both the pop and country fields, topping both charts for six and ten weeks, respectively. Ironically, this song consisted of new lyrics put by Arkansas school teacher Jimmie Driftwood to a traditional fiddle tune, "The Eighth of January," that had commemorated the battle. Successive saga hits— "Johnny Reb," "Sink the Bismarck," and "North to Alaska"—kept Horton high on the charts for another year and a half, several months after his tragic death in an automobile wreck.[12]

The Nashville establishment seemed a bit slow to get caught up in the rockabilly movement, although the record industry seems to have grasped its significance somewhat quicker than that of the *Grand Ole Opry*. Session guitarists, such as Chet Atkins, Grady Martin, and Hank Garland, did not take long to adapt their licks for those of the rockers, much as Merle Travis and Joe Maphis had grasped it in California. Most of the current *Opry* people responded with a rocker or two, including such traditionalists as Little Jimmy Dickens with "Blackeyed Joe's," "Salty Boogie," and "I Got a Hole in My Pocket." Cowboy Copas tried it with "Circle Rock," and Red Sovine offered up "Juke Joint Johnnie." Most were not successful, but a few did remarkably well at the newer styles.[13]

One who accommodated very well was the Arizona-born Marty Robbins (1925–1982). After making a positve impact in Phoenix, Robbins came to Nashville with a style somewhere between that of the country crooners and the honky-tonk singers. From 1952 onward, he was on the country charts regularly for the rest of his life. However, one might also say that he "re-invented" himself regularly and effectively. He experienced his first hit with his third Columbia release, "I'll Go on Alone" in the winter of 1952–1953. He made five more appearances over the next two years and after sharing a show date with Elvis Presley in the latter part of 1954 recorded a cover of "That's All Right," which peaked at number seven. He also covered Chuck Berry's "Maybellene" successfully in 1955. His purest rockabilly effort was probably a song called "Tennessee Toddy," but it did little. "Singing the Blues" proved to be one of his biggest hits, and "Knee Deep in the Blues" did nearly as well. Turning to what one might term rock-and-roll ballads, he scored number ones in country and in the top thirty in pop with "A White Sport Coat," "Just Married," and "The Story of My Life."

When the fad for saga songs hit at the end of the decade, Robbins turned to what he termed *Gunfighter Ballads* and had one of his biggest ever hits with the Spanish-flavored "El Paso," which was actually his only number one pop listing. He also experienced success with "Running Gun," "Big Iron," "Five Brothers," and "The Cowboy in the Continental Suit." When the Nashville Sound began to dominate the country scene in the early 1960s, he came to the forefront again with such major hits as "Don't Worry" and "Devil Woman." Meanwhile, he recorded albums of Hawaiian songs and even an album of such old-time numbers as "The Little Rosewood Casket" and "The Letter Edged in Black," with only his guitar as accompaniment (from which only a four song EP was released in his lifetime). During a period when he switched to Decca in the mid-1970s, he even did some credible bluegrass songs. As an actor of sorts, he made country music movies in the 1960s, such as *The Road to Nashville*. A man of varied interests, he became a racecar driver and survived several crashes but ultimately died of heart failure only weeks after his induction into the Country Music Hall of Fame, having made the country charts ninety-four times and the pop top forty thirteen times. The Robbins rockabilly years may have been just one phase of many, but whatever he did, he did well.[14]

Those country singers who dabbled in rockabilly and who recorded in Nashville, but were not necessarily associated with the *Opry*, were fairly numerous. Some merit passing mention. Among the more significant were Missouri-born Ronnie Self (1938–1981), who earned the nickname "Mr. Frantic" for his stage presence. Self had a midlevel hit with "Bop-a-Lena" and toured with the Phillip Morris Caravan. Kentucky's Jimmie Logsdon (b. 1922) sang hard country on Decca in the Hank Williams style, but his Roulette rockabilly efforts under the name "Jimmy Lloyd" made him a minor legend. Virginia-born James "Roy" Hall (1922–1984) came to Nashville by way of Detroit, played a boogie-woogie piano, and had recorded for Fortune before coming to Tennessee. There he and a black musician, David Williams, co-authored "Whole Lotta Shakin' Goin' On," and Hall recorded it for Decca over a year before the better known hit version by Jerry Lee Lewis (but after the R & B rendition by Big Maybelle). Rusty York (b. 1935) was closely linked through much of his career with Cincinnati-based country singer Jimmie Skinner (1909–1979). His musical roots were mostly in bluegrass, but he had a modest hit with "Sugaree." He also played on national television's *American Bandstand* and played a package show at the Hollywood Bowl.

The principal Nashville contribution to the rockabilly scene probably came in the harmony duets of the Everly Brothers—Don (b. 1937) and Phil (b. 1939)—who made all of their early recordings in Nashville. Most of their early hits came from the compositions of the Nashville song-writing team of Boudleaux and Felice Bryant. Sons of Ike Everly, a guitar picker from the same area that produced Merle Travis, the Everlys sang in radio with their parents in places like KMA in Shenandoah, Iowa, and developed some of the best harmony ever heard. A 1955 single on Columbia went nowhere, but a string of singles on the Cadence label beginning in the spring of 1957 established them as both country and pop stars. They were equally adept at rockers like "Bye Bye Love," Wake Up Little Susie," and "Bird Dog" or slow ballads of teenage love, such as "All I Have to Do Is Dream," and "Cathy's Clown," and even tragic songs geared to teens typified by "Ebony Eyes." Like Presley, the Everlys ultimately made a bigger impact in pop music, but even more than he, their initial identification was with country all the way. They displayed their heritage in a 1959 album of old-time country numbers titled *Songs Our Daddy Taught Us* that displayed a harmony reminiscent of the Bailes or Louvin Brothers, but with folk guitar-style accompaniment. Later efforts by the Everlys continued to make the pop charts, but their impact declined after they moved to California. The duo split in 1973 and reunited a decade later.[15]

In retrospect, Nashville country stars had more success in following Johnny Horton's venture into the fad for saga songs than they experienced with rockabilly. Marty Robbins's string of gunfighter ballads were in essence saga songs with western themes. So, too, was Jim Reeves's "The Blizzard" (Reeves was already finding greater success with what was becoming known as the Nashville Sound). Carl Smith had a hit with "Ten Thousand Drums." Eddy Arnold scored with Jimmy Driftwood's "Tennessee Stud," as did Hawkshaw

Hawkins with "Soldier's Joy" (another example of Driftwood putting lyrics to a traditional fiddle tune). A relative newcomer, Stonewall Jackson (b. 1932) had crossover success with the rock-flavored "Waterloo" (in a sense, almost a parody of the saga genre) and the Civil War–inspired rewrite of an old spiritual, "Mary Don't You Weep."[16]

ROCKABILLY ELSEWHERE

Among other rockabilly figures, Gene Vincent (1935–1971), whose real name was Vincent Craddock, ranks as one of the most significant. At the time he burst on the musical scene in mid-1956, Vincent was a Virginia-born Navy veteran who had injured his leg in a motorcycle accident in 1955. A meeting with Elvis Presley later that year influenced his musical style, and after winning a local talent contest, he signed with Capitol and made his first recordings in Nashville in May 1956, a four-song session that yielded his signature number, "Be-Bop-a-Lula," with his band the Blue Caps. While that song scored in the top ten on both country and pop charts, his other two hits, "Lotta Lovin'" and "Dance to the Bop," scored only on the latter. Vincent suffered injuries in the same 1960 auto crash that killed Eddie Cochran, and his career declined thereafter, partly because of his alcoholism and a variety of other problems largely self-induced. He remained popular in England and Europe after his popularity faded in the United States. Bleeding ulcers caused his death, but he remained something of a legendary figure, and the Blue Caps played to sold-out audiences in England, France, and Germany in both 1982 and 1993.[17]

Conway Twitty (1933–1993), whose real name was Harold Jenkins, was born in Mississippi and grew up in Helena, Arkansas, where he was exposed to both country and blues influences. His early efforts as a rockabilly on Sun remain unreleased, and his two similar discs on Mercury had but little success, "I Need Your Lovin'" reaching the ninety-third spot on the pop charts. A switch to M-G-M proved beneficial, and his "It's Only Make Believe," which was not really a rocker, went to the top in the latter weeks of 1958. Over the next four years, he had seven more songs in the pop top forty. However, with the advent of the Beatles and changing trends in that field, Twitty reinvented himself as a mainstream (i.e., Nashville Sound) country singer from 1965 and went on to amass some ninety-seven appearances on the *Billboard* country charts, forty of them reaching the top spot, with "Hello Darlin'" and "You've Never Been This Far Before" being among the more memorable.[18]

QUEENS OF ROCKABILLY

Not all rockabillies were men, and in fact several female vocalists came to the Sun studios in Memphis—including Wanda Ballman, Barbara Pittman, the Miller Sisters, and Maggie Lee Wimberly—but none ever got the record that elevated them to becoming major performers. Three young ladies did, however, reach major status. None ever quite attained the stardom of an Elvis Presley or the Everly Brothers, but the "Rockabilly Queens," as they were termed in a book title by Bob Garbutt, did prove to be survivors of a sort.[19]

The first to make it into the recording studio, Wanda Jackson (b. 1937) worked on radio in Oklahoma City, where she and her high school buddy Norma Jean Beasler aspired to musical careers. She signed with Decca in 1954 and recorded straight honky-tonk country in 1954 and 1955. Her only hit, "You Can't Have My Love," a duet with Billy Gray, made it to number eight. Moving to Capitol after finishing high school, her half country, half rockabilly "I Gotta Know" dented the charts briefly in 1956. Touring with Elvis Presley helped lead Jackson to doing some rocking numbers along with more mainstream country. Her best rocking songs, such as "Fujiyama Mama," "Honey Bop," and "Let's Have a Party," rank among the finest ever cut in that style. From 1961, her hits "Right or Wrong" and "In the Middle of a Heartache" brought her back to straight country, more often made in Hollywood than in Nashville. Jackson's Capitol singles and albums were consistent successes through the 1960s, and in 1971, she slowed down a bit, took her Christian conversion seriously, and did more gospel material while still doing rockabilly songs on tours, especially those on the European continent.[20]

If anything, Brenda Lee (b. 1944), born in Georgia as Brenda Mae Tarpley, gained even more success than Jackson. A child prodigy from the age of six, she first won a national audience with her appearances on the *Ozark Jubilee* in 1956. Short of stature and strong of voice, Lee's first Decca release, "Jambalaya"/"Bigelow-6200," established her as a coming force. Her third release, "One Step at a Time," made both the pop and country charts. By this time, she had earned the nickname that stuck with her for several years: "Little Miss Dynamite." From 1958, her "Rockin' Around the Christmas Tree" became a perennial holiday season favorite. Through the 1960s, Lee experienced twenty-nine appearances on the pop top forty, but from 1969, her recordings graced the country charts regularly for the next sixteen years. Her most notable number, "Big Four Poster Bed," peaked at number four.[21]

The third "rockabilly queen," Janis Martin (b. 1940), had no hits but made numerous singles for RCA Victor from 1956 through 1958. A native of Virginia, Martin joined the cast of WRVA's *Old Dominion Barn Dance* at thirteen. At sixteen, she made her first recording, "Drug Store Rock and Roll"/"Will You, Willyum," which while not charting did well enough to encourage more sessions. Meanwhile, with RCA contractee Elvis Presley riding a major wave of stardom, the record company began billing Martin as "the female Elvis," and she even cut a song called "My Boy Elvis." However, with no hits, an early marriage, and motherhood, RCA dropped her after a session of July 22, 1958. After four additional sides for the smaller Palette Records in 1960, Martin retired. Later efforts to rekindle her career made only minor headway in the United States, but she did better in periodic visits to Europe.[22]

RETROSPECT

By 1960, the rockabilly era of country music history had begun to wear thin. Elvis Presley had gone to Hollywood to make motion pictures, and Johnny Cash and numerous other performers moved backed toward a country mainstream that they were helping to change and alter as they went. Rockabilly had been essentially a youth-oriented style, and as those who listened to it matured into adults, their musical tastes changed. While many eschewed the rough-edged honky-tonk sounds of a decade earlier, they found comfort in what New England-born, Texas-migrant George H. W. Bush might have termed a "kinder, gentler" country music that would be typified by what came to be known as the Nashville Sound. Others (myself included) observed the success of the Kingston Trio in 1958 with their urban-folk version of the old murder ballad "Tom Dooley." In looking for the folk roots of this new craze, these maturing adults not only rediscovered the "old-time music" of the pre–World War II era and its surviving practitioners but also the modern manifestation of it that critic Alan Lomax described as "folk music with overdrive" or what had more commonly become known as "bluegrass." This latter sound had been around for more than a decade and drew its roots from the older music of both Southern blacks and whites. Seemingly, rockabilly and the emerging Nashville Sound had marginalized it, but bluegrass had its devotees and loyalists. They hailed from diverse backgrounds. Bluegrass thrived in the hills and hollows of Appalachia, in the hillbilly bars of Midwestern cities, and increasingly among a small but zealous band of collegians, who saw it as an evolving relic of America's vanishing agrarian and early industrial past.

NOTES

1. For a brief definition of the genre, see Rich Kienzle, "Rockabilly," in Paul Kingsbury, ed., *The Encyclopedia of Country Music* (New York: Oxford University Press, 1998), 453; see also Craig Morrison, *Go Cat Go! Rockabilly Music and Its Makers* (Urbana: University of Illinois Press, 1996), 24–53. For Bill Haley, see John Swenson, *Bill Haley: The Daddy of Rock and Roll* (New York: Scarborough Books, 1982).

2. Literature on Presley is voluminous, but the most useful are the two books by Jerry Hopkins, *Elvis: A Biography* (New York: Warner Brothers, 1972), and *Elvis: The Final Years* (New York: St. Martin's Press, 1980), and the two by Peter Guralnick, *Last Train to Memphis: The Rise of Elvis Presley* (Boston: Little, Brown, 1994), and *Careless Love: The Unmaking of Elvis Presley* (Boston: Little, Brown, 1998). For details on the early recordings, see the booklet by Peter Guralnick, *Elvis: The Complete 50's Masters* (New York: BMG Music, 1992).

3. See Carl Perkins and David McGee, *Go, Cat, Go! The Life and Times of Carl Perkins, the King of Rockabilly* (New York: Hyperion, 1996).

4. Although several Cash books exist, the more significant include his own, Johnny Cash, *Man in Black* (Grand Rapids, MI: Zondervan Publishing House, 1975), and an essay by Frederick Danker, "Johnny Cash," in Bill C. Malone and Judith

McColloh, eds., *Stars of Country Music* (Urbana: University of Illinois Press, 1975), 289–308.

5. Perhaps because of his bizarre lifestyle, Jerry Lee Lewis has attracted considerable attention from writers. See especially Nick Tosches, *Hellfire: The Jerry Lee Lewis Story* (New York: Dell Publishing, 1982). A more sobering personal account is by former wife Myra Lewis, *Great Balls of Fire: The Uncensored Story of Jerry Lee Lewis* (New York: Quill, 1982).

6. Ellis Amburn, *Dark Star: The Roy Orbison Story* (New York: Lyle Stuart/Carol, 1990).

7. See Colin Escott, Martin Hawkins, Hank Davis, *The Sun Country Years: Country Music in Memphis, 1950–1959* (Bremen, West Germany: Bear Family Records, 1989); see also Morrison, *Go Cat Go!*, 73–110.

8. Quoted in Kienzle, "Rockabilly," 453; Morrison, *Go Cat Go!*, 140–168.

9. John Goldrosen, *The Buddy Holly Story*, 2nd rev. ed. (New York: Quick Fox, 1979), is the standard biography.

10. Morrison, *Go Cat Go!*, 169–182.

11. Ibid., 173–175. See also Colin Escott, *Hop, Skip and Jump* (Vollersode, Germany: Bear Family Records, 1991).

12. Morrison, *Go Cat Go!*, 135–139, 161–163. For a good vignette of Horton, see Horace Logan with Bill Sloan, *Elvis, Hank and Me: Making Musical History on the Louisiana Hayride* (New York: St. Martin's Press, 1998), 189–206.

13. Morrison, *Go Cat Go!*, 114–116.

14. Despite his broad significance, Marty Robbins has not attracted a biographer. For now, the best introduction is the booklet for the Time-Life reissue series by Patricia Hall, *Marty Robbins* (Alexandria, VA: Time-Life Records, 1983). His rockabilly material is discussed in Morrison, *Go Cat Go!*, 116–119.

15. Morrison, *Go Cat Go!*, 111–116, 119–122. A brief sketch of the Everlys may be found in Colin Escott, "Everly Brothers" in Kingsbury, *The Encyclopedia of Country Music*, 167–168.

16. The best discussion of saga songs remains Bill C. Malone's *Country Music, U.S.A.* 2nd rev. ed. (Austin: University of Texas Press, 2002), 283–285.

17. Morrison, *Go Cat Go!*, 122–126.

18. Like Marty Robbins, Conway Twitty lacks an adequate biographer, but a sketch is provided by Robert K. Oermann, "Conway Twitty," in Kingsbury, *The Encyclopedia of Country Music*, 553–554, and Barry McCloud, "Conway Twitty," *Definitive Country: The Ultimate Encyclopedia of Country Music and Its Performers* (New York: Perigee Books, 1995), 826–828.

19. Mary A. Bufwack and Robert K. Oermann, *Finding Her Voice: The Saga of Women in Country Music* (New York: Crown Publishers, 1993), 214–239.

20. Ibid., 234–237; Bob Garbutt, *Rockabilly Queens* (Toronto: Ducktail Press, 1979), 15–26; Colin Escott, *Wanda Jackson: Right or Wrong* (Vollersode, Germany: Bear Family Records, 1992).

21. Garbutt, *Rockabilly Queens*, 38–54; Morrison, *Go Cat Go!*, 129–130; Bufwack and Oermann, *Finding Her Voice*, 223–227.

22. Bufwack and Oermann, *Finding Her Voice*, 222–223; Garbutt, *Rockabilly Queens*, 27–37.

7

Bluegrass Pickin' and Singin'

If rockabilly music represented a fusion of honky-tonk country music with African American rhythm and blues, it also reflected a trend toward the amalgamation of both of these musical forms with mainstream popular music. The development of bluegrass as a country music subtype could almost be said to represent a merger of honky-tonk country with pre–World War II old-time music. Bluegrass music emphasized the acoustical stringed instruments of guitar, fiddle, mandolin, string bass, finger-picked five-string banjo, and sometimes a resonator guitar, with high lead and harmony vocals. The earliest bluegrass bands were generally regarded as part of the country music scene, but by the end of the 1950s, they were more or less considered as somewhat apart from the country music mainstream, particularly as the Nashville Sound came to emphasize electric instrument leads and a smoother more poplike sound. Initially, bluegrass audiences were most common in the rural South, especially the Appalachian areas. However, bluegrass also found audiences in those urban areas where numerous southern and mountain people had migrated, such as Cincinnati, Detroit, and Washington, D.C. When collegians began to discover folk music in the late 1950s, bluegrass won acceptance on many campuses as one of folk's forms.

The person usually credited with being the originator of bluegrass music, William Smith "Bill" Monroe (1911–1996), had been the younger half of the Monroe Brothers. When Bill and Charlie Monroe continued their separate

Bill Monroe, the "Father of Bluegrass Music" (second from right), is shown here with his band, the Bluegrass Boys. *Courtesy of Photofest.*

careers, both moved toward a larger string band sound, although not immediately. From his childhood as a lonely introverted youngster, Bill Monroe drew musical inspiration from a variety of sources, including his old-time fiddler, "Uncle Pen[dleton Van Diver]," and an itinerant western Kentucky bluesman, Arnold Schultz, and later had familiarity with the Carolina string bands of J. E. Mainer, Wade Mainer, Byron Parker, and Roy Hall. By October 7, 1940, when Bill made his first solo recordings, his band the Blue Grass Boys consisted of guitar, fiddle, string bass, and his own mandolin, but what became known as the "bluegrass sound" had not yet fully evolved. Later recordings moved closer to bluegrass, but the process was not completed until the right band members were in place. Lester Flatt (1914–1979) joined the Blue Grass Boys in the spring of 1945, and Earl Scruggs (b. 1924) joined in September of that year. Robert "Chubby" Wise (1915–1996), a former fiddler with Monroe, returned in March 1946, and Howard "Cedric Rainwater" Watts replaced "Cousin Wilbur" Wesbrooks on bass. In September 1946, the cast was complete with the assemblage of Monroe on mandolin, Flatt on guitar, Scruggs on banjo, Wise on fiddle, and Watts on bass. Monroe and Flatt handled most of the vocals, with each singing solo on certain songs and Flatt singing lead on the chorus and Monroe singing tenor. Some numbers also had trio and quartet parts. While many Monroe songs dealt with the typical subject of broken romances, others consisted of newer sentimental lyrics of mother and home or came from the earlier years of country music, including blues numbers associated with Jimmie Rodgers, and other old songs, such as "Goodbye Old Pal," "Footprints in the Snow," "Molly and Tenbrooks," and "Girl in the Blue Velvet Band." Sacred songs and instrumentals also formed important parts of the Monroe musical repertoire. In fact, the repertoire pattern set by the Blue Grass Boys in the 1940s remained pretty much the standard for the next half century.

In addition to their recordings first on Bluebird and then on Columbia, Bill Monroe and his Blue Grass Boys had an advantage of being on WSM and the *Grand Ole Opry*, which was fast gaining an ever larger national audience. With the growing audience for country music at the end of World War II, the aforementioned band members were in a better position than prior aggregations to enhance their popularity. The combination of Monroe, Flatt, Scruggs, and Wise provided the Blue Grass Boys with just the right sound that would characterize nearly all their future recordings. To be sure, there was still room for some innovation, such as the use of twin and even triple fiddles (one session even used an electric organ, although it is uncertain whether this was the band's idea or that of the record producer). After recording twenty-eight numbers with this band, Flatt and Scruggs departed and soon formed their own band. Monroe found new musicians who played in that style and went forward, moving to Decca after one final session with Columbia in October 1949. In fact, this process of finding new bluegrass musicians who played in the established Monroe style would be repeated many times in the next forty-five years. Some would later become leaders or parts of other noted bluegrass bands.

BLUEGRASS IN APPALACHIA AND THE PIEDMONT

Bluegrass music moved from being exclusively associated with Bill Monroe fairly rapidly. In 1946, the Stanley Brothers, Ralph (b. 1927) and Carter (1925–1966), from mountainous southwest Virginia and newly returned from wartime service, put together a band known as the Clinch Mountain Boys. In addition to the brothers, the band included Harold "Pee Wee" Lambert (1924–1965) on mandolin and a veteran fiddler, Leslie Keith (1906–1978?). The Stanley band played on radio at WCYB Bristol, a station with a more limited reach than WSM, but one that still had a sizable audience in central Appalachia. At first, the Stanley sound seemed more like that of a typical mountain string band, but when with Lambert's lead vocal, the band recorded—on the tiny Rich-R-Tone label—"Molly and Tenbrooks," a song that the Monroe band had performed on radio and during personal appearances, bluegrass became a style. Monroe's disc of the song had not yet been released, but the Stanley rendition of it clearly demonstrated Monroe's influence.

Bill Monroe did not initially appreciate the fact that other musical groups emulated this style and is said to have become disenchanted with Columbia Records when they signed the Stanleys to a contract. He became even more upset in 1948 when his former sidemen Lester Flatt and Earl Scruggs started a group called the Foggy Mountain Boys that also played in the style of the Blue Grass Boys. In fact, many years passed before Monroe came to appreciate that he had developed a unique musical style that had spread around the world. A proud and introverted musical genius, his first reaction was to resent his direct or indirect protégés and term them imitators or copiers.

Over the decades, those who worked with Monroe in some capacity and became virtual legendary figures as leaders or co-leaders of their own bands included Don Reno, Mac Wiseman, Jimmy Martin, Carter Stanley, Carl Story, Sonny Osborne, and Del McCoury. Like Flatt and Scruggs and the Stanley Brothers, the style of these figures had some similarity to that of Monroe, but they were also just different enough to have a sound that was uniquely their own. Although bluegrass was not traditional music, it contained enough tradition that it appealed to those who looked back toward the folk roots of early-day country music and just enough newness and innovation to fascinate many younger people. Ironically, those who found the music most appealing tended to be older folks, particularly those of Appalachian origin—including those who migrated to the cities—and young urbanites and collegians who had been captivated by either the commercial folk music of groups like the Kingston Trio or the urban folk singers like Woody Guthrie and Pete Seeger. Sometimes they managed to make common ground despite their generational and cultural differences.

But prior to its discovery by urban folk enthusiasts at the end of the 1950s, bluegrass music was simply part of the country scene. Only after the rise of rockabilly did it seem dated and old-fashioned. Bill Monroe and his Blue Grass Boys continued to work regularly at the *Grand Ole Opry* and record for Decca. The Stanley Brothers worked periodically at WCYB and other radio venues while moving from Columbia to Mercury to record. Flatt and Scruggs worked on radio at a variety of stations either in the Appalachian region or the nearby Piedmont. In 1951, they switched from Mercury to Columbia. They also formed a sponsor partnership with Martha White Mills and began a daily early morning radio program on WSM, although Monroe's opposition kept them off the *Opry* until 1955.

In the early years of bluegrass, three bands—those of Monroe, Flatt and Scruggs, and the Stanley Brothers—dominated the music. Monroe was of course the original. Flatt and Scruggs tended a little more to the country mainstream, and the Stanleys adhered closer to their Appalachian roots. By the end of the 1940s, all had recordings on major labels: Monroe on Victor, then Columbia; Flatt and Scruggs on Mercury; and the Stanleys on Rich-R-Tone, then Columbia.[1]

Bill Monroe continued to be musically active until March 1996, but his career experienced several ups and downs during those years. Through the early 1950s, he continued to produce quality music and work the *Opry*. But with the advent of rock and roll, the more traditional acts such as his own were not in demand. Retaining band members on the low wages he paid always seemed a problem. Still he persisted with his music and enjoyed something of a comeback when urbanites began to see him as a folk icon. Initially, he remained aloof from the folk movement until Ralph Rinzler took charge of his career and found work for him in the larger world of folk festivals. By the end of the 1960s, bluegrass festivals gained a degree of popularity, providing venues where he could play most weekends in the warmer months. Monroe even started several festivals himself—most notably, at Beanblossom, Indiana, where he had owned a country music park since 1951. While he never enjoyed the commercial success of his chief rivals—Flatt and Scruggs—numerous honors eventually came to him, including induction into the Country Music Hall of Fame in 1970 and a National Heritage Fellowship Award in 1982. He had the honor of playing for four presidents (Carter, Reagan, Bush, and Clinton) and, perhaps most significant of all, received widespread recognition as "the Father of Bluegrass Music."[2]

Thanks to their relationship with Martha White Mills and, after 1955, the *Grand Ole Opry*, Lester Flatt and Earl Scruggs enjoyed relative prosperity for bluegrass musicians. Their sponsors put them on a chain of television stations in the Appalachian region (Chattanooga, Knoxville, Bluefield, Huntington, and Wheeling), and they played live shows in the immediate region almost nightly before returning to the *Opry* on Saturday nights. As a result, their band enjoyed more stability than the Blue Grass Boys. They also benefited from the managerial skills of Earl's wife, Louise. Beginning in 1962, they furnished "The Ballad of Jed Clampett" as theme music for a hit CBS network TV sitcom, *The Beverly Hillbillies*; the song became a number one hit. Six years later, their old Mercury recording of "Foggy Mountain Breakdown" became background music for the hit motion picture *Bonnie and Clyde*, a film based loosely on the lives of Depression-era outlaws Bonnie Parker and Clyde Barrow.

Many of the more noted bluegrass musicians worked as part of the Foggy Mountain Boys, including such fiddlers as the aforementioned Chubby Wise (1915–1996), Benny Martin (1928–2002), and, for many years, Paul Warren (1918–1978). John "Curley" Seckler (b. 1919) played mandolin minimally but gave many years of yeoman service as a tenor vocalist on many of their harmonies. Jake Tullock (1922–1988) played bass and did comedy, while Burkett "Uncle Josh" Graves (b. 1928) also did some comedy but also (from 1955) played the resonator guitar (or Dobro from its brand name). Although this instrument had been used earlier in traditional country music and occasionally in bluegrass, it became much more common after the Foggy Mountain Boys made it part of their sound.

Although Flatt and Scruggs contributed many standard songs and original banjo tunes to bluegrass music almost from the beginning of their recordings on Mercury, they never really had a bona fide hit until 1959, when their rendition of the nostalgic "Cabin in the Hills" spent thirty weeks on the *Billboard* charts. After *The Beverly Hillbillies* of 1962, they were on the charts with some regularity. But many of these numbers ranked more in the novelty vein, such as "Nashville Cats" and "California Up Tight Band," as opposed to the true bluegrass numbers that endeared them to country traditionalists. The songs that had sustained them through the 1950s, like "We'll Meet Again Sweetheart," "Salty Dog Blues," "I'll Go Stepping Too," and other banjo originals typified by "Earl's Breakdown" and "Flint Hill Special," had virtually disappeared from their repertoire, and bluegrass versions of true old-time songs like "Legend of the Johnson Boys" barely registered in *Billboard*.

Personal and musical tensions began to wear on the team, and they split early in 1969. Flatt believed they were getting too far from their traditional roots. Earl increasingly favored working with his sons and moving in new musical directions. Thereafter, Lester and his group renamed the Nashville Grass adhered more to traditional bluegrass while continuing the Martha White connection, playing for festivals, and recording mostly for RCA Victor. The Earl Scruggs Revue played a more eclectic mix of bluegrass, urban folk, country, and rock for a number of years prior to Earl's virtual retirement from 1980. In 1985, Flatt and Scruggs joined Monroe in the Country Music Hall of Fame. The three entered the Bluegrass Hall of Honor at the same time in 1991.[3]

The Stanley Brothers alternated between bases in Bristol and Live Oak, Florida. They recorded more than their two principal rivals, but after departing from Mercury in 1958, much of their output was for lesser companies, such as Starday, King, and even smaller labels like Wango and Rimrock. They played some on the folk festival circuit in the early 1960s but increasingly found their work confined to smaller country music parks and clubs (actually what have been termed "hillbilly bars" in cities frequented by Appalachian migrants). They, too, experienced difficulty retaining band members because of the meager financial rewards, and Carter's drinking problems contributed to his declining health and death at the age of forty-one.

Nonetheless, there was still a market for Stanley-style bluegrass music, and Ralph Stanley soon emerged with a reformed version of the Clinch Mountain Boys. Over the years, his band included some strong musicians, such as longtime fiddler "Curly Ray" Cline (1923–1997), and notable lead singers, such as Larry Sparks (b. 1946), Keith Whitley (1954–1989), the tragic homicide victim Roy Lee Centers (1947–1974), and, most recently, Ralph Stanley II (b. 1978)—Stanley has managed to maintain a quality band. If anything, he has become even more traditional. In addition, the popularity of bluegrass festivals have provided Ralph Stanley with a level of financial stability that the Stanley Brothers never experienced, even when they were becoming legends in the field. In 2000, his singing of the old sacred song "Oh Death" on the soundtrack of the popular motion picture *O Brother, Where Art Thou?* won him an ever-widening audience, several awards, and *Grand Ole Opry* membership. With the other earliest pioneers of bluegrass either deceased or retired, Ralph Stanley has truly gained star status in his mid-seventies. As Ron Thompson once remarked, "he [Ralph Stanley] has finally aged into the archaic voice he has had since early adulthood."[4]

The early 1950s brought about the emergence of other bluegrass bands. One of the first was the Lonesome Pine Fiddlers, hitherto a traditional country band operating out of WHIS in Bluefield, West Virginia. Ezra Cline (1907–1984), a bass fiddle player of limited talents, headed this group that had worked locally since the late 1930s with as its main members Ezra's cousins "Curly Ray" (1923–1997) on fiddle, Ireland or "Lazy Ned" (d. 1944) on tenor banjo, and Charlie Cline (b. 1931), who played several instruments. According to most persons who heard them, their sound closely resembled that of the Delmore Brothers. Around 1949, Charlie and Ray temporarily dropped out of the band, and Ezra hired Bob Osborne (b. 1931) and Larry Richardson (b. 1928) as replacements, giving the group a bluegrass sound that they displayed on four recordings for the small Cozy label in 1950. One of their songs, "Pain in My Heart," subsequently recorded by Flatt and Scruggs, became one of the classics of early bluegrass. The duo of Osborne and Richardson moved on within a few months, but Ezra retained the bluegrass sound by hiring two teenagers, Paul Williams (b. 1935) and Ray Goins (b. 1936), as replacements and securing a contract with RCA Victor, thus becoming that label's first bluegrass band. Although the Fiddlers' recordings of such songs as "You Broke Your Promise," "Windy Mountain," and "Dirty Dishes Blues" rank among the classics of early bluegrass, the band never attained wide popularity, partly because with the exception of several months in Detroit, they remained based in locales with limited audiences, such as Bluefield and Oak Hill, West Virginia, and Pikeville, Kentucky. In the early 1960s, they did television in Bristol, Virginia, and recorded for Starday with Ezra and Ray Cline together with Ray and Melvin Goins (b. 1933) as personnel. In later years, their sound survived in the bands of the Goins Brothers, while Paul Williams and Charlie Cline became key figures in other bands.[5]

When Bobby Osborne departed from the Lonesome Pine Fiddlers, he briefly teamed up with sometime member of Monroe's Blue Grass Boys Jimmy Martin (1927–2005) to form the Sunny Mountain Boys. With the help of Curly Ray and Charlie Cline, they cut four sides on King in August 1951 before dissolving. Meanwhile, Bobby's younger brother, Roland, nicknamed "Sonny" (b. 1937), worked as a banjo player for Bill Monroe through much of 1952. Bobby himself spent some time in military service during which time Sonny recorded some covers of Flatt and Scruggs and Bill Monroe numbers for the Gateway company of Cincinnati (Bobby was present on some of these sessions). Later, with Bobby back from Korean War duty, they went to work on radio again, briefly teaming up a second time with Jimmy Martin and working on the *Big Barn Frolic* at WJR radio in Detroit. In November 1954, they recorded six songs for RCA Victor, including such later bluegrass standards as "20/20 Vision" and "That's How I Can Count on You." A few months later the partnership ended, with the Osbornes returning to Dayton, Ohio, and Martin remaining in Detroit with newly recruited musicians and retaining the name Sunny Mountain Boys.

Martin soon signed a contract with Decca and recorded four songs in May 1956, including one of his signature numbers: "Hit Parade of Love." By the time of his second recording session in December, he had taken on the two band members who would define the sound of the Sunny Mountain Boys: mandolinist, tenor singer, and former Lonesome Pine Fiddler Paul Williams and eighteen-year-old banjo picker James Dee "J. D." Crowe (b. 1938). Martin filled out his band on record with session musicians from Nashville, and Crowe and Williams appeared on most of Martin's best-known songs, including "Ocean of Diamonds," "Sophronie," "Rock Hearts," and "Home Run Man." Over eighteen years, Martin would record some 140 songs for Decca, and while he included typical bluegrass fare in his repertoire, he also demonstrated— more than other bluegrass vocalists—some preference for novelty songs. His base of operations shifted from Detroit to Shreveport and KWKH in 1957 and to Wheeling and WWVA in 1959. In 1962, hoping to become an *Opry* regular, Martin moved to Nashville but never got more than an occasional guest spot. From the early 1960s on, despite Martin's band members changing with some regularity, his personality always dominated. As Chris Skinker wrote, "Martin's music reflected his personality—brash, bold and aggressive."[6]

After the Osborne Brothers split with Martin, they continued to be musically active. After working a few months as band members for Charlie Bailey at WWVA Wheeling, they began to develop a solid trio with the help of Harley "Red" Allen (1930–1993), who like themselves was a Kentuckian, transplanted to Dayton, Ohio. They became regulars on the Wheeling *Jamboree* and began recording for M-G-M in July 1956, cutting one of their signature tunes, "Ruby (Are You Mad)," an old number from a decade earlier by Cousin Emmy (Carver). The Osborne Brothers and Red Allen continued to work at the Wheeling *Jamboree* and to record for M-G-M through 1958, doing other significant numbers such as "Once More" and "Ho Honey Ho." After Allen's departure, the Osbornes continued with other partners in their trio. While doing bookings through WWVA and working the *Jamboree*, they continued to reside in Dayton and supplemented their musical income by working as taxi drivers. In 1963, they switched to Decca Records and in 1964 moved to Nashville and became *Grand Ole Opry* regulars.

When they went to Decca and joined the *Opry*, the Osbornes accommodated somewhat more than other bluegrass acts to the emerging Nashville Sound by using drums and amplified instruments on their recordings to sound more like modern country music. Bluegrass purists complained, but their popularity if anything increased. While other bluegrass acts had virtually vanished from the charts, Bobby and Sonny Osborne made the *Billboard* listings fifteen times between 1966 and 1976, and their better known numbers, such as "Tennessee Hound Dog," "Rocky Top," and "Georgia Pineywoods," became some of the best-known numbers in the field. By the end of the 1970s, they had moved back to a more traditional approach to their music and remained there for the next quarter century.[7]

Shortly after the Stanley Brothers had started their careers on radio at Bristol, another duo from southwestern Virginia began playing music on the newly opened WNVA in Norton. Jim (1927–2002) and Jesse (b. 1929) McReynolds from Coburn started out as a simple mandolin/guitar harmony duet, playing in the style of the Monroe Brothers. True success came slowly for the boys as they struggled to make a living from their skills and talents. While they sometimes had additional musicians on their program, such as fiddler Marion Sumner, they remained essentially a duet group and worked briefly—for a few months each—on radio stations extending from West Virginia to Kansas. In 1951, they made a few recordings on the Gateway label under the name Virginia Trio with a third musician, Larry Roll. But their first recordings of consequence were made in June 1952 when they secured a contract with Capitol while working at WVLK Versailles, Kentucky. At the time, they had John "Curley" Seckler and banjoist Hoke Jenkins as a band supplemented in the studio by fiddler Sonny Loden and a bass player. Their first session as Jim and Jesse and the Virginia Boys resulted in eight recordings, including "Are You Missing Me" and a Korean War song, "Purple Heart," written and performed primarily by Seckler. They were not able to do much promotion because Jesse was called to military service shortly afterward, although they did manage to make more recordings, eventually making twenty sides for Capitol.

After Jesse's military service, they resumed their careers in the waning days of live radio with minimal financial rewards. They did somewhat better at Live Oak, Florida; did some television programs in Alabama and North Florida for Martha White Flour and its subsidiary for livestock, Fortune Feed; and cut a few numbers for Starday in 1958. After a brief association with Columbia Records and a longer one with its subsidiary label, Epic, they finally had a midlevel hit with "Cotton Mill Man" in 1964, which led to membership on the *Grand Ole Opry*. Like the Osborne Brothers, Jim and Jesse made some concessions to modern country music on their recordings, which allowed them to get some airplay on the country radio stations with numbers like the trucker song "Diesel on My Tail" and a revival of Hank Snow's railroad number "The Golden Rocket." Their excellent harmony and Jesse's innovative mandolin picking, along with pleasing dispositions, helped them retain favor with fans into the new millenium. Like the Osbornes, the McReynolds boys moved back toward a more traditional band sound when chart success became less meaningful. Both encountered health problems that eventually led to Jim's demise, but Jesse continues on as an active *Opry* performer and festival favorite.[8]

Malcolm "Mac" Wiseman (b. 1925), another Virginian with a winning personality and pleasing voice who often favored old songs, won a following among bluegrass fans. Although he generally sang with whatever instrumentation (or even no instrumentation other than his own guitar), most of his early recordings did make use of bluegrass instruments. Wiseman grew up in the Shenandoah Valley listening to radio station WSVA in Harrisonburg, where he was influenced by solo country singers, such as Blaine Smith (1915–2000) and especially Buddy Starcher (1906–2001), who favored old songs delivered in a simple straightforward manner. He served an apprenticeship as a featured vocalist with Starcher and then Molly O'Day, playing bass on her 1946 Columbia recordings. He then worked and did one session each with Flatt and Scruggs on Mercury and with Bill Monroe on Columbia. By and large, however, he preferred being a solo singer and pursued that goal on a variety of large and small radio stations.

In May 1951, Mac Wiseman finally got the opportunity to record on his own with the small and relatively new Dot label of Gallatin, Tennessee. He was based at KWKH in Shreveport at the time and did his first session there with mandolin, banjo, fiddle, and bass accompaniment, with his most notable number being an old song once featured by McFarland and Gardner (or Mac and Bob): " 'Tis Sweet to Be Remembered." Thereafter, Mac recorded in Gallatin or Nashville, backed most often by Nashville studio musicians and harmony occasionally provided by such figures as Ted Mullins or Jimmy Williams. Dot followed a practice of releasing a single disc every six weeks, and so by the end of 1952, Wiseman had some ten singles on the market. About that time, Arlington, Virginia, disc jockey Don Owens gave Mac a nickname that he would use throughout his career. Owens dubbed him "the voice with a heart." From 1955, his recordings—including all those that ever appeared on *Billboard* charts—often had mainstream country and even popstyle backing, but he continued to win favor with traditionalists, partly because he still recorded many old songs along with newer ones. Eventually he left Dot and made recordings for Capitol, M-G-M, and RCA Victor as well as smaller labels.[9]

Another bluegrass band that had a considerable impact during the 1950s and early 1960s was that of Don Reno (1926–1984) and Arthur "Red" Smiley (1925–1972). Reno, a South Carolinian and World War II veteran, had been an early convert to the Scruggs-style banjo and in fact had replaced Scruggs in the Blue Grass Boys (although he never recorded with them), but he had more experience working out of Charlotte with Arthur "Guitar Boogie" Smith. Smiley grew up in Asheville, North Carolina, and worked there with local groups at WWNC. The two met in 1949 at WDBJ Roanoke and first worked together in a short-lived band headed by fiddler Tommy Magness and another led by Toby Stroud. Reno and Smiley recorded four sides for Federal (a King subsidiary) as part of Magness's Tennessee Buddies in March 1951. The Reno and Smiley band, the Tennessee Cut-Ups, went to Cincinnati in January 1951 and cut sixteen sacred, secular, and instrumental numbers for Syd Nathan's King label—most notably, an original gospel song, "I'm Using My Bible for a Roadmap." The Tennessee Cut-Ups were not initially a touring band with a regular radio or television base but were simply a recording group. However, the discs sold well, and Don and Red subsequently returned to record additional numbers, even though Reno continued as part of Arthur Smith's band while Smiley labored in a nonmusical job.

Not long after the sessions of November 1954, the group became a regular performing outfit with Mac Magaha on fiddle and John Palmer on bass and did a daily morning program at WDBJ-TV in Roanoke and the *Old Dominion Barn Dance* in Richmond. A little later, Don's oldest son, Ronnie (b. 1947), joined but played with the band on an irregular basis. They continued recording on King (and also did a session on Dot in 1957) for another decade. Several of their numbers attained bluegrass classic status, including "Talk of the Town," "Trail of Sorrow," "Let's Live for Tonight," "Barefoot Nellie," and "I Know You're Married (but I Love You Still)." In addition, they turned out a number of original sacred songs, including "The Lord's Last Supper," "Let in the Guiding Light," and the first bluegrass number to feature a recitation, "Someone Will Love Me in Heaven." Reno also contributed a goodly share of original banjo tunes, such as "Banjo Signal," "Choking the Strings," and "Crazy Finger Blues." Reno also adapted tunes from other types of music to bluegrass; these were typified by "Limehouse Blues" and "Beer Barrel Polka." Equally adept on guitar, he also recorded a number of solos with that instrument. Until their capacity for originality began to wear thin in the early 1960s, prior to their split at the end of 1964 Don Reno and Red Smiley had one of the most innovative bluegrass bands in the country.[10]

After their split, both continued to play bluegrass music. Smiley kept the TV show, retained Palmer on bass, and hired new musicians, including fiddler Clarence "Tater" Tate and banjo pickers David Deese and Billy Edwards. As Red Smiley and the Bluegrass Cut-Ups, they recorded four long-play albums, but WDBJ-TV changed hands in March 1969 and terminated their program. Smiley, whose health was precarious, voluntarily retired. The band members continued as the Shenandoah Cut-Ups for another decade. In the last two years of his life, Smiley subsequently played several reunion concerts and recorded two additional albums with Reno on the festival circuit.[11]

Don Reno also continued in bluegrass, recording briefly with a new version of the Tennessee Cut-Ups that briefly included fiddler Benny Martin and for a longer period (1966–1976) with a new partner, Bill Harrell (b. 1934). By this time, bluegrass festivals had become popular, and they were quite active on the circuit and in recording studios. In 1976, the two split, with Harrell reforming his old band the Virginians while Reno's new band was built around his younger sons, Dale and Don Wayne Reno. After his father's demise, Ronnie Reno (b. 1947) rejoined his younger half brothers, and they maintained the family tradition as the Reno Brothers.[12]

Other bluegrass bands appeared from time to time. Carl Story (1916–1995) and the Rambling Mountaineers, based alternately in Knoxville, Asheville, and Charlotte, played a brand of traditional country on numerous Mercury and Columbia recordings from 1947 that bore some resemblance to bluegrass. The band often featured the mandolin and vocals of William "Red" Rector (1929–1990), but Story did not really add a banjo to his efforts until 1955. Most but not all of his repertoire was sacred music, and he earned the title "Father of

Bluegrass Gospel Music." He was particularly effective on songs like "Light at the River," "My Lord Keeps a Record," and "You Don't Love God if You Don't Love Your Neighbor." Frank "Hylo" Brown (1922–2003), an Eastern Kentucky native transplanted to Springfield, Ohio, worked locally with old-timer Bradley Kincaid but secured a contract with Capitol in 1954. He recorded some excellent bluegrass and traditional country sides over a five-year period, including a fine album with his band the Timberliners that featured Red Rector and Tater Tate. Brown also worked as a featured vocalist with Flatt and Scruggs and made some good albums on Starday and lesser ones on Rural Rhythm in the 1960s, but his ability to hit natural high notes waned with advancing age. The Lilly Brothers, Everett (b. 1924) and Mitchell B. (1921–2005), started as an old-time harmony duet, but after adding banjo picker Don Stover (1928–1996) and fiddler Benjamin "Tex" Logan (b. 1929) to their ranks did much to popularize bluegrass in New England. Bill Clifton (b. 1931) started the Dixie Mountain Boys, a band based largely in northern Virginia that recorded extensively for Starday and became one the first bands to search for and use material found on pre–World War II old-time country songs. Jim Eanes (1923–1995) from Martinsville, Virginia, alternated between bluegrass and country. Finally, a gospel-singing family from Lincolnton, Georgia, named Lewis brought bluegrass instrumentation into southern gospel, particularly through the banjo work of youngest sibling "Little" Roy Lewis (b. 1942). From the mid-1950s, the Lewis Family recorded a long string of albums on the Starday, Canaan, and Benson labels. Their quality showmanship and Little Roy's brand of humor made them favorites on the bluegrass festival circuit from the late 1960s, even among people who expressed a distaste for gospel music.[13]

BLUEGRASS IN APPALACHIAN MIGRANT CITIES

While traditional bluegrass as heretofore discussed developed as a significant subtype of mainstream country music, the audience for it seemed strongest in the depths of Appalachia and in cities that absorbed large numbers of Appalachian migrants. These cities included Cincinnati, Dayton, Detroit, and Columbus in the Midwest and the Baltimore–Washington area to the east. It flourished in the clubs and hillbilly bars that catered to the migrant audience in those locales. Bands in the midwestern cities often patterned themselves more along the lines of the Stanley Brothers or the Osborne Brothers and Red Allen, the latter themselves Kentucky-born products of the migrant culture in Dayton. Those particularly in the Washington, D.C., area soon began to exhibit some degree of creativity that ultimately led to a newer type of bluegrass.

Early practitioners of bluegrass in the nation's capital included Benny and Vallie Cain, Buzz Busby, and a band that became known as the Bluegrass Champs. Leading personnel in the Bluegrass Champs were also the children of country music pioneer Ernest Stoneman. The principal leader was innovative fiddle virtuoso Scott Stoneman (1932–1973), but the band also included sister Donna (b. 1934) on mandolin, brother Jimmy (1937–2002) on bass, and somewhat later younger sister Veronica (b. 1938), known as "Roni," on banjo as well as a couple of nonfamily members. In 1956, the Champs appeared and became winners on the national TV program *Arthur Godfrey's Talent Scouts*. With the passage of time, they added the retired Ernest (by now known as "Pop") and younger brother Van (1940–1995) to their group. In 1963, they relocated briefly to Houston, then California, and in 1965 to Nashville where as the Stonemans they won some acclaim with their exciting blend of country bluegrass and folk music. Virtually all of the Washington, D.C.,–area bands often interchanged members, including some Stonemans with a newly formed band in 1957 that became known as the Country Gentlemen.[14]

The only constant member of the Country Gentlemen throughout their near half century of existence has been guitarist and lead vocalist Charlie Waller (1935–2004), a Louisiana native transplanted to D.C. Other key early members included mandolin picker and tenor singer John Duffey (1934–1996) and banjo player Bill Emerson (b. 1938). Initially, the Gentleman played bluegrass that differed little from that of other bands, but they eventually came to incorporate elements of urban folk and, later, rock music into their sound. One of their earlier innovations was to turn the Lord Byron poem "When We Two Parted" into a bluegrass lyric retitled "Silence or Tears." They recorded for Starday, Folkways, and Mercury and eventually had a long stint with the small bluegrass-oriented Rebel label. Emerson left the band late in 1958 but returned a dozen years later. In the meantime, Pete Kuykendall came in to play banjo for a brief period and was followed by Eddie Adcock (b. 1938) for a decade. The band employed numerous bass players over the years, with Tom Grey, Ed Ferris, and Bill Yates ranking among the better known. Most of their recordings did not use a fiddle, something that many supposedly urban sophisticates tended to identify with what they derisively termed "hillbilly music." The Country Gentleman pioneered a style that would become known as progressive bluegrass or newgrass, although they would not move the style as far from its origins as some later practitioners of the art. Although clubs in the Washington area served as their home base, the band also began playing outside of the area when opportunities arose. Although not oriented to chart action in the manner of Nashville-based groups, their Rebel single "Bringing Mary Home," a ghostly song version of the vanishing hitchhiker folktale, peaked at number forty-three in 1965. Other musicians associated with the group at various times included Jim Gaudreau, Doyle Lawson, Jimmy Bowen, and Ed McGlothlin.[15]

By the later 1960s, other bands adopted many of the features of the Gentlemen. One of the first was that of former member Bill Emerson, who started a band with Cliff Waldron (b. 1941) that was known as the Lee Highway Boys and made three albums for Rebel. Although short-lived, the Emerson and Waldron team made an impact of consequence by introducing the British rock song "Fox on the Run" into bluegrass, where it soon ranked with "Blue Moon of Kentucky," "Foggy Mountain Breakdown," "Rocky Top," and "Uncle Pen" among the best-known bluegrass numbers. When Emerson returned to the Country Gentlemen in 1970, Waldron continued on, renaming the group the New Shades of Grass and making several albums of his own for Rebel.[16]

John Duffey also left the Country Gentlemen in 1969 but soon returned with a new band known as the Seldom Scene, which soon ranked as one of the premier progressive groups. They, too, began recording for Rebel (as did traditionalist Ralph Stanley). The name derived from the fact that the Seldom Scene intended to be only a part-time band. Guitarist and lead singer John Starling was an army surgeon by trade, while banjo picker Ben Eldridge and Dobro player Mike Auldridge—who had been part of the New Shades of Grass—also held professional day jobs, and former Country Gentleman Tom Grey was a cartographer with the National Geographic Society. However, from a once-a-week club appearance, the Scene quickly became favorites on the circuit for a limited number of festival appearances. Even more than the Country Gentlemen, the band broadened the horizon of bluegrass to include material from other types of music but demonstrated that they could handle bluegrass standards, too, as on their rendition of Jimmy Martin's "Hit Parade of Love." They recorded several albums, first for Rebel and then for Sugar Hill, and like other bands eventually had their share of personnel changes. The band continued after Duffey's death, with Dudley Connell (b. 1956), formerly of the traditional Johnson Mountain Boys, among the most prominent members.[17]

CALIFORNIA BLUEGRASS

Bluegrass also had a life on the West Coast, much of it an outgrowth of the folk music fad. The Dillards probably constituted the best-known and most succesful of these. Missourian in background, the band came to Los Angeles in 1962 and included two brothers, Rodney (b. 1942) and Douglas Dillard (b. 1937), on guitar and banjo, respectively; Dean Webb (b. 1937) on mandolin; and Mitch Jayne (b. 1930) on bass, who also contributed a witty form of emcee work to their show. In addition to well-crafted albums on the Elektra label, the Dillards appeared several times on the *Andy Griffith Show* as "the Darlings," a family of mentally challenged bucolics who played an exciting brand of bluegrass. Another California-based band, the Kentucky Colonels, boasted guitarist Clarence White (1944–1973), who made a big impact with his lead and rhythm work before becoming a member of the country-rock band the Byrds. Other West Coast bands included the Golden State Boys; the Hillmen; Ken Orrick's Lost Highway; the Butch Waller-led High Country; and the duo of Vern (Williams) and Ray (Park), who after the latter's exodus was succeeded by the Vern Williams Band.[18]

THE RISE OF BLUEGRASS FESTIVALS AND
THE NATIONALIZATION OF THE MUSIC

Once the folk boom had subsided, interest in bluegrass waned somewhat except among hard-core fans. Furthermore, Carter Stanley had died; Reno and Smiley had split; Flatt and Scruggs were quite popular, but their newer recordings were considered awful; the Osbornes and McReynolds bands were accommodating to the Nashville Sound; and Mac Wiseman often distanced himself from bluegrass. Major record labels were either dropping their acts, turning out poorly produced goods, or forcing modernization on their contractees. It often seemed that even name acts had no venues other than the hillbilly bars or small jamboree barns in which to play. David Freeman, a New Yorker who had started a mail-order record firm called County Sales in 1965, seemed pessimistic in the January–February 1969 edition of his newsletter as he referred to "these sad, dying days of bluegrass." Although perhaps not readily apparent at the time, positive changes were already in the making.[19]

The man responsible for the changes was Carlton Haney (b. 1928), a North Carolinian who had once worked in a battery factory and had been a booking agent for Bill Monroe and a manager for Reno and Smiley. He also promoted country package shows in big city auditoriums. Inspired by the Newport Folk Festival, Haney began to conceive an idea for a weekend festival built around the music of Monroe and his former sidemen now in other bands. He would call it "the Bluegrass Story." Earlier efforts, such as the July 4, 1961, all-bluegrass show of Bill Clifton, had been held, but Haney wanted a whole weekend. For three years, he toyed with the idea, with Ralph Rinzler providing both encouragement and information. Finally in 1965, Haney approached Monroe and began to line up other bands to play. The event was scheduled for Labor Day weekend at Cantrell's Horse Farm at Fincastle, Virginia, near Roanoke. Although described as an artistic success and attracting a crowd estimated as somewhere between 500 and 1,000, the first festival lost money, but the idea caught on and expanded.[20]

Another promoter had a festival at Warrenton, Virginia, in July 1966. Not only Monroe but his archrivals Flatt and Scruggs both appeared at that one, although not together. Haney held another festival at Roanoke on Labor Day weekend. Monroe himself started a festival at his park in Bean Blossom in June 1967. Haney had festivals at Berryville, Virginia (the first to actually turn a profit), in 1968 and at Norwalk, Ohio. There were five festivals in 1969, and the numbers expanded thereafter. By 1998, Richard Smith estimated that there were as many as 600 worldwide. Ironically, in the same issue that he described bluegrass as "dying," David Freeman also praised Haney for beginning the festivals. Little did the perceptive Freeman realize that the festival movement would reinvigorate the "dying" bluegrass even more than he could have imagined.[21]

Another factor in the revitalization of bluegrass came with the 1966 founding of the monthly magazine *Bluegrass Unlimited*. Originally started as a mimeographed newsletter printed on legal size paper, it developed into a small format magazine and then into an 8½-by-11-inch format by 1971 when Pete and Marion Kuykendall took over the editing and publishing role as a full-time operation. Bluegrass enthusiasts in the suburban Washington area led by Richard Spottswood had started the magazine, but it soon outgrew its origins and required a regular, albeit small, staff. It contained schedules of bluegrass shows, listings of clubs where the music was featured, information on instruments, reviews of shows and new recordings, letters from readers, and, increasingly, articles and discographies on both current and historical figures and bands. By 1973, it had about 9,000 subscribers, a number that eventually grew to more than 20,000. The success of this magazine soon attracted competition. In 1970, Carlton Haney started *Muleskinner News* under the editorship of Fred Bartenstein, a Harvard student who often assisted Haney in the summer months. The following year, Bill Monroe's son James started the short-lived *Bluegrass Star*, and in 1974, a New York publisher initiated another one called *Pickin'*. Only *Bluegrass Unlimited* among early competitors lasted for more than a decade. In 1991, *Bluegrass Now* began publication based in Rolla, Missouri. A third magazine, *Bluegrass Music Profiles*, put out its first issue in March 2003 as a bimonthly and within a year and a half had reached a circulation of 3,000.[22]

As the number of festivals multiplied into the hundreds, not all were successful. Many were initiated by persons with little business knowledge and unrealistic expectations of financial reward. Some of the larger and more prestigious attracted crowds of perhaps 10,000 or more, but most were smaller. A few of the earlier ones attempted to book nearly every name act in the field, but the wisest soon learned to balance their talent rosters to have a maximum of two or three major bands, a few midlevel groups, and perhaps a few up-and-coming or lesser ones. Still, it would be possible to hit a rainy or cold weekend and literally "lose your shirt." A rule of thumb followed by many promoters came to be not to expect to turn profits until perhaps the third year.

By the end of 1970, Carlton Haney and Bill Monroe came to a parting of the ways in a reputed dispute over money. For a time, they each ran several rival festivals, but both managed to survive. Haney countered his split with Bill Monroe by bringing the long-retired Charlie Monroe back onto the scene in 1972, where the more extroverted Charlie quickly became a favorite. Charlie's comeback ended in 1975 when he lost a bout with cancer.[23]

In addition to the growth of festivals, record labels that specialized in bluegrass music took an increasingly significant role. The aforementioned David Freeman of County Sales also had a record label, County, that pushed old-time music and some bluegrass. Dick Freeland had Rebel Records, which primarily had the Country Gentlemen but added Ralph Stanley and the newly founded Seldom Scene as well as some lesser groups. In 1979, Freeland sold Rebel to Freeman, who continued with both labels. A Freeman protégé, Barry Poss, started Sugar Hill. In Massachusetts, Ken Irwin, Marian Leighton, and Bill Nowlin started Rounder as a collective, and it subsequently grew to become one of the principal bluegrass labels. Other small companies also issued bluegrass material, such as Vetco in Cincinnati, Old Homestead in Michigan, Atteiram in Georgia, Flying Fish in Chicago, and Arhoolie in California. Some of these companies also reissued old-time music or other kinds of folk-related music, but bluegrass became a main staple for all.[24]

While the established bluegrass groups usually became the top headliners at bluegrass festivals, a number of new groups rose to prominence, many of which had some background as band members for the older stars. For instance, the Goins Brothers Melvin and Ray had both been part of the now defunct Lonesome Pine Fiddlers, and Melvin had also been an early member of Ralph Stanley's Clinch Mountain Boys. Larry Sparks had been Ralph Stanley's lead singer for over two years before leaving to form his own band, the Lonesome Ramblers. The Shenandoah Cut-Ups made up of what had been the Red Smiley band at WBDJ-TV continued on without Red for another decade led by fiddler Clarence Tate, with the addition of mandolinist Herschel Sizemore, an Alabama native who had worked with a Deep South band of the early 1960s and had also toured with Jimmy Martin. Cliff Waldron reorganized the New Shades of Grass, playing a tasteful mixture of old and new grass. Farther south, Charlie Moore (1935–1979), Bill Napier (1935–2000), and the Dixie Pardners played on daily television shows from various locales and recorded several albums for King before splitting in the late 1960s. Moore then reorganized the band and turned out several more good albums—becoming best known for his "Legend of the Rebel Soldier"—before his premature death hastened by alcoholism. Former Monroe sideman Del McCoury (b. 1939) had the Dixie Pals in Pennsylvania and Maryland for a number of years before moving to Nashville, where he reorganized as the Del McCoury Band in 1987, a group that included his grown sons Ron and Rob, and eventually gained *Grand Ole Opry* membership and virtual star status.[25]

A few new grass groups also came to the forefront. In retrospect, two Kentucky-based bands made the direction of the Country Gentlemen and the Seldom Scene look conservative by comparison. The Kentucky Mountain Boys had been organized in Lexington, Kentucky, for regular work in a Holiday Inn. They featured such strong musicians as Red Allen on guitar, J. D. Crowe on banjo, Doyle Lawson on mandolin and tenor vocal, and former Kentucky Colonel left-handed fiddler Bobby Slone usually on bass. Essentially traditional in approach, they made a fine album as such: *Bluegrass Holiday*. However, when Allen departed, Doyle Lawson took over the lead role, and the band moved slightly toward a more progressive sound on its next two albums.

Lawson's departure in 1971 to join the Country Gentlemen brought about another change, and the band was renamed the New South and took on a new image. Comparing them to the "outlaw" movement then current on the country scene, Marian Leighton and Ken Irwin of Rounder Records contend that Crowe "picks out the most compelling elements of modern folk, bluegrass, and progressive country music, coming up with the perfect blend to make the

New South the band often imitated, but never equalled [sic]." Musicians who passed through the New South included Larry and Tony Rice, Keith Whitley, Ricky Skaggs, and Jerry Douglas, among others. The New South made one album for Starday and a half dozen for Rounder, winning acclaim in some quarters but causing the more traditional wing of bluegrass fandom to cringe. Crowe announced retirement in 1989, but it proved temporary, and he became a 2003 inductee to the Bluegrass Hall of Honor. By 2004, the Crowe band—with all new members—had reverted to a more traditional sound.[26]

Louisville, Kentucky, was the birthplace of another progressive group, initially known as the Bluegrass Alliance. This band was founded by Lonnie Peerce, a country fiddler who had worked with Jimmie Logsdon, but its first instrumental star was guitarist Dan Crary. However, he soon departed, and the prime members included Sam Bush (b. 1952) on mandolin, Danny Jones on guitar, Courtney Johnson on banjo, and Ebo Walker on bass. Tony Rice replaced Jones, who was in turn replaced by Curtis Burch. A quarrel with Peerce soon resulted in the band splitting into two groups. Peerce kept the name Bluegrass Alliance and continued to work out of Louisville for several years with a band that at one point included future country star Vince Gill.[27]

Bush, Burch, Johnson, and Walker started the New Grass Revival and soon relocated to Nashville and recorded an album for Starday. Their counterculture image and ultra progressive approach alienated some fans but also won new ones. Personnel changes took place until only Bush, who earned widespread admiration for his mandolin work, remained. A later banjo picker, Bela Fleck (b. 1958), also won wide admiration. They signed with Capitol and ultimately placed a half-dozen numbers on the country charts, none higher than thirty-seven. The band dissolved in 1989, with Bush becoming a session musician and Fleck forming a new band, the Flecktones.[28]

The continuing growth of bluegrass and the festival movement into the 1980s, in spite of minimal radio airplay, led some of the more far-seeing persons to believe that if the music was to continue and grow, more direction and leadership might be necessary in the future. This led to the 1985 founding of the International Bluegrass Music Association (IBMA), which was patterned after the Country Music Association (CMA), which had been founded in 1958. In the words of Bill C. Malone, the IBMA functioned "essentially as a chamber of commerce, clearinghouse and showcase for bluegrass musicians."[29] One concern widely expressed was over what was termed "the graying of the bluegrass audience" and the belief that the music needed to become more appealing to younger people. Initially based in Owensboro, Kentucky, but later in Louisville and from 2005 in Nashville, every October the IBMA sponsored an awards ceremony, trade show, and concerts all designed to promote the music and to bring together persons with a common interest in some form of the bluegrass business. In 1991, the IBMA started inducting individuals into a Hall of Honor, beginning with Bill Monroe, Lester Flatt, and Earl Scruggs, and established a museum and archives to preserve and protect important artifacts in the music's history. Whether because of the IBMA or on their own, *Bluegrass Unlimited* and *Bluegrass Now* soon began publishing monthly charts. This could hold potential pitfalls—the same problems for which mainstream country music has received criticism—less experienced deejays seem prone to primarily make up their playlists from these types of charts. It also led to a heavier reliance on newly published songs, although some artists continued to mine the seemingly inexhaustible lode of forgotten country songs that would adapt to bluegrass arrangements. After nearly two decades, it can safely be said that the organization is achieving many of its goals, particularly that of broadening the bluegrass audience.

The post-IBMA decades witnessed the rise of a new wave of what one might term "bluegrass stars." One already well on the way by 1985 was Doyle Lawson (b. 1944) and Quicksilver. A Kingsport, Tennessee, native, Lawson had well over a decade of professional experience behind him, beginning with a brief stint playing banjo for Jimmy Martin in 1963. He followed with three years with the Kentucky Mountain Boys (1968–1971) and seven with the Country Gentlemen (1972–1979). Adept on several instruments but most comfortable on mandolin, Lawson learned a great deal from his work with others, including band management, arrangements, and song choice. He also favored a repertoire containing more sacred song and numerous a cappella quartets than that of most bands, and despite fairly rapid turnover of band members, he always maintained high standards and presented top-flight stage shows and a tight sound on all his recordings, mostly on the Sugar Hill label. One experienced bluegrass deejay recently stated that Lawson's music regularly "came closest to perfection."[30]

Another band that rose to prominence, IIIrd Tyme Out, formed in 1991 and led by Russell Moore, was initially primarily made up of persons who trained under Lawson. They straddled a middle position between more traditional and newer groups, a stance that won them the IBMA Vocal Group of the Year award seven straight times from 1994, while Moore took the Male Vocalist award in 1994 and 1997. While placing numerous songs on the *Bluegrass Unlimited* Charts, they have become especially known for their version of a Platters song, "Only You."[31]

Two slightly older bands also gained wide recognition. The Nashville Bluegrass Band, founded in 1984 by guitarist Pat Enright and banjoist Alan O'Bryant, also mixed traditional and more modern sounds. Later they added veteran Roland White on mandolin after Mark Hembree suffered injuries. Recording for Rounder, they took the vocal group award at IBMA four times before IIIrd Tyme Out monopolized it. They also became the first bluegrass band to tour the People's Republic of China. When White retired in 2001, Hembree rejoined them. One of their major innovations was to adapt songs by old-time African American gospel acts to bluegrass. The Lonesome River band, based in Ferrum, Virginia, was founded by guitarist Tim Austin and bassist Jerry McMillan and recorded several albums for Rebel and later Sugar

Hill. In 1995, Austin departed to start Doobie Shea Records. Several other musicians passed through the band, including Don Rigsby and Dan Tyminski. By 2001, none of the original band remained, but banjo picker Sammy Shelor, who had joined for the second time in 1993, reorganized them and continued. While no vocal awards came their way, several members won IBMA awards as instrumentalists.[32]

Some newer bands retained a strong traditional image. The Dry Branch Fire Squad emphasized the lonesome mountain style that characterized the Appalachian migrant bands of southwest Ohio but were dominated by mandolin picker Ron Thomason (b. 1944), whose brand of wit made him one of the most popular emcees around. The Johnson Mountain Boys, based in Montgomery County, Maryland, after some early years as low-key performers burst on the scene as preservers of hard-driving, traditional grass. Although they, too, experienced personnel changes, guitarist Dudley Connell and fiddler Eddie Stubbs were constant members. After 1989, they performed only on a limited basis, with Connell eventually joining the Seldom Scene and Stubbs becoming a WSM late-night deejay and *Opry* announcer. Oklahoma-based Bill Grant and Delia Bell made the male-female duet tradition viable in bluegrass. In addition, Grant's festival at Hugo, Oklahoma, came to rank as probably the largest event of its kind in the trans-Mississippi region. The Traditional Grass, another southwest Ohio group, built its sound around the fiddle of deejay Paul Mullins (b. 1936) and his banjo-picking son Joe (b. 1965). By the 1990s, they were becoming major figures on the scene, but the group ultimately dissolved as Joe went into radio station ownership and management in Xenia, Wilmington, and Eaton, Ohio. By the turn of the century, the major bearer of the traditional approach—other than Dry Branch—was Karl Shiflett and the Big Country Show. Not only did they sound like a band from the late 1940s, they even dressed that way, sang and played into one microphone (labeled KSBC), used mannerisms of that era, and at one point even traveled in a 1947 Chrysler with bass fiddle attached to the top. However, they could also play with skill and precision.[33]

If bluegrass music had a dominant figure by the turn of the century, it had to be the former country star who returned to his bluegrass roots: Ricky Skaggs (b. 1954). A native of Lawrence County, Kentucky, Skaggs had made his first mark on the bluegrass scene in 1970 when he appeared as half of a duet with Keith Whitley (1954–1989) within Ralph Stanley's Clinch Mountain Boys. He had also worked with the Country Gentleman and a short-lived band called Boone Creek before becoming a sideman with country star Emmy Lou Harris. He emerged as a factor on the country scene in 1980 and had a string of ten number one hits between 1982 and 1986, four of them tasteful, well-crafted country versions of bluegrass standards: "Crying My Heart out over You" (from Flatt and Scruggs), "I Wouldn't Change You If I Could" (Jim Eanes and Reno and Smiley), "Don't Cheat in Our Hometown" (Stanley Brothers), and "Uncle Pen" (Bill Monroe). Other old standards and lesser hits helped fill out his albums. Thus, while becoming a country star, he retained the respect of bluegrass fans.

By the end of the decade, Skaggs's country chart position began to slip, and he left Epic Records, had a couple of minor hits on Atlantic, and then moved back toward a full bluegrass band. He started his own label, Skaggs Family Records, in 1997 and turned out a series of a half-dozen bluegrass compact discs bearing such titles as *Bluegrass Rules*, *Soldier of the Cross*, and *Ancient Tones*, with the latter containing an eight-minute, fifteen-verse rendition of "Little Bessie," an 1875 song that is essentially a vision of a dying child and had been recorded several times in the 1920s. In 2000, he made a project of Bill Monroe songs with a number of guest stars drawn from mainstream country and rock musicians. Most Skaggs albums have contained a tasteful mixture of older bluegrass standards along with some newer songs.[34]

After experimenting with neo-traditional country music—a blend of bluegrass and western swing—Ricky Skaggs returned to his original bluegrass style, where he remains popular. *Courtesy of Photofest.*

Another recent trend in bluegrass came with the emergence of all-girl bands and female bandleaders. As members of family bands, female musicians dated back to the Stonemans in the mid-1950s, and Bill Monroe even had a female band member—Sally Ann Forester—for a time in the mid-1940s. The duo of Hazel Dickens and Alice Foster had made duet recordings in the early 1960s. However, all-girl bands had less success primarily because of shifting personnel problems. The New Coon Creek Girls in 1980, based in Renfro Valley, Kentucky, were the pioneers in this field but eventually took in male members. Founder Vicki Simmons lamented, "The big problem has been Nashville," meaning that country superstars kept hiring away her band members. Finally, the band "integrated" in 1997 and became Dale Ann Bradley and Coon Creek. Andrea Campbell Roberts led Petticoat Junction for a decade, but it disbanded in 1998. The Wildwood Girls flourished for several years, although never really hitting the top. The Dixie Chicks, originally based in Dallas, began as a bluegrass group but found stardom only after they turned to country.[35]

Female bandleaders compiled a much better track record of commercial success than the all-girl outfits. Allison Krauss (b. 1971) proved to be the pacesetter in this area, although she played in a more contemporary and progressive style than most musicians in the field. Illinois-born, she first earned distinction as a twelve-year-old fiddle champion and at sixteen had her first solo album on Rounder, for which she was encouraged to sing. By 1993, when her *Now That I've Found You: A Collection* went double-platinum, she and her band Union Station became *Grand Ole Opry* members. A gospel album with the Louisiana-based Cox Family, *I Know Who Holds Tomorrow*, demonstrated that she could fit in with traditional sounds. Krauss further added to her laurels on the same *O Brother, Where Art Thou?* soundtrack album that elevated Ralph Stanley to the status of mainstream media star.[36]

Rhonda Vincent (b. 1962) fell closer to the bluegrass mainstream. Missouri-born, she had started playing bluegrass with her family band, the Sally Mountain Show, with whom she recorded eleven albums over a period of years. In 1992, she went solo and veered toward mainstream country with limited success. In 1998, she returned to bluegrass, organizing a band called the Rage and turning out a quality album, *Back Home Again*, on Rounder. Rewarded with the IBMA Female Vocalist of the Year award in both 2000 and 2001, she also won the IBMA Entertainer of the Year award. Her subsequent albums, *The Storm Still Rages* (2001) and *One Step Ahead* (2003), have generally followed a pattern of mixing older and newer songs.[37]

One of the longest-lived female-led groups—the Lynn Morris (b. 1948) Band—formed in 1988. Morris, born in Texas and reared in Colorado, won several banjo-picking contests, moved east, and joined the Pennsylvania band Whetstone Run in 1980. Her own band took in some former Johnson Mountain Boys, including her husband Marshall Wilburn, and she won the IBMA Female Vocalist award three times in the 1990s and recorded for Rounder. However, her health problems have left the band's future in doubt.[38]

In recent years, several other female-led bands played the circuits. These include Laurie Lewis and Grant Street, the Emma Smith Band, Valerie Smith and Liberty Pike, Claire Lynch and the Front Porch String Band, Honi Deaton and Dream, and Sally Jones and the Sidewinders. While all have proven themselves competent, their longevity as groups remains indeterminate.[39]

Bluegrass, like other musical forms, is in a constant state of evolution and change. Certainly in the early years of the twenty-first century there are more bands, more musicians, and more festivals than ever before. A look at the charts in mid-2004 showed bands with names like Pine Mountain Railroad, King Wilkie (named for Bill Monroe's Horse), Kane's River, and Mountain Heart. Ironically, other than two entries by the Del McCoury Band, the most familiar name on the list was that of Sam Bush, thought of as revolutionary three decades ago but now viewed as somewhere near the center of the mainstream. Traditionalists could note that, in addition to McCoury, names like Larry Stephenson, Karl Shifflet, the Warrior River Boys, and Open Road showed that the traditional older style as pioneered by Monroe was alive and well. So-called middle-of-the-road bands or artists that retained some elements of traditional bluegras, such as IIIrd Tyme Out, Tim O'Brien, Rhonda Vincent, Rarely Herd, Larry Cordle, and Lonesome Standard Time, were also well represented. Some were more in the progressive or "new grass" styles, and others could not be easily classified.[40]

The boundaries of the music also seem to be stretching farther from the Monroe-created sound than ever before. In 2002, older fans wondered if the hot new group on the scene Nickel Creek was really bluegrass. If so, it would be the first band to be without a banjo.[41] A decade earlier, some wondered the same about Allison Krauss and Union Station, but she ultimately won acceptance. At some point, a band stops being bluegrass or never is one in the first place. One supposes that eventually a line will be drawn.

NOTES

1. This account is condensed largely from that in Neil V. Rosenberg, *Bluegrass: A History* (Urbana: University of Illinois Press, 1985), 40–94. See also Richard D. Smith, *Can't You Hear Me Callin': The Life of Bill Monroe, Father of Bluegrass* (Boston: Little, Brown, 2000), 47–86. Good general works on bluegrass of a popular nature are Bob Artis, *Bluegrass* (New York: Hawthorn Books, 1975), and Richard D. Smith, *Bluegrass: An Informal Guide* (Chicago: A Cappella Books, 1995).

2. Smith, *Can't You Hear Me Callin'*. A short but excellent essay on Monroe is Ralph Rinzler, "Bill Monroe," in Bill C. Malone and Judith McCulloh, eds., *Stars of Country Music* (Urbana: University of Illinois Press, 1975), 202–221. For detailed data on Monroe's recordings through 1973, see Neil V. Rosenberg, *Bill Monroe and His Blue Grass Boys: An Illustrated Discography* (Nashville, TN: Country Music Foundation Press, 1974).

3. Neil V. Rosenberg, "Lester Flatt and Earl Scruggs," in Malone and McCulloh, *Stars of Country Music*, 255–273. A somewhat uncritical biography of Flatt is Jake Lambert with Curly Sechler, *A Biography of Lester Flatt: "The Good Things Out Weigh the Bad"* (Hendersonville, TN: Jay-Lyn Publication, 1982). See also Pete Kuykendall, "Lester Flatt & the Nashville Grass," *Bluegrass Unlimited* 5 (January 1971), 3–6.

4. Although not a biography, the best work on the Stanley Brothers and Ralph Stanley is John Wright, *Traveling the High Way Home: Ralph Stanley and the World of Traditional Bluegrass Music* (Urbana: University of Illinois Press, 1993). See Thompson's quote on 145–146; Penny Parsons, "The Renaissance of Ralph Stanley," *Bluegrass Unlimited* 29 (May 1995), 16–22. For updates on Stanley and other musicians and groups discussed herein, see Wayne Rice, *Bluegrass Bios: Profiles of the Stars of Bluegrass Music* (Lakeside, CA: Bluegrass Specialties, 2003); entries are alphabetical.

5. Ivan M. Tribe, "The Goins Brothers, Melvin and Ray: Maintaining the Lonesome Pine Fiddler Tradition," *Bluegrass Unlimited* 8 (May 1974), 11–18. Their Cozy and RCA Victor recordings may be found on *The Lonesome Pine Fiddlers: Windy Mountain* (ECD 501).

6. The best work on Martin is currently Chris Skinker, *Jimmy Martin and the Sunny Mountain Boys* (Hamburg, Germany: Bear Family Records, 1994), 27. Also good is Brett F. Devan, "The High Lonesome Sound of Jimmy Martin: The King of Bluegrass," *Bluegrass Unlimited* 30 (December 1995), 16–23.

7. The best work on the Osborne Brothers is currently Neil V. Rosenberg with Edward L. Stubbs, *The Osborne Brothers, 1956–1968* (Hamburg, Germany: Bear Family Records, 1995). See also Rosenberg's earlier work, "The Osborne Brothers I," *Bluegrass Unlimited* 6 (September 1971), 5–10, and "The Osborne Brothers II," *Bluegrass Unlimited* 6 (February 1972), 5–8.

8. An uncritical biography is Nelson Sears, *Jim and Jesse: Appalachia to the Grand Ole Opry* (n.p.: privately printed, 1976). See also Dale Vinicur, *Jim & Jesse: Bluegrass and More* (Hamburg, Germany: Bear Family Records, 1993).

9. The definitive work is Charles Wolfe and Eddie Stubbs, *Mac Wiseman: 'Tis Sweet to Be Remembered* (Hamburg, Germany: Bear Family Records, 2003).

10. See Gary B. Reid, *Don Reno & Red Smiley and the Tennessee Cut-Ups, 1951–1959* (Dearborn, MI: Highland Music, 1993).

11. For Smiley's later career, see Ivan M. Tribe, "A Quarter Century of Bluegrass Fiddling: Clarence 'Tater' Tate," *Bluegrass Unlimited* 8 (November 1973), 7–11. Tate played fiddle for Smiley during most of this time.

12. Linda Stanley, "Don Reno: A Bluegrass Family Tradition," *Bluegrass Unlimited* 15 (August 1980), 17–23.

13. See Ivan M. Tribe, "Carl Story: Bluegrass Pioneer," *Bluegrass Unlimited* 9 (January 1975), 8–14; Tribe, "Hylo Brown: The Bluegrass Balladeer," *Bluegrass Unlimited* 9 (August 1974), 10–13; Tribe, "Pros Long Before Boston: The Entire Career of the Lilly Brothers," *Bluegrass Unlimited* 9 (July 1974), 8–17; Pete Kuykendall, "Smilin' Jim Eanes," *Bluegrass Unlimited* 7 (February 1973), 7–11. Of many articles on the Lewis Family, one of the more comprehensive and informative is Brett F. Devan, "Still Making Bluegrass History: The Sensational Lewis Family," *Bluegrass Unlimited* 30 (September 1995), 34–38.

14. See Rosenberg, *Bluegrass: A History*, 138–139.

15. Steven Robinson, "The Country Gentlemen . . . in the Truest Sense," *Bluegrass Unlimited* 18 (June 1984), 14–23.

16. H. Lloyd Whittaker, "Cliff Waldron and the New Shades of Grass," *Bluegrass Unlimited* 5 (April 1971), 5; Joe Ross, "Bill Emerson: Banjo Player Extra Ordinaire," *Bluegrass Unlimited* 26 (March 1992), 20–32.

17. Bill Vernon, "Part-Time Professionals: The Seldom Scene," *Muleskinner News* (March 1973), 6–8. See also Jack Tottle, "Don't Wait for Them to Buy—Sell It: John Duffey and His Music," *Bluegrass Unlimited* 9 (November 1974), 8–13. For a more up to date view, see Penny Parsons, "The Seldom Scene: All This and Fun, Too," *Bluegrass Unlimited* 29 (December 1994), 16–24.

18. George B. McCeney, "And the Dillards Came to Grass," *Bluegrass Unlimited* 6 (November 1971), 5–6; Peter V. Kuykendall, "The Kentucky Colonels," *Bluegrass Unlimited* 3 (April 1969), 3–4; George Martin, "High Country," *Bluegrass Unlimited* 6 (June 1972), 7–11; Matt Dudman, "Vern & Ray," *Bluegrass Unlimited* 38 (August 2003), 32–35.

19. Quoted in David Freeman, *County Sales Newsletter* 23 (January–February 1969), 3.

20. For Haney and the origins of bluegrass festivals, see Rosenberg, *Bluegrass: A History*, 203–212; Smith, *Can't You Hear Me Callin'*, 200–207.

21. Rosenberg, *Bluegrass: A History*, 272–304; Smith, *Can't You Hear Me Callin'*, 221–224; Freeman, *County Sales Newsletter* 23, 2–3.

22. See Rosenberg, *Bluegrass: A History*, 224–230, 285–289.

23. Smith, *Can't You Hear Me Callin'*, 216, 222–223, 226–227. For Charlie Monroe's career, see Ivan M. Tribe, "Charlie Monroe," *Bluegrass Unlimited* 10 (October 1975), 12–19.

24. For typical articles on the bluegrass specialty record labels, see Charles K. Wolfe, "Dave Freeman and County Records," *Bluegrass Unlimited* 15 (December 1980), 50–55; Wayne Erbsen, "Barry Poss and Sugar Hill Records," *Bluegrass Unlimited* 17 (October 1982), 28–33; Eric Zorn, "A Homestead for Using Talent," *Bluegrass Unlimited* 14 (December 1979), 24–26.

25. Tribe, "The Goins Brothers," 11–18; Doug Green, "Larry Sparks," *Bluegrass Unlimited* 7 (December 1972), 7–8; Bob Allen, "Larry Sparks: A Man unto His Own Time, and His Own Music," *Bluegrass Unlimited* 35 (November 2000), 34–37; Pete Kuykendall, "Charlie Moore," *Bluegrass Unlimited* 7 (January 1973), 5–9; Ivan M. Tribe, "The Shenandoah Cutups: Classic Bluegrass from a Newer Group," *Bluegrass Unlimited* 11 (December 1976), 8–12; Gwen Taylor, "Del McCoury," *Bluegrass Unlimited* 7 (June 1973), 17–19; David Royko, "Del McCoury Band," *Bluegrass Unlimited* 36 (December 2001), 28–31.

26. An early look at J. D. Crowe's new approach is Mary Jane Bolle, "Happy Medium: J. D. Crowe & the New South," *Bluegrass Unlimited* 8 (February 1974), 7–9; Douglas Fulmer, "J. D. Crowe," *Bluegrass Unlimited* 29 (April 1995), 16–20; quote from Marian Leighton, Ken Irwin, *J. D. Crowe and the New South* (Starday SLP 489, 1977), liner notes.

27. For an early look at the Bluegrass Alliance, see John Kaparakis, "The Bluegrass Alliance," *Bluegrass Unlimited* 4 (October 1969), 12–14.

28. Stephanie P. Ledgin, "New Grass Revival: A Timeless Tradition of Innovation," *Bluegrass Unlimited* 19 (April 1985), 14–19.

29. For the founding of the IBMA, see Bill C. Malone, *Country Music, U.S.A.*, 2nd rev. ed. (Austin: University of Texas Press, 2002), 454.

30. The first notable article on Doyle Lawson's group is Jack Tottle, "Doyle Lawson and Quicksilver," *Bluegrass Unlimited* 15 (November 1980), 16–22; Les McIntyre, "Doyle Lawson and Quicksilver: The First 20 Years," *Bluegrass Unlimited* 34 (June 2000), 36–40. The quote is from deejay Ron Vigue, "D28+5" WOUB-FM, Athens, Ohio, August 1, 2004.

31. Geoffrey Himes, "IIIrd Tyme Out: Leading the Way," *Bluegrass Unlimited* 34 (May 2000), 42–46.

32. Art Menius, "The Nashville Bluegrass Band's American Lancao," *Bluegrass Unlimited* 21 (October 1986), 14–20; Penny Parsons, "Lonesome River Band: It's About Excitement!," *Bluegrass Unlimited* 28 (February 1994), 22–30.

33. Don Rhodes, "Band on the Run: The Johnson Mountain Boys," *Bluegrass Unlimited* 16 (December 1981), 12–17; Art Menius, "Dry Branch Fire Squad's Quest for Lonesome," *Bluegrass Unlimited* 20 (July 1985), 14–20; Barry Brower, "Living Life the First Time Around: Bill Grant & Delia Bell," *Bluegrass Unlimited* 23 (September 1988), 16–18; Marty Godbey, "Ten Years of the Traditional Grass," *Bluegrass Unlimited* 28 (December 1993), 16–21.

34. Bob Allen, "Ricky Skaggs: Musical Evangelist, Record Label Executive with a Cause," *Bluegrass Unlimited* 35 (August 2000), 30–34.

35. For a good survey of women in bluegrass music, see Robert Oermann and Mary Bufwack, *Finding Her Voice: The Saga of Women in Country Music* (New York: Crown

Publishers, 1993), 454–461. See also F. Paul Haney, "Women in Bluegrass from the Women's Point of View," *Bluegrass Unlimited* 24 (December 1989), 20–28.

36. Jack Tottle, "Allison Krauss and Union Station," *Bluegrass Unlimited* 25 (June 1991), 20–27; Thomas Goldsmith, "Allison Krauss and Union Station, 1995," *Bluegrass Unlimited* 29 (June 1995), 42–48.

37. Arlie Metheny, "Missouri's Vincent Family and Their Sally Mountain Show," *Bluegrass Unlimited* 23 (July 1988), 24–26; Loretta Sawyer, "Rhonda Vincent: She's Come Full Circle and Her Future Looks Bright," *Bluegrass Now* 9 (October 1999), 22–25, 42.

38. Geoffrey Himes, "Lynn Morris: She Will Be the Light," *Bluegrass Unlimited* 34 (August 1999), 26–31.

39. For a light look, see Murphy Henry, "Women in Bluegrass: Keynote Address," in Thomas Goldsmith, ed., *The Bluegrass Reader* (Urbana: University of Illinois Press, 2004), 298–305. See also the entries on these groups in Rice, *Bluegrass Bios*.

40. Data herein come from Lee Michael Demsey, comp., "The Bluegrass Unlimited National Bluegrass Survey," *Bluegrass Unlimited* 39 (August 2004), 75.

41. For Nickel Creek, see Julie Koehler, "Nickel Creek: It Takes a Village...," *Bluegrass Unlimited* 36 (February 2002), 22–28.

8

The Nashville Sound and
More Since 1958

If one had to date the beginning of the modern era of country music, the year 1958 is a likely choice. The Country Music Association, commonly known as the CMA, came into existence that year as a trade organization "by which country music could attain respectability and achieve a wider popularity." For the most part, the association defined its mission as being one almost exclusively of "economic[s] and public relations." Definition and aesthetics of country music was left largely to musicians, fans, and listeners, although certain actions by the CMA undoubtedly influenced developments within the field.[1]

Around this time, some recent country songs had displayed considerable strength in the pop field and were termed crossover hits. In addition to the pure rockabilly items by the likes of Jerry Lee Lewis and the slower numbers by Johnny Cash and Marty Robbins with wide teen appeal, these included items like "A Rose and a Baby Ruth" by George Hamilton IV, "Young Love" by Sonny James, and "Gone" by Ferlin Husky. Many record producers began to make minimum use of or eliminate altogether the hillbilly sounding fiddle and the twangy steel guitars that had helped define the honky-tonk sounds that had brought success to Hank Williams and Webb Pierce only a few years earlier. Fiddlers like Tommy Jackson, who had once made a comfortable living doing record sessions, increasingly found little demand for their services. Vocal chorus backup increasingly appeared on many recordings supplied by the Jordanaires, the Anita Kerr Singers, or other groups, some of whom worked in southern gospel quartets. Record producers made a conscious appeal to preserve the flavor of country, or what Bill Malone called "the feel and ambience," but to make it commercially appealing to pop music fans. Adult supporters of older forms of popular music believed their preferences were being obliterated by the rock-and-roll sounds increasingly defined by teenage tastes. The results of these changes came to be known as "the Nashville Sound," a term first used in 1958 in *Music Reporter*.[2]

The person most responsible for the creation of the Nashville Sound was Chet Atkins (1924–2000), a superb country guitarist and recording artist from east Tennessee who Steve Sholes, the chief of RCA Victor's country division, made his assistant in 1952 and the head of operations in Nashville in 1957. Atkins's favorite session musicians, such as Bob Moore on bass, Floyd Cramer on piano, Buddy Harman on drums, and sometimes Boots Randolph on saxophone, were among the other prime creators of the musical blend that Atkins preferred. Other Nashville session musicians also quickly perfected these techniques, including lead guitarists Grady Martin and Hank Garland, rhythm guitarist Ray Edenton, and pianist Hargis Robbins. Other Nashville record producers, such as Columbia's Don Law, Capitol's Ken Nelson, and Decca's Owen Bradley, also played a role in the development of the Nashville Sound. Of course, Eddy Arnold, who had been moving away from hard country sounds for some years, had largely been recording sessions virtually akin to that already.

As musicians in the recording studios were creating what was becoming known as the Nashville Sound, the CMA encouraged the development of radio stations with all-country-music formats. By this time, the days of live country music on the radio were practically over as far as daytime programming was concerned, except of course for the Saturday night jamboree programs that survived, such as the *Grand Ole Opry* at WSM Nashville and the *World's Original Jamboree* at WWVA Wheeling (soon to be renamed *Jamboree USA*). Disc jockeys playing records during all the broadcasts hours with news headlines on the hour characterized most stations, and by 1967, there were 328 of them around the nation, plus additional stations that programmed one or two hours of country daily. Since many of the deejays were only vaguely familiar with the music and its traditions, they tended to play from playlists usually built around the *Billboard* charts. Thus, the music became more standardized than before.[3]

Some of the earliest hits to come out of the Nashville Sound on the RCA Victor label included songs by Florida-born Hank Locklin (b. 1918), such as "Send Me the Pillow That You Dream on," "It's a Little More Like Heaven Where You Are," and his biggest success, "Please Help Me I'm Falling" which spent fourteen weeks at number one in 1960 and made the top ten on the pop listings as well. His later songs appeared regularly on the charts through 1971, and he gained long-standing popularity in the British Isles as well. Don Gibson (1928–2003), who came from North Carolina by way of Knoxville, also scored big in 1958 with "Oh Lonesome Me," "I Can't Stop Loving You," and "Blue Blue Day," all of which demonstrated crossover appeal as well. Personal problems dimmed Gibson's success from 1961, but he had at least one song on the charts every year through the 1960s on RCA Victor, and then on Hickory with some regularity until 1980, including a few duets with Dottie West and Sue Thompson. A trio composed of a brother and two sisters—Jim Ed, Maxine, and Bonnie Brown—performing as the Browns also had a million-selling crossover hit with "The Three Bells."[4]

However, the biggest country star RCA turned out with the Nashville Sound was Texas-born Jim Reeves (1924–1964), who like Webb Pierce and Faron Young had come to Nashville by way of the *Louisiana Hayride*. Reeves had started out in baseball as a minor league pitcher in the vast St. Louis Cardinal farm system, but a 1947 injury ended his athletic career, and his pleasant voice helped secure work as a radio announcer and deejay who could also sing a little. He made a few recordings on the Macy label in 1949 but had no real success until signing with Abbot in 1953, where his second release, a country novelty song "Mexican Joe," became a hit and was followed by "Bimbo," a song about a cute little boy. In 1955, he moved on to RCA Victor and the *Grand Ole Opry*, and from then until his premature death in a plane crash in 1964, he just kept scoring one hit after another.

The early Reeves hits on Abbot and RCA Victor differed but little from the standard honky-tonk songs produced in mid-1950s Nashville. They included "Yonder Comes a Sucker" and a revival of Jimmie Rodgers's "Waiting for a Train." However, the number that really served as the crossover breakthrough for Reeves was "Four Walls" in 1957, which spent six months on the country listings, eight weeks of that at the top, and reached number eleven in pop. Over the next year, he had four more songs make the top ten, and then in the latter part of 1958, he scored two major hits in succession with "Blue Boy" and "Billy Bayou." His biggest crossover hit, released late in 1959, "He'll Have to Go," spent thirty-four weeks on the country charts; fourteen at the top; and twenty in the pop top forty, reaching number two. Although Reeves had no more number one hits in his lifetime, he had thirteen more in the top ten, most of which exhibited some crossover action, and starred in a motion picture in South Africa, *Kimberley Jim*. His recordings also sold well in foreign markets, even non-English-speaking ones, causing one journalist to write, "The resonant purr from the honeyed larynx of Jim Reeves has an almost hypnotic effect."

Reeves also has the distinction of scoring more posthumous hits than anyone in country music history, even Jimmie Rodgers and Hank Williams. "I Guess I'm Crazy" had just entered the charts at the time of his death on July 31, 1964, reached number one the last week of August, and remained there until mid-October. Since RCA Victor had a considerable backlog of his material in their vaults, he had two number one hits each in 1965 and 1966 and another in 1967. Thanks to the marvels of modern technology, two duets of Jim Reeves and Patsy Cline, who had preceded him in death by over a year, made the country charts, one from his label and one from hers (MCA as successor to Decca).[5]

Even while Jim Reeves was still dominating the charts, RCA Victor found another vocalist who possessed an ideal voice for the Nashville Sound: Charley Pride (b. 1938), a Mississippi-born Montana resident who also became the first African American country music star. Country singers Red Sovine and Red Foley had first heard Pride sing in 1962. Encouraging him to pursue a musical career, they eventually got the attention of Chet Atkins, who signed him to a contract and held a first session in August 1965. His first single, "Snakes Crawl at Night," attracted some notice, but his third release, "Just Between You and Me," became his first real hit, peaking at the ninth spot. Then and only then was his racial background made public. Country fans accepted him, and beginning in 1969 with "All I Have to Offer You Is Me," he ran up a string of twenty-nine number one hits over the next fourteen years and a total of fifty-nine chart entries in a twenty-year period with RCA. His most memorable songs probably were "Is Anybody Goin' to San Antone" and "Kiss an Angel Good Morning," in 1970 and 1971, respectively. Changing to 16th Avenue Records in 1987, his songs continued to make the *Billboard* listings through 1989.[6]

Another RCA Victor artist whose recordings increasingly reflected the Nashville Sound was Porter Wagoner (b. 1927), known as "the Thin Man from West Plains [Missouri]." Wagoner began to play irregularly on KWPM radio in his hometown in the late 1940s and gained a regular program in 1950. The following year, he landed at spot at KWTO in Springfield, which had several live country acts, most under the guidance of enterprising entrepreneur E. E. "Si" Siman, whose business endeavors included a transcription operation, "RadiOzark," and later the network television *Ozark Jubilee*. In 1952, Siman managed to get Wagoner a contract with RCA Victor, but Wagoner's earliest releases made little impression on the broader market. Finally, two of his 1954 efforts gained hit status: "Company's Comin'" and the inspirational number "A Satisfied Mind," which made number one in mid-1955. Meanwhile, Wagoner became one of the early cast members of the *Ozark Jubilee* and in 1957 moved to the *Grand Ole Opry*.

In April 1959, Chet Atkins added characteristics of the Nashville Sound to Wagoner's recordings while retaining the fiddle and steel, but the initial results yielded no major hits. As quoted in Dale Vinicur's *Porter Wagoner: The Thin Man from the West Plains*, Wagoner himself said, "We tried really hard to record a hit. Chet, in fact worked very hard, tried his best. But we just didn't come up with anything." Ironically, he finally did come with a hit in September 1961 with "Misery Loves Company," when Atkins was out of town and Wagoner arranged the session on his own, personally believing that hiring Jimmy Day on steel guitar was the decisive factor. Another reason for Wagoner's ascent to major stardom came that same month when he launched the syndicated *Porter*

Wagoner Show on eighteen TV stations. Sponsored by the Chattanooga Medicine Company, it became the most successful program of its type during the decade and undoubtedly played a major role in his growing popularity. The television show was unabashedly country, retained fiddle and steel in its sound, and included cornball comedy featuring "Speck" Rhodes. It also had until mid-1967 featured songs by female vocalist "Pretty Miss Norma Jean" Beasler (b. 1938), who became one of the top female country vocalists of the decade. When Beasler left the program, her replacement, Dolly Parton (b. 1946), eventually attained a level of stardom that eclipsed that of Wagoner, who retained the TV show until 1980.

While Porter Wagoner's recordings reflected many of the trappings of the Nashville Sound, they also retained more of a country feel than did those of Reeves by retaining the fiddle and steel guitar. While his hits had little or no crossover appeal, they consistently ranked high on the country charts, as illustrated by "I've Enjoyed as Much of This as I Can Stand," "Green Green Grass of Home," "The Cold Hard Facts of Life," and "The Carroll County Accident." By the end of the decade, his duets with Parton, such as "The Last Thing on My Mind" and "Daddy Was an Old Time Preacher Man," began to do as well or better than his solo offerings, which may have been a factor in their 1975 split. Ironically, some of his most popular TV numbers like "Trouble in the Amen Corner" and "Legend of the Big Steeple" never made the charts at all, reflecting the continuing appeal of nostalgia to traditional country audiences.[7]

Television also played a role in the rise to stardom of one of Columbia's new stars of the early 1960s, Jimmy Dean (b. 1928), although the circumstances were quite different. Of Texas birth, Dean worked local television in the Washington, D.C., area with his band the Texas Wildcats, including a six-month-long weekday morning on the CBS network. In the early days, his only noteworthy appearance on disc was in 1953 with "Bumming Around" on the 4 Star label. Signing with Columbia in the early 1960s, he had hits with a pair of saga songs, one a fictional tale about a coal miner who sacrificed his life for others, "Big Bad John"; and "PT 109," a true lyric about the World War II adventure of then President John Kennedy. Both demonstrated crossover strength, with the former song being number one in both fields. He had other hits, such as "Little Black Book" and "The First Thing Every Morning." By the time the latter hit number one, Dean also had a prime-time ABC-TV network variety show—based in New York—which ran for three years from 1963 to 1966. Although *The Jimmy Dean Show* seldom had high ratings, the mere fact that a major network carried the program for nearly three years ranked as something of a milestone in country and western annals.[8]

Most of Columbia's other stars had been with the label prior to the rise of the Nashville Sound. Johnny Cash's accompaniment never had much fiddle or steel guitar music on them, and so his music fit in well and he had already shown crossover potential with some of his Sun efforts. One of his first

Columbia hits, the western saga song "Don't Take Your Guns to Town," was backed with "I Still Miss Someone," which Cash scholars have identified with the Nashville Sound. Other Cash hits, such as "Ring of Fire" and his duet with wife June Carter, "Jackson," have also exemplified that approach as well, although in many respects Cash can hardly be pigeonholed into any one style. Marty Robbins also did well with the new style continuing through the 1960s and 1970s with a string of hits typified by "Devil Woman," "Ribbon of Darkness," and "Don't Worry (About Me)."[9]

Ray Price (b. 1926) also belatedly bought into the newer style. A typical honky-tonk singer, he first became known for such songs as "Talk to Your Heart," "Release Me," and "I'll Be There (If You Ever Want Me)." When other Columbia artists were experimenting with rockabilly and the Nashville Sound, Price clung to the older styles with only slight modification and had some of his biggest hits in the later 1950s with "My Shoes Keep Walking Back to You," "Crazy Arms," "The Same Old Me," and "Heartaches by the Number." Many of these were characterized by what became known as the "shuffle" sound that would later be incorporated into the music of Buck Owens.

Tidbits of the Nashville Sound began creeping into Price's recordings, however, and in September 1962, he incorporated a string section composed of members of the Nashville Symphony (one of whom was Cecil Brower, a former member of western swing pioneer Milton Brown's band). By 1966, when he recorded the Irish song "Danny Boy," Price had full orchestra accompaniment. Fans who had idolized his earlier "keeping it country" approach felt betrayed, and some even walked out of his concerts. Nonetheless, he persisted and even required a minimum of a twenty-piece orchestra at his declining number of appearances. His recordings continued to make the charts, but most peaked at lower levels than his pre-1966 efforts. By the early 1970s, he returned to the top, turning out four number one hits, most notably, "For the Good Times," which became his first real crossover hit, and "I Won't Mention It Again." As one of the real country music giants of the last half of the twentieth century, he continued to make the charts regularly throughout the 1980s.[10]

Other record companies bought into the Nashville Sound almost as rapidly as RCA Victor and Columbia. One of the first, Decca, demonstrated the influence of Owen Bradley (1915–1998), who became the head of its Nashville division in 1958. In addition to Kitty Wells and Webb Pierce, both of whom had numerous top ten hits in the early 1960s, Bradley had moderate success with the already established Wilburn Brothers and new figure Warner Mack (b. 1938). However, he also developed a new major male star in South Carolina native Bill Anderson (b. 1937), who had written "City Lights," a Ray Price hit of 1958. Signed to Decca, Anderson had his first session in August 1958 and had his first chart maker later that year with "That's What It's Like to Be Lonesome," which peaked at number twelve. He joined the *Opry* in 1961 and soon afterward had two consecutive number one hits: the nostalgic "Mama Sang a Song" and "Still," a crossover hit of broken love that continues to be a favorite country and pop music theme. A series of additional hits—"8 × 10," "Bright Lights and Country Music," "I Get the Fever," "Wild Week-End," and "My Life"—cemented his position as one of the leading new stars of the 1960s. In addition, he and duet partner Jan Howard (b. 1930) also began a series of charted songs of which "For Loving You" and "If It's All the Same to You" ranked highest.[11]

Anderson was still high on the charts when former rockabilly-pop singer Conway Twitty (1933–1993) returned to his country roots and signed with Decca in 1965. His initial recordings were best described as moderate hits because some country DJs were skeptical, but by 1968, he had a number one hit, and in 1970 "Hello Darlin'" went to the top for four weeks. Much of Twitty's success derived from a large and loyal legion of fans that would help give him a record total of forty number one hits. In addition, some of his popularity may also have derived from clever song titles and lyrics that seemed suggestive at a time when society trended toward more permissive attitudes. Several of his hits were with female star Loretta Lynn (b. 1935), including "After the Fire Is Gone" and "Louisiana Woman, Mississippi Man," which not surprisingly sounded more country than his solo efforts. He also developed a tourist complex near Nashville known as Twitty City. By the time of his death, he had amassed a total of ninety-seven country chart listings.[12]

After Faron Young left Capitol for Mercury in 1962, Sonny James (b. 1929) became Capitol producer Ken Nelson's leading male artist in Nashville. Born James Loden in Alabama, Sonny James worked on radio with his sisters as part of a family group. After Korean War service, he signed with Capitol and made his first appearance on the charts in 1953 with "That's Me Without You," which was also a hit for Webb Pierce. He did not score high again until 1957, when his "Young Love" proved a crossover success and so to a lesser degree did "First Date, First Kiss, First Love." He left Capitol for other labels but eventually resigned with Ken Nelson in 1963. For the next decade, he accumulated a string of high-ranking hits, twenty-two of which made number one. The most memorable were "You're the Only World I Know," "I'll Never Find Another You," and "Empty Arms." James had a voice that accommodated well to the Nashville Sound and that, like Eddy Arnold's, pop music fans found quite pleasing. In fact, several of James's bigger hits were soft country versions of pop hits from a few years earlier. Nicknamed "the Southern Gentleman," James was by all accounts the personification of that sobriquet. He generally avoided involvement in country music politics and controversy, kept to himself, and, when he retired about 1986, went back to a cattle farm in Alabama and expressed little care or concern about his legacy.[13]

Other country stars prospered with the Nashville Sound. Faron Young moved from Capitol to Mercury in 1962 and continued to rack up hit records until the early 1980s—most notably, "It's Four in the Morning" in 1971. Tall Georgia-born Roy Drusky (1930–2004) after a brief association with Decca joined the Mercury roster in 1963 and charted thirty times in a decade with that company, including eight in the top ten. But Mercury's biggest star in the late sixties, Tom T. Hall (b. 1936), a former deejay from Olive Hill, Kentucky, demonstrated unusual skills initially as a composer but eventually as a vocalist. Hall's talent derived largely from his ability to write skilled story songs on unusual subjects, often with an ironic twist, which soon inspired his nickname, "the Storyteller." For instance, his first top ten single, "Ballad of Forty Dollars," told the story of a beer-drinking gravedigger looking over at the attractive widow while lamenting that the deceased still owes him "forty bucks." "A Week in a Country Jail" related the narrator's arrest for speeding and spending a week in a small lockup waiting for the local justice to try his case. His best-known song, "The Year that Clayton Delaney Died," consisted of a nostalgic memoir about a guitar picker the narrator had known in earlier days. Hall also wrote songs for other artists—most notably "Harper Valley P.T.A.," which was a gold record and crossover hit for Jeannie C. Riley in 1968. In the later 1970s, the fad for Hall's story songs began to fade, but he still made the lower echelons of the charts with titles like "Back When Gas Was Thirty Cents a Gallon" and "Everything from Jesus to Jack Daniels." By the dawn of the new century, he had begun writing songs for bluegrass artists.[14]

Other new stars had their moments of success in the 1960s and 1970s, virtually all with music that featured some variation of the Nashville Sound. Roger Miller (1936–1992) had three very strong years in the mid-1960s with songs in a humorous vein, such as "Dang Me," "Chug-a-Lug," "King of the Road," and "England Swings," all of which were crossover hits. Starting with an advantage of name recognition, Hank Williams, Jr. (b. 1949), had his first session in 1963 and had numerous hits in the country mainstream but then in the mid-1970s recast his image to fit the "outlaw movement." Mel Tillis (b. 1932), had long been noted as a songwriter before his own recordings began to attract major attention in the early 1970s. Ironically, a stuttering problem, which failed to affect his singing, made him a popular figure on talk shows and probably helped give him an enhanced celebrity status. He ranked as the most consistent country chart maker on M-G-M Records other than Hank Williams, Sr. and Jr.[15]

Other stars who gained their initial fame in earlier decades continued to do well in the 1960s and 1970s, especially George Jones, but also Eddy Arnold, Hank Snow, and Kitty Wells. Ernest Tubb made less accommodation to the newer sounds than did the others. But the real major change that came to country in the 1960s along with the Nashville Sound and the growth of Bakersfield was the increasing numbers of top-ranking female performers.[16]

The original purveyor—and later patron saint—of the new woman vocalist was the short-lived Patsy Cline (1932–1963), who died in a March 1963 plane crash along with Cowboy Copas and Hawkshaw Hawkins. A native of near Winchester, Virginia, where she was born Virginia Hensler, Cline gained her early experience with local groups, signing with Decca in 1955. Her first three releases on the Coral subsidiary made little impact, but her second Decca disc, "Walkin' After Midnight," became a major hit in 1957, also made the pop charts, and clearly demonstrated crossover appeal. A couple of slack years followed, and then came "I Fall to Pieces," "Crazy," and "She's Got You" in rapid succession. These were the songs that really elevated her to stardom, and like her first hit, all showed crossover strength, with "Crazy" reaching number nine on the *Billboard* pop charts. At the time of her fatal crash, "Leavin' on Her Mind" was climbing the charts and eventually peaked at number eight. She had a pair of posthumous hits with "Sweet Dreams" (which became the title of a motion picture based on her life) and a revival of the Bob Wills classic "Faded Love." Overall, the significance of Patsy Cline would seem to rest not so much on her relatively small number of hit records but on the impact that she undoubtedly had on female singers who followed in her footsteps and the larger-than-life legend that developed after her death.[17]

Whether based on Cline's legendary image or the continuing impact of Kitty Wells, the 1960s saw a number of singing country girls come to the forefront, two of whom ultimately became superstars. Several others gained a level of middle rank among the stars. Of the superstars, Loretta Lynn (b. 1935) had a steady ascent to stardom throughout the 1960s and peaked in the early 1970s. A native of poverty-stricken Eastern Kentucky, Lynn became one of the great Appalachian success stories. Born a coal miner's daughter, she married at thirteen and moved to far-off Washington State with her serviceman husband and after having several children made her first record at twenty-five on the tiny Zero label. Surprisingly, through self-promotion her song "I'm a Honky-Tonk Girl" climbed to fourteen on the *Billboard* charts and landed her a contract with Decca, a job as vocalist on the syndicated *Wilburn Brothers TV Show*, *Grand Ole Opry* membership in 1962, and encouragement from the soon-to-be-sainted Patsy Cline. Beginning in 1962, she soon accumulated several top ten hits that included "Before I'm Over You," "Blue Kentucky Girl," and "You Ain't Woman Enough (to Take My Man)." While her recordings were firmly in the Nashville Sound mode and style, Lynn's voice was pure unapologetic country and had little of the crossover appeal that Cline personified. Her Appalachian accent and uninhibited country mannerisms endeared her to fans, even those who were more sophisticated.

Loretta Lynn, one of country's most acclaimed female vocalists, often writes songs that reflect the viewpoint of strong women who choose to be independent. *Courtesy of Photofest.*

Lynn had her first number one hit in early 1967 with "Don't Come Home a-Drinkin' (with Lovin' on Your Mind)." "Fist City," "Woman of the World (Leave My World Alone)," and "Your Squaw Is on the Warpath" all cast the singer as an aggressive woman who could deal equally with either erring husbands or women who tried to tempt them. Her songs from the early 1970s, such as the autobiographical "Coal Miner's Daughter" and "One's on the Way," which might be termed a working-class housewife's view of the women's lib movement, probably represented the peak of her success, but she continued to score high on the charts all through the 1970s. Duets first with Ernest Tubb and especially with Conway Twitty added to her laurels as did several CMA awards. Various relatives also launched musical careers—most notably, younger sister Crystal Gayle (b. 1951). In the meantime her autobiography, *Coal Miner's Daughter*, and the popular motion picture version of it, which won an Oscar for actress Sissy Spacek, made her much more of a household name than Kitty Wells or Patsy Cline had ever been.[18]

Decca had some other country girls on their talent roster, but their success paled compared with that of "the Coal Miner's Daughter." One of the best was probably Jan Howard (b. 1930), the former wife of well-known country songwriter Harlan Howard (1929–2003). A native of West Plains, Missouri, where she was born Lulu Grace Johnson, Howard endured two bad marriages, moved to California, and first hit the charts on Challenge Records on a duet with Wynn Stewart. When third husband Harlan Howard came to Nashville to pursue his writing career, Jan came, too, and although their marriage soon disintegrated, her career thrived and she joined the Bill Anderson touring unit in 1965 and the *Grand Ole Opry* in 1971. Her biggest numbers on Decca were duets with Anderson, but she had top ten solo numbers with "Evil on Your Mind" and "Bad Seed." Howard also wrote a quality autobiography, *Sunshine & Shadow*, in 1989.[19] Other women singers who experienced varying degrees of success with Decca included Jeannie Seely, Wilma Burgess, Margie Bowes, and Marion Worth, all of whom also recorded for other labels at some point in their careers.

The first country girl to score hits on RCA Victor was Kentuckian Skeeter Davis (1932–2004), who was born Mary Frances Penick but formed a duet with teenage friend Betty Jack Davis as the Davis Sisters. They had a hit record with "I Forgot More Than You'll Ever Know" in 1953, but Betty Jack died in an auto crash that year, and some time passed before Skeeter got her career back on track in 1958 with "Lost to a Geisha Girl." She had another hit in 1961 with "(I Can't Help You) I'm Falling Too," an answer to the Hank Locklin hit. Her best effort, "The End of the World," went to number two in both pop and country, remaining on the latter listings for twenty-four weeks. She had eight other top ten country hits during the 1960s and spent several decades as a *Grand Ole Opry* regular.[20]

Another RCA Victor contractee, Dottie West (1932–1991), hailed from McMinnville, Tennessee, but came to Nashville by way of Cleveland, Ohio, where she had appeared on local television prior to returning to her home state. Early recording efforts on Starday and Atlantic did little more than attract attention. When she signed with RCA in 1963, her career took off in a bigger way following "Love Is No Excuse," a hit duet with Jim Reeves, and she joined the Opry in 1964. After a string of hits characterized by "Paper Mansions" and "Country Sunshine," she moved to United Artists in 1977 and had fewer but bigger successes, including both solo numbers ("A Lesson in Leavin'" and "Are You Happy Baby?") and duets with Kenny Rogers ("Every Time Two Fools Collide," "All I Ever Need Is You," and "What Are You Doin' in Love"). Meanwhile, West reinvented her image into that of a middle-aged sex symbol that included two marriages to much younger men, each of which lasted about seven years. The failure of her third nuptial, however, coincided with financial reversals that included a bankruptcy and troubles with the IRS. But she still had the Opry, although sadly, she perished after a fatal auto crash on her way to an appearance there.[21]

West may have had more chart entries, but the biggest hit by a country girl in the 1960s came from the voice of Connie Smith (b. 1941). Born in Indiana, Smith grew up in West Virginia and Ohio and gained some experience on local TV programs in the Ohio River cities of Huntington and Parkersburg. However, her big break came when Bill Anderson heard the young housewife sing at Frontier Ranch, a country music park near Columbus, Ohio. Within a year—July 1964—she had her first session. Her first single written by Anderson, "Once a Day," hit the charts in September, was number one by late November, and remained there for eight weeks, becoming the virtual song of the year. Although Smith never had another hit reach the top of the charts, she managed to place a total of twenty-seven of them on the Billboard listings through 1972, many of them in the top ten, including "Then and Only Then," "Cincinnati, Ohio," and "You and Your Sweet Love." Her strong pure country voice led her successor as RCA's top country female, Dolly Parton, to later remark, "There's only three real female singers: Barbra Streisand, Linda Ronstadt, and Connie Smith. The rest of us are only pretending."[22]

Smith found her success to be extremely stressful. Two broken marriages and a considerable amount of mental depression led her to a religious conversion in 1968 and a conscious effort to cut back on career obligations. In 1973, she signed with Columbia and had two top ten hits over a five-year period and ten lesser ones, but the label permitted her to record more religious music. With Monument in the later 1970s, her chart numbers tended to be on the lower end, but she continued to play the Opry and found life more satisfying. Other than some custom albums, Smith's only major record deals were brief—with Epic in 1985 and Warners in 1996—and they yielded little in the way of hits, although the latter could certainly be termed an artistic success. Still she continued to play the Opry; work some show dates; and, as one scholar of her music, Colin Escott—echoing the title of one of her early albums—wrote, "few were born to sing as Connie Smith was born to sing."[23]

The *Porter Wagoner Show* produced two female country stars who recorded for RCA Victor, one of whom attained a stature that surpassed all of her competitors. The first, Oklahoma-born Norma Jean Beasler, known simply as "Norma Jean," came to Nashville as a vocalist with Wagoner's touring unit after brief liasons with both the *Big D Jamboree* in Dallas and the *Ozark Jubilee* in Springfield. After a short stay with Columbia, she signed with RCA in 1963 and remained with the label for a decade, making the charts some twenty-one times, but her best solo numbers, both ranking at the eighth position, were "Go Cat Go" and "I Wouldn't Buy a Used Car from Him." Whether by accident or design, many of her songs took an assertive attitude that engaged in "man-bashing" from a variety of angles. She left the show in 1967 to return to Oklahoma, and with less national exposure her chart ratings declined. However, she eventually returned to Nashville and more recently Branson, Missouri, where she continues to sing.[24]

Norma Jean's replacement, Dolly Parton, eclipsed all other female country women. She had appeared on the *Billboard* country charts over 100 times by the end of 1997, has experienced several crossover hits, has had television specials, owns her own theme park, and has starred in big-budget motion pictures. Born near Sevierville, Tennessee, to a family of Appalachian mountain folk, Parton cut her musical teeth on the *Cas Walker Farm and Home* program on early morning TV in Knoxville and took a bus to Nashville the day after her high school graduation in 1964. After scoring a pair of modest hits on the Monument label, she joined the Wagoner show in 1967 and signed with RCA Victor, where she had her first taste of success later that year with the duet "The Last Thing on My Mind." Her solo efforts made only modest hits until 1970, when her version of "Mule Skinner Blues" followed by "Joshua" and the autobiographical "Coat of Many Colors" established her as a star in her own right.

Dolly Parton left Wagoner in 1974 but continued to accumulate hit records and additional honors. Among the former were the gold records for "Here You Come Again" and "9 to 5," the latter of which also served as the theme for her film about female office workers. Accolades included being named the 1975 and 1976 CMA Female Vocalist of the Year and the 1978 CMA Entertainer of the Year. Moving to Columbia in 1989, she immediately hit the top again with "Why'd You Come in Here Lookin' Like That," "Yellow Roses," and a duet with Ricky Van Shelton, "Rockin' Years." Hit films included *9 to 5*, *Steel Magnolias*, and *The Best Little Whorehouse in Texas*. By the dawn of the new century, Parton was making albums for Sugar Hill with bluegrass accompaniment. Her name helped to launch musical careers for her brother Randy and sister Stella. Parton's theme park, Dollywood, near her hometown of Sevierville, provides hundreds of seasonal jobs for Appalachians and attracts hundreds of thousands of tourists annually. In fact, Dollywood may represent the ultimate in entertainers using their name and wealth to help their home region. Small wonder that the people of Sevier County had a life-size statue of her erected in front of the local courthouse.[25]

Columbia Records and subsidiary label Epic entered the female country singer sweepstakes somewhat late but ultimately turned out a pair of major figures. Lynn Anderson (b. 1947), a native of North Dakota, was the daughter of songwriter Liz Anderson (b. 1930), who had turned out several charted songs on RCA Victor. At age nineteen, Lynn signed with Chart Records and first hit the *Billboard* listings at the end of 1966 with "Ride, Ride, Ride." Several other midlevel hits followed over the next four years, some of which ranked higher, such as "Promises, Promises" and "If I Kiss You, Will You Go Away." Moving over to Columbia in 1970, where her records were produced by husband Glenn Sutton, she soon had a super hit with "Rose Garden," a song allegedly inspired by a popular novel about mental illness, *I Never Promised You a Rose Garden.* The song exhibited strong crossover appeal, being number three on the pop charts as well as spending five weeks at the top in country, and earned Anderson the CMA award as 1971 Female Vocalist of the Year. Over the next three years, she had four more number one hits and numerous lesser ones, but none could ever match the popularity of "Rose Garden," and none ever reached higher than sixty-three on the pop listings. From the mid-1970s, her hits fell back to midrank status, and she went on other labels in the 1980s.[26]

Tammy Wynette (1942–1998) had more staying power, scoring number one hits scattered over a nine-year period and remaining with her original label Epic for a quarter century. A Mississippi-born former hairdresser, Wynette came to Nashville after her first marriage ended and had her first minor hit, "Apartment #9," only weeks after Lynn Anderson's first appearance. She scored even more in 1967 with "Your Good Girl's Gonna Go Bad," "I Don't Wanna Play House," and "My Elusive Dreams," the latter a duet with male country vocalist David Houston (1938–1993). If anything, her 1968 hits "D-I-V-O-R-C-E" and "Stand By Your Man" won her even more acclaim, including the CMA Female Vocalist of the Year honors, an award she received for three consecutive years. In 1969, she married male superstar George Jones, and their stormy six-year marriage provided almost as much fuel for the gossip columns as activities of Hollywood film stars. The Jones-Wynette combination also produced a number of excellent duets, such as "We're Gonna Hold On," "Golden Ring," and "Two Story House."

Wynette's 1979 autobiography, *Stand by Your Man*, dealt frankly with her professional and personal life, including five marriages, and it appeared as a TV movie in 1981. Most of her later chart appearances fell into the middling rank. Part of this decline could be credited to recurring health problems, but she continued to maintain an active presence and win some accolades for simply being a survivor. By the mid-1990s, she was touring and recording with George Jones again, but health problems continued and she expired at the age of fifty-five.[27]

Another female singer who began her ascent to stardom in the late 1960s, Texas-born, California-reared Barbara Mandrell (b. 1948), grew into a country music career from childhood as part of a family group and a talent for being able to play about any type of musical instrument associated with country. Coming to Nashville in 1968, Mandrell signed with Columbia and had a low-level chart entry in 1969 with "I've Been Loving You Too Long" and a more successful duet with David Houston in 1970 with "After Closing Time." She had other midlevel entries both with Houston and by herself, but her first real solo hit came with a cheating song in 1973, titled "The Midnight Oil." Her peak period of popularity came in the later 1970s with such number one hits as "Sleeping Single in a Double Bed," "(If Loving You Is Wrong) I Don't Want to Be Right," and "I Was Country When Country Wasn't Cool." The latter song exemplified the "country-politan" approach (a blend of pop and country) that led this fan of the older, more traditional hard country sound to remark that the song might have been "cool but wasn't very country." Despite her flair for performing songs dealing with cheating and adultery, Mandrell herself lived a lifestyle that epitomized middle-class respectability. She also left Columbia/Epic for ABC/Dot Records and eventually MCA.

From 1980 to 1982, Barbara Mandrell, along with sisters Louise (b. 1954) and Irlene (b. 1957), starred in an NBC Network variety show, *Barbara Mandrell & the Mandrell Sisters*. The program retained popularity but apparently put a great deal of stress and physical strain on the petite blonde star, and she canceled it on her own initiative. In 1984, she suffered severe injuries in an auto crash. The accident seemed to slow her momentum, although she continued to have hit records through the 1980s. In the 1990s, she did a few TV specials and tried her hand at acting, including a dramatic guest spot on the beach adventure series *Baywatch*.[28]

Another popular country girl, Texas-born, Arizona-reared Tanya Tucker (b. 1958), started with Columbia and had hits as a teenager with songs like "Delta Dawn" and "What's Your Mama's Name" in 1972 and 1973, respectively. Somewhat like Conway Twitty, she often favored songs with suggestive titles typified by "Would You Lay With Me (in a Field of Stone)." Switching to MCA, she continued to have hits with the western swing-flavored "San Antonio Stroll" and "Texas (When I Die)." Moving to Capitol in the 1980s, she scored four more number one hits, including "Strong Enough to Bend" and "Just Another Love." She also kept her name in the tabloids with a much publicized romance with Glen Campbell, among other diverse activities. Experiencing more career longevity than many country singers, Tucker still made the top ten a quarter century after "Delta Dawn."[29]

Capitol Records through the 1960s and into the early 1970s continued reliance on its previously contracted female vocalists Wanda Jackson and Jean Shepard. The former began recording in Nashville in 1960 and had a hit the following year with "In the Middle of a Heartache" and continued regular appearances on the charts, mostly in the midlevel category, through 1972. Jackson tended to be more popular in the western states. She left the label to give more emphasis to sacred music after 1973 but also still performed country material. Both she and Shepard also concentrated on the album market to a considerable degree. Shepard, who had been a fixture at the *Opry* since 1955, also recorded with the Nashville Sound from 1958 and had numerous midlevel hits and sometimes better with numbers like "Second Fiddle to an Old Guitar" in 1964. By 1973, she began to feel increasingly lost in the shuffle at Capitol and switched to United Artists, where she had a career rejuvenation with "Slippin' Away" before falling back to lower levels again. Nonetheless, she remained solidly entrenched at the *Opry*.[30]

Meanwhile, Capitol signed some other women, including Texas-born Billie Jo Spears (b. 1937), who had success with "Mr. Walker, It's All Over" and less so with "Marty Gray," one of the first songs to deal the increasing problem of teenage pregnancy. In 1974, Spears followed Shepard to United Artists, where she had a number one hit with "Blanket on the Ground." Other Capitol female singers of the 1970s included Susan Raye (b. 1944), who often toured with Buck Owens and LaCosta Tucker (b. 1951), the older sister of Tanya Tucker.

Other country women had their moment of success. Jeannie C. Riley (b. 1946) had a number one crossover hit with "Harper Valley, P.T.A.," a Tom T. Hall song about middle-class hypocrisy that also won her the CMA Single of the Year award. Despite several other hits, Riley could not build lasting chart success in spite of talent, personality, and all-around charisma. Bobbie Gentry (b. 1944) also had a million seller with "Ode to Billy Joe" but made the charts

only five more times. Melba Montgomery (b. 1938) sang some outstanding duets with George Jones, including her own "We Must Have Been out of Our Minds," and had numerous charted singles before finally having a number one hit with "No Charge" in 1974. With the passage of time, her skills as a songwriter proved more sustaining. Margie Singleton (b. 1935) also had successful duets with Jones, but her highest-ranking solo number reached only number eleven.[31]

While Nashville retained its significance as the major country music center in the 1960s, other challenges to its dominance would surface in later decades. Certainly one of the advantages that "Music City, U.S.A." had over other centers was the ability that its music business executives had to absorb characteristics associated with rivals into its own structure. For instance, in the early 1970s, the construction of a new home for the *Grand Ole Opry* and the adjacent Opryland theme park that

Tom T. Hall wrote "Harper Valley, P.T.A." for singer Jeannie C. Riley. The song won her the Country Music Awards Single of the Year.
Courtesy of Photofest.

opened in 1972 helped make the city a family tourist attraction for more than just attending the *Opry* on a Friday night or a Saturday night. Kids and adults could enjoy the rides and listen to not only country but other types of mainstream American musical groups in the little theater venues scattered over the grounds.

Other things helped keep Nashville as the major country center, including the continuing popularity of the aforementioned syndicated television program *Hee Haw*, where filming took place twice a year. In addition to Roy Clark and Buck Owens, the show had regular guest stars and an array of beautiful women, typified by Gunilla Hutton, Barbie Benton, Misty Rowe, and Marianne Gordon, and country comics, such as Archie Campbell, Roni Stoneman, Stringbean (until 1973), and Grandpa Jones, who performed in a variety of skits, much of it old and rather corny to urban critics but popular nonetheless. In March 1983, The Nashville Network (better known simply as TNN) brought a cable TV network into millions of American homes that featured a variety of country shows, including a segment of the *Opry* as well as talk programs with country stars as guests hosted by such individuals as longtime WSM deejay Ralph Emery (b. 1933) and the popular duo of Charlie Chase (b. 1952) and Lorianne Crook (b. 1957). Unfortunately, the sale of TNN in 1997 to a larger communications conglomerate led to most of the country music programming being canceled by 2000 when it became the National Network. Country Music Television, or CMT, began about a year after TNN as a medium for country music videos, but after 2000, it, too, began "to decrease its emphasis on music in favor of 'lifestyle programs,'" leaving its future as a venue for country music programming in doubt.[32]

THE BAKERSFIELD SOUND

Capitol Records, with its country division headed by Ken Nelson (b. 1911), remained active on the California scene as well as Nashville but had more success on the West Coast, at least with male artists. For instance, the leading country star of the 1960s as defined by compilations in *Billboard* was Texasborn, Arizona-reared Alvis "Buck" Owens (b. 1929), who more than any other artist put Bakersfield on the map as a country music center. Owens gained attention first as a session guitarist at Capitol for artists like Ferlin Husky, Jean Shepard, and Tommy Collins while playing nights at a club in Bakersfield called the Blackboard. He did a few recordings for small labels in the mid-1950s—some under the name Corky Jones—before signing with Capitol in 1957 but did not see any chart action until 1959, when his song "Second Fiddle" peaked at number twenty-four. Like the efforts of Ray Price in the late 1950s, many of Owens's best songs made use of the "shuffle beat." Over the next three years, he placed eight numbers in the top ten and finally got a number one song with the Johnny Russell composition "Act Naturally" in 1963. From 1963 through 1969, he chalked up a total of nineteen number one songs. Some of the more memorable included "I've Got a Tiger by the Tail," "Waitin' in Your Welfare Line," "My Heart Skips a Beat," and, the most successful of all, "Love's Gonna Live Here," which spent sixteen weeks at the top. All this time, he recorded virtually all of his sessions at the Capitol Towers in Hollywood and avoided the studios in Nashville and utilized little if any of the Nashville Sound.

In 1969, Buck Owens did come to Nashville as a costar with Roy Clark (b. 1933) in the CBS television show *Hee Haw*, which started out as a summer replacement program and lasted for twenty-five years, all but two of them in syndication. Buck remained with it until 1986 but even then continued to mostly work out of Bakersfield and from 1970 did most of his recordings in his own studio. His high-level hits began to taper off in the 1970s as he found himself doing humorous numbers like "On the Cover of the Music City News" and "(It's a) Monster's Holiday," but they still made the top ten. A switch in

Roy Clark starred in the CBS hit show *Hee Haw*, a syndicated television program that helped to keep Nashville as a major center for country music.
Courtesy of Photofest.

labels to Warner Brothers in 1976 saw his rankings drop even lower, but a 1988 duet with neotraditional newcomer Dwight Yoakam, the song "Streets of Bakersfield," saw him briefly back on top and led to a comeback tour and some new recordings for Capitol. But for the most part, he has been happily retired from music for nearly two decades and looks after his extensive business activities.[33]

Other Capitol artists associated with Bakersfield included Wynn Stewart (1934–1985), who had several noted songs, especially "Wishful Thinking" and "It's Such a Pretty World Today," and J. C. "Red" Simpson, who favored truck driver songs. However, the only one who really gained long-lasting stardom was Merle Haggard, who eventually accumulated more hits than Owens. Haggard may have found irony in his situation in the 1960s in that he started the decade as a convict in San Quentin and ended it as an emerging country superstar.[34]

Merle Haggard (b. 1937) was born in Bakersfield of working-class parents who had migrated from Oklahoma during the Great Depression (the Haggards, however, always refuted the picture painted in John Steinbeck's novel *Grapes of Wrath*, arguing that they and most Okies were not nearly that poor). Merle grew up an unruly child, got into problems with the law, and eventually wound up in prison for armed robbery, serving two and one-half years. Released in 1960, he went to work as a laborer for his brother, worked in clubs at night, and served a stint as band member for Wynn Stewart. Recording for the small Tally label, his second release, "Sing a Sad Song," peaked at nineteen and a third, "Sam Hill," at forty-five. A duet with Bonnie Owens (former wife of Buck and future wife of Haggard) also made the charts, and "(My Friends Are Gonna Be) Strangers" hit the top ten early in 1965. By that time, he had moved on to Capitol, where he had his first session in April 1965. "Swinging Doors" and "The Bottle Let Me Down," a pair of barroom ballads, ranked high in 1966, and in early 1967, "The Fugitive" gave him his first number one. Many of Haggard's recordings, whether written by him or someone else, identified closely with his own troubled background, such as "Branded Man," "Mama Tried," and "Sing Me Back Home."

In 1969, the Merle Haggard song "Okie from Muskogee" followed by "The Fightin' Side of Me," whatever their meaning, were taken by much of middle America as patriotic songs at a time when political dissension over the Vietnam conflict was rampant. Controversial or not, they elevated the ex-convict to the top ranks of country music stardom, where he remained for the next fifteen years. He shied away from politically controversial material but continued to favor songs that dealt with hard times, such as "Daddy Frank" and "Grandma Harp." Haggard also paid tribute to country music greats of the past with a double album tribute to Jimmie Rodgers, *Same Train, Different Time*; and one to Bob Wills, *A Tribute to the Best Damn Fiddle Player in the World*. Another song, "Leonard," paid tribute to one of his Bakersfield mentors, Tommy Collins. By the time he left Capitol in 1976, he had given that label some two-dozen number one hits.

After a troublesome adolescence that landed him in jail, Merle Haggard found his way through country music. Haggard was most successful for his controversial views of patriotism that he expressed through his songs. *Courtesy of Photofest.*

Merle Haggard continued his period of stardom on MCA and Epic Records. While his efforts from this period were not as memorable as his late 1960s songs, thirteen of them made number one, and his tribute albums to Elvis Presley, Hank Williams, and Lefty Frizzell (the latter two combined in one album) reflected his appreciation for those who came before him. He continued to be a regular on the *Billboard* charts until 1990.[35]

The success of Buck Owens and Merle Haggard and their brand of hard country music notwithstanding, the Bakersfield Sound failed to replace Nashville as the main center of country music. Besides, with each man making the pop top forty one time, neither Owens nor Haggard demonstrated much crossover appeal.

Capitol's West Coast department did produce one star who exhibited a great deal of crossover appeal, but his only connection to Bakersfield seems to have been appearing on some of Haggard's sessions in 1966. Arkansan Glen Campbell (b. 1936) came from as much of a plain-folk background as the Bakersfield stars but went to California only after reaching adulthood. His talents as a guitarist provided him with session work with such pop figures as Elvis Presley, Ricky Nelson, and Frank Sinatra. In 1962, he did a bluegrass-flavored album with a group called the Green River Boys that produced a moderate hit of an old Merle Travis song, "Kentucky Means Paradise," but attracted little more attention until 1966—other than TV guest spots on *Shindig*—when he revived a Jack Scott song, "Burning Bridges." The following year, he had a true crossover hit with "By the Time I Get to Phoenix" and did even better in 1968 with "I Wanna Live" and "Wichita Lineman." Soon after, he had a prime time CBS network TV show, *The Glen Campbell Goodtime Hour*, followed by another major crossover hit with "Galveston." Dabbling in motion picture acting, he appeared in the legendary John Wayne classic *True Grit*. After his TV show ended in 1972, he came back with a revival of Pee Wee King's "Bonaparte's Retreat" and had his biggest hit in 1975 with "Rhinestone Cowboy," which was number one in both pop and country. So, too, was "Southern Nights" in 1977, but for a briefer time. Thereafter his chart ratings slipped a bit, but he continued to have songs on the charts through 1991, even after leaving Capitol for Atlantic America in 1981 and MCA in 1987. Although fan support for Campbell seems not to run as deep as for some artists, one can hardly ignore the fact that he had seventy-five songs on the country charts between 1962 and 1994 as well as twenty-one appearances on the pop top forty lists.[36]

AUSTIN AND THE COUNTRY "OUTLAWS"

In the 1970s, the biggest challenge to Nashville dominance came from the so-called outlaw movement, which developed largely in Austin, Texas, although several mainstream artists with Nashville connections had more than a hand in it. The origins of the Austin scene have been traced to an older bar called Threadgill's and to newer clubs, such as the Armadillo World Headquarters, which opened in a former national guard armory in August 1970. An early figure on the Austin scene was Jerry Jeff Walker (b. 1942), who located there in 1970, but the most famous in the long run was Willie Nelson (b. 1933), who moved there in 1972 after varying flirtations with fame in Nashville. In the words of Bill Malone, the outlaws "were a group of musicians who sought artistic autonomy and the right to roam freely for material and style." In other words, they tended to be more freewheeling than the tighter musical structures associated with the sameness of what the Nashville Sound had become.[37]

A native of Fort Worth, Willie Nelson had been largely reared on a farm by his grandparents and had deejay and songwriting experience in the Lone Star State prior to his 1960 move to Nashville. Some of his songs, such as "Hello Walls" and "Crazy," became hits for others, but his own recordings for Liberty, such as "Touch Me," and then for RCA Victor, like "Blackjack County Chain," made much less of an impact. In 1972, he returned to Texas, shed his clean-cut Nashville image, grew a beard, let his hair grow, and in 1975 scored a huge hit with "Blue Eyes Crying in the Rain," a Fred Rose composition from the mid-1940s. Ironically, some of Nelson's biggest hits that followed came from revivals of old country songs typified by "Remember Me" and "If You've Got the Money I've Got the Time"; but also gospel tradition, such as "The Uncloudy Day"; and one-time pop standards, like "Blue Skies" and "Georgia on My Mind." Still, he continued to have hits with new songs as well, such as "On the Road Again." Several of his songs showed strong crossover appeal, and he was elected to the Country Music Hall of Fame in 1993. Nelson also had duet hits with the other principal symbol of the country outlaw movement, Waylon Jennings: "Good Hearted Woman" and "Mammas Don't Let Your Babies Grow Up to Be Cowboys."[38]

The aforementioned Waylon Jennings (1937–2002) ranked as the second superstar created by the outlaw fad. Like Nelson, Jennings was a native Texan, born in Littlefield and reared in Lubbock, who had brief experience as a band member for Buddy Holly and experience as a deejay. Signing with RCA in 1965, he made the country charts eighteen times in the next five years, scoring number two and three hits with "Only Daddy That'll Walk the Line" and "Brown Eyed Handsome Man," respectively. Yet, like Nelson, he grew increasingly disenchanted with the Nashville establishment and the well-groomed image it had created for him. From 1972, he began producing his own records, used his own band on sessions, increasingly identified with the outlaw movement, and occasionally recorded with Willie Nelson.

As an outlaw, Jennings turned out some major hits, such as "Luckenbach, Texas," "Amanda," and "I've Always Been Crazy," as well memorable tribute songs to past country stars in "Are You Sure Hank Done It This Way" and "Bob Wills Is Still the King." His "Theme from the Dukes of Hazzard (Good Ol' Boys)" resulted in a gold record and his highest ranking on the pop charts. He also had some successful duets with his wife, Jessi Colter (b. 1947), of which "Suspicious Minds" ranked highest at number two. Although Jennings had a number one hit with "Roses in Paradise" in 1987, his popularity waned somewhat thereafter, and he vanished from the charts after 1991.[39]

A third figure associated with the Austin outlaw movement, Tompall Glaser (b. 1933), had earlier been part of the more mainstream country group known alternately as the Glaser Brothers and as Tompall and the Glaser Brothers.

They had enjoyed moderate success on Decca and M-G-M records prior to splitting up in 1973. Glaser had no monumental hits during his fling as a solo artist but did see some chart action with "Put Another Log on the Fire (Male Chauvinist National Anthem)" and a revival of the old Jimmie Rodgers favorite "T for Texas." As the outlaw fad began to wane, the Glaser Brothers reunited in 1979 and had a genuine hit in 1981 with a revival of a Kris Kristofferson pop song, "Lovin' Her Was Easier (Than Anything I'll Ever Do Again)."[40]

Another belated convert to the outlaw image, although not really part of the Austin scene, was Hank Williams, Jr. (b. 1949), who had ridden his family name to fame as a teenage country singer in the late 1960s and early 1970s, but in the mid-1970s, he began to turn to a brand of country rock and grew a beard—partly as a result of a serious facial injury suffered on a Montana hunting trip—and adopted an outlaw appearance. Despite a well-publicized effort to escape from the style and image associated with the original Hank Williams, his most memorable songs often continued to deal with his father in some manner, such as "Family Tradition," "Whiskey Bent and Hell Bound," and "All My Rowdy Friends Have Settled Down." Later efforts included a duet with his father (from an acetate disc) of "There's a Tear in My Beer" and a topical number directed against Saddam Hussein's 1990 invasion of Kuwait entitled "Don't Give Us a Reason."[41]

BACK IN NASHVILLE, NEOTRADITIONAL COUNTRY

Even while the outlaw movement garnered much attention, it could hardly be said to have dominated the country scene, even at its height. For instance, blind pianist Ronnie Milsap (b. 1946), a native of Robbinsville, North Carolina, who personified the tendency of pop and country music to become increasingly similar, had thirty-five number one hits between 1974 and 1989, a figure that almost equaled the combined totals of Nelson and Jennings. While few of Milsap's hits, typified by such songs as "Pure Love" and "Day Dreams about Night Things," seem to have come close to having the impact of "Mammas Don't Let Your Baby's Grow Up to Be Cowboys" or "Luckenbach, Texas" and many seem in retrospect to have been easily forgettable, there is no doubt that he had some fifteen years of high-ranking popularity and that if the Nashville establishment faced something of a challenge from the outlaw movement, it was not about to be replaced.[42]

The early 1980s saw the rise of a movement that also had its day in the sun— what might be termed the neotraditional era. Although some journalists used the term "new country," long-standing observers of the music recognized something of a return of the music to its roots, albeit with some of the smoothness of the Nashville Sound. New-country artists were mostly relative youngsters, often born in the 1950s, who had a feel for the music of their parent's generation.

Although receiving little of the credit, perhaps indirectly the mother figure of the movement was Emmylou Harris (b. 1947). Born in Alabama to a military family that moved frequently, Harris had an early interest in urban folk music before coming to the country field. She had been influenced by Gram Parsons (1946–1973), a former member of the Byrds and the Flying Burrito Brothers and a rock musician with a genuine feel for traditional country, who had worked at fusing the two musical forms prior to his death from a drug overdose. Harris signed a contract with Reprise Records and had a hit in 1975 with a Louvin Brothers composition, "If I Could Only Win Your Love," and another in duet with rocker Linda Ronstadt, "The Sweetest Gift," a song about a mother visiting her son in prison from the 1940s that had been written by Mississippi gospel composer J. B. Coats and recorded by such traditional duets as James and Martha Carson, the Bailey Brothers, and the Blue Sky Boys. Although Harris recorded newer songs, too, and had hits with them, her renditions of such older numbers through the years as "Together Again," "Sweet Dreams," "Making Believe," "Satan's Jeweled Crown," "I'm Movin' On," and "Blue Kentucky Girl" endeared her to traditionalists.[43]

In 1977, young Ricky Skaggs, a veteran of Ralph Stanley's Clinch Mountain Boys and other bluegrass groups, joined Harris's traveling band. Apparently during this period, Skaggs learned something about how to make more traditional songs and music sufficiently acceptable for the Nashville scene of the early 1980s. Skaggs made an album with Harris's help on the Sugar Hill label in 1979, from which a single cut, "I'll Take the Blame," cracked the charts in the spring of 1980. This led to a contract with Epic in 1981, which produced a string of hit songs. Although his music contained more of a western-swing flavor than either bluegrass or honky-tonk, many of his songs came from those latter two styles. For instance, "Crying My Heart out over You," "I Wouldn't Change You if I Could," "Don't Cheat in Our Hometown," and "Uncle Pen" had all been bluegrass standards, while "I Don't Care," "Honey (Open That Door)," "I've Got a New Heartache," and "I'm Tired" were honky-tonkers, three from the repertoire of Webb Pierce. Other hits were new songs, including "Heartbroke," "Highway 40 Blues," "Cajun Moon," "Country Boy," and "Lovin' Only You." He took CMA awards as Male Vocalist of the Year in 1982 and Entertainer of the Year in 1985. Skaggs's hit production dropped sharply after the 1980s, but he continued to be popular on the *Opry* and by the later 1990s had pretty much returned to his bluegrass roots.[44]

If Ricky Skaggs ultimately retreated from superstardom to the sounds of his origins, he fared better than his one-time teenage companion Keith Whitley (1954–1989). Like Skaggs, Appalachian Kentucky native Whitley had cut his musical teeth on the sounds of the Stanley Brothers. He served not one but two stints as a Clinch Mountain Boy and another with J. D. Crowe, but he also admired the vocal styles of Lefty Frizzell and George Jones. Coming to Nashville and signing with RCA in 1984, he had his first chart entry that September. Within two years, his singles were making the top ten, and in 1988, he had a pair of number one hits with "Don't Close Your Eyes" and "When You Say Nothing at All." His third top hit, "I'm No Stranger to the Rain," had just peaked when he died from alcohol poisoning on May 9, 1989. Two posthumous top hits followed along with a number thirteen duet with his wife, Lorrie Morgan (b. 1959), who had been an *Opry* regular since 1984 but did not really experience any top hits, such as "What Part of No," until the early 1990s.[45]

After Ricky Skaggs, the next neotraditional performer to hit the big time was North Carolinian Randy Travis (b. 1959), who emerged as Skaggs was hitting his peak in the mid-1980s. While Ricky Skaggs's repertoire mixed older and newer songs, Travis recorded mostly new songs. His first chart offering released under his real name, Randy Traywick, peaked at number ninety-one in 1979, but "On the Other Hand," "Diggin' up Bones," and "Forever and Ever, Amen" all went number one in 1986 and 1987. He took the CMA Male Vocalist of the Year honors in 1987 and 1988. Early in 1990, his "Hard Rock Bottom of Your Heart" remained at number one for four weeks, an unusual accomplishment in an era when a song seldom lasted at the top for more than a week. In 1993, he cut an album of western songs, *Wind in the Wire*, which placed a couple of songs on the charts and had another top hit with "Whisper My Name," suggesting that he had more longevity in mainstream country than Skaggs.[46]

A third neotraditional figure was Texas-born George Strait (b. 1952), who demonstrated more long-lasting success than either Skaggs or Travis, amassing some thirty-two number one songs and making fifty-four chart appearances between 1981 and 1997, all of them for MCA (the successor to Decca). Strait's music had more of a western-swing flavor than the others and a frequent tendency to mention either Texas or some Lone Star State city in his lyrics. Illustrations of this can be found in such titles as "Amarillo By Morning," "Does Fort Worth Ever Cross Your Mind," and "All My Ex's Live in Texas." He also revived some classic oldies, including Bob Wills's "Right or Wrong" and Tommy Collins-composed, Faron Young hit song "If You Ain't Lovin' (You Ain't Livin')." By 2004, when he had accumulated nearly forty number one songs, MCA released a two-compact disc set containing all of them.[47]

Mother Naomi Judd (left) and daughter Wynonna Judd (right) rocked the country music world with their harmony and glamorous looks.
Courtesy of Photofest.

Female vocalists also made their mark among the neotraditionalists. Like George Strait, Oklahoman Reba McEntire (b. 1954) had a western background. In fact,

In 1996, Patty Loveless won the Country Music Award for Female Vocalist of the Year.
Courtesy of Photofest.

she and her family had rodeo experience, both as entertainers and riders. As a Mercury recording artist from 1976 until 1983, McEntire's early recordings were more in the Nashville Sound vein and only moderate hits, although she did eventually hit the top twice with "Can't Even Get the Blues" in 1982 and with "You're the First Time I've Thought about Leaving" in 1983. Switching to MCA in 1984, she adopted what Mary Bufwack termed a more "back to basics style" and soon had even bigger hits beginning with "How Blue." Through 1997, McEntire had accumulated twenty number one hits, with "Is There Life out There" being perhaps the most significant. In addition, she perhaps has done more as an actress on television than any other female country star being the central figure as a stressed housewife and divorcée in the Warner Brothers cable network sitcom *Reba*. Still, she remains at her roots a country singer.[48]

The atypically successful mother-daughter duo the Judds also attained fame with their harmony duet. Naomi (b. 1946) and daughter Wynonna (b. 1964) had both been born in the northeast Kentucky city of Ashland but moved to California in 1968 and then back east, where they developed their harmonies from listening to records by the bluegrass-folk duet of Hazel Dickens and Alice Gerrard. Settling in Nashville in 1979, they signed with RCA and first hit the charts in 1983 with "Had a Dream (for the Heart)" and a number one in 1984 with "Mama He's Crazy." Thirteen more top hits followed as well as several lesser ones. Glamour played some role in the Judds' success, with Naomi being the more aesthetically attractive of the duo. Naomi retired in 1991, but Wynonna Judd continued as a solo act, known simply by her first name from 1995 on. In her first five years as a single act, Wynonna made the *Billboard* listings nineteen times, including four at number one.[49]

Patty Loveless (b. 1957), another product of Appalachian Kentucky came on the scene. By the 1990s, U.S. Route 23, which ran through the region, of her birth, was becoming known as the "Country Music Highway" because so many noted country and bluegrass music figures had grown up near it. Loveless first hit the charts in 1985 but did not really attain star status until the end of the decade. Songs like "Blue Side of Town" and "Don't Toss Us Away" placed her among the best neotraditional country artists, and with the 1993

"Blame It on Your Heart," she provided writer Harlan Howard with another number one hit. Loveless won the CMA 1996 Female Vocalist of the Year award and by the end of that decade as a guest on a Ralph Stanley and Friends album displayed that she could sing a gutsy traditional rendition of the murder ballad "Pretty Polly" with as much authority as Lily May Ledford. She proved equally adept at such traditional gospel songs as "Daniel Prayed." Not long afterward, she recorded her own bluegrass album.[50]

COUNTRY-POLITAN

By the 1990s—while neotraditional country artists continued to do well—something of a reaction of moving toward a more pop-country mixture also developed. The principal figure to become a superstar in the decade, Oklahoma-born Garth Brooks (b. 1962), exhibited many of the "country-politan" characteristics, although his hit recordings never made anything but the country charts. Brooks's first notable release, "Much Too Young (to Feel This Damn Old)," reached the eighth spot in the spring of 1989, and by the end of 1990, he had accumulated four number one hits—most notably, "The Dance," which spent three weeks at the top, and his best-known song, "Friends in Low Places," which spent the entire month of October atop the *Billboard* listings. In 1991, 1992, 1997, and 1998, he took the CMA Entertainer of the Year award.[51]

Brooks may have been the most commercially successful of the new male stars, but he was actually only one out of many. A pair of Georgians were regulars on the charts through the 1990s: Alan Jackson (b. 1958), who had six million-selling albums to his credit and such hit songs as "Don't Rock the Jukebox" and "Chattahoochie," and Travis Tritt (b. 1963), with the hit song "Here's a Quarter (Call Someone Who Cares)." Oklahoman Vince Gill (b. 1957), who had some background in bluegrass, won five straight CMA Male Vocalist of the Year awards from 1991 through 1995, while fellow Sooner State native Toby Keith (b. 1961) also accumulated a number of hit records, including "Have You Forgotten," that struck a

Native Canadian Shania Twain's status as a country music superstar was achieved when her second album sold over 9 million copies in 1997, making her the all-time top-selling female artist in her field.
Courtesy of Photofest.

patriotic chord with many listeners in the tense moments that followed the September 11, 2001, attacks on the World Trade Center and the Pentagon. Billy Ray Cyrus (b. 1961)—a native of the same region of eastern Kentucky as Skaggs, Whitley, Lynn, and the Judds—had a phenomenal hit in 1992 with "Achy Breaky Heart," and although not a one-hit wonder, he could never seem to equal his initial effort. By the new century, still more new stars, such as east Tennessee's Kenny Chesney (b. 1968), were attaining hit records and accumulating awards.

If the new male superstars of the 1990s may have leaned a bit toward the country side, the new breed of country women tended more toward pop-rock music. The most dynamic of the newcomers, Shania Twain (b. 1965), perhaps illustrated this best. Born Eileen Edwards in Canada and reared mostly in remote Timmins, Ontario, she did exhibit many of the same characteristics of a working-class background with occasional hardship as displayed by such past country icons as Lynn and Parton, but much less of it came through in her music. Signed by Mercury in 1993, her earliest recordings had only limited success, but after marrying rock producer Robert "Mutt" Lange later that year, her recording of "Any Man of Mine" soared to the top in mid-1995 and became a million seller, and her success became phenomenal. Two more number one country hits and another gold record for "Love Gets Me Every Time" made her star shine even brighter. Several of her efforts scored high on the pop charts and her compact disc album releases also sold in the millions. Possessing considerable beauty and displaying a bare midriff in music videos also boosted her career, while her photograph adorned the covers of such mass-market magazines as *People* and *TV Guide*. In the earlier years of her stardom, Twain eschewed touring but eventually did so—and quite profitably, one might add. By 1999, she and her husband resided in a Swiss villa near Lake Geneva, and she had reportedly sold more records than any female in country music history. While her style may be more on the pop side, an appearance with Dolly Parton on the *Oprah Winfrey Show*, where they rendered as fine a rendition of "Coat of Many Colors" as ever heard, suggests than she can indeed belt out a quality version of a country song, just as Ralph Stanley and Patty Loveless can do bluegrass.[52]

Faith Hill (b. 1967), a Mississippi-born blonde, vied with Twain as a country singer and international sex symbol. Her first chart maker, "Wild One" in 1993, went to number one and remained there for an atypical four weeks. Seven more top ten numbers followed. In 1999 the video version of her song, *Breathe*, was described by one writer as being "as glamorous and sexy as a Victoria's Secret commercial." She took the CMA Female Vocalist of the Year award in 2000. A 2002 album, *Cry*, allegedly sold 472,000 copies the first week after it was released. She made her movie debut in *The Stepford Wives* in 2003. After she married Tim McGraw (b. 1967) in 1996, their duet of "It's Your Love" went to the top for five weeks. McGraw had a number of hits on his own, and they became one of the top country duet acts.[53]

Martina McBride (b. 1966) also combined glamour with musical talent, and although she did not make the *FHM Magazine* "One Hundred" sex-symbol list (as did Twain and Hill), she did play a dramatic role as a country singer on "Western Exposure," an episode of *Baywatch*. One of her early chart makers, "Independence Day," in 1994 struck a favorable chord with female listeners, particularly those concerned with abusive men. A native of Kansas, she has been RCA's top country girl for a decade even through it took ten chart appearances for her to hit number one with "Wild Angels" in 1995 and then with "A Broken Wing" in 1997. In 1995, she became an *Opry* member. By 2004, McBride had accumulated six number one hits and taken the CMA Female Vocalist of the Year in 1999, 2002, 2003, and 2004 and was the December 2004 *Redbook* magazine cover girl.[54]

As with male stars, the parade of new country ladies seems endless. Among the better known have been West Virginia's Kathy Mattea (b. 1959), who had a major hit with "Eighteen Wheels and a Dozen Roses" in 1988 and was CMA Female Vocalist of the Year in 1989 and 1990; and Ivy-League educated Mary Chapin Carpenter (b. 1958) with the Cajun-flavored "Down at the Twist and Shout" in 1991, who won CMA Female Vocalist of the Year that year and the next. Other country women who had their moments of glory included Deana Carter, Terry Clark, Sara Evans, Mindy McCready, Jo Dee Messina, Lee Ann Womack, Chely Wright, Michelle Wright, and Trisha Yearwood. Most recently, Gretchen Wilson with a major hit in "Redneck Woman" has been the rage.

Vocal groups also did remarkably well in the generation of the Nashville Sound and after. They also displayed more longevity in the limelight than many single acts. One of the most successful, the Statler Brothers, came out of the Shenandoah Valley town of Stanton, Virginia, to become longtime favorites in Music City and across the nation. Only two of the "Statlers" were really brothers: Harold (b. 1939) and Don Reid (b. 1945). The others included Phil Balsley (b. 1939) and Lew DeWitt (1938–1990), who was replaced in 1982 by Jimmy Fortune (b. 1955). The Statler repertoire included a variety of country, gospel, and pop songs often done in quartet arrangements. More than any other country act, they drew much of their style from such slick singing southern gospel groups as the Blackwood Brothers and the Statesmen Quartet. In 1964, they joined Johnny Cash's touring unit as a feature act and signed with Columbia, where they had their first hit in 1965 with "Flowers on the Wall," a song about loneliness. They did well with "Ruthless" and "You Can't Have Your Kate and Edith, Too" in 1967, but later recordings did not do as well, and Columbia dropped them. However, when they signed with Mercury in 1970, their career went through a rejuvenation with the song "Bed of Roses." Through the remainder of the decade, they scored a string of hits with nostalgia themes, such as "Pictures," "Do You Remember These," "The Class of '57," "Whatever Happened to Randolph Scott," and "Do You Know 'You Are My Sunshine.'" Between 1972 and 1984, they took the CMA Vocal Group of the Year award seven times.

After DeWitt's health problems forced his retirement, the Statlers continued to score hits, some of them written by Fortune, such as "Elizabeth," "My Only Love," and "More Than a Name on a Wall," and did revivals of Ricky Nelson's "Hello Mary Lou" and the Four Knights' "Oh Baby Mine." In 1991, they started a Saturday night variety show on TNN that attracted a large audience and ran until 1999. Not long afterward, the Statlers—who had always retained residence in Stanton, where they were quite active in church and community affairs—chose to retire after thirty-five years of commercial success. In their day, however, as Edward Morris pointed out, the Statlers "were the Great Suburbanizers of country music... who never made the slightest pretense of being dislocated farm boys."[55]

The Oak Ridge Boys rivaled the Statler Brothers as a four-man vocal group. Whereas the latter had been much influenced by southern gospel acts such as the Blackwood Brothers, the Oaks had a considerable background as such, being a descendent of Wally Fowler's Oak Ridge Quartet that dated back to 1945. Over the years, the group went through numerous personnel changes and even disbanded a couple of times. In 1962, they took the name Oak Ridge Boys and in the early 1970s decided to also start doing secular music. By this time, their members consisted of William Lee Golden (b. 1939), Duane Allen (b. 1943), Richard Sterban (b. 1943), and Joe Bonsall (b. 1948). Early efforts on Columbia yielded little success, and they alienated many of their gospel fans when they went to worldly music, but in 1977 their switch to ABC/Dot brought them a major hit with "Y'All Come Back Saloon," and more hits followed, including "You're the One" and "I'll Be True to You." In 1978, they wrested the CMA Vocal Group award from the Statlers.

Moving to MCA in 1979, they had a whole string of hits over the next decade, including sixteen that reached number one. The more notable were typified by "Trying to Love Two Women," "American Made," "Elvira," and "Bobbie Sue," the latter two of which also ranked as pop hits. In 1987, Golden, whose long gray hair and beard made him the most identifiable individual within the Oaks—departed the band and Steve Sanders (1952–1998) replaced him. The group had one of its biggest hits at the end of 1989 with "No Matter How High," but the next year they moved to RCA Victor and their chart ratings began to drop, with only "Lucky Moon" making the top ten in 1991. William Golden returned in 1995, replacing Sanders, who subsequently committed suicide. The Oaks signed with Capitol when Golden resumed his old place in the foursome, but their best days seem to be behind them.[56]

A third vocal group to attain major stardom—Alabama—arrived on the scene at the end of the 1970s, after having had earlier names of Young Country (1969–1972) and Wildcountry (1972–1977). The band was built around three cousins: Randy Owen (b. 1949), Jeff Cook (b. 1949), and Ted Gentry (b. 1952), all of whom hailed from Fort Payne, Alabama, and played instruments in addition to being primarily singers. The fourth man in the group had varied, but by the time they attained status in the music world, Mark Herndon (b. 1955) had filled this spot. They had a couple of minor hits on smaller labels before signing with RCA Victor in 1980, where they had the first of more than thirty number one hits in midyear with "Tennessee River." Among their more notable other big numbers were "Mountain Music," "Love in the First Degree," "Forty Hour Week (for a Livin')," "If You're Gonna Play in Texas (You Gotta Have a Fiddle in the Band)," and "Jukebox in My Mind." Along the way, the group took the CMA Vocal Group award three times and the Instrumental Group award twice.

While achieving stardom and winning awards, Alabama also sold records far in excess of their rivals. Their first *Greatest Hits* album chalked up sales of five million, while two more sold four million each and another one sold three million. A Christmas album sold two million, and eleven others sold at least a million. In 1982, they began an annual June Jam festival in Fort Payne that over a period of fifteen years raised three million dollars for local charities. Critics sometimes complained that they were insufficiently country and "all but indistinguishable from pop." Like the Statlers, Alabama ultimately chose to retire while still at the top.[57]

Several other male vocal groups made some impact on the country scene during the 1980s and 1990s. Among the more notable were the Kentucky-based Exile led by J. P. Pennington (b. 1949), the son of one-time Coon Creek Girl Lily May Ledford of *Renfro Valley Barn Dance* fame. Exile scored several hits in the mid-1980s—most notably, "Give Me One More Chance" in 1984. Diamond Rio included six musicians, none of whom were southerners, sometimes exhibited bluegrass influences, and had a number one hit in 1991 with "Meet in the Middle," the group's first chart entry. Despite their Virginia-sounding name, Shenandoah hailed from Muscle Shoals, Alabama, and boasted several hits—most notably, "Next to You, Next to Me" in 1990. The Four Guys hailed from the Steubenville, Ohio/Wheeling, West Virginia, area, and although they had only three minor chart entries, they performed for many years on the *Grand Ole Opry* from 1967 and also at their own dinner theater in Nashville. Other groups who tasted commercial success bore such colorful names as Confederate Railroad, Kentucky Headhunters, McGuffey Lane, Pirates of the Mississippi, and Restless Heart. The most notable duet of the era was that of Kix Brooks and Ronnie Dunn.

By contrast, female vocal groups did less well. The four Georgia-born Forester Sisters probably did best, making the charts twenty times between 1985 and 1992, five of which—most notably, "Just in Case"—reached the top. A Sevierville, Tennessee, sister trio, the McCarters, had seven chart listings between 1988 and 1990, their best number being "The Gift," which peaked at number four. Two sisters, Janis and Kristine Oliver, performing as Sweethearts of the Rodeo made the charts a dozen times, with "Midnight Girl/Sunset Town" and "Chains of Gold" both reaching number four in 1986 and 1987, respectively. A trio of Texas girls performing as the Dixie Chicks may outdo all the other female; groups they moved toward stardom in the early years of the twenty-first century.[58]

The California music scene that provided country music with a range of stars, from the Hollywood movie cowboys to the Bakersfield honky-tonkers, produced only one major figure in the post-Nashville sound era. Transplanted Appalachian, Kentucky-born Dwight Yoakam (b. 1956) burst on the scene a little later than Ricky Skaggs, Randy Travis, and George Strait and remained somewhat apart from them, in spite of considerable similarity in their musical approach. In 1986, Yoakam had two major hits on the Reprise label, with the second release, a new version of Johnny Horton's "Honky Tonk Man," actually hitting first. "Guitars, Cadillacs, and Hillbilly Music" gained hit status a few weeks later. By 1988, he succeeded in getting Buck Owens out of retirement to do a duet version of one of Buck's lesser numbers, "Streets of Bakersfield," and it hit number one. Later that year, he had another top hit with "I Sang Dixie." Yoakam continued on the charts for another decade, having three songs that peaked at the second spot in 1993, but thereafter his rankings slipped somewhat, although he remains the West Coast's principal contribution to the neotraditional era.[59]

RETROSPECT

Meanwhile, the parade of old and new country stars continues onward. Some artists' careers have faded while others have retained status. In 1993, *Country America* magazine named a dozen individuals as stars of the future. However, after twelve years, only two—Tim McGraw and Shania Twain—have reached the heights of success, and two others—Tracy Bird and John Michael Montgomery—have done quite well. The others have had much less to show for their efforts, and one has not even made the charts at all. Fame in the music business, country or otherwise, tends to be fickle and fleeting. To paraphrase a line from one of Carl Butler's songs from a generation earlier, each evening at sundown in Nashville, they sweep broken dreams off the street.[60]

Still, country music continues to flourish. Like all of American society through eight decades, it has changed in many respects from what it had been in the beginning. If Fiddlin' John Carson and Henry Whitter were alive today, they might not recognize the sounds of the music in an industry they helped to create. Yet the music contains a few threads of content that might still be recognizable. Writer Edward Morris, a longtime reporter on the Nashville scene for *Billboard* who had been musically weaned in his youth on the live country music played on stations like WMMN and WPDX in northern West Virginia, wrote an essay titled "Can Country Survive?" for the magazine *Country Music* in 2000. Noting how the rural environment that initially nurtured the music had nearly vanished and the tendencies of musical forms and styles to amalgamate, Morris nonetheless thought that certain attitudes remained constant. He wrote:

In spite of its endless adaptations, country has values and conventions that have never changed. Nor do they have to. These conventions hold that a simple life is preferable to a lavish one; love is a big deal and not an evening's recreation; poverty is morally superior to wealth; home is where you're from rather than where you are; hard work is ennobling; experience is better than book-learning; family is more a comfort than a burden; and Mom and Dad were right all along. These notions will prevail in country music long after the once-serviceable images of remote farms, dirt roads, coal mines, log cabins and Mama-at-the-stove have been plowed under with hot-rod Fords and two-dollar bills.[61]

Morris obviously thinks that country music will survive, as it has already gone through varied evolutionary change. One hopes he is correct, but only time will tell.

NOTES

1. Bill C. Malone, *Country Music, U.S.A.*, 2nd rev. ed. (Austin: University of Texas Press, 2002), 264–267.

2. Ibid., 256–261.

3. See Chet Atkins with Bill Neely, *Country Gentleman* (Chicago: Henry Regnery, 1974), especially chap. 20, 184–195. See also Bill Ivey, "The Nashville Sound," in Paul Kingsbury, ed., *The Encyclopedia of Country Music* (New York: Oxford University Press, 1998), 371–372.

4. Hank Locklin's musical legacy is well explored in two booklets that accompany his boxed sets: Kevin Coffey, *Hank Locklin: Send Me the Pillow That You Dream On* (Hamburg, Germany: Bear Family Records, 1996), and Otto Kitsinger, *Hank Locklin: Please Help Me I'm Falling* (Hamburg, Germany: Bear Family Records, 1995). One should note that it was the second recording of "Send Me the Pillow That You Dream On" for RCA Victor in June 1957 that helped define the Nashville Sound, rather than the earlier 1949 effort on 4 Star. For Don Gibson, see Richard Weize and Charles Wolfe, *Don Gibson: A Legend in His Own Time* (Vollersode, Germany: Bear Family Records, 1987).

5. Reeves has been understudied by scholars, but a good short sketch is Chet Hagen, *Country Music Legends in the Hall of Fame* (Nashville, TN: Thomas Nelson Publishers, 1982), 92–97; journalist quoted in John Rumble, "Jim Reeves," *Encyclopedia of Country Music*, 435.

6. Ann Malone, "Charley Pride," in Bill C. Malone and Judith McCulloh, eds., *Stars of Country Music* (Urbana: University of Illinois, 1975), 340–356, is the best study, although it is somewhat dated. For a brief update, see *Official Opry History Picture Book* (Nashville, TN: Gaylord Entertainment, 2001), 100–101.

7. Steve Eng, *A Satisfied Mind: The Country Music Life of Porter Wagoner* (Nashville, TN: Rutledge Hill Press, 1992), covers Wagoner's life and TV show. For more detail on his recordings, see Dale Vinicur, *Porter Wagoner: The Thin Man from the West Plains* (Hamburg, Germany: Bear Family Records, 1993).

8. See Jimmy Dean and Donna Meade Dean, *Thirty Years of Sausage, Fifty Years of Ham: Jimmy Dean's Own Story* (New York: Berkley Books, 2004), especially 77–93, which cover his prime-time network TV program.

9. For an excellent analysis of Columbia Records and the label's place in the Nashville Sound, see Rich Kienzle, *The Nashville Sound* (Columbia Records, CT 46032), liner notes. See also Patricia Hall, *Marty Robbins* (Alexandria, VA: Time-Life, 1983).

10. Rich Kienzle, *Ray Price and the Cherokee Cowboys* (Hamburg, Germany: Bear Family Records, 1995), is the best study of Price and his music.

11. Bill Anderson, *Whisperin' Bill: An Autobiography* (Atlanta: Longstreet Press, 1989).

12. John Pugh, "Conway Twitty: Sexy Songs and Good Deeds Keep Him on Top," *Country Music* 5 (March 1977), 39–40; see also Malone, *Country Music, U.S.A.*, 381–382.

13. Beyond lists of his major recordings, few data on Sonny James have been published, but a good start is Robert Adels, "Sonny James: At All Times, in All Ways, the Southern Gentleman," *Country Music* 2 (September 1973), 46–49; see also "Sonny James/Everybody's No. 1," *Country Song Roundup* 24 (March 1972), 8–12.

14. Hall is profiled in William C. Martin, "Tom T. Hall," in Malone and McCulloh, *Stars of Country Music*, 357–376. See also Bob Allen, "Tom T. Hall's Struggle for Balance," *Journal of Country Music* 9:3 (1983), 4–8.

15. For a good view of Roger Miller at the height of his career, see William Price Fox, Jr., "Dang Him," *TV Guide* 14 (November 12–18, 1966), 10–13; his later activity is covered in Barry McCloud, "Roger Miller," in Barry McCloud, ed., *Definitive Country: The Ultimate Encyclopedia of Country Music and Its Performers* (New York: Perigee Books, 1995), 544–546.

16. See Mary A. Bufwack and Robert K. Oermann, *Finding Her Voice: The Saga of Women in Country Music* (New York: Crown Publishers, 1993), 270–277.

17. Ellis Nassour, *Patsy Cline: An Intimate Biography* (New York: Tower Books, 1981), contains a great deal of information, although it is somewhat sensationalized and contains a lot of likely fictional conversation.

18. See Loretta Lynn, *Coal Miner's Daughter* (New York: Warner Books, 1976), and her more recent *Still Woman Enough: A Memoir* (New York: Hyperion, 2002). For a detailed analysis of her pre-1980 recordings, see Laurence J. Zwisohn, *Loretta Lynn's World of Music* (Los Angeles: John Edwards Memorial Foundation, 1980).

19. Jan Howard, *Sunshine and Shadow* (New York: Eagle Publishing, 1987).

20. Skeeter Davis, *Bus Fare to Kentucky: The Autobiography of Skeeter Davis* (New York: Birch Lane Press, 1993).

21. Bufwack and Oermann, *Finding Her Way*, 258–264.

22. Quoted in Colin Escott, *Connie Smith: Born to Sing* (Hamburg, Germany: Bear Family Records, 2001), 3.

23. Ibid., 30; Patrick Carr, "20 Questions with Connie Smith," *Country Music* 178 (March/April 1996), 68–69.

24. Ivan M. Tribe, "Norma Jean: Country Sweetheart of the Sixties," *The Journal* 31 (February 1996), 16–17. See also the German biography by Rainer H. Schmeissnear, *"Pretty Miss" Norma Jean: Das All-American Girl Der Country Music* (Regensburg, Germany: North Country Publications, 1994).

25. The first Parton biography is Lola J. Scobey, *Dolly Parton: Daughter of the South* (New York: Zebra Books, 1977), followed by Alanna Nash, *Dolly* (Los Angeles: Reed

Books, 1978). More insightful is Dolly Parton's autobiography, *My Life and Other Unfinished Business* (New York: HarperCollins, 1994).

26. Bufwack and Oermann, *Finding Her Way*, 390–392.

27. Tammy Wynette, *Stand by Your Man: An Autobiography* (New York: Pocket Books, 1979).

28. Mandrell literature is voluminous. See Charles Paul Conn, *The Barbara Mandrell Story* (New York: Berkley Books, 1989); Louise Mandrell and Ace Collins, *The Mandrell Family Album* (New York: Signet Books, 1983); and Barbara Mandrell, *Get to the Heart: My Story* (New York: Bantam Books, 1991). For a typical magazine piece, see Neil Pond, "Busy B," *Country America* 3 (September 1992), 34–37.

29. Daniel Cooper, Tanya Tucker: Almost Grown," *Journal of Country Music* 17:1 (1994), 10–25; Valerie Hansen, "The Truth about Tanya," *Country America* 6 (October 1995), 42–45.

30. Colin Escott, *Wanda Jackson: Right or Wrong* (Hamburg, Germany: Bear Family Records, 1992); Escott, *Wanda Jackson: Tears Will Be the Chaser for Your Wine* (Hamburg, Germany: Bear Family Records, 1997); Chris Skinker, *Jean Shepard: The Melody Ranch Girl* (Hamburg, Germany: Bear Family Records, 1996).

31. Bufwack and Oermann, *Finding Her Voice*, 315–316, 321, 323–325, 353, 376–377.

32. For background on *Hee Haw*, see Sam Lovullo and Marc Eliot, *Life in the Kornfield: My 25 Years at Hee Haw* (New York: Boulevard Books, 1996); see also Tim Brooks and Earle Marsh, *The Complete Directory to Prime Time Network and Cable TV Shows, 1946–Present*, 8th ed. (New York: Ballantine Books, 2003), 177, 520–521, 1163.

33. Rich Kienzle, *The Buck Owens Collection, 1959–1990* (Los Angeles: Rhino Records, 1995), contains the best analysis of Owens's career, and the accompanying three compact disc set is the best anthology of his recordings.

34. Rich Kienzle, *Wynn Stewart: Wishful Thinking* (Bear Family BFD 15261, 1988), liner notes; see also Mark Humphrey, "Bakersfield," in Kingsbury, *The Encyclopedia of Country Music*, 26. For a good contemporary look at the Bakersfield scene, see Jeff Young, "Buck, Bakersfield, and the Talent Boom: A Music Empire in the West," *The Best of Country Music*, 1 (1974), 106–115.

35. Merle Haggard's early life and career are discussed in Dale Vinicur, *Untamed Hawk* (Hamburg, Germany: Bear Family Records, 1995). See also Paul Hemphill, "Merle Haggard," in Malone and McCulloh, *Stars of Country Music*, 326–339; and Merle Haggard, *Sing Me Back Home* (New York: Quadrangle Books, 1981).

36. Quality material on Campbell is scant and rarely goes beyond fan magazine fluff. For instance, Freda Kramer, *The Glen Campbell Story* (New York: Pyramid Books, 1970), is of little value and dated; it does provide some outline of his early life but generally is no more than what the book's cover blurb calls "the warm, wonderful story of how an obscure singer became" a star. See also "Glen Campbell: A Conversation," *Country Song Roundup* 21 (September 1969), 8–11.

37. For a general discussion of the Austin scene and Outlaw Movement, see Malone, *Country Music, U.S.A.*, 393–404, in particular.

38. The first Nelson biography was Michael Bane, *Willie: An Unauthorized Biography of Willie Nelson* (New York: Dell Books, 1984), followed by Willie Nelson with Bud Shrake, *Willie: An Autobiography* (New York: Pocket Books, 1988). A good

interview article is Bob Allen, "Interview: Willie Nelson," *Journal of Country Music* 8 (1980), 3–28. For a recent look at Nelson, see Robert Baird, "Full Nelson," *Country Music* (June/July 2002), 34–38.

39. R. Serge Denisoff, *Waylon: A Biography* (Knoxville: University of Tennessee Press, 1983), is controversial but covers much of the main part of Jennings's career. See also Waylon Jennings with Lenny Kaye, *Waylon: An Autobiography* (New York: Warner Books, 1996).

40. Mickey Lane, "Tompall—The Outlaw with Style and Flavor," *Nashville Sound* 2 (November 1976), 18–21, 36.

41. See Hank Williams, Jr., with Michael Bane, *Living Proof: An Autobiography* (New York: Putnam, 1979), which is updated somewhat in Bane, "Hank Williams, Jr.: A Country Boy Has Survived," *Country Music* 121 (September/October 1986), 24–29.

42. Bob Allen, "Ronnie Millsap: Feast or Famine," *Country Music* 120 (July/August 1986), 36–40.

43. For good articles on Harris, see Amy Worthington Hauslohner, "Emmylou Harris: Goin' Back to Bluegrass School," *Bluegrass Unlimited* 27 (September 1992), 18–22; Bobby Reed, "Unfettered Angel," *Country Music* 200 (December 1999), 30–32, 34.

44. Geoffrey Himes, "Roots and Wings," *Country Music* (June/July 1999), 54–57, is a good review of Skaggs as both a bluegrass and country star.

45. Robert K. Oermann, "No Stranger to the Rain: Keith Whitley's Promising Rise and Tragic Fall," *Journal of Traditional Country Music* (February 2002), J4–J7.

46. Michael Bane, "Randy Travis: Technicolor Dreams," *Country Music* 179 (May/June 1996), 30–34.

47. Daniel Cooper, "George Strait: The Enigmatic Cowboy," *Journal of Country Music* 18:1 (1996), 15–26; Curt Goettsch, "George Strait," *Country America* 4 (May 1993), 56–59; Michael McCall and Hazel Smith, "Seeing Strait in a Different Light," *Country Music* (April/May 2001), 34–39.

48. Literature on McEntire is voluminous. Biographies include Don Cusic, *Reba McEntire: Country Music's Queen* (New York: St. Martin's Press, 1991); and Carol Leggett, *Reba McEntire: The Queen of Country* (New York: Fireside Books, 1991); as well as the autobiography Reba McEntire with Tom Carter, *Reba: My Story* (New York: Bantam Books, 1994). Typical periodical literature includes Bob Allen, "Reba McEntire: Country Music's Got Another First Lady," *Country Music* 120 (July/August 1986), 26–30; Patrick Carr, "Reba: Still Learning After All These Years," *Country Music* 191 (May/June 1998), 30–34.

49. The Judds attracted considerable biographical attention. For instance, see Bob Millard, *The Judds: A Biography* (New York: Dolphin Books, 1988); and George Mair, *The Judds: The True Story of Naomi, Wynonna, and Ashley* (Secaucus, NJ: Birch Lane Press, 1998). See also the autobiography Naomi Judd with Bud Schaetzle, *Love Can Build a Bridge* (New York: Fawcett Crest Books, 1993). For Wynonna as an individual performer, see Neil Pond, "Wynonna: 'I Am Alone,' Says the Now Solo Judd," *Country America* 4 (June 1993), 28–30; Bob Allen, "Mighty Wynonna Returns," *Country Music* 178 (March/April 1996), 30–34; Gerry Wood, "Wynonna's Starting over after 15 Years," *Country Weekly* 4 (October 21, 1997), 12–16.

50. For an early sketch of Loveless, see Andrew Vaughn, *Who's Who in New Country* (New York: St. Martin's Press), 52–55. For an update, see the Web site www.pattyloveless.com.

51. Brooks has received considerable press, much of it of limited value. Typical is Neil Pond, "Daddy Wants to Stay Home," *Country America* 4 (January 1993), 42–45; and Neil Pond, "Garth's Biggest Fear," *Country America* 5 (May 1994), 50–53. A more useful—albeit somewhat dated—study is that of Robert K. Oermann, "How Garth Conquered America: Marketing the New Nashville," *Journal of Country Music* 14:3 (1992), 16–21.

52. A popular biography written when Twain emerged as a superstar is Scott Gray, *On Her Way: The Shania Twain Story* (New York: Ballantine Books, 1998). Typical of the mass media press on Twain is Nick Krewen, "Shania Twain," *Country Weekly* 4 (October 7, 1997), 20–23; Jeremy Helligar, "Against All Odds," *People* 51 (June 14, 1999), 108–116; Mary Murphy, "The Secret World of Shania Twain," *TV Guide* (November 7, 2004), 38–42.

53. Holly George-Warren, "Change of Faith," *Country Music* (February/March 2003), 22–27; Joanna Connors, "Face to Face with Faith," *Redbook* (October 2004), 142–148.

54. Jancee Dunn, "For Martina McBride There's No Place Like Home," *Redbook* (December 2004), 54–58. See also the Web site: www.martina-mcbride.com.

55. Charles K. Wolfe has a chapter on the Statler Brothers in *Classic Country: Legends of Country Music* (New York: Routledge, 2001), 221–235. See also Brooks and Marsh, *The Complete Directory to Prime Time Network and Cable TV Shows, 1946–Present*, 1128; Edward Morris, "Can Country Survive?," *Country Music* (Winter 2000), 43.

56. See Kimmy Wix, "The Oak Ridge Boys: They've Been Through It All," *Music City News* 30 (September 1992), 8; Bob Millard, "20 Questions with the Oak Ridge Boys," *Country Music* 179 (May/June 1996), 68–69.

57. Alabama is profiled in Valerie Hansen, "Mellowing Megastars," *Country America* 4 (March 1993), 50–54; quoted from, *Baltimore Sun* by Geoffrey Himes in *Encyclopedia of Country Music*, 8.

58. The Forester Sisters are profiled in Michael McCall, "The Forester Sisters," *Country America* 4 (January 1993), 46–49. For the Dixie Chicks, see Bill Friskics-Warren, "There's Your Trouble," *Country Music* (June 2003), 34–38.

59. Tom Lanham, "Dwight Stuff," *Country Music* (April/May 2001), 72–75.

60. Neil Pond, "Most Likely to Succeed," *Country America* 4 (March 1993), 44–49; Butler paraphrased from "Sundown in Nashville," on *Temptation Keeps Twisting Her Arm* (Chart CHS-1051, 1972).

61. Morris, "Can Country Survive?," 42–43.

Biographical Sketches

Acuff, Roy (1903–1992). Roy Acuff became known as the "King of Country Music" during a career that spanned nearly six decades. A native of Union County, Tennessee, Acuff developed a serious interest in music as a profession after a bout with ill health in early adulthood that sidetracked his interest in playing baseball. He worked in medicine shows and on radio at WNOX Knoxville, where he led a band called the Crazy Tennesseans from the mid-1930s. The band played a variety of old-time country mixed with newer pop-influenced sounds. In 1936, the band began recording for the American Record Corporation, where Acuff's first session turned out a variety of numbers—most notably, a holiness-style gospel song, "The Great Speckle[d] Bird." Continuing to record, Roy moved with his band to WSM Nashville and the *Grand Ole Opry* in 1938, where with the increasing popularity of the program on network radio, he became its best-known personality and a major star from the early 1940s.

Roy Acuff appeared in several motion pictures as well as becoming the best-known *Opry* star and a best-seller with Columbia Records. Other well-known songs included "Wabash Cannonball," "The Precious Jewel," "Wreck on the Highway," and "Lonely Mound of Clay." Many of his numbers had sad, sentimental themes. Although his star quality waned somewhat from the early 1950s, he remained a major figure for another generation and the dean of *Opry* performers. He continued recording for such firms as Capitol, M-G-M, Decca, and Hickory and cofounded the Acuff-Rose Publishing Company, one of the first music publishers in Nashville. His band, renamed the Smoky Mountain Boys, contained such popular figures as Beecher (Bashful Brother Oswald) Kirby, fiddler Howard "Howdy" Forester, and harmonica wizard Jimmy Riddle. Active as an *Opry* performer until a few months before his death, Roy Acuff became in 2003 one the few country music figures to be honored with his picture on a postage stamp. Also active in politics, he ran unsuccessfully for governor of Tennessee in 1948.

Recommended Recordings: Roy Acuff: King of Country Music, Properbox 70, 2004 (four-CD set containing 101 of his 1936–1950 recordings); *Roy Acuff: The King of Country Music*, Bear Family BCD 15652, 1993 (two-CD set containing his 1953–1958 recordings).

Allen, Rex (1920–1999). Elvie (nicknamed Rex) Allen became known as the "Arizona Cowboy" and enjoyed a lengthy career, primarily as a western-styled singer, and a few years of motion picture stardom in the latter days of B western films. Allen grew up near the town of Willcox in southeast Arizona and aspired to a career as a radio singer. After minimal success in such varied locales as West Virginia and New Jersey, he finally found security at the WLS *National Barn Dance* in Chicago from the mid-1940s and became an early recording artist for the Mercury label. In 1950, Republic Pictures decided to add another singing cowboy to its film roster, and Allen went on to star in nineteen movies until the studio discontinued the series in 1954. He also starred in a syndicated television program, *Frontier Doctor*, in 1958 and narrated a number of Walt Disney nature films.

Meanwhile, Allen continued to make his mark as a singer, having hits with "Crying in the Chapel" on Decca in 1953 and "Don't Go Near the Indians" with Mercury in 1962. Allen also had a number of successful albums of western music with these firms. Semiretired in the 1980s and 1990s, he lived on a ranch near Tucson, Arizona, in his later days. Allen died as a result of a freak auto accident in 1999, when his driver backed over him. During the 1970s and 1980s, his son Rex Allen, Jr. (b. 1947), also had a fine career as a country and western singer.

Recommended Recordings: Rex Allen: The Arizona Cowboy, BACM CD 013, 2002; *Rex Allen: Songs of the Hills*, BACM CD 051, 2003 (both from Mercury); *Rex Allen: The Last of the Great Singing Cowboys*, Soundies SCD 4101, c. 2000 (from M. M. Cole Transcriptions).

Arnold, Eddy (b. 1918). Eddy Arnold, a west Tennessee native, first gained fame as a mainstream country singer from the mid-1940s. He became known through his appearances on the *Grand Ole Opry* and a string of hit RCA Victor records as the "Tennessee Plowboy," a nickname that reflected his humble origins as a Chester County sharecropper's son. As time went by, Arnold moved away from a hillbilly image to a more pop-country style that appealed mainly to middle-class adults.

After gaining experience by singing for local functions, Eddy Arnold worked on radio in Jackson, Tennessee, and St. Louis, Missouri, until 1940 when he joined Pee Wee King's Golden West Cowboys at WSM and the *Grand Ole Opry*. Branching out on his own as a solo performer in 1943, he began recording for RCA the next year, first for Bluebird and then for Victor. A near instant success, he had numerous hit records—most notably, "Cattle Call," "I'll Hold You In My Heart," "Anytime," and "Bouquet of Roses." In 1948, Arnold left the *Opry* and subsequently starred in a pair of country music movies—*Hoedown* and *Feudin' Rhythm*. While his popularity faded somewhat in the 1950s, he continued to have at least one hit record in every year except 1958. During the mid-1960s, he scored some of his biggest successes with numbers like "Make the World Go Away" and "What's He Doing in My World," which also did well on the pop music listings. Through 1983, Arnold had placed 145 songs on the *Billboard* country charts. Largely retired in recent years, the man who now prefers to be known as "the Last of the Love Song Singers" still made occasional concert appearances into the beginning years of the twenty-first century.

Recommended Recordings: Eddy Arnold: The Tennessee Plowboy, Bear Family, BCD 15726, 1998 (four-CD boxed set); *Last of the Love Song Singers: Then and Now*, RCA Victor 66046 2, 1993 (two-CD boxed set).

Asleep at the Wheel. Asleep at the Wheel is a country band best known for its role in the revival of interest in western swing music. Throughout its existence, the only constant member has been guitarist Ray Benson (b. 1951), a native of Philadelphia who grew up in Paw Paw, West Virginia, and formed the band in 1969 with Reuben Gosfield on steel, Danny Levin on fiddle, and Chris O'Connell as female vocalist. They moved to San Francisco in 1973, where they did their first album, *Comin' Right at Ya'*, for United Artists and then relocated to Austin in 1974, which has remained their principal base. Their best-known songs have included "The Letter That Johnny Walker Read," "Miles and Miles of Texas," and "The House of Blue Lights." Through its thirty-five years of existence, Asleep at the Wheel has undergone numerous changes in personnel but has maintained a consistent sound quality with western swing dominating but also including some honky-tonk and rhythm and blues in its style. The band has had numerous albums on the charts, including a fine tribute to the music of Bob Wills and his Texas Playboys.

Recommended Recordings: Western Standard Time, Epic 44213, 1988; *Tribute to the Music of Bob Wills and the Texas Playboys*, Liberty 81470, 1993.

Atkins, Chet (1924–2001). The fame of Chet Atkins rests primarily on his talents as a suburb guitarist. But as a record producer, he may have been even more influential as one of the major creators of what became known as "the Nashville Sound." A native of Lutrell in rugged east Tennessee, Atkins worked both as a fiddler and guitarist, helping make records with such now forgotten figures as "Pappy Gube" Beaver when barely out of his teens. After a solo session on Bullet Records in 1946, he began recording for RCA Victor in 1947, singing on a few numbers but mostly doing guitar instrumentals. Although he had a few charted hits beginning with his adaptation of the pop standard "Mr. Sandman" in 1955, he placed thirty-two long-play albums on the listings over the next four decades. Working as a session musician, he played on record sessions for many country, rockabilly, and even pop artists. As Atkins progressed, he became considerably more than a country guitarist, excelling in many musical styles.

On the business end of country music, Atkins became manager of RCA Victor's Nashville operation, and something of a protégé of Steve Sholes, who headed Victor's country division. There he labored to make country music more acceptable to middle-class and pop audiences as a prime developer of the Nashville Sound. Eventually, he became a vice president of RCA until he left the company in 1982 and signed with Columbia. Nonetheless, Chet remained a significant—if semiretired—figure on the music scene through the 1980s and 1990s.

Recommended Recording: Chet Atkins & His Gallopin' Guitar, Bear Family BCD 15714, 1993 (four-CD set).

Autry, Gene (1907–1998). Orvon "Gene" Autry ranks as one of the great American success stories. Starting out in adult life as a relief telegrapher for the Frisco Railroad who sang and played guitar for the fun of it, he built a career as a radio recording artist and motion picture cowboy into that of a television producer and multimillionaire businessman who became principal owner of an American League baseball franchise. A native of Tioga, Texas, who grew up in Oklahoma, Autry launched his career in 1928 as a radio singer at KVOO in Tulsa and then went on to New York. His early recordings were more in the style of a white blues singer of the Jimmie Rodgers–Jimmie Davis mold, but he eventually developed his own more western approach to a song. The 1931 recording of "That Silver-Haired Daddy of Mine," a duet with Jimmy Long, marked his emergence as a major musical figure.

In December 1931, Gene Autry became a regular on the *National Barn Dance* at WLS in Chicago. In the summer of 1934, he made a guest appearance as a singing cowboy in the Ken Maynard film *In Old Santa Fe*, which in turn led to him becoming the star in a long series of films first for Republic and later for Columbia. By 1937, he had become the most popular star in western movies, a position he retained until entering the Army Air Corps in World War II. All this time, he continued to have hit records with such songs as "Mexicali Rose," "The Last Roundup," "Back in the Saddle Again," and "Be Honest with Me." He also had a popular CBS network radio program, *Melody Ranch*, from 1940 through 1956 (with time out for military service in 1942–1945), which combined songs with a little comedy and drama.

While his motion picture and recordings continued in the postwar years, his biggest successes came with children's holiday songs, such as "Here Comes Santa Claus," "Rudolph the Red-Nosed Reindeer," "Peter Cottontail," and

"Frosty the Snow Man." From the late 1950s, he recorded sparingly and concentrated more of his time on business ventures and his baseball team. However, his impact on the nation's popular culture from the mid-1930s through the 1950s remains immense.

Recommended Recordings: Gene Autry Blues Singer, 1929–1931, Columbia CK 64987, 1996; *The Essential Gene Autry, 1933–1946*, Columbia CK 48957, 1992.

The Blue Sky Boys: Bill Bolick (b. 1917) and Earl Bolick (1919–1998). Bill and Earl Bolick, who were professionally known as the Blue Sky Boys, personified the brother-duet style that tended to be prevalent in the later 1930s. Natives of Hickory, North Carolina, the Bolicks' soft but tight harmonies, tasteful mandolin, and guitar accompaniment coupled with a repertoire containing old ballads, folk songs, and traditional hymns have long made them favorites with lovers of traditional rural music. Their radio career began in 1935 when they were in their teens as did their recordings for Bluebird in June 1936. With the exception of time spent in military service during World War II, they continued with Bluebird and RCA Victor until 1950, usually working on radio at such locales as WGST Atlanta, WCYB Bristol, and KWKH Shreveport, among others. Their post–World War II recordings featured some backup fiddle, usually played by Curly Parker, and a studio musician on bass fiddle. Their most successful songs date from that period—one a cover of Karl and Harty's "Kentucky" and the other a cover of the Bailes Brothers' "Dust on the Bible." They retired from music in 1951 but did play a few concerts in the 1960s and 1970s, when they recorded again with the same quality as in their prime years. In musical retirement, Bill Bolick worked for the post office in his native North Carolina while Earl returned to the Atlanta area.

Recommended Recording: The Blue Sky Boys: The Sunny Side of Life, Bear Family BCD 15951, 2003 (six-CD boxed set).

Boyd, Bill (1910–1977). Together with his band the Cowboy Ramblers, Bill Boyd, a native of Fannin County, Texas, had one of the best western swing bands and the top-ranking one on Bluebird/RCA Victor. Ironically, Boyd seldom worked the Texas dance hall circuits like the other groups but worked solo as a radio artist at WRR Dallas, assembling the band primarily for recording sessions. Many of the Cowboy Ramblers actually doubled as band members with the Light Crust Doughboys and Roy Newman's Boys, among others. The band recorded well over 225 numbers between 1934 and 1951. Afterward, he worked primarily as a deejay. Boyd also costarred in a short series of western movies as part of a three-man team known as the Frontier Marshals with sometime Cowboy Rambler Art Davis and Lee Powell. Throughout much of his career, Bill Boyd's brother Jim Boyd (1914–1993) worked as a western swing musician with the Cowboy Ramblers as well as other groups, including that of Roy Newman, the Light Crust Doughboys, and briefly his own Men of the West.

Recommended Recordings: The Golden Age of Bill Boyd and His Cowboy Ramblers, Cattle Compact CCD 229, 2000; *Swing with Bill Boyd & His Cowboy Ramblers,* Cattle Compact CCD 234, 2000; *Bill Boyd & His Cowboy Ramblers Singing & Swinging,* BACM CD 049, 2003.

Britt, Elton (1913–1972). Elton Britt had the first certified country music million-selling record and the single most popular World War II song with "There's a Star Spangled Banner Waving Somewhere." A native of Arkansas, where he was born as Elton Baker, the fledgling star began his professional career in 1930 as a member of the California-based Beverly Hill Billies, where he took the stage name "Elton Britt." He later worked with another group called the Wenatchee Mountaineers and recorded his classic yodel song, "Chime Bells," in 1934.

In 1937, Britt signed with RCA and over the next five years cut several numbers for its Bluebird label. His history-making number was recorded on March 19, 1942, slightly over four months after the attack on Pearl Harbor. His other notable patriotic numbers included his 1944 cover of Red River Dave McEnery's "I'm a Convict with Old Glory in My Heart" and "Korean Mud" in 1951. He had several other chart makers for RCA Victor in the years after World War II, some of them duets with Rosalie Allen (1924–2003). His hit production slowed down after 1950, and he left that label in 1955, later recording for ABC Paramont and back with RCA in the late 1960s, where he had a midlevel hit with "The Jimmie Rodgers Blues." He died in 1972 and was buried in Pennsylvania.

Recommended Recording: Elton Britt: The RCA Years, Collectors' Choice Music CCM 031, 1997.

Brooks, Garth (b. 1962). Garth Brooks, a native of Luba, Oklahoma, emerged as the top country star of the 1990s as well as the most successfull recording artist in country music history in terms of sales. Through 1997, his first eight compact discs had accumulated certified sales of fifty-nine million. Recording for Capitol, Brooks had his first hit in the spring of 1989 with "Much Too Young (to Feel This Damn Old)." A string of number ones followed, including "Friends in Low Places," "Two of a Kind, Workin' on a Full House," and "American Honky-Tonk Bar Association."

Brooks's popularity in part derives from his dynamic stage performance, which includes pyrotechnics, such as lights and smoke, that give him some of the same appeal with younger fans as that associated with rock stars. His music contains elements of country-rock, swing, and honky-tonk styles, and his third album, *Ropin' the Wind,* became a spectacular success with four million orders prior to release, becoming the first in the country field to debut at number one. Through 2001, his charted *Billboard* hits numbered eighty-five, and although his last number one came in 1998 with "To Make You Feel My Love," he remained on the charts almost continually for the next three years.

Recommended Recordings: No Fences, Capitol CD 93866, 1990; *Ropin' the Wind,* Capitol CD 96330, 1991; *The Hits,* Liberty CD 98742, 1994.

Brown, Milton (1903–1936). Milton Brown ranks with Bob Wills as one of the major pioneers of western swing music, and had he not died at an early age, he might have become as well known as Wills to later generations of fans and musicians. Brown grew up in Stephensville, Texas, and moved as a teenager to Fort Worth, where he met Bob Wills in 1930. They worked in local bands, such as the Aladdin Laddies and the Light Crust Doughboys, prior to Brown forming his Musical Brownies band in September 1932. Milton served as bandleader and vocalist. His band at various times included such noted swing musicians as Cecil Brower and Cliff Bruner on fiddle, Fred Calhoun on piano, Ocie Stockard on tenor banjo, Bob Dunn on steel guitar, and Wanna Coffman on bass, as well as Milton's younger brother Durwood. Brown's group displayed a great deal of jazz and popular music influences. The addition of Dunn to the band late in 1934 marked the first time that an electrified instrument was used on a country music recording.

The Musical Brownies played Fort Worth radio daily on KTAT and then WBAP. They worked dances regularly at the Crystal Springs Dance Pavillion on the outskirts of town as well as at more distant locales. They made their first recordings on the Bluebird label in 1934 and then switched to the newer Decca Company in 1935 and 1936. In all, they made an even 100 numbers. Milton died as the result of injuries received in an automobile accident in April 1936. Durwood tried to carry on with the Brownies, but the band soon split up and went their separate ways, with fiddler Cliff Bruner achieving some success as a bandleader a few years later in Houston and Beaumont.

Recommended Recording: Milton Brown and the Musical Brownies, 1932–1937, Texas Rose TXRCD 1-5, 1995 (five-CD set includes all recordings that featured Milton and Derwood Brown).

Bruner, Cliff (1915–2000). After the death of Milton Brown, fiddler Cliff Bruner, a native of Texas City, returned in the summer of 1936 to the Gulf Coast, where he formed his own western swing band, the Texas Wanderers, who made their first Decca recordings in February 1937. He had not yet celebrated his twenty-second birthday. Like other former Musical Brownies, Bruner's music demonstrated a great deal of jazz and popular influences. Significant members of Bruner's band included steel guitarist Bob Dunn; vocalist Dickie McBride; Leo and Randall Raley on mandolin and guitar, respectively; and the colorful Aubrey "Moon" Mullican on piano. Although there was some continuity in membership, Bruner changed his band's name in 1939 to simply Cliff Bruner and his Boys. Among the most significant of his 100-plus recordings were the first version of the country standard "It Makes No Difference Now"; an early trucking song, "Truck Driver's Blues"; a swing version of Bill Cox's "Sparkling Blue Eyes"; and Bruner's own instrumental showpiece, "Jessie."

Bruner remained with Decca through 1944, although he had broken up his band earlier and worked briefly with W. Lee O'Daniel and longer with Jimmie

Davis in Shreveport, Louisiana. After the war, he had a session with Mercury in 1947 and with the regional label Ayo in 1949 and 1950. Widowed in the latter year, he left music on a full-time basis and went into the insurance business. In retirement, he did continue to participate in musical activity, particularly when interest in western swing revived and he came to be regarded as something of a living legend in the genre.

Recommended Recording: Cliff Bruner and His Texas Wanderers, Bear Family BCD 15932, 1997 (five-CD boxed set containing all 1937–1950 recordings).

Carlisle, Cliff (1904–1983) and Bill (1908–2003). The Kentucky-born and reared Carlisle Brothers, sometimes working together and sometimes working separately, carved out significant careers for themselves in country music during the 1930s and 1940s. After Cliff retired in 1950, Bill continued on chiefly as a performer on the *Grand Ole Opry*, where he enjoyed several hits, mostly in the comic novelty vein. Cliff had some experience in vaudeville in the 1920s and became a master of the acoustic steel guitar. His early radio experience was gained at WHAS Louisville, and he began recording for Gennett in 1930 with a partner named Wilbur Ball. In 1932, he moved to the American Record Corporation. Many of his earlier songs were blues numbers in the style of Jimmie Rodgers but with original lyrics on such subject matter as the railroad and hobo and cowboy themes, sometimes on the risqué side. Bill began recording in 1933; many of his songs were in a vein not unlike that of his older brother. "Rattle Snake Daddy" was his most noteworthy number. Both brothers recorded for Bluebird in 1936 and 1937 and for Decca in 1938 and 1939 and then went back to Bluebird. Their radio base moved from Louisville to Charlotte; Asheville; Charleston, West Virginia; and Knoxville, where they remained through most of the 1940s and where Bill developed a comic alter-ego named "Hot-Shot Elmer." Cliff and Bill recorded for King in the mid-1940s.

By the time Bill Carlisle joined the *Opry* in 1953, Cliff had retired to become a painter in Lexington, although he sometimes joined in on record sessions. The Carlisles' Mercury efforts in the early 1950s produced some major hits, including "Too Old to Cut the Mustard," "Iz Zat You Myrtle," "Knothole," and "No Help Wanted." Bill continued performing on the *Opry* until a short time before his death at ninety-four.

Recommended Recordings: Cliff Carlisle: Blues Yodeler & Steel Guitar Wizard, Arhoolie/Folk Lyric CD 7039, 1996; *Cliff Carlisle: A Country Legend*, JSP 7732, 2004 (four-CD set); *Bill Carlisle: Duvall County Blues, Early Recordings, 1933–1939*, BACM 034, 2002.

The Carter Family: A. P. (1891–1960), Sara (1898–1979), Maybelle (1909–1978). The Carter Family of Scott County, Virginia, ranks among the all-time greats of country music for the vast legacy of song they recorded between 1927 and 1941. In addition, later generations of Carters continued the family musical traditions into the twenty-first century. The original Carters were A. P. and his wife, Sara, and sister-in-law Maybelle. They journeyed to Bristol in 1927 to begin their musical careers, a career that continued through A. P. and Sara's ultimate separation and divorce. They recorded extensively for Victor until 1934, and then in 1935 and 1940 for the American Record Corporation, for Decca from 1936 to 1938, and finally back to Victor in 1941. Their vast repertoire of song included such numbers that became standards as "Wildwood Flower," "Jimmy Brown, the Newsboy," "Thinking Tonight of My Blue Eyes," "Wabash Cannonball," and "Foggy Mountain Top."

The Carters continued recording through the 1930s even though A. P. and Sara's marriage collapsed early in the decade. In the late 1930s, they worked on radio on the Mexican border stations and in the early 1940s at WBT Charlotte. Sara, who had remarried, moved to California, and A. P. returned to Virginia, where he ran a country store. Maybelle remained in music performing with her three daughters Helen, June, and Anita in such locales as WRVA Richmond and KWTO in Springfield, Missouri. By the early 1950s, they were based in Nashville, where they performed both together and as individuals. Maybelle gained considerable renown in later years for guitar and autoharp skills. June became known somewhat for her comedy work but even more known for her work with husband Johnny Cash, whom she married in 1968. A. P. and Sara's children Janette and Joe maintained a more traditional sound and played regularly on weekends at the Carter Family Fold, built adjacent to where A. P. had his store, near the hamlet of Hiltons, Virginia.

Recommended Recording: In the Shadow of Clinch Mountain, Bear Family BCD 15865, 2000 (twelve-CD boxed set).

Carter, Wilf (1905–1996). Canadian vocalist Wilf Carter, who was also known as "Montana Slim," turned out a steady stream of recordings for a half century beginning in 1933. Although born and reared in the maritime province of Nova Scotia, Carter built an identity for himself associated with the Canadian West, particularly Alberta. While he sang all sorts of country songs, his yodeling cowboy numbers dominated his repertoire, and he eventually composed many of the western songs that he favored. Carter's first recordings dated from 1933 and included the topical "Capture of Albert Johnson" and the yodeling song "My Swiss Moonlight Lullaby." For a time from the mid-1930s until 1940, he also had a CBS network radio program from New York, and he was best known as Montana Slim, particularly in the United States.

In spite of his lengthy career, Carter's life had some tragic moments. In April 1940, he had a serious auto accident and was inactive for more than a year. He spent much of World War II raising cattle on his Alberta ranch but resumed recording in 1944. After RCA dropped him, he signed with Decca in 1954 but returned around 1960 to RCA-Canada, where he continued to record albums until 1988. He also did albums for Apex in Canada and two for Decca in the United States. In addition to his ranch and regular tours, he also operated a motel in Florida for several years. Widowed in 1989, he lived has last years in Arizona but continued to do an annual summer tour in Canada through 1993.

Recommended Recordings: Wilf Carter: The Dynamite Trail, Bear Family BCD 15507, 1990 (1954–1958 Decca masters); *A Prairie Legend*, Bear Family BCD 15754, 1993 (four-CD boxed set containing 1944–1952 Victor recordings); *Cowboy Songs*, Bear Family BCD 15939, 1997 (eight-CD boxed set containing 1933–1941 Bluebird recordings).

Cash, Johnny (1932–2003). Johnny Cash, who grew up poor in Dyess, Arkansas, became a major figure in country music in the mid-1950s. After serving in the U.S. Air Force, Cash embarked on a musical career while still employed as a vacuum cleaner salesman and began recording for Sun Records in 1955. Although part of the rockabilly scene, his songs remained more in a country vein than such contemporaries as Elvis Presley and Jerry Lee Lewis. After four number one country hits on Sun—most notably, "I Walk the Line" and "Ballad of a Teenage Queen"—he moved in 1958 to Columbia, where his string of hits continued, beginning with the western-flavored "Don't Take Your Guns to Town." He remained consistently at or near the top of the charts until the early 1970s and also pioneered in thematic albums on topics ranging from prison songs, comedy numbers, railroads, western ballads, and the plight of Native Americans.

Through all of this, Cash endured and eventually conquered a number of personal problems, married June Carter of Carter Family fame, experienced a religious conversion, and enjoyed high ratings on a network television program from 1969 until 1971. After 1972, he had fewer high-ranking hits but remained in the mid- and lower charts through the mid-1980s, when he began to slow down. Plagued by chronic health problems in his latter years, he continued to remain a revered figure in the country music world even after his death.

Recommended Recordings: The Man in Black, 1954–1958, Bear Family BCD 15517, 1991; *The Essential Johnny Cash, 1955–1983*, Columbia CK 47991, 1991; *16 Biggest Hits*, Columbia CK 69739, 1999 (good sampler of Columbia recordings).

Cline, Patsy (1932–1963). Patsy Cline, who was born Virginia Hensley, has often been considered the all-time number one female in country music. However, much of her greatness derives more from the influence she had on others and from her tragic death, as her own career in the limelight was relatively brief. She grew up in Winchester, Virginia, and its environs and sang with local bands in that vicinity and on the Washington, D.C., scene. In 1954, she signed with Four Star Records, where she experienced a hit in 1957 with "Walkin' After Midnight," which had been leased to Decca. Thereafter her career languished until Owen Bradley assumed direction of her recordings and she experienced another major success in 1961 with "I Fall to Pieces." Other hits followed, including "She's Got You," "Crazy," and "Sweet Dreams." By the time the latter song climbed the charts, Cline had died in a plane crash along with Cowboy Copas and Hawkshaw Hawkins.

Patsy Cline's stature improved immensely in the years following her death. Despite only thirteen appearances on the charts through 1964, she became the first female inductee into the Country Music Hall of Fame in 1973. Loretta Lynn helped make her a legend with the credit she gave her for providing her with encouragement when she first came to Nashville both in her book, *Coal Miner's Daughter*, and in the motion picture of the same name. Cline's life also inspired the biographical film *Sweet Dreams* in 1985, and her recordings have remained in print.

Recommended Recording: The Patsy Cline Collection, MCA 10421, 1991 (four-CD boxed set).

Cooley, Spade (1910–1969). Donnell "Spade" Cooley became a key figure as a western swing bandleader in the middle and late 1940s and as the "King of Western Swing" even helped give the musical style its name. However, his star faded quickly during the 1950s, and after killing his wife received a life sentence behind bars. An Oklahoma-born and Oregon-reared classy fiddler and bandleader, Cooley's career was marked by alternating high and low points.

Even after her tragic death in 1963, Patsy Cline's legacy influenced fellow country musicians. She posthumously became the first woman to be inducted into the Country Music Hall of Fame in 1973.
Copyright © Corbis.

Cooley first gained attention as a fiddler with different western music groups in the Los Angeles area and recorded as a sideman with both Gene Autry and Roy Rogers. During World War II, he organized his Western Swing band, which featured Tex Williams (1917–1985) on vocals, and had several successful hits on Columbia Records—most notably, "Shame on You" in 1945. He also had one of the first popular TV programs on the West Coast and appeared in motion pictures. Within a year, however, Williams left to form his own group, and Cooley had to reorganize. His later efforts on Victor and Decca—while of high musical quality—yielded no hits, and compounded by a drinking problem, his popularity began to wane. On April 3, 1961, Cooley killed his wife during a drunken rage and received a life term in the state prison at Vacaville, California. Eventually, he became a model prisoner and died during a seventy-two-hour leave, two months before his scheduled parole.

Recommended Recordings: The Essential Spade Cooley, Columbia CK 57932, 1994; *Shame On You*, Bloodshot Revival SCD 08022 2, 1996.

Copas, Cowboy (1913–1963). Lloyd "Cowboy" Copas emerged as a major figure in country music in the mid-1940s, but his popularity waned after a

Cowboy Copas came on to the country music scene in the 1940s and again with renewed success in 1960. Copas died tragically in the same plane crash as Patsy Cline in 1963. *Courtesy of Photofest.*

decade. He bounced back with renewed success in 1960, only to die a tragic death in a 1963 airplane crash. An Adams County, Ohio, farm boy by birth and background, "Cope" carved out a western image for himself after several years of musical experience on small radio stations in Ohio and West Virginia.

In his early years, Copas often appeared in conjunction with fiddler Lester Storer, who was known professionally as "Natchee the Indian." His rise to prominence began when he replaced Eddy Arnold as lead vocalist in Pee Wee King's Golden West Cowboys at the *Grand Ole Opry*. He had a solo hit record with "Filipino Baby" at the end of World War II, which launched a separate career and such follow-up numbers as "Signed Sealed and Delivered," "Down in Nashville, Tennessee," "Tragic Romance," and the sacred song "Purple Robe." His career declined in the mid-1950s, and he even tried his hand with the rockabilly flavored "Circle Rock" on Dot. After signing with Starday, his 1960 song "Alabam," a reworking of an old 1926 Frank Hutchison number "Coney Isle," spent twelve weeks at number one, and he had several other midlevel hits on Starday prior to his death.

Recommended Recordings: Copasetic: The Cream of the King–Starday Recordings, 1944–60, Westside WESF 115, 2001; 20 Song Gospel Collection, King KG 0534 2, 2003.

The Country Gentlemen. The Country Gentlemen constituted the first and the most significant of what has come to be known as "progressive" bluegrass bands experimenting with types of music not ordinarily associated with the style. Formed in Washington, D.C., in July 1957, the Gentlemen also played a key role in making that area something of a bluegrass center. Until his death in August 2004, guitarist Charlie Waller (1935–2004) provided the leadership in the group as well as being its only constant member. Other key personnel over the years included mandolinist-tenor John Duffy (1934–1996), banjoists Bill Emerson (b. 1938) and Eddie Adcock (b. 1938), and bass players Tom Grey, Bill Yates, and Ed Ferris.

Early recordings of the Country Gentlemen appeared on the Starday and Folkways label, and while they had one album on Mercury, most of their numerous albums came out on Rebel Records, although they also cut for

Vanguard and Sugar Hill. Their one entry on the *Billboard* country charts came in 1968 when "Bringing Mary Home," a song version of the vanishing hitchhiker folktale, reached number forty-three. Nontheless, their wide-ranging repertoire of folk, rock, and older and newer renditions of country songs rearranged for bluegrass have made them favorites on the club and festival circuits for more than forty years. Waller's untimely death in late summer of 2004 put the band's future in doubt, but with new group members they continued to make appearances into 2005.

Recommended Recordings: High Lonesome: Complete Starday Recordings, Starday CD 3510, 1998; *Country Gentlemen: The Early Rebel Recordings, 1962–1971*, Rebel REB 4002, 1998 (four-CD boxed set).

Dalhart, Vernon (1883–1948). Vernon Dalhart, the best-known pseudonym of Marion T. Slaughter, could in a sense be termed the first country superstar, although many would also argue that he was not really a country singer at all. His rather stiff, formal vocal style could be termed country only by some stretch of the imagination, although many of his songs recorded between 1924 and 1930 found favor with rural folk. Born and reared in Texas, Slaughter received some formal training at the Dallas Conservatory of Music and came to New York in 1910. He soon began making stage appearances and recordings by 1915, singing a variety of popular material.

In 1924, his Victor renditions of "The Wreck of the Old 97" and "The Prisoner's Song" became one of the first million-selling discs. For the rest of the decade, he found success with similar material, much of it of a topical nature, including "The Death of Floyd Collins," "The Santa Barbara Earthquake," "The Wreck of Number Nine," and "The Convict and the Rose." Many of these songs were composed by writers like Carson Robison and Andrew Jenkins, who had a feel for material that country folks found appealing. He made discs for virtually all the major companies of the time under a wide range of pseudonyms, including Al Craver, Tobe Little, and Jep Fuller. From about 1930, his popularity declined rapidly, and he made his last recordings in 1939. His last years were spent in relative obscurity working as night clerk in a Bridgeport, Connecticut, hotel, where he died.

Recommended Recordings: The Wreck of the Old '97 and Other Early Country Hits, Old Homestead OHCD 4167, 1999; *Ballads and Railroad Songs*, Old Homestead OHCD 4129, 2000.

Davis, Jimmie (c. 1899–2000). Jimmie Davis not only had a lengthy career as a country and gospel singer but also served two terms as governor of Louisiana. During his long life, Davis held other public offices; starred in a motion picture depicting his own life; and proved an excellent interpreter of white blues, traditional country, cowboy, and southern gospel songs. He even worked for a time as a history professor. Born in humble circumstances at Beech Springs, he struggled to get a formal education and ended up as a legend. Above all else, he became identified with two of the most memorable songs in country music history, "Nobody's Darling But Mine" in 1935 and "You Are My Sunshine" in 1940.

Davis began his recording in earnest in 1929 for Victor. His sixty-eight sides for that label included both sentimental and blues numbers, but most had modest sales because of the Depression. After signing with Decca in 1934, he began to do fewer rowdy blues songs and veered more toward the sentimental as well as western songs. Since he held a full-time job as a court clerk in Shreveport, Davis was not wholly dependent on record and radio work for his primary source of income, but he became one of Decca's best sellers in the country field. Meanwhile, he was elected public safety commissioner in Shreveport in 1938 and to the state public service commission in 1942. Even after becoming governor, Davis continued to make recordings, and only after his term expired did he become a full-time vocalist. His successful recordings continued with songs typified by "Sweethearts or Strangers" and "There's a New Moon over My Shoulder." From the mid-1950s, his songs included more sacred lyrics, such as "Supper Time" and "Taller Than Trees." He recorded numerous gospel albums on Decca and later Canaan and Plantation. After being widowed, Davis married Anna Carter Gordon of southern gospel's legendary Chuck Wagon Gang. Although the exact year of his birth is unknown, he apparently passed the century mark prior to his death.

Recommended Recordings: Nobody's Darlin' But Mine, Bear Family BCD 15943, 1998 (five-CD boxed set); *You Are My Sunshine,* Bear Family BCD 16216, 1998 (five-CD boxed set).

The Delmore Brothers: Alton (1908–1964) and Rabon (1916–1952). During the 1930s, when harmony duets usually sung by brothers dominated much of the country music scene, the Delmore Brothers ranked among the most popular and influential. With their intricate guitar work, close harmony, and numerous original compositions, Alton and Rabon Delmore set a high standard for other brother teams to follow. Natives of northern Alabama, the brothers grew to adolescence and developed their duet style in an economically poor but culturally rich area of the south, making their first record for Columbia in 1931, when Rabon was only fifteen.

Their next stop was radio station WSM and in 1933 the *Grand Ole Opry* in Nashville, where they gained a national audience and began a seven-year recording career with Bluebird. It was there that their songs typified by "Brown's Ferry Blues," "Gonna Lay Down My Old Guitar," and "Weary Lonesome Blues" gained standard status and where their influence peaked. However, they never really felt like they were accepted by *Opry* management and departed in September 1938 for a series of short stays at radio stations in various parts of the South and powerful WLW in Cincinnati. The Delmores left Bluebird for Decca in 1940, and in 1944 they began recording for King, where they remained until Rabon's death. During their stay with the latter firm, they actually made their best-known song, "Blues Stay Away from Me," as well as a number of songs associated with the country boogie fad of the latter 1940s, such as "Freight Train Boogie" and "Mobile Boogie." Alton Delmore's son Lionel later became a songwriter of some renown in Nashville.

Recommended Recordings: The Delmore Brothers: Classic Cuts, 1933–41, JSP 7727, 2004 (four-CD disc set); *Sand Mountain Blues,* County CCS 110, 1987; *Freight Train Boogie,* Ace CDCH 455, 1993 (latter two discs from King masters).

Dickens, Little Jimmy (b. 1920). James C. Dickens, of short physical stature (4'11"), made use of his size to create a stage persona of a diminutive but brash vocalist who specialized in country novelty songs but could also render a sentimental love song with convincing authenticity. A native of Raleigh County, West Virginia, Dickens began his lengthy career on newly opened WJLS in Beckley in 1939 and after a decade of experience in locales ranging from Ohio and Michigan to Kansas came to Nashville and the *Grand Ole Opry* in 1949. He also signed with Columbia Records and turned out a series of humorous numbers typified by "Take an Old Cold Tater and Wait," "Sleepin' at the Foot of the Bed," "I'm Little but I'm Loud," and "Out Behind the Barn." These songs defined his image and held him in good stead during a period of years in the later 1950s and early 1960s when his recordings made minimal impact.

Dickens bounced back in 1965 and revived his career with another comical song, "May the Bird of Paradise Fly up Your Nose," which he followed with some lesser hits typified by "Country Music Lover." He then switched to Decca and later United Artists, both with modest success. In 1975, he rejoined the *Opry* after an eighteen-year absence. Although he has had increasing bouts with ill health, he remains an occasional performer on the program at age eighty-five.

Recommended Recordings: Country Boy, Bear Family BCD 15848, 1997 (four-CD boxed set); *Out Behind the Barn,* BCD 16218, 1998 (four-CD boxed set).

The Everly Brothers: Don (b. 1937) and Phil (b. 1939). The Everly Brothers were in some respects the most country oriented of the Nashville-based musical groups to find success in the pop field during the early years of rock and roll. As the sons of Ike Everly, a Kentucky contemporary of Merle Travis, the Everlys were reared on country music and came to Nashville as teenagers, having an unsuccessful single on Columbia in 1955. Signing with Cadence Records in 1957, they scored a succession of crossover hits, many of them composed by Boudleaux and Felice Bryant, which critic Colin Escott described as "teenage playlets." These included "Bye Bye Love," "Wake Up Little Susie," "All I Have to Do Is Dream," and "Bird Dog." During the late 1950s, they also recorded an album of old-time country songs in a folk style, which demonstrated their capacity for traditional country harmony on numbers like "Oh So Many Years" and "The Lightning Express."

In 1960, the Everlys switched to Warner Brothers Records, where their hits continued with the more pop-oriented "Cathy's Clown" and "Ebony Eyes." Not long afterward, both brothers entered military service, and they never quite recovered their earlier momentum. They split in 1973 but reunited a decade later and performed several reunion concerts.

Recommended Recording: The Everly Brothers: Classic, Bear Family BCD 15618, 1989 (three-CD boxed set).

Flatt, Lester (1914–1979) and Scruggs, Earl (b. 1924). The team of Lester Flatt and Earl Scruggs together with their Foggy Mountain Boys were the most commercially successful bluegrass band during the 1950s and 1960s. As alumni of Bill Monroe's Blue Grass Boys, Flatt and Scruggs made numerous recordings for Mercury and Columbia that featured Lester's heartfelt vocals and Earl's three-finger banjo-picking style that virtually defined the bluegrass style. They dissolved their partnership in 1969, but each continued solo careers, with Flatt moving back to a more traditional sound while Scruggs and his sons as the Earl Scruggs Revue played a more experimental form of folk-rock music.

Flatt had hailed from Sparta, Tennessee, and Scruggs from Flint Hill, North Carolina, and although both had played in other bands, they met in 1945 as members of Monroe's band. After playing the *Grand Ole Opry* and recording for Columbia with the Blue Grass Boys, they left in 1948 and soon formed the Foggy Mountain Boys, playing on various radio stations in the Appalachians and recording for Mercury from 1948 and for Columbia from 1950. In 1953, they came to WSM on a daily early morning show sponsored by Martha White Flower. However, they did not join the *Opry* until 1955, allegedly because of objections from their former employer Bill Monroe. That same year, they also began a series of weekly television shows in various locales, initially done live but later syndicated on videotape. While the duo gained immense popularity among bluegrass devotees, their emergence as major stars resulted from their appearances, first on the soundtrack of the CBS-TV network comedy *The Beverly Hillbillies* from 1962 until 1969 and second on the soundtrack of the popular motion picture *Bonnie and Clyde* in 1967, which had originally been a 1949 Mercury recording. Ironically, this success also took them further from traditional bluegrass sounds to songs aimed at commercialism and ultimately led to the tensions that brought about their breakup in 1969. Both did well on their own, with Flatt moving to RCA Victor and Scruggs remaining with Columbia, but neither produced the quality of music that had made them so endearing during the 1950s.

Recommended Recordings: Flatt & Scruggs, 1948–1959, Bear Family BCD 15472, 19919 (four-CD boxed set); *Flatt & Scruggs, 1959–1963*, Bear Family BCD 15559, 1992 (five-CD boxed set).

Foley, Clyde "Red" (1910–1968). From the mid-1940s through the late 1950s, Red Foley seemed to be the country star with whom much of the pop music mainstream felt most comfortable. A native of Berea, Kentucky, Foley came to initial prominence at WLS and the *National Barn Dance*, subsequently moving to WLW Cincinnati and briefly to the *Renfro Valley Barn Dance* before returning to Chicago. In 1946, he began a longer stay at WSM and the *Opry*, where he became host of the NBC network portion of the program. Although he made some records in Chicago for the American Record Corporation, his first major success came with his 1941 Decca recording of the sentimental dog song "Old Shep." Later in Nashville, he had other hits, such as "Smoke on the Water," "Tennessee Saturday Night," "Chattanooga Shoe Shine Boy," and "Peace in the Valley," reputedly the first country sacred song to sell a million copies.

In 1954, Foley left Nashville for Springfield, Missouri, where he became host of the ABC-TV network show *Ozark Jubilee* (later called *Country Music Jubilee* and *Jubilee USA*), a program that ran for five years. In 1962–1963, he had a dramatic role in the short-lived situation comedy *Mr. Smith Goes to Washington.* He then returned to Nashville and continued to tour until his death.

Recommended Recording: Country Music Hall of Fame Series: Red Foley, MCA 10084, 1991.

Ford, "Tennessee Ernie" (1919–1991). During the years 1949 to 1956, Tennessee Ernie Ford gained considerable renown on the West Coast with his brand of country music and a vocabulary loaded with down-home phrases and philosophy. A native of east Tennessee, Ford first gained some attention as an announcer and deejay on KXLA radio in Pasadena from 1946, which led to his joining the cast of Cliffie Stone's live program, *Hometown Jamboree.* In 1949, he began recording for Capitol and had successes with country boogie numbers like "Shotgun Boogie" and "Blackberry Boogie," as well as with novelty songs typified by "Mule Train" and "Cry of the Wild Goose." He demonstrated versatility by doing songs with pop songstresses like Ella Mae Morse and Kay Starr. Ford moved first into daytime television and then after his giant crossover hit, "Sixteen Tons," in 1955 moved into NBC prime-time variety from 1956 until 1961. By that time, Ford and his music had moved some distance from his original country image. His 1956 album of sacred songs simply titled *Hymns* became one of Capitol's all-time best sellers, and several other gospel albums followed.

"Tennessee Ernie" Ford became popular in the early 1950s with his innovative style and "down home" philosophy. His versatility throughout the years allowed him to sing pop duets and even gospel music.
Copyright © Corbis.

Tennessee Ernie remained on network television until 1961 and with Capitol Records until 1977, but his days of hit records tapered off after 1956, although his albums continued to do moderately well into the 1960s. A combination of efforts to recast him for the pop audience and the coming of rock and roll terminated his days at the top. In later years, he appeared several times on the *Hee Haw* syndicated TV show.

Recommended Recording: Vintage Collections, Capitol 54319, 1995.

Frizzell, "Lefty" (1928–1975). William Orville "Lefty" Frizzell ranked as one of country music's most original stylists during the era when honky-tonk sounds predominated. Growing up in Texas as the son of an oil field worker, Frizzell was exposed to a rough life and country music at an early age. Married at sixteen, Frizzell sang in clubs and on radio in Paris, Texas, and Roswell, New Mexico, where he wrote some of his better known early songs. In the summer of 1950, he made his first recordings in Dallas, a session that would produce two of his more memorable songs, "If You've Got the Money, I've Got the Time" and "I Love You a Thousand Ways." Frizzell had other top hits over the next two years with "Always Late," "I Want to Be with You Always," "Mom and Dad's Waltz," and "Give Me More More More of Your Kisses." After 1954, he dropped out of the top ten until 1959, when his rendition of "The Long Black Veil" reached number six. He had another number one hit in 1964 with "Saginaw, Michigan." In the last two years of his life, he switched labels to ABC Paramount, and while the critics praised his music from that era, no song ranked higher than twenty-one on the *Billboard* listings. His vocal manner at what his biographer Daniel Cooper termed an "intimate, vowel-bending style of singing" gave him a uniqueness.

Despite his major successes in his first two years with Columbia, Frizzell failed to maintain his momentum. Bad management decisions and personal problems associated with a rowdy lifestyle have often been blamed for his inability to sustain a long career at the top. Nonetheless, he has been credited as a major influence on many other honky-tonk singers who followed in his footsteps, ranging from Merle Haggard to Keith Whitley. In addition to Lefty's work, his younger brothers Allen and especially David also had significant careers as country singers.

Recommended Recording: Lefty Frizzell: Life's Like Poetry, Bear Family BCD 15550, 1992 (Complete recordings in twelve-CD boxed set).

Haggard, Merle (b. 1937). Merle Haggard, along with Tommy Collins and Buck Owens, put Bakersfield on the map as a significant country music center for a decade from the mid-1960s. Overcoming an adolescence laced with criminal behavior that ultimately landed him in prison, he eventually found his niche as a country singer. His first appearances on the *Billboard* charts came in 1963 on the small Tally label, but when his song "(My Friends Are Gonna Be) Strangers" in 1965 made the top ten, it landed him a contract with Capitol, and from 1966, the hits began to flow like water, beginning with "Swinging

Doors." Haggard's most successful songs that attracted widespread attention were "Okie from Muskogee" and "The Fightin' Side of Me," controversial lyrics that were either tongue-in-cheek views of patriotism or captured the frustrations of the "silent majority." Haggard himself has made ambivalent efforts to explain them. Either way, they elevated his fame.

While Merle Haggard's fame and success earned him a full pardon from Governor Reagan of California in 1972 and he accumulated thirty-eight number one hits over two decades and over 100 numbers on *Billboard* charts over thirty years, he continued to be plagued with occasional problems, including a two of failed marriages (both to country singers, Bonnie Owens and Leona Williams), business difficulties, and what might be described as "lifestyle challenges." Along the way, he made some fine tribute albums to the music of such past greats as Jimmie Rodgers, Bob Wills, Hank Williams, and Lefty Frizzell.

Recommended Recording: Untamed Hawk: The Early Recordings of Merle Haggard, 1962–1968, Bear Family BCD 15744, 1995 (five-CD boxed set).

Hawkins, Harold "Hawkshaw" (1921–1963). Nicknamed "Eleven Yards of Personality," Hawkshaw Hawkins demonstrated himself to be one of the best honky-tonk singers in country music in the generation following World War II. Unfortunately, his death in a plane crash cut short a career that deserves to be better remembered. A native of Huntington, West Virginia, Hawkins had some early experience on local radio there and in nearby Charleston and Ashland, Kentucky. After army service in World War II, he signed with King Records and secured a spot at the *World's Original Jamboree* at WWVA Wheeling, where with brief exceptions he remained until 1953. Some of his more memorable recordings from this period included "Sunny Side of the Mountain" and "Moonlight on My Cabin." In addition, he performed tasteful covers of other artists' hits, especially Ernest Tubb, but also Hank Williams and Pee Wee King. Seeking new territory he went to the *Ozark Jubilee* and then to the *Grand Ole Opry* in 1955.

While he proved a popular entertainer who could not only charm an audience but render convincing renditions of almost any kind of song from old-time and country boogie to saga and rockabilly, a signature hit eluded him. Moving to RCA Victor in 1953 and to Columbia in 1959 before returning to King in 1962, he finally found it with "Lonesome 7-7203." However, by the time it peaked at four weeks atop the charts in May 1963, Hawkins had died in a March 7, 1963, airplane tragedy that also took the lives of Patsy Cline and Cowboy Copas. Hawkins's widow, Jean Shepard (b. 1933), also had a lengthy and successful career in country music.

Recommended Recordings: Hawkshaw Hawkins: 22 Greatest Hits, DeLuxe DCD 7812, 1997 (King masters); *Hawk*, Bear Family BCD 15591, 1991 (three-CD boxed set containing RCA Victor and Columbia masters).

Hay, George D. (1895–1968). A nonmusician but a significant figure, George D. Hay, who was nicknamed "The Solemn Old Judge," is best known as the man who formed and directed the *Grand Ole Opry* through somewhat more than its first twenty years as a radio institution. A native of Indiana, Hay went into newspaper work after World War I and soon became a popular radio announcer. At WLS Chicago in 1924, he worked as an emcee on what soon became the *National Barn Dance*. When he came to WSM a few months later as radio director, Hay began inviting persons who played traditional music to appear, and from November 1925 it became a regular program, taking the name *Grand Ole Opry* in 1927. For the next several years, he pretty much had charge of the show. With the passing of time, his influence began to wane, although he appeared in the 1940 motion picture *Grand Ole Opry*. By the end of the 1940s, he had pretty much left the show, and he eventually moved to Virginia Beach, where he died.

Hofner, Adolph (1916–2000). Adolph Hofner led western swing bands in south Texas for more than fifty years. Of a German-Czech ethnic background, his brand of Texas swing sometimes reflected this influence, and he made some recordings of that type of music as well. Both Adolph and his brother Emil (b. 1918) also developed an interest in Hawaiian music, and the latter became quite proficient on the steel guitar. As swing musicians, both Hofners worked and recorded with Jimmy Revard and his Oklahoma Playboys around San Antonio. Adolph also recorded for Bluebird as solo act from 1938 and formed his own band the Texans in 1939. Brother Emil and top-notch swing fiddler J. R. Chatwell became key figures in most of Hofner's band lineups over the years.

In 1940, Adolph had a hit with "Maria Elena" and soon switched to OKeh and Columbia, where his band took the name the San Antonians. He went to California for a time, where he was known as Dub Hofner, but by 1946 had returned to San Antonio. In 1950, the band received another name, the Pearl Wranglers, for their sponsor Pearl Beer. Hofner recorded in the 1950s for Decca and Imperial and afterward for the Sarg label. Hofner and the band remained active well into the 1990s, but age and declining health ultimately began to take its toll on the venerable band leader.

Recommended Recording: Adolph Hofner: South Texas Swing, Arhoolie CD 7029, 1994.

Jackson, Wanda (b. 1937). Wanda Jackson began her musical career as a teenager in Oklahoma City in the early 1950s and matured into one of the top female singers of the 1960s. In addition to being a fine singer of straight country songs, Wanda had a capacity to deliver rockabilly-style songs perhaps more convincingly than any other female performer. She also had much more sex appeal than any other country girl of her generation.

Wanda Jackson began regular radio appearances on KLPR radio in Oklahoma City and made guest appearances at the Trianon Ballroom with Hank Thompson and his Brazos Valley Boys. This led to a contract with Decca Records and a first session in March 1954, six months prior to her seventeenth birthday. Her only Decca recording to gain much attention was the duet "You Can't Have My Love" with Thompson's front man Billy Gray. Moving to

Capitol, she had more success with both country and rockabilly, and while none of the latter achieved real hit status, songs like "Fujiyama Mama," "Honey Bop," and "Let's Have a Party" are regarded as classics of the genre. Her country songs, such as "Right or Wrong" and "In the Middle of a Heartache," gave her consistent chart placings for a dozen years from 1960 through 1973. Jackson also did some quality concept albums during the mid-1960s. From the mid-1970s, she focused more attention on sacred music in the Uniteds States, but she still toured Europe with some frequency, where her rockabilly fans continued to turn out in droves for her concerts. Leaving Capitol in 1973, Jackson turned to gospel music and had several quality albums for Word and Myrrh. In demand for rockabilly concerts in Europe, she did not entirely forsake that type of music and continued to perform in both styles well into the 1990s from her base in Oklahoma City.

Recommended Recordings: Right or Wrong, Bear Family BCD 15629, 1992 (four-CD boxed set of Decca and Capitol recordings through 1962); *Tears Will Be the Chaser for Your Wine*, Bear Family BCD 16114, 1997 (eight-CD boxed set containing 1963–1973 Capitol recordings).

Jennings, Waylon (1937–2002). Along with Willie Nelson, Waylon Jennings became a key figure in the country music "outlaw" movement of the 1970s. Growing up in Littlefield, Texas, Jennings's first taste of show business came with a radio show in Lubbock, and his first taste of the big time came as a sideman with rock-and-roll legend Buddy Holly. After Holly's tragic death, it took Jennings some time to reascend the musical ladder, but he took a major step when he began recording for RCA Victor in March 1965. His songs consistently made the charts through the later 1960s—most notably, "Only Daddy That'll Walk the Line" and "Brown Eyed Handsome Man." Nonetheless, the singer felt increasingly straitjacketed by the Nashville establishment and desired to get control over his own recording sessions, which eventually met with success.

Along with Willie Nelson at Columbia, Jennings emerged as the leading beneficiary of the country outlaw era of the middle and late 1970s. Jennings and Nelson's duet single of "Good Hearted Woman" took the CMA Single of the Year award, and they had an even bigger hit with "Mammas Don't Let Your Babies Grow up to Be Cowboys" in 1977. Jennings also had major solo hits with "Luckenbach, Texas," "I've Always Been Crazy," and "Amanda." He continued to rank high on the charts though the early 1980s but began slowing down somewhat as the decade progressed, making his last chart appearance in 1991. Jennings's wife, known professionally as "Jessi Colter" (b. 1943), also had a noteworthy career, making the charts several times, some of them being duets with Waylon.

Recommended Recording: The Essential Waylon Jennings, RCA Victor 668572, 1996.

Jim and Jesse (McReynolds) (1927–2002/b. 1929). The brother duet of Jim and Jesse McReynolds, together with their band the Virginia Boys, attained status as one of the finest bluegrass acts in a career that spanned some fifty years. Natives of Coeburn, Virginia, the brothers began under the influence of the popular duets of the 1930s, developing a tight harmony with mandolin-guitar accompaniment. Jim and Jesse began their radio careers at Norton, Virginia, in 1947, played at numerous stations over the next several years, and began recording in 1951 as two-thirds of the Virginia Trio. Signing with Capitol in 1952, they became a full bluegrass band and recorded twenty songs over the next three years. Later they recorded for Starday and Columbia and worked radio and television in Alabama, Florida, and Georgia. Through the 1960s, they had several albums and singles on the Epic label, seven of which made the *Billboard* charts, some that were a mixture of country and bluegrass. As favorites on the festival circuit, they were known for their high standard of professionalism, flawless harmony, and Jesse's unique mandolin style. Both brothers encountered health problems in the later 1990s, but Jesse continued on after Jim's death, with a Virginia Boys band that included his grandson Luke McKnight.

Recommended Recordings: Jim & Jesse, 1952–1955, Bear Family BCD 15635, 1992; *Jim and Jesse: Bluegrass and More*, Bear Family BCD 15716, 1993 (five-CD set containing all Columbia and Epic recordings); *The Old Dominion Masters*, Pinecastle PRC 9001, 1999 (four-CD set).

Jones, George (b. 1931). In a career that has stretched through a half-century, George Jones has encountered several highs and lows while gaining the status of a living legend in the process. For better or worse, he not only became the quintessential honky-tonk singer but frequently lived the life of his songs. Growing up in Beaumont, Texas, Jones began singing at an early age (on radio from 1949) and also acquired the drinking habits that would periodically plague him into middle age. After a hitch in the Marine Corps, he returned to Beaumont and made his first record for Starday in January 1954. By the fall of 1955, he experienced his first hit with "Why Baby Why." Moving on to Mercury in 1957, he had his first number one in 1959 with "White Lightning."

In the early 1960s, Jones moved on to United Artists and then to Musicor and finally to Epic in the 1970s. He continued to experience hit records with all of the labels, such as "The Race Is On" and "Walk Through this World with Me." He also had notable numbers with duet partners—most notably, Melba Montgomery (b. 1938). In 1969, he married Tammy Wynette (b. 1943) and both during and after their stormy six-year marriage had successful duets with her typified by "We're Gonna Hold On" and solo hits such as "The Grand Tour." Nonetheless, failure to control his drinking ultimately ended their marriage, and he hit another personal low following the divorce but had the CMA single of the year and one of his biggest hits in 1980 with "He Stopped Loving Her Today." A fourth marriage in 1983 brought more stability to his personal life and still more hit songs, such as "Who's Gonna Fill Their Shoes" and "The One I Loved Back Then (The Corvette Song)." His 1996 autobiography, *I Lived to Tell It All*, made the best-seller lists. Perhaps the most heavily recorded figure in country music history, his *Billboard* chart appearances alone through 2001 totaled 165, with 142 in the top forty and 78 in the top ten, but only twelve at the first spot (including the duets).

Recommended Recordings: George Jones: 50 Years of Hits, Bandit 220/22-2, 2004 (three-CD set); *The Best of George Jones, 1955–1967*, Rhino 70531, 1991.

Jones, Louis M. "Grandpa" (1913–1998). Grandpa Jones had one of the longest and most notable careers in country music history as a musician and comedian in spite of having almost no hit records. A longtime radio, recording, and television artist, Jones earned widespread respect as an advocate for traditional country music. A native of western Kentucky who grew to adulthood in Akron, Ohio, Jones began his radio career in Cleveland in 1929, worked with Bradley Kincaid in 1935, went on his own in 1937 at WWVA Wheeling, and appeared on other radio stations, including WSM and the *Opry* in 1946–1951, 1952–1956, and from 1959 until his death.

Grandpa Jones began recording for King in 1944, both as a solo artist and in company with Merle Travis and the Delmore Brothers as the Brown's Ferry Four. While he had no hits as such, most of the songs that made him famous were done for this label, including "Good Old Mountain Dew," "Old Rattler," "Tragic Romance," and "Eight More Miles to Louisville." Later on he went with RCA Victor, Decca, Monument, and finally CMH. His only hit records were a 1959 spoof on the rock-and-roll song "The All-American Boy" and a 1962 revival of Jimmie Rodgers's "T for Texas." While many of his numbers ranked in the humorous vein, he could render heart songs, hymns, and traditional ballads with authority, sometimes in duet with his wife Ramona (b. 1925) and other family members. Jones may well have gained his widest audience on the television show *Hee Haw*, on which he appeared as a regular during the program's entire twenty-four-year run (1969–1993). His 1984 autobiography, *Everybody's Grandpa*, ranks among the most astutely written books of its type.

Recommended Recordings: Grandpa Jones: Everybody's Grandpa, Bear Family BCD 15788, 1992 (five-CD boxed set containing all Monument recordings); *Country Music Hall of Fame Series*, MCA D 10549, 1992.

Kincaid, Bradley (1895–1989). Bradley Kincaid, the "Kentucky Mountain Boy," is the first person to become a country star on the basis of his radio appearances. A native of Garrard County, Kentucky, he had limited opportunity for education until entering Berea Academy at the age of nineteen. After military service in World War I, he returned to Berea and completed his secondary education and then went on to attend the YMCA College in Chicago. While in the Windy City, he began singing at WLS radio's *National Barn Dance* in 1926. Kincaid's rendition of old ballads like "Barbara Allen" and Victorian songs like "The Letter Edged in Black" struck a favorable chord with listeners. His appearances there, which were heard nationwide, made him a popular figure, and the profits from the sale of his songbooks enabled him to pay college expenses and graduate with money in the bank. In 1930, he moved on to WLW Cincinnati and then to other stations, mostly in the northeastern United States. He later returned to WLS and then in 1944 to WSM and the *Grand Ole Opry*.

Kincaid also had an extensive recording career beginning with Gennett, then Brunswick, Bluebird, Majestic, and, last, Capitol in 1950. However, his fame rested more on radio programming and sale of songbooks. In 1949, he went to Springfield, Ohio, where he ran a radio station and a music store and retired from active performing in the early 1950s. In 1963, he made a series of long-play albums for the Bluebonnet label and during the 1970s made some limited personal appearances.

Recommended Recording: Mountain Ballads & Old-Time Songs, Old Homestead OHCD 4107, 2001.

King, Frank "Pee Wee" (1914–2000). Pee Wee King (born Francis Kuczynski) was a Polish American accordion player who led a western-style band. As a composer, his song "Tennessee Waltz" ranked as one of the most successful country songs of all time and ranked high on the popular charts as well. With his Golden West Cowboys, King played a significant role in both the spread and modernization of country music in the decade following World War II. A native of Wisconsin, where he worked in a polka band as a teenager, King entered country music as part of a backup band supporting *National Barn Dance* star Gene Autry on tours, which took him to Louisville. He next went on his own to Knoxville and then to Nashville and WSM, where he led the Golden West Cowboys. The band undoubtedly benefited from the management skills of Joe L. Frank, who became Pee Wee's father-in-law. King himself led the band, but it usually depended on others for lead vocals, including such figures as Eddy Arnold, Lloyd Copas, and eventually Henry Redd Stewart (1921–2003), who also served as cowriter on many of the songs associated with Pee Wee.

The Golden West Cowboys really came into their own at the end of World War II when they began recording for RCA Victor. Over the years, their hits included—in addition to "Tennessee Waltz"—"Bonaparte's Retreat," "Slow Poke," "You Belong to Me," and "Changing Partners." King took his band to Louisville in 1947, where they had a quality TV show for a decade and had programs on other stations as well. The popularity of King's brand of music began to erode after the coming of rock and roll, but he continued to work extensively through the 1960s and to be a revered figure, from his Louisville home, among the elder statesmen of the music scene.

Recommended Recording: Pee Wee King and His Golden West Cowboys, Bear Family BCD 15727, 1994 (six-CD boxed set containing all RCA Victor recordings).

Krauss, Allison (b. 1971). Allison Krauss is the best representative of the younger breed of bluegrass musicians. A fiddler from Illinois, Krauss became something of a child prodigy on that instrument. In 1987, she signed with

Rounder Records and soon displayed her prowess as a vocalist. Many younger persons felt attracted to her folksy soprano voice. Her third album, *I've Got That Old Feeling*, in 1990 with her band Union Station placed an emphasis on newer material and helped earn her membership on the *Grand Ole Opry* in July 1993, even though her only chart appearance had been "Steel Rails," which appeared for one week at the seventy-third spot. Later, in 1995, her rendition of "When You Say Nothing at All" reached number three and took the CMA Single of the Year award as well as the Female Vocalist of the Year award.

In 1993, Krauss did a somewhat more traditionally oriented gospel album with the Cox Family of Cotton Valley, Louisiana. By November 1997, Krauss's *Now That I've Found You: A Collection* racked up certified sales of two million copies—the only bluegrass album in history to achieve this distinction (the soundtrack of *O Brother, Where Art Thou?*, on which Krauss appeared, later also sold two million). Her work as a session musician and harmony vocalist has also been in demand.

Recommended Recordings: I've Got That Old Feeling, Rounder CD 0275, 1990; *Now That I've Found You: A Collection*, Rounder CD 0325, 1995.

Lee, Brenda (b. 1944). Brenda Lee (born Brenda Tarpley) first gained fame as a child prodigy in the mid-1950s on the *Ozark Jubilee*, where she earned the nickname "Little Miss Dynamite." A native of Georgia whose father died when she was nine, Brenda's music helped support her widowed mother and put her siblings through college. After her TV appearances, she signed with Decca in 1956 and cut country favorites like "Jambalaya" and rockabilly like "Bigelow 6200." She had a modest crossover success with "One Step at a Time" and the holiday classic "Rockin' Around the Christmas Tree" all under her belt before she turned sixteen. During the 1960s, most of her music was aimed at the pop market, where she had thirty-seven numbers in the top forty from 1960 to 1967, including "I'm Sorry" and "I Want to Be Wanted." Popular in Europe as well as America, Lee's versatility enabled her to sing everything convincingly, from pop oldies to country and rock.

In 1967, Brenda Lee returned to the country charts with "Johnny One Time." She remained there through the mid-1980s, with nine of her songs making the top ten. "Big Four Poster Bed" came in highest at number four. Known for her dynamic stage show and ceaseless activity, Lee became one of the few figures to be inducted into both the Country Music Hall of Fame and the Rock and Roll Hall of Fame.

Recommended Recording: Brenda Lee: Little Miss Dynamite, 1956–1963, Bear Family BCD 15772, 1995 (four-CD boxed set).

Lewis, Jerry Lee (b. 1935). Jerry Lee Lewis is known as one of the most dynamic and unpredictable figures in American musical history. Emerging on the national scene in 1957 with his "pumping piano" and wild rockabilly vocals, he took the music world by storm and then came crashing down after the story of his marriage to his thirteen-year-old cousin became known.

Nonetheless, Lewis slowly rebuilt his career and became a country star again in the later 1960s, although not without a share of controversy and bizarre incidents that continued to plague him. Still, the so-called Killer manages to come across for better or worse as a true American original.

A native of Ferriday, Louisiana, Lewis had ample exposure to both hillbilly and African American music styles in his youth. Moving to Memphis in 1956, he signed with Sun Records, and his rendition of "Whole Lotta Shakin' Going On" became a top crossover hit early in 1957, as did the follow-up, "Great Balls of Fire." Then, while on a British tour in late May 1958, the facts of his December 12, 1957, marriage to Myra Brown became public. Shortly afterward, the tour was canceled and the Killer's career virtually collapsed, going from big concert halls to one-nighters in the Deep South. But he slowly came back, and from 1968, he appeared on the country charts again with regularity, as highlighted by such major hits as "What's Made Milwaukee Famous," "To Make Love Sweeter for You," "There Must Be More to Love Than This," "Me and Bobby McGee," and "Chantilly Lace." He never really recaptured his strength in the pop market, and his rocky lifestyle continued to be marred by tragedy, scandal, illness, and narrow escapes from death. Age has finally slowed the Killer down, but as author Jimmy Guterman once concluded, "he remains unquenched."

Recommended Recordings: Classic Jerry Lee Lewis: Complete Sun Recordings, Bear Family BCD 15420, 1992 (eight-CD boxed set); *Mercury Smashes*, Bear Family BCD 15784, 2000 (ten-CD boxed set).

The Light Crust Doughboys. The Light Crust Doughboys constituted one of the longest-lived western swing aggregations. Sponsored by Burrus Mills Light Crust Flour, early members included Bob Wills and Milton Brown, who rank as the main creators of the style. When this twosome departed to start their own groups, manager W. Lee O'Daniel (1890–1968) hired other musicians and continued on with radio programs and a Vocalion recording contract. After O'Daniel left to form his own company, the Doughboys remained under Burrus Mill sponsorship. Key members over the years included tenor banjo player Marvin Montgomery, fiddlers Clifford Gross and Kenneth Pitts, guitarists Muryel Campbell and Jim Boyd, and pianist John "Knocky" Parker.

The Doughboys disbanded during World War II but reorganized in 1946 and have continued to exist in some form ever since. Montgomery was considered the leader until his death in 2001. The band recorded steadily for the American Record Corporation until 1941 and again in 1947 for King. Their connection with Burrus Mill ended about 1952, but they kept the name and continued playing as a part-time group. In 1969, they even began to record again and did a 1997 album with gospel legend James Blackwood.

Recommended Recordings: The Light Crust Doughboys: Western Swing Memories (1936–1941). Bronco Buster CD 9019, 1997; *Lone Star State Swing; 26 Original Tracks from 1935 to 1941*, Cattle Compact CCD 261, 2002.

The Louvin Brothers: Ira (1924–1965) and Charlie (b. 1927). The Louvin Brothers took the brother duet style of the 1930s through the post-World War II era of country music into the 1960s. With Ira's mandolin and high tenor vocals along with Charlie's guitar and vocal leads, the Louvins (original name Loudermilk) probably reached the pinnacle of the style. After their split in 1963 and Ira Louvin's tragic death in 1965, Charlie Louvin carried on with success for some years as a solo country singer and *Grand Ole Opry* star.

Natives of the Sand Mountain area of northern Alabama, Ira and Charlie started their radio career in Chattanooga in 1942. They continued on a variety of stations in Knoxville, Memphis, and Birmingham until joining the *Opry* in February 1955. After recording briefly for Apollo and Decca in 1947 and 1949, respectively, they had a longer stay with M-G-M in 1951 and Capitol from 1952 until their dissolution. Ira's original songs, both sacred and secular, typified respectively by "The Family Who Prays" and "When I Stop Dreaming," contributed to their success. Despite their musical quality and numerous original songs, the coming of rock-and-roll influences also limited their commercial appeal. The resurgence of country during the rise of the Nashville Sound era undoubtedly contributed to Charlie's strengths and his hit Capitol recordings in the later 1960s and 1970s. Interest in Louvin songs has continued to uphold their reputation as a musical force, and their recordings have remained in print.

Recommended Recording: Close Harmony, Bear Family BCD 15561, 1992 (eight-CD boxed set).

Lynn, Loretta (b. 1935). Loretta Lynn's life has often been hailed as one of the great American success stories; she was a girl who rose from the poverty of Appalachian Kentucky and an early marriage to fame and wealth as a country singer. But Lynn also became one of the two most significant female vocalists in the history of the music. Her achievements as a singer along with her triumphs over adversity and occasional tragedy have become symbolic of the inner strengths found in American womanhood.

A native of Johnson County, Kentucky, Loretta Webb resided in the coal camp of West Van Lear until she married Oliver "Mooney" Lynn in 1949 and moved to the state of Washington. Ten years and four children later, she made some recordings for the tiny Zero label and promoted them through her own and Mooney's efforts. The song made the charts and led to a contract with Decca and a move in 1961 to Nashville, where she joined the cast of *The Wilburn Brothers* TV show and in 1962 the *Grand Ole Opry*. From 1962, she was constantly on the charts for the next twenty-four years and had sixteen number one hits. Her peak period of popularity came in the later 1960s and early 1970s, when her hits included such songs as "You Ain't Woman Enough (to Take My Man)," "Don't Come Home a-Drinkin' (with Lovin' on Your Mind," "One's on the Way," and the autobiographical "Coal Miner's Daughter." The latter also became the title of her best-selling autobiography, which also became a 1980 motion picture hit. Many of Lynn's songs reflected the viewpoint of a woman who chose to cease being a victim, and although she was hardly a part of the women's liberation movement, listeners probably identified her with it to some degree. While her recordings have nearly vanished from the charts, she remains a living legend on the country scene. Recently widowed, phase two of her life story is told in the book *Still Woman Enough*.

   Recommended Recording: *Honky-Tonk Girl: The Loretta Lynn Collection*, MCA 11070, 1994 (three-CD set).

McBride, Martina (b. 1966). Along with Faith Hill and Shania Twain, Martina Schiff McBride ranks as one of a triumvirate of female singers to reach superstar status in the 1990s. A native of Kansas, she went to Nashville and sold T-shirts for Garth Brooks until signing with RCA Victor, where she had her first chart maker with "The Time Has Come" in May 1992. However, her 1994 song of domestic abuse, "Independence Day," garnered the most atten-

tion from critics, and "Wild Angels" provided McBride with her first number one hit. Other top hits followed, including "A Broken Wing," "Wrong Again," "I Love You," and "Blessed." She joined the cast of the *Grand Ole Opry* in November 1995 and took her first of four CMA Female Vocalist of the Year awards in 1999.

   Recommended Recordings: *Wild Angels*, RCA Victor 66509, 1995; *Evolution*, RCA Victor 67516, 1997; *Timeless*, RCA Victor 724252, 2005.

McEntire, Reba (b. 1954). From the mid-1980s to the mid-1990s, Reba McEntire reigned as the queen of country music, amassing four CMA Vocalist of the Year awards in that period and sixteen of her twenty-one number one hits in that decade. Oklahoma-born and the product of a rodeo background, where she worked with a family group called the Singing McEntires, Reba signed with Mercury in 1975 and had her first chart entry the following May. Most of her early efforts had only modest success until 1980, when "(You Lift Me) Up to Heaven" rose to number eight. After that, fans took more notice, and in 1982–1983, she had back-to-back top hits

Oklahoma-born Reba McEntire earned four Country Music Awards for Vocalist of the Year between the mid-1980s and the mid-1990s. In addition to singing, she has proven herself as an actress on the Warner Brothers sitcom, *Reba*. *Courtesy of Photofest.*

with "Can't Even Get the Blues" and "You're the First Time." Not long afterward she signed with MCA, where her signature song "How Blue" hit the top in January 1985. The next week she joined the cast of the *Grand Ole Opry* and took home the first of her CMA awards that fall.

Reba McEntire's career peaked in 1987, but she remained almost as high for the next three years. Her last Mercury album sold more than a half million copies, but fourteen of her MCA albums sold at least a million each, with her *Greatest Hits Volume Two* selling at least four million. In 1990, she began to appear in made-for-TV movies and from 2001 starred in her own sitcom, *Reba*, on the Warner Brothers cable network.

Recommended Recordings: The Best of Reba McEntire, Mercury 824342, 1985; *Greatest Hits*, MCA 5979, 1987; *Greatest Hits Volume Two*, MCA 10906, 1993.

Macon, Uncle Dave (1870–1952). David Macon, known as "Uncle Dave," is remembered as the first real star on the *Grand Ole Opry* and also as one the major recording artists of the first years of commercial country music. Less obvious, but no less significant, is the role that Macon played as a link between the music of the nineteenth-century minstrel tradition and country music. As a banjo player with a flair for comic songs, Macon served as an inspiration for later figures that included Grandpa Jones, David "Stringbean" Akemon, "Old Joe" Clark, and LeRoy Troy.

A native of Warren County, Tennessee, Macon spent part of his youth growing up in Nashville, where his parents ran a hotel favored by theatrical, vaudeville, and minstrel performers, which gave young David a chance to learn the songs, music, and techniques he later brought to the country entertainment world. As an adult, he farmed, ran a freight hauling business for a time, and then became a vaudeville artist himself. He became one of the first country recording artists—for Vocalion—in 1924 and went on to also make discs for Brunswick, Gennett, OKeh, and finally Bluebird and was quite active until 1938. Perhaps even more important, he became a regular on the *Opry* from late in 1925 until a few weeks before his death in 1952. He also appeared in the 1940 Republic picture *Grand Ole Opry* as a featured performer. His best-known songs included such numbers as "Keep My Skillet Good and Greasy," "Late Last Night When Willie Came Home," and "Rock About My Saro Jane."

Recommended Recordings: Keep My Skillet Good and Greasy, Bear Family BCD 15978, 2004 (nine-CD set containing complete recordings and DVD of 1940 film *Grand Ole Opry*); *Country Music Hall of Fame Series*, MCA CD 10546, 1991 (sample of Vocalion–Brunswick cuts).

Mainer's Mountaineers: J. E. Mainer (1898–1971) and Wade Mainer (b. 1907). Mainer's Mountaineers proved to be an important musical link between the older fiddle bands of the 1920s and what emerged in the mid-1940s as bluegrass music. Actually, except for a brief period in the mid-1930s, there were two Mainer groups, one led by the older brother J. E., a competent if somewhat rough fiddler, and the other often styled the Sons of the

Mountaineers led by two-finger-banjo picker Wade. The Mainers hailed from rugged Buncombe County, North Carolina, but were residents of the Piedmont town of Concord, near Charlotte. They started in radio about 1932 at WBT Charlotte under the sponsorship of Crazy Water Crystals, but at one time or another were also based in Raleigh; Asheville; Columbia, South Carolina; and other radio stations in southern cities.

In August 1935, Mainer's Mountaineers—featuring both brothers, Zeke Morris, and John Love—made their first recordings for Bluebird. One song, "Maple on the Hill," featured Wade and Zeke in a duet and became a hit. Not long after their second session, J. E. and Wade formed separate groups, and later, Zeke Morris and his brother Wiley formed the Morris Brothers. J. E.'s most frequent recording group included DeWitt "Snuffy" Jenkins, George Morris, and Leonard Stokes. Wade's key band members included Clyde Moody, Jay Hugh Hall, and Steve Ledford. Both Mainers made numerous influential recordings for Bluebird through 1941. In the 1940s, both recorded seperately for King. J. E. remained based in Concord with a band that sometimes included his children. He continued recording until his death, most frequently for Rural Rhythm. Wade moved to Michigan in 1953 and played only in a few churches for some years. After retirement, he and his wife Julia made numerous recordings, mostly for Old Homestead, and personal appearances. Both remained semiactive into the early years of the twenty-first century, and at the age of ninety-seven, Wade put on a full show to entertain well wishers at his birthday party.

Recommended Recordings: Wade Mainer's Mountaineers: Volume I, 1935–1936, Old Homestead OHCD 4043, 2004 (actually includes both J. E. and Wade); *Wade Mainer: Early and Great Sacred Songs*, OHCD 4013 (1935–1941 recordings); *J. E. Mainer's Mountaineers: Run Mountain*, Arhoolie CD 456 (1962 recordings); *Wade and Julia Mainer: In the Land of Melody*, June Appal JA0065, 1992 (1991 recordings).

Martin, Jimmy (1927–2005). Former Bill Monroe band member Jimmy Martin built a fifty-year career as leader of a bluegrass group that emphasized a strong hard-driving traditional sound that earned him the nickname "King of Bluegrass." Martin displayed his musical strengths during an eighteen-year career with Decca and MCA Records along with stints as a regular on both the *Louisiana Hayride* and *Wheeling Jamboree*. A longtime favorite on the bluegrass festival circuit, Martin also displayed an ill-timed talent for demonstrating a brash attitude that likely limited his success at crucial moments.

Martin hailed from Sneedville in Appalachian Tennessee and honed his skills on radio in Knoxville before joining Monroe's Blue Grass Boys in 1949 and subsequently recording several sessions with him on Decca. Along the way, he had a short liason with Bobby Osborne on King Records and a somewhat longer one with the Osborne Brothers on RCA Victor. On his own from 1955, Jimmy Martin and the Sunny Mountain Boys signed with Decca and began making bluegrass history with the help of such band members as Paul Williams on mandolin-tenor vocal and J. D. Crowe on banjo. Martin's rendition of such numbers as "Hit Parade of Love," "Sophronie," "Sunny Side of the Mountain," and the trucker song "Widow Maker" all became classics of the genre. Band members came and went, but the Sunny Mountain Boys—augmented by Martin's strong vocal and perfect timing on rhythm guitar—maintained a consistent quality in sound and style. After 1974, he left MCA, which had absorbed Decca, and continued to record quality material for Gusto. In recent years, health problems slowed him down, and early in 2005, he was diagnosed with terminal cancer. He passed away in May 2005.

Recommended Recording: Jimmy Martin and the Sunny Mountain Boys, Bear Family BCD 15705, 1994 (five-CD boxed set containing all RCA Victor and Decca/MCA recordings).

Monroe, Bill (1911–1996). Bill Monroe is best remembered as the "Father of Bluegrass Music," but before that he made up half of the Monroe Brothers. Bill with his brother Charlie (1903–1975) had one of the most influential mandolin-guitar harmony duet teams of the mid-1930s. After each Monroe went his own way in 1938, both had innovative successful careers, but that of Bill and his Blue Grass Boys evolved by the mid-1940s into what became widely recognized as bluegrass music. For a half-century, Monroe and a succession of band members pursued the development of the style. It is hardly surprising that many of the best-known figures in bluegrass served their apprenticeships with the master-creator.

The Monroes were natives of the hamlet of Rosine in southwestern Kentucky and received exposure to a wide variety of musical styles that became ingredients in bluegrass, including old-time fiddle bands and African American blues. After their parents' deaths, the brothers sought work in Hammond, Indiana, which eventually led them into show business during the Depression. Bill and Charlie worked at various radio stations in Iowa and the Carolinas. In 1936, they began recording for Bluebird, eventually placing sixty numbers on disc—most notably, "What Would You Give in Exchange for Your Soul?"—before their breakup in 1938. Bill then organized the Blue Grass Boys, working on different stations and recording for Bluebird until arriving at WSM Nashville in 1940. His music was not yet bluegrass, although it did contain many elements of the style. His first true bluegrass band crystalized about 1946 with such members as Earl Scruggs on banjo, Lester Flatt on guitar, Chubby Wise on fiddle, and Howard Watts on bass. They recorded for Columbia, turning out such standards as "Blue Moon of Kentucky," "Little Cabin Home on the Hill," "Will You Be Loving Another Man," and a number of sacred songs. After the initial band broke up, Monroe hired other musicians, including Mac Wiseman, Jimmy Martin, Carter Stanley, and Don Reno. In 1950, Monroe switched to Decca, continuing to turn out such standards as "Uncle Pen," "My Little Georgia Rose," and "Highway of Sorrow." Continuing to record, to perform at the *Opry*, and from the mid-1960s to play at bluegrass festivals, Monroe remained musically active into the 1990s as a generally uncompromising advocate for the style he had created.

Recommended Recordings: The Essential Bill Monroe, Columbia CD 52478, 1992; *Bill Monroe: Blue Moon of Kentucky*, Bear Family BCD 16399, 2002 (six-CD boxed set containing all Bluebird and Columbia recordings); *Bill Monroe: Bluegrass, 1950–1958*, Bear Family BCD 15423, 1989 (four-CD boxed set containing Decca recordings).

Montana, Patsy (1908–1996). Patsy Montana (born Ruby Blevins) became country music's first female solo star and created the image of the yodeling cowgirl in the process. Born in Hot Springs, Arkansas, she went to California at seventeen and had her first experience in show business with a cowgirl act as part of Stuart Hamblen's program. Later returning to Arkansas, she met and briefly recorded with Jimmie Davis on Victor. In 1933, she auditioned for WLS at Chicago and became a female vocalist with accompaniment by the Prairie Ramblers. In 1935, her American Record Corporation cut of "I Wanna Be a Cowboy's Sweetheart" became the first major hit by a female singer in the country and western field. Although Montana recorded a wide variety of other songs, such as "Rodeo Sweetheart," "I Wanna Be a Cowboy's Dream Girl," "The She Buckaroo," and "Swing Time Cowgirl," none matched the popularity of her biggest hit.

Patsy left Chicago in 1940 but continued to be active for a number of years, recording for Decca and RCA Victor. In 1939, she appeared in the movie *Colorado Sunset* with Gene Autry. Her radio base varied from Los Angeles to Hot Springs, Arkansas. In 1952, she settled in Los Angeles, which became her home thereafter, and she remained semiactive musically into her eighties and made albums for Sims and Birch records.

Recommended Recording: The Best of Patsy Montana, Collector's Choice CCM-185, 2001.

Nelson, Willie (b. 1933). Through 1997, Texas-born Willie Nelson could claim the distinction of having had the most gold and platinum albums of any other country artist (George Strait may have surpassed this record by the time of the next compilation). He also ranks with Waylon Jennings as a prime mover and shaker in the "country outlaw" era. Nelson had some achievements as a mainstream country songwriter and artist in Nashville during the 1960s. However, only after his return to Texas in 1970 did he adopt a counterculture image and really emerge as a major star. Ironically, with the exception of his duets with Waylon, the songs that really thrust him to the top were four songs from a generation earlier: "Blue Eyes Crying in the Rain," "Remember Me," "If You've Got the Money I've Got the Time," and the gospel favorite "The Unclouded Day."

Willie Nelson gained attention as a songwriter with compositions like "Hello Walls," "Crazy," and "Fuzzy How Time Slips Away," but with two exceptions on Liberty and a contract with RCA Victor, none of his other charted recordings hit the top ten. However, from 1975, he began turning out hits regularly for the next sixteen years. These included a mixture of old pop songs, such as "Blue Skies" and "Georgia on My Mind," as well as new songs typified by "On the Road Again" and "My Heroes Have Always Been Cowboys." By 1993, he had accumulated a total of 114 listings on the *Billboard* charts, twenty of which had been number one. Nelson's creativity has taken some personal toll as he has encountered domestic problems, tax troubles, persistent rumors of drug usage, and the suicide of a son. Yet, he has proven himself a survivor.

Recommended Recording: Willie Nelson: Super Hits, Columbia CK 64184, 1994.

O'Day, Molly (1923–1987). Molly O'Day (born Lois LaVerne Williamson) could likely have been country music's first female superstar had she not opted to leave the commercial music world for evangelistic work after less than a dozen years. Nonetheless, Molly and her husband Lynn Davis (1914–2000) left a small but significant legacy of hard country Appalachian-styled solos and duets made for Columbia between 1946 and 1951. Her style and repertoire also made an impact on other female singers of her generation, most notably, Wilma Lee Cooper and Rose Maddox of Maddox Brothers and Rose fame.

As a native of Pike County, Kentucky, Molly absorbed the music of the few country females she heard on radio during the middle and late 1930s, such as Lulubelle Wiseman, Patsy Montana, Texas Ruby, and Lily May Ledford, as well as the traditional sounds of Appalachia and combined them into a style uniquely her own. At the age of sixteen, she began singing on WCHS radio in Charleston, West Virginia, and subsequently at Williamson, Beckley, and Bluefield, where she married guitarist Leonard "Lynn" Davis in April 1941. They subsequently worked on other stations in Louisville, Birmingham, and Dallas before coming to WNOX Knoxville in mid-1945. In 1946, she signed with Columbia, where she cut such signature songs as "Tramp on the Street," "Matthew 24," "Poor Ellen Smith," and "Don't Sell Daddy Any More Whiskey." However, following a 1950 conversion experience, both she and Lynn eschewed secular music, and she finished her contract singing only sacred songs. As part of their evangelistic work, the couple made gospel albums in 1962 and 1968 and later had a gospel radio program broadcast from their home in Huntington, West Virginia.

Recommended Recording: Molly O'Day, Lynn Davis and the Cumberland Mountain Folks, 1946–1951, Bear Family BCD 15565, 1992 (two-CD set).

The Osborne Brothers: Bobby (b. 1931) and Sonny (b. 1937). Although they sometimes departed from the pure acoustical sound, the Osborne Brothers constituted one of the most influential bluegrass groups during the 1960s and 1970s. Natives of Hyden, Kentucky, who grew up near Dayton, Ohio, the Osbornes first played bluegrass music in southwestern Ohio, developed a tight harmony trio, and took it first to the *Wheeling Jamboree* and then in 1964 to the *Grand Ole Opry*. Recording initially on local labels and then for longer stints with M-G-M and Decca, Bobby and Sonny created some good original bluegrass, including their rendition of Cousin Emmy's "Ruby, Are You Mad" and one of the best-known bluegrass classics, "Rocky Top."

Older brother Bobby entered the professional music world by first joining the Lonesome Pine Fiddlers in 1949 at WHIS Bluefield and recording with them on Cozy Records. A little later when Bobby was in military service, Sonny worked as a sideman with Bill Monroe and recorded for Gateway in Cincinnati, sometimes with Bobby when he was on leave. Back from service in 1953, the Osbornes formed a team first with Jimmy Martin and then with Red Allen (1930–1993). They developed their trio sound with Allen as the third member, recorded for M-G-M, and had a moderate hit with "Once More." After Allen's departure, others took the third vocal part—most notably, Benny Birchfield and Dale Sledd. After coming to Nashville, the Osbornes added electric steel and drums to their recordings and were consistently on the charts from 1967 through 1973, although none of their offerings scored higher than number twenty-eight ("Tennessee Hound Dog"). After leaving MCA in the mid-1970s, the Osbornes reverted to a more standard bluegrass approach to their music and recorded for such companies as CMH and Pinecastle. In 2004, Sonny Osborne announced his retirement from working the road but would still play on the *Grand Ole Opry*.

Recommended Recordings: The Osborne Brothers, 1956–1968, Bear Family BCD 15598, 1995 (four-CD boxed set of M-G-M, RCA, and early Decca material); *The Osborne Brothers, 1968–1974*, Bear Family BCD 15748, 1997 (includes later Decca and MCA material).

Owens, Buck (b. 1929). Buck Owens developed and perfected the Bakersfield Sound that rivaled the country music developed in Nashville during the 1960s. Originally known more as a session guitarist, Owens stepped to the forefront as a vocalist for Capitol Records at the end of the 1950s and amassed forty-six hits during the 1960s, nineteen of which reached number one. He also costarred in and hosted the TV show *Hee Haw* for seventeen of the program's twenty-four years on the air. In 1986, he retired for a couple of years to look after his numerous business interests but then made a brief comeback after making a final number one hit in duet with Dwight Yoakam.

Owens made his first solo recorded efforts on the small Pep label but signed with Capitol in 1957 and made his first appearance on the charts in 1959 with "Second Fiddle." However, his major successes came in 1963, beginning with songs like "Act Naturally" and continuing with "Love's Gonna Live Here" (sixteen weeks at number one), "Together Again," "Before You Go," and "I've Got a Tiger by the Tail." He kept a top-notch band, the Buckaroos, on the road and with him in the recording studios and may have been the first to ask and receive $10,000 per show date. He continued turning out hits, such as "Waitin' in Your Welfare Line," "Sam's Place," and "Who's Gonna Mow Your Grass." A couple of years after joining the cast of *Hee Haw*, his hit production tailed off somewhat, and his songs like "On the Cover of the *Music City News*" and "Monsters' Holiday" began to fall more into the comic novelty vein, although they still made the top ten. In 1976, he left Capitol for Warner Brothers, and his releases fell to the lower end of the rankings. He left *Hee Haw* in 1986 and retired for a couple of years until his "Streets of Bakersfield" duet with Dwight Yoakam went to number one. At that point, he resigned with Capitol, had a few more minor hits in the late 1980s, and made a comeback tour. But by 1990, he had gone back to Bakersfield to look after his extensive business interests.

Recommended Recording: The Buck Owens Collection, 1959–1990, Rhino 71016, 1992 (three-CD boxed set).

Parton, Dolly (b. 1946). Along with Loretta Lynn, Dolly Parton has emerged as an icon as the living image of the rags-to-riches country girl. Born near Sevierville, Tennessee, at the edge of the Smoky Mountain National Park, Parton moved from adolescent vocalist on early morning television in Knoxville to major stardom in less than a decade. Beginning in 1967, she had at least one charted hit yearly, coming in a total of 106 times. Two dozen of these made it to the top. In addition, she added several starring movie roles and ownership of a theme park to her laurels.

The day after her high school graduation, Parton took the bus to Nashville, leaving her days on *Cas Walker's Farm and Home Hour* behind. Her first big break came when she signed with Monument Records and had minor hits with "Dumb Blonde" and "Something Fishy." Then she joined the *Porter Wagoner Show* as female vocalist, replacing Norma Jean. After moving to Wagoner's RCA Victor label, Parton and Wagoner had a top ten duet with "The Last Thing on My Mind." Thereafter, Parton appeared on the charts regularly but attained her first number one early in 1971 with "Joshua." Other major hits included "Jolene," "Love Is Like a Butterfly," "The Bargain Store," and her first gold record with "Here You Come Again" in 1977. By that time, she had split with Wagoner and gone on her own, although they continued to do duets on occasion. In 1980, she had first starring film role in *9 to 5*, the title song of which also went number one. Other notable films included *The Best Little Whorehouse in Texas* and *Steel Magnolias*. Meanwhile, she shifted to Columbia in 1987 and continued to score notable hits. In 1985, she obtained the theme park known as Dollywood near Pigeon Forge, and it has become one of the South's most popular tourist attractions, furnishing seasonal and even full-time employment to hundreds of Appalachians. No wonder there is a life-size statue of Parton in front of the Sevier County Courthouse! In recent years, she has recorded albums for Sugar Hill with bluegrass accompaniment.

Recommended Recordings: The Essential Dolly Parton, RCA Victor 665332, 1995; *The Essential Dolly Parton, Volume 2*, RCA Victor 669332, 1997; *Super Hits*, Columbia CK 69086, 1998.

Pearl, Minnie (1912–1996). For fifty years, Minnie Pearl (born Sarah Ophelia Colley) reigned as the virtual queen of country comedy, widely known for her stage creation of a rustic, man-hungry old maid. She first created the role in 1939 and began portraying it on the *Grand Ole Opry* in November 1940, and within a month she had become a regular. Minnie often did her *Opry* routines with male comedian Rod Brasfield (1910–1958) from 1948 until his death. Her stories concerned her relatives from the fictional hamlet of Grinder's Switch, and her customary greeting of "Howdee! I'm just so proud to be here!" became one of the best-known lines in American entertainment.

Although not known for recordings, Minnie Pearl did make several sides for RCA Victor in the early 1950s, some of which were duets with Grandpa Jones. In the 1960s, some of her monologues appeared on Starday albums, and she had a midlevel hit with the recitation "Giddyup Go-Answer." In addition to the *Opry*, she also appeared often on the television program *Hee Haw* from 1970. Minnie gave her last performances in 1991. After suffering a stroke, she was confined to a nursing home until her death.

Recommended Recording: Minnie Pearl: The Starday Years, Starday 3509-3-2, 1997 (three-CD set).

Peer, Ralph S. (1892–1960). As an employee of record companies and a pioneer publisher of country songs, Ralph Peer played a key role in the early development of both African American and country music. Peer was born in Kansas City, but his father owned a furniture store in nearby Independence that sold both phonographs and records. As a result of this connection, Peer went to work briefly for Columbia and then in 1919 for the General Phonograph Company, which manufactured the OKeh label. In 1921, he was instrumental for his company in making the first recordings of black songstress Mamie Smith and two years later of Fiddlin' John Carson, which marked the real beginning of the fad for country music. He also recorded such key individuals as Ernest Stoneman and the original Hillbillies. In 1926, he switched his employment to Victor Talking Machine, taking Stoneman with him. Among his other key discoveries in 1927 were the "Blue Yodeler" Jimmie Rodgers and the Carter Family.

Simultaneous with his work for the record companies, Peer got into the business of copyrighting songs and of music publishing. He founded Southern Music in 1928 as an ASCAP firm and later Peer International as a BMI affiliate. For years, these companies were among the largest in the field. Peer himself seems to have cared little for country music except as a business operation. But whatever his personal tastes, his contributions to the field were of major consequence.

Perkins, Carl (1932–1998). Carl Perkins ranked among the most significant rockabilly musicians, although he became overshadowed by fellow Sun recording artists, such as Johnny Cash, Jerry Lee Lewis, and Elvis Presley. A native of west Tennessee, where he was influenced by both country and blues music, Perkins first recorded for Sun's subsidiary Flip in October 1954. His third recording, "Blue Suede Shoes," made him a star, but he was sidelined for a month in an auto accident in the spring of 1956, which cost him a certain degree of momentum. Still, he recorded other fine rockabilly songs for Sun, such as "Boppin' the Blues" and "Dixie Fried." In 1957, he left Sun for Columbia and later Decca, but most of his recordings on these labels failed to click, with "Pink Pedal Pushers" doing best at seventeen in country and ninety-one on the pop charts.

In 1965, Perkins joined the Johnny Cash entourage for a decade. During this time, he composed the Cash hit "Daddy Sang Bass," but his own efforts on Dollie and Columbia were more modest. His later efforts made the charts twice in 1986 and 1987, at which latter time he was chosen for the Rock and Roll Hall of Fame. He died of a stroke at sixty-five.

Recommended Recording: The Classic Carl Perkins, Bear Family BCD 15494, 1990 (five-CD boxed set containing all Sun, Columbia, and Decca recordings).

Pierce, Webb (1921–1991). In the early 1950s, Webb Pierce emerged as a major figure in country music. A native of Monroe, Louisiana, he began performing at KTBS and KWKH Shreveport on the *Louisiana Hayride*. His earliest recordings were for Pacemaker and Four Star, but in December 1951, he signed with Decca and soon had a major hit with an updated arrangement of the Cajun song "Wondering." He followed with a dozen more number one hits, such as "Back Street Affair," "It's Been So Long," "There Stands the Glass," "More and More," and his most memorable numbers, "Slowly," and "I Don't Care." His revival of Jimmie Rodgers's "In the Jailhouse Now" spent twenty-one weeks atop the *Billboard* charts. The rise of rockabilly dimmed his stardom a little, but songs like "Teenage Boogie," "Honky-Tonk Song," and "I Ain't Never" still held up remarkably well.

Although Pierce had no giant hits in the 1960s, he still made the charts consistently through 1972. A true individualist, his silver-dollar-studded Cadillac and guitar-shaped swimming pool not only became symbols of success but also demonstrated a form of conspicuous consumption that rankled some within the Nashville establishment. Adept at business, he and Jim Denny formed the Cedarwood Publishing Company, which came to own several of country music's biggest hits of that era. He also invested in a chain of radio stations in rural Georgia. Largely retired in later years, he died from pancreatic cancer and heart failure.

Recommended Recording: Webb Pierce: The Wondering Boy, 1951–1958, Bear Family BCD 15522, 1990 (four-CD boxed set).

Poole, Charlie (1892–1931). Charlie Poole and his North Carolina Ramblers helped define the quality sound of old-time string band music with their Columbia recordings of the late 1920s. Poole, who played banjo, came out of the North Carolina Piedmont textile mill culture. With a lead fiddle played first by Posey Rorer and then by Lonnie Austin and a guitar played most often by Roy Harvey, the North Carolina Ramblers ranked as perhaps the best and most creative band of their era. With the onset of the Great Depression, the market for Poole's music began to erode, and he died following a prolonged drinking spree.

The North Carolina Ramblers visited the Columbia studios in mid-1925, where they recorded their best-known songs, "Don't Let Your Deal Go Down

Blues" and "Can I Sleep in Your Barn Tonight, Mister," which subsequently sold over 100,000 copies. From then onward through 1930, the Ramblers recorded twice yearly, with a repertoire consisting of Victorian sentimental numbers, minstrel show pieces, and a variety of other songs and tunes. "There'll Come a Time," "Goodbye Liza Jane," "White House Blues," and an adaption of a Bret Harte poem, "Bill Mason," ranked among their best-known songs. Although he has been deceased for more than seventy years, interest in Poole's music remains high.

Recommended Recordings: Charlie Poole and the North Carolina Ramblers: Old Time Songs, County CO-CD 3501, 1993; *Charlie Poole: Volume Two,* County CO-CD 3508, 1996; *The Legend of Charlie Poole: Volume 3,* County CO-CD 3516, 1999.

The Prairie Ramblers. The Prairie Ramblers reflected some of the most versatile country music talent of the 1930s and 1940s. Initially known as the Kentucky Ramblers, they began their careers as an old-time string band; shifted to western swing a little later, although they could still do old-time numbers with authority on occasion; recorded country novelty and risqué songs as the Sweet Violet Boys; and eventually became a polka band as Stan Wolowic and the Polka Chips in 1956. They disbanded in 1960.

As the Kentucky Ramblers, Charles "Chick" Hurt (1901–1969), Jack Taylor (1901–1962), Floyd "Salty" Holmes (1909–1970), and Fiddler Shelby "Tex" Atchison began their professional careers at WOC radio in Davenport, Iowa. In 1933, they came to WLS Chicago, took the name Prairie Ramblers, and remained there until 1956, except for brief stints in New York (1934–1935) and Cincinnati (1949–1950). After recording a few sides for Victor in 1933, they signed with the American Record Corporation and recorded the bulk of their material for that company, including the numerous recordings they made with female vocalist Patsy Montana. After World War II, they recorded for Mercury. Fiddler Tex Atchison left the band in 1938 and was replaced by Johnny Crockett, and Salty Holmes was later replaced by Rusty Gill. Other band members at later times included Wade Ray and Wally Moore. Hurt and Taylor remained with the group throughout, including after they became the Polka Chips. They ranked among the most frequently recorded groups of the 1930s and among the most popular on radio.

Recommended Recordings: Swinging Down the Old Orchard Lane with the Prairie Ramblers, Bronco Buster CD 9038, c. 1996; *The Oregon Trail,* BACM CD D 048, 2003.

Presley, Elvis (1935–1977). Although he is remembered today more as the "King of Rock and Roll" and for his string of musical motion pictures, Elvis Presley began his career in country music and managed to have eighty-five appearances on the country charts over a forty-year period. Born in Tupelo, Mississippi, and a resident of Memphis from the age of thirteen, Presley had ample exposure to and was influenced by a wide variety of both African American and white musical styles. In a broader sense, he fulfilled the alleged prophecy of his manager Colonel Tom Parker that a white person who sang like a black person would someday revolutionize the music world.

Presley's first recording as a nineteen-year-old truck driver for Sun Records was an up-tempo adaptation of Bill Monroe's "Blue Moon of Kentucky," backed by bluesman Arthur Crudup's "That's All Right." Other early recordings included such country standards as the Shelton Brothers' "Just Because" and Leon Payne's "I Love You Because." Much of his initial exposure to live audiences came on the KWKH *Louisiana Hayride* in Shreveport. His music soon transcended country, particularly after signing with RCA Victor in late 1955. However, he managed to keep something of a country following and recorded such country songs as "Little Cabin Home on the Hill," "Faded Love," "Tomorrow Never Comes," and "I Washed My Hands in Muddy Water." While a full treatment of Presley's career is unwarranted here, his 1998 election to the Country Music Hall of Fame seems altogether justified.

Recommended Recordings: Elvis: The Complete 50's Masters, RCA Victor 66050, 1992 (five-CD boxed set); *Elvis Country*, RCA Victor 4460, 1971.

Price, Ray (b. 1926). After four or five years of moderate success, Ray Price emerged as a major figure in country music in 1956 with his hit song "Crazy Arms." At a time when rock-and-roll influences seemed to be obscuring the type of country that prevailed earlier in the decade, Price remained firmly within the country fold, although he did move toward what became known as the Nashville Sound with a "rhythmic brand of honky-tonk" and songs like "My Shoes Keep Walking Back to You," "Heartaches by the Number," "City Lights," and "The Same Old Me." Ironically, when the country mainstream was settling in for a degree of renewed vigor, Price moved toward a more pop-country sound in the manner of Eddy Arnold and scored major hits in the early 1970s with "For the Good Times" and "I Won't Mention It Again."

Reared primarily in Dallas, Price came to Nashville as a World War II veteran and dropout from North Texas State College, recorded a single for Bullet, and signed with Columbia in 1951. His first real hit was "Talk to Your Heart" in 1952, followed by the two-sided "I'll Be There" and "Release Me" in 1954. But it took twenty weeks at the top for "Crazy Arms" to make him a major star. The follow-up hits kept him at the top, but his 1967 rendition of the old Irish song "Danny Boy" launched him in a pop-country mode that was not immediately successful but eventually won favor with fans. Even after he left Columbia in 1974, Price continued to have midlevel chart entries through the later 1970s and 1980s with various labels.

Recommended Recordings: The Essential Ray Price, 1951–1962, Columbia CK 48532, 1991 (good sample of his best work); *Ray Price and the Cherokee Cowboys*, Bear Family BCD 15843, 1995 (ten-CD boxed set containing all 1950–1966 recordings).

Pride, Charley (b. 1938). Charley Pride entered the history books by becoming country music's first (and to date only) African American superstar. A native of the Mississippi Delta, which was most famous for being the home of the blues, Pride had more exposure to country in his youth through his sharecropper father's musical preferences. Leaving home to play baseball at sixteen, Pride was actually living and working in Montana when he first attracted notice from Red Sovine and Red Foley. Signed by RCA Victor in 1965, Pride's race remained something of a secret until his third single release, "Just Between You and Me," gained hit status in 1966. By then, he had managed to gain a high, if not quite universal, degree of acceptance.

Between 1969 and 1983, Charley Pride accumulated twenty-nine number one hits, of which "All I Have to Offer You Is Me," "Is Anybody Goin' to San Antone," "Wonder Could I Live There Anymore," "Kiss an Angel Good Morning," and a cover of Hank Williams's "You Win Again" rank among the more memorable. After fifty-nine chart appearances in twenty-two years with RCA Victor, Pride signed with 16th Avenue South Records and charted eight more times in the late 1980s, of which "Shouldn't It Be Easier Than This" came in highest at number five. In 1993, as his career was winding down, he became a *Grand Ole Opry* regular.

Recommended Recording: The Essential Charley Pride, RCA Victor 07863, 1997.

Reeves, Jim (1923–1964). In the late 1950s, Jim Reeves emerged as a country star who exhibited wide crossover appeal, and had he not died in a 1964 plane crash, he might have exhibited the same type of long-term middle of the road acceptance as Eddy Arnold. As it was, he still showed himself to be a top artist for a dozen years. In fact, "Gentleman Jim" accumulated five number one hits after his death.

Jim Reeves grew up in east Texas, played minor league baseball in the St. Louis Cardinal farm system, and did his first recording on the tiny Macy's label about 1949. His climb to success, however, came when he signed with Abbot Records in 1952. He experienced a pair of hits with "Mexican Joe" and "Bimbo" in 1953, which landed him on the cast of the *Louisiana Hayride* in 1954 and the *Grand Ole Opry* and RCA Victor in 1955. His first RCA hit, "Yonder Comes a Sucker," and songs like "I've Lived a Lot in My Time," demonstrated his skills at hard country material, but beginning with "Four Walls" in 1957, he turned more to a soft country-pop approach and had a crossover hit. He hit his peak in early 1960 when "He'll Have to Go" got him a gold record and spent fourteen weeks at the top spot in country and number two on the pop charts. In addition to his American success, Reeves proved to be atypically popular in Europe. His other notable achievements included starring in a motion picture in South Africa entitled *Kimberley Jim.*

Recommended Recordings: Gentleman Jim, Bear Family BCD 15439, 1990 (four-CD boxed set containing recordings from Reeves's peak period); *Welcome to My World*, Bear Family BCD 15656, 1992 (sixteen-CD boxed set containing all 447 Reeves recordings); *The Essential Jim Reeves*, RCA Victor 665892, 1995 is a good sampler of his work.

Reno, Don (1926–1984) and Smiley, Arthur "Red" (1925–1971). Don Reno and Red Smiley led one of the most creative and innovative bluegrass bands during the 1950s and early 1960s. Somewhat atypically, they worked as a recording group for three years before they actually toured and worked together with their band, the Tennessee Cut-Ups. After a decade spent working daily television in Roanoke, they split and each had his own band. Still later, they reunited for a time. Reno also worked as a duet with Bill Harrell and in a band with his sons, who continued in music after their father's death.

Don Reno grew up in the South Carolina Piedmont and Red Smiley in the mountainous Asheville area, where each received their respective musical influences. The two met and formed their duet when they were band members in Tommy Magness and his Tennessee Buddies, with whom they recorded on Federal. In January 1952, Reno and Smiley made their first recordings as a duet act for King, including their original bluegrass gospel classic "I'm Using My Bible for a Roadmap." Although they did not tour, they continued recording and in 1955 finally formed their band, which included fiddler Mack Magaha and bassist John Palmer. Later, Don's son Ronnie was added on mandolin. Some of their better known efforts for King included "I Know You're Married (But I Love You Still)," "Love Please Come Home," "Let's Live for Tonight," and "Trail of Sorrow." They also did some recordings for Dot. After their 1964 split, Smiley continued on daily television in Roanoke until 1969, while Reno formed a ten-year partnership with Bill Harrell beginning in 1966. Smiley, usually in frail health, died in 1972 after playing several reunion concerts in 1970 and 1971. Reno continued working with his sons until health problems ultimately ended his career and life.

Recommended Recordings: Don Reno & Red Smiley, 1951–1959, King 7001, 1993 (four-CD boxed set); *Reno & Smiley: Bluegrass Hits*, Copper Creek CCRS 7009, 2004 (Dot masters).

Riders in the Sky. Riders in the Sky has become known as the group that revived the kind of western trio music once made famous by groups like the Sons of the Pioneers and Foy Willing's Riders of the Purple Sage. Led by Douglas "Ranger Doug" Green (b. 1946), who himself gained recognition as the leading scholar and historian of cowboy and western music, Riders in the Sky combined pleasing vocal harmonies and old and new songs along with a degree of humor to lead what might be termed the rennaissance of cowboy music. Green gained help along the way from friends Fred "Too Slim" LeBour (b. 1948) and Woody Paul (b. 1949), known as the "King of Cowboy Fiddlers." In later years, they added an accordion player, Joey Miskulin (the "Cowpolka King"), to their unit.

Riders in the Sky originated in 1977 as a part-time group playing in a Nashville club once a week. As demands for their music picked up, they began recording on Rounder, with their first album, *Three on the Trail*, in 1979. Three years later they gained *Grand Ole Opry* membership and in 1983 began hosting *Tumbleweed Theater* on TNN for the next three years. Later they recorded for MCA; had a Saturday morning program on CBS-TV and another weekend program, *Riders Radio Theater* on NPR; but eventually returned to Rounder.

Recommended Recordings: Cowboy Songs, EasyDisc 7005, 1996; *Yodel the Cowboy Way*, EasyDisc 7055, 1998; *Always Drink Upstream from the Herd*, Rounder CD 0360, 1995.

Ritter, Tex (1905–1974). Tex Ritter ranked as one of Hollywood's best-known singing cowboys. While his films never enjoyed the popularity of those of Gene Autry and Roy Rogers, he was generally considered a more authentic vocalist than either. After his film career ended, he starred on the *Town Hall Party* in California and eventually moved to Nashville and joined the cast of the *Grand Ole Opry*.

Maurice "Tex" Ritter grew up in Texas and went to college as a pre-law student, but his interests shifted to folklore, music, and cowboy songs. In 1928, he went to New York and sang on radio and in plays. In 1932 and 1933, he recorded a few numbers for the American Record Corporation and then in 1935 for Decca. Movie producer Edward Finney was looking for a singing cowboy, found one in Ritter, and signed him for a series of pictures for Grand National. Ritter continued recording for Decca, and when Grand National entered bankruptcy, he moved to Monogram and eventually to other studios. While his popularity never equaled that of Gene Autry, his pictures were competent albeit low budget. He became one of the first contractees at newly established Capitol Records in 1942 and remained with that label for the remainder of his life. Ritter had hit records with songs like "I'm Wasting My Tears on You," "You Two Timed Me Once Too Often," and "I Dreamed of a Hillbilly Heaven," but his ultimate success was probably the theme from the award-winning western film *High Noon*. He moved to Nashville in 1964, joined the *Opry*, had several lesser hits for Capitol, and remained active until his death.

Recommended Recordings: Blood on the Saddle, Bear Family BCD 16260, 1999 (four-CD boxed set including all 1932–1947 recordings); *Tex Ritter: Vintage Collections*, Capitol CD 7243, 1996 (good sampling of Capitol recordings).

Robbins, Marty (1925–1982). In a career that included three decades in the limelight, Marty Robbins demonstrated a capacity for effectively rendering just about any type of music ranging from hard country to rockabilly, pop-country, western, Hawaiian, and even a little bluegrass. A native of Arizona, he had attained some regional stature when he signed with Columbia in 1951, came to Nashville, and joined the cast of the *Grand Ole Opry* in January 1953.

Robbins's first real hit came when his third Columbia release, "I'll Go on Alone," began climbing the charts late in 1952 and became the first of sixteen to ultimately reach the top. By 1955, he was dabbling in rockabilly, doing covers of Elvis and Chuck Berry as well as numbers of his own like "Tennessee Toddy," Guy Mitchell's "Singing the Blues," and ballads like "A White Sport Coat" and "The Story of My Life," the latter two of which showed strong appeal on the pop charts. When saga songs came into vogue, Marty did even better with new western numbers like "El Paso," "Big Iron," and "Five

Brothers." When straight country resurged with the Nashville Sound in the early 1960s, Robbins scored big with "Don't Worry" and "My Woman, My Woman, My Wife." By the 1970s, his enthusiasm for racecars almost engulfed his musical career, but he often arrived in time to close the *Opry*. Plagued by heart problems in later years, he died only a few weeks after his election to the Country Music Hall of Fame.

Recommended Recordings: The Essential Marty Robbins, 1951–1982, Columbia CK 48537, 1991 (two-CD boxed set, an excellent sampler); *Marty Robbins: Country, 1951–1958*, Bear Family BCD 15570, 1991 (five-CD boxed set of all early recordings).

Rodgers, Jimmie (1897–1933). Jimmie Rodgers, who became known as "the Singing Brakeman" and as "America's Blue Yodeler," was the first country singer to really gain a widely recognized star status. With his railroad songs, African American-tinged blue yodels, and a number of sentimental ballads, Rodgers also became the first legendary figure the music produced, a process augmented by an early demise from the ravages of tuberculosis. The Mississippi-born former railroader experienced a short six-year career, with just over 100 recordings.

Rodgers's railroading came to an end in 1924, when he was diagnosed with the dreaded TB and his frail physique could not sustain heavy labor. His efforts to establish himself as an entertainer yielded minimal results until his opportunity to make recordings for Victor in Bristol in August 1927. Called back for a second session in November, his "Blue Yodel" or "T for Texas" became a major hit and made him a star. He followed with more hits, such as "Waiting for a Train," "In the Jailhouse Now," "Any Old Time," and a whole series of additional "Blue Yodels." He toured on the bigger theater circuits and did quite well until the effects of the Great Depression took its toll on his health and prosperity. A move from humid Mississippi to the dryer climate of south Texas may have slowed his growing weakness but could not stop his physical decline. He died in May 1933 while in New York for what proved to be his final recording session. Numerous other country singers, including such major figures as Gene Autry, Jimmie Davis, Ernest Tubb, and Hank Snow, all began their careers heavily influenced by "the Blue Yodeler" Rodgers style. Rodgers later became the first country singer to be pictured on a postage stamp.

Recommended Recording: The Singing Brakeman, Bear Family BCD 15540, 1992 (six-CD boxed set).

Rogers, Roy (1911–1998). Roy Rogers (born Leonard Slye in Ohio) earned the nickname "King of the Cowboys" from his fifteen years of popularity in a long series of Republic Pictures. His first taste of musical success came as a member of the Sons of the Pioneers. While his numerous recordings for the American Record Corporation, Decca, and RCA Victor were all popular and sold well, somehow they never quite attained the hit status of those of the other singing cowboys, such as Gene Autry, Tex Ritter, and Jimmy Wakely.

Rogers's family had relocated from Scioto County, Ohio, to California during the Great Depression. Working initially as a laborer, he fell in with various local singing trios, especially the Pioneers. In 1937, he auditioned for a newly created singing cowboy series and soon became a close rival to Gene Autry. While his series met with success, he never really eclipsed Autry as a star until the latter entered military service in World War II. From then on, the King of the Cowboys ruled at the box office for the remainder of the B western era. Many of his better-known songs were written as title themes for his movies, such as "Don't Fence Me In," "Along the Navajo Trail," "Home in Oklahoma," and "Roll on Texas Moon." He also had a popular radio program and a TV program that always ended with "Happy Trails to You," which he and his costar wife, Dale Evans (1912–2001), sang. In later years, Rogers recorded some for Capitol and operated his popular museum in Victorville, California. Roy and Dale also sang a considerable amount of sacred songs that reflected their deep Christian faith.

Recommended Recordings: Roy Rogers: Country Music Hall of Fame Series, MCA CD 10548, 1992; *Peace in the Valley*, Pair PDC-2-1352, 1996 (double CD with Dale Evans); *Happy Trails: The Roy Rogers Collection, 1937–1990*, Rhino CD 75722, 1999 (three-CD boxed set from recordings, radio, and TV, and motion picture soundtracks).

Satherley, Arthur (1889–1986). Art Satherley was a talent scout and record producer under whose tutelage some of the biggest and best country music stars did their finest work. Of English birth, Satherley began his work in America by grading lumber and by 1918 became involved with recording labels, such as Paramount, but soon moved to the American Record Corporation and its successor company Columbia. During the 1930s and 1940s, he played a prime role in the business of recording both country and blues artists.

The biggest name country artists associated with development under Satherley's direction included Roy Acuff, Gene Autry, Bill Monroe, and Bob Wills. However, he also recorded such significant but now largely forgotten artists as Billy Cox and Asa Martin. Satherley retired in 1952 and lived out a long retirement in California, with much of his work being carried on by another English immigrant, Don Law (1902–1982), who had assisted the older man for several years.

Shepard, Jean (b. 1933). Jean Shepard rose to prominence among country female singers about the time the Korean War ended and remained a leading figure in the field for a quarter century. The Oklahoma-born, California-reared Shepard has also proved to be a durable fixture at the *Grand Ole Opry*, having celebrated her fiftieth year on the venerable program. She started out in Visalia, California, as a teen singing with a female group called the Melody Ranch Girls. One day, Hank Thompson and his Brazos Valley Boys played a show in the same venue and worked through Ken Nelson of Capitol Records to get her a contract at the label, where she had her first session in late September 1952.

However, it was a song with a recitation, "A Dear John Letter," that elevated Jean Shepard to stardom. The song also had Ferlin Husky on it, and it went to number one in country and to number four on the pop charts. It still ranks as her biggest hit, although she made the charts thirty more times in her twenty years with Capitol. With her status in the industry enhanced by a hit, she moved on to the *Ozark Jubilee* in January 1955 and then on to Nashville and the *Opry* that November. Continuing to record steadily, her more memorable numbers included "A Satisfied Mind," "Beautiful Lies," and "Second Fiddle to a Steel Guitar." Her 1956 album, *Songs of a Love Affair*, is said to have been the first concept LP by a country female singer. In 1973, Shepard left Capitol and went to United Artists, where she had another notable success with "Slippin' Away," but thereafter her rankings dropped into the lower end of the charts. However, she has continued to record, play regularly, and turn out such creditable numbers as "I'm Only a Phone Call Away." In recent years, Shepard has been termed one of the "Grand Ladies of the *Grand Ole Opry*."

Recommended Recordings: Jean Shepard: Honky-Tonk Heroine, Country Music Foundation CMF 021D/521-18589, 1995 (good sampling of her Capitol recordings); *Jean Shepard: The Melody Ranch Girl*, Bear Family BCD 15905, 1996 (five-CD boxed set).

Skaggs, Ricky (b. 1954). After spending his late adolescence and early adult years as a bluegrass musician, Ricky Skaggs emerged in the early 1980s as a champion of what came to be called neotraditional country with a fresh-sounding blend of bluegrass and western swing that yielded several hit records on the Epic label. By the 1990s, however, as his chart listings began to decline, he switched to Atlantic Records with little success. As the old century ended and the new century dawned, he returned to the bluegrass sounds of his youth and continues as a popular figure in that field.

As a native of eastern Kentucky, Skaggs formed a duet in his midteens with the late Keith Whitley (1954–1989), singing in the style of the Stanley Brothers. Later, both joined Ralph Stanley's band. Skaggs worked a stint with the Country Gentlemen as well and later came to Nashville as a member of the Emmylou Harris band. After signing with Epic in 1980, he had a string of hits which fell into three categories: new arrangements of bluegrass standards (e.g., "Crying My Heart over You," "Uncle Pen," and "Don't Cheat in Our Hometown"), old Webb Pierce hits (e.g., "I Don't Care," "Honey [Open that Door]," "I'm Tired"), and new songs (e.g., "Heartbroke," "Highway 40 Blues," and "Cajun Moon"). Skaggs became a *Grand Ole Opry* regular in 1982. In 1997, he marked his return to bluegrass tradition with his own Skaggs Family Records and a fine album entitled *Bluegrass Rules*. Others of a similar nature followed.

Recommended Recordings: Don't Cheat in Our Hometown, Epic EK 38954, 1983; *Bluegrass Rules*, Skaggs Family/Rounder CD 0801, 1997; *Soldier of the Cross*, Skaggs Family SKFR CD 5001, 1998; *Ancient Tones*, Skaggs Family SKFR CD 1001, 1999.

The Skillet Lickers. The Skillet Lickers constituted the best known of the Georgia fiddle bands of the late 1920s and early 1930s. While several musicians worked in the band, the basic unit was built around the threesome of fiddler

Gid Tanner (1885–1960), guitarist-vocalist Riley Puckett (1894–1946), and lead fiddler Clayton McMichen (1900–1970). Tanner, a chicken farm operator who played fiddle and did comedy routines, and Puckett, who was a blind street-corner musician, teamed on Columbia Records as early as 1924 after gaining attention at fiddling contests in Atlanta. McMichen, a younger fiddler who had earlier recorded for OKeh with his Hometown Boys, joined them in 1926, and for the next five years, they produced some of the most popular country releases on Columbia. Puckett also recorded a wide variety of solo numbers and made duets with others (especially McMichen, under his pseudonym, "Bob Nichols"). Other musicians who were part of the Skillet Licker entourage at various times included banjoist Fate Norris and fiddlers Bert Layne and Lowe Stokes.

Skillet Licker recordings were dominated by fiddle tunes, sometimes with Puckett doing vocal refrains, but they also included some ballads and numerous comedy skits. A fourteen-part series of skits that proved especially popular was entitled "A Corn Licker Still in Georgia," which concerned the trials and tribulations of a fictional group of Appalachian moonshiners. After their October 1931 session, the original Skillet Lickers disbanded, partly as a result of declining record sales and of McMichen forming his own band, the Georgia Wildcats. However, in 1934, Tanner and Puckett formed a newer edition of the band that included mandolinist Ted Hawkins and Tanner's son Gordon on fiddle. This group recorded two dozen more numbers for Bluebird, with the fiddle tunes "Down Yonder"/"Back Up and Push" allegedly going on to sell a million copies over the next several decades. This session proved to be the last hurrah for the Skillet Lickers, although Riley Puckett continued to record on a regular basis for Bluebird and Decca until 1941.

Recommended Recording: The Skillet Lickers: Complete Recorded Works in Chronological Order, Volumes 1–6, Document DOCD 8056-8061, 2000.

Smith, Carl (b. 1927). As a vocalist, Carl Smith had a style that marked him as one of the country crooners, yet unlike Eddy Arnold, he never made any efforts to accommodate to the popular audience and always remained well within the traditional honky-tonk style. A native of the same east Tennessee mountain community as Roy Acuff, Smith gained much of his early professional experience on radio at WROL Knoxville and signed with Columbia Records in 1950, the same year he came to Nashville and WSM and the *Grand Ole Opry*. Although his first release made little impact, one side of his second, "I Overlooked an Orchid," became a country standard. From his fourth release onward, "Let's Live a Little," "Mr. Moon," "If Teardrops Were Pennies," "Let Old Mother Nature Have Her Way," and "Don't Just Stand There," among others, all became hits.

In late 1956, Carl Smith left the *Opry* to tour with the Philip Morris Country Music Show for the next eighteen months. Although he never returned to that program, he did appear regularly on *Jubilee U.S.A.* for a time and had a network

TV program in Canada called *Carl Smith's Country Music Hall* from 1964 to 1969. His Columbia recordings continued to be on the *Billboard* charts steadily until 1973, although only "Deep Water" in 1967 cracked the top ten. From 1974 through 1978, he recorded for Hickory, but none of his seven entries ranked higher than sixty-seven. After that, he generally eschewed interest in touring and settled into the life of a gentleman farmer and horse breeder from his extensive acreage near Franklin, Tennessee. Married twice—his first wife was June Carter of Carter Family fame—he recently became a widower after the passing of Goldie Hill (1933–2005), who had a brief fling with country stardom in the mid-1950s.

Recommended Recordings: Satisfaction Guaranteed, Bear Family BCD 15849, 1995 (five-CD set containing all Smith recordings from the 1950s); *The Essential Carl Smith, 1950–1956*, Columbia CK 47996, 1991 (good sampler of his best work).

Smith, Connie (b. 1941). Although she had some earlier experience on local television in Parkersburg and Huntington, West Virginia, Connie Smith shot to sudden stardom in 1964 with the success of her first RCA Victor release, "Once a Day." As events worked out, she never had another hit with the impact of that song, but Smith did turn out a string of top ten recordings over the next decade. She also has been a constant performer at the *Grand Ole Opry* since 1971, after having been a regular earlier in the mid-1960s.

Born in Indiana as Constance Meador, she was reared in West Virginia and Ohio, where she completed high school and then worked as a store clerk. She married Jerry Smith in 1961, had her first child in 1963, and began working on the weekly TV programs. Country star Bill Anderson, however, made the connection for her to receive her RCA Victor contract and also furnished her with his composition "Once a Day," which topped the charts for eight weeks at the end of 1964. Other high-ranking Smith hits included "Cincinnati, Ohio," "Then and Only Then," "The Hurtin's All Over," and "Ain't Had No Lovin'." After a born-again religious experience in 1968, she made a conscious decision to slow down the pace of her career, although she still had periodic hit records, including a revival of Don Gibson's "Just One Time" in 1971 and "Just for What I Am" in 1972. Moving to Columbia in 1973, her chart rankings generally dropped to lower levels, although two made the top ten. She later recorded for Monument and briefly returned to Columbia in 1985 and went with Warner Brothers in 1998. In 1997, she married her fourth husband, the much younger male country star Marty Stuart (b. 1958).

Recommended Recording: Connie Smith: Born to Sing, Bear Family BCD 16368, 2001 (four-CD boxed set containing 1964–1967 recordings).

Snow, Clarence E. "Hank" (1914–1999). Nova Scotia-born Hank Snow became one of RCA Victor's longest running artists as a fixture from 1936 until 1980. His early efforts appeared on the Canadian Bluebird label as "Hank, the Yodeling Ranger" and then as "Hank, the Singing Ranger." After World War II, he made two unsuccessful efforts to make it in the United States, finally succeeding on his third try. From the end of 1949 on, Snow was a regular on the *Grand Ole Opry* and on the charts at least once a year until early 1980, with the exceptions of 1971 and 1972.

Snow had a difficult childhood as a result of his parents' divorce and an abusive stepfather. As a result, he went to sea, where he also encountered difficult times. In 1933, he began singing on radio in Halifax and made his first recordings in October 1936. Still, his escape from poverty came slowly. Early efforts to make it in the United States had limited success and he had almost decided to return to Canada, when in 1950 his railroad-flavored song of broken love, "I'm Moving On," went to number one for twenty-one weeks. Other top hits followed, including "The Golden Rocket," "The Rhumba Boogie," "I Don't Hurt Anymore," and a cover of the pop hit "Let Me Go, Lover." Numerous others made the top ten. He also continued making successful recordings through the 1960s and 1970s, although he had only one at the top, "I've Been Everywhere" and "Hello Love," in each decade, respectively. After a dispute with RCA Victor in 1981, he left the label and did not record thereafter, except for guest appearances with others. He played the *Opry* until his last years as health permitted.

Recommended Recordings: The Singing Ranger, 1949–1953, Bear Family BCD 15426, 1988 (four-CD boxed set); *The Singing Ranger Vol. 2, 1953–1958*, Bear Family BCD 15476, 1990 (four-CD boxed set); *Hank Snow: The Yodeling Ranger*, Bear Family BCD 15587, 1993 (five-CD boxed set of 1936–1947 Canadian recordings).

The Sons of the Pioneers. The Sons of the Pioneers were the best-known western vocal group from the mid-1930s for more than a generation. In addition to numerous recordings for Decca, the American Record Corporation, and RCA Victor, they appeared in western films, providing musical and a bit of acting support. Songs associated with the Pioneers that went on to become standards in the field included "Cool Water," "Tumbling Tumbleweeds," "Happy Rovin' Cowboy," and "Way Out There." Although the original members are all long deceased, the group has had a continuous existence for some seven decades.

The original Sons of the Pioneers vocal trio included Bob Nolan (1908–1980), Tim Spencer (1908–1974), and Len Slye (1911–1998), who left in 1937 to become movie cowboy star Roy Rogers. Lloyd Perryman (1917–1977) came in early as a replacement. Other early members were fiddler Hugh Farr (1903–1980) and guitarist Karl Farr (1909–1961). In addition to radio work in the Los Angeles area, they began their recording career in 1934 and appeared in films from 1935. In 1937 and 1938, they switched to the American Record Corporation but then returned to Decca in 1940. After World War II, they went with RCA Victor and remained with the label until 1969, with the exception of a brief period with Coral in 1954. From the late 1950s, they concentrated on albums, many of a thematic nature. Other than the aforementioned members of the group, significant members of the Sons of the Pioneers included Tommy

Doss, Luther Nallie, Shug Fisher, Ken Carson, Pat Brady, Ken Curtis, and Dale Warren. By the 1990s, the Sons of the Pioneers were regular performers at Branson, Missouri.

Recommended Recordings: Sons of the Pioneers: Wagons West, Bear Family BCD 15640, 1993 (four-CD boxed set containing all 1945–1954 recordings); *Country Music Hall of Fame Series*, MCAD 10090, 1991 (Decca recordings).

Sprague, Carl T. (1895–1979). More than anyone else, Carl Sprague qualifies as the first real singing cowboy to record. Unlike the movie and radio cowboys, he had been the real thing in his late adolescence. Born in Brazoria County, Texas, he worked on ranches that mostly belonged to relatives and learned many of the songs he sang firsthand prior to enrolling in college at Texas A&M. He left school to serve in World War I and returned to receive his degree in 1922. Thereafter, he worked for the institution primarily as an ath-letic trainer until 1937, when he opened a grocery store and insurance business.

During his time with the athletic department, Sprague began to record for Victor in August 1925, a session that included his best-known song, "When the Work's All Done This Fall." He continued to record through 1929, having a total of twenty-four released sides. These numbers included "Following the Cow Trail," "If Your Saddle Is Good and Tight," "Last Great Round Up," "The Last Long Horn," and "The Mormon Cowboy." Sprague did not record again until the early 1970s, by which time folklorists and old-time music enthusiasts had sought him for interviews and folk concerts.

Recommended Recordings: Cowtrails, Longhorns and Tight Saddles, Bear Family BCD 15979, 2003 (complete Victor recordings); *Classic Cowboy Songs*, Bear Family BCD 15456 (recordings from the 1970s).

The Stanley Brothers: Carter Stanley (1925–1966) and Ralph Stanley (b. 1927). The Stanley Brothers and their Clinch Mountain Boys probably rank as the most Appalachian and the most tradition-oriented among the better-known bluegrass bands. Organized in 1946, they began recording in 1947 and remained quite active for some twenty years until Carter Stanley's death. After a few months, Ralph Stanley decided to continue and with the popularity of bluegrass festivals and the intense interest in traditional music that followed release of the 2000 motion picture *O Brother, Where Art Thou?* has won more acclaim than at any earlier time in his career.

Following their service in World War II, Carter and Ralph Stanley, natives of mountainous Dickinson County, Virginia, began their careers as moun-tain string-band leaders at newly opened WCYB radio in Bristol and began recording for Rich-R-Tone in 1947. They soon evolved into a bluegrass band and signed with Columbia in 1949, moving on to Mercury in 1953. Later, they made most of their recordings for the King label in Cincinnati as well as with smaller firms. Despite their popularity with hard-core bluegrass fans and in small Appalachian enclaves, the Stanleys often found it challenging to win acceptance in the broader world of country music. Nonetheless, they managed to place over 400 recordings on disc in their twenty-year career, and there is an indeterminate number of recordings from live shows. A few months after Carter's death, Ralph Stanley had a new group of Clinch Mountain Boys back on the road, with Larry Sparks (b. 1947) as lead vocalist. He has generally kept a quality band together for more than thirty-five years. Initially, Ralph recorded for King but mostly for Rebel and other labels as well, including a return to Columbia in 2002. In addition to the popularity of bluegrass, his association with the aforementioned film undoubtedly gave his appeal a significant boost.

Recommended Recordings: The Stanley Brothers, 1949–1952, Bear Family BCD 15564, 1991 (Columbia recordings); *The Stanley Brothers & the Clinch Mountain Boys, 1953–1958 & 1959*, Bear Family BCD 15681, 1993 (two-CD set of Mercury and Blue Ridge recordings); *Ralph Stanley: Poor Rambler*, King KC3D-0951, 2002 (King and Gusto recordings from 1967–1969 and 1980); *Ralph Stanley*, Columbia CK 86625, 2002.

Stoneman, Ernest "Pop" (1893–1968) and Family. The story of the Stoneman Family is one of two prosperous decades, the 1920s and 1960s, with low periods in between and afterward. A native of Carroll County, Virginia, Ernest "Pop" Stoneman became one of country music's top artists in the 1925–1929 period. However, his career virtually collapsed in the Great Depression. With the help of his talented children, Pop slowly rebuilt his career to the point that the Stoneman Family won the CMA Vocal Group of the Year award in 1967. In the years after his death, the family slowly faded from the limelight in the Nashville scene.

Ernest Stoneman began his musical career as a thirty-one-year old carpenter who became convinced that he could do as well or better than Henry Whitter, another recording artist he had heard. He journeyed to New York and proved his point by placing his ballad "The Titanic" and other songs on disc. Until Depression conditions curtailed his activity, he made numerous recordings for OKeh, Victor, Edison, and Gennett, including both solo numbers and others with string band accompaniment. Finally, as his career phased out and debtors closed in, he moved his large family to the Washington, D.C., area and survived years of dire poverty before slowly coming back. In the late 1940s, his family won an amateur contest at Constitution Hall, and in 1956, the Bluegrass Champs, which included the Stonemans, were winners on Arthur Godfrey's Talent Scouts. Beginning in 1962, they recorded successively for Starday, World Pacific, and M-G-M and were named CMA award winners, with five charted hits. The most active children included champion fiddler Scott (1932–1973), mandolinist Donna (b. 1934), bassist Jimmy (1937–2002), banjoist Veronica or "Roni" (b. 1938), and guitarist Van (1940–1995). After Pop died, older daughter Patsy (b. 1925) joined on guitar and autoharp. In 1969, the group signed with RCA Victor and later recorded for RPA, CMH, and Old Homestead. Roni left the group in 1971, eventually becoming a TV regular on *Hee Haw*, and Donna left in 1972 to do evangelistic work, but the group continued on with their tasteful mixture of country and bluegrass under Patsy's leadership. Age and health took their toll on the group, but Patsy, Donna, and Roni still play on occasion.

Recommended Recordings: Ernest V. Stoneman: Edison Recordings, 1928, County CD 3510, 1996; *Ernest V. Stoneman: With Family and Friends, Vol I and Vol II*, Old Homestead OH CD 4172 and 4173, 2000; *The Stoneman Family: 28 Big Ones*, King 28CD 4119, 2000 (Starday material).

Strait, George (b. 1952). As of the fall of 2005, George Strait approached Conway Twitty's record of forty number one charted *Billboard* hits. Strait, a no-nonsense Texan, began his atypical achievement of chart success—all with MCA—in 1981 with "Unwound," which went to number six. In the late 1970s, he had recorded with his band, Ace in the Hole for D, but the records made little impact outside of Texas. At any rate, Strait's artful blend of western swing and honky-tonk with a touch of contemporary country has proven not only successful but long-lasting, going nineteen straight years with at least one top hit, and eighty-seven chart appearances in a twenty-year period. Through 1997, Strait had twenty albums that sold a minimum of one million copies each.

In many ways, Strait lived the life of a typical male Texan. He joined the military after high school, married and had children, attended college and obtained an agricultural education degree in 1979, and played music part-time until landing his MCA contract. With such a large number of hits, only a few can even be mentioned here, but the more memorable would certainly include "Right or Wrong" (an old song from the repertoire of Emmett Miller and Bob Wills), "Ocean Front Property," "All My Ex's Live in Texas," "Does Fort Worth Ever Cross Your Mind," "Love without End, Amen," and a revival of the Tommy Collins song "If You Ain't Lovin' (You Ain't Livin')." In a career that is far from over, George Strait perhaps has proven that one can stick with a true style, remain unbowed by the record production establishment, and still come out a winner.

Recommended Recordings: Strait out of the Box, MCA 11263, 1995 (four-CD boxed set); *George Strait: 50 Number Ones*, MCA 80000459-02, 2004 (two-CD set; the title seems a misnomer as a few of the songs, while ranking high, failed to reach number one on the *Billboard* charts).

Thompson, Hank (b. 1925). Hank Thompson carried the sound of western swing through the 1950s and 1960s at a time when that musical type seemed like a fading form. After breaking up his band in 1966 and working as a solo performer, Thompson continued to place songs on the charts through 1981 and kept recording into the twenty-first century, becoming one of the few country artists to record in seven decades. Above all he remains best-known for his honky-tonk classic "The Wild Side of Life," which spent seven months on the charts in 1952, with fifteen weeks at number one.

Hank Thompson kept western swing alive during the 1950s and 1960s, a time during which interest in the musical style seemed to be fading.
Courtesy of Photofest.

Thompson had programs around his home area of Waco, Texas, while still in high school and after navy service in radio technology returned to a local radio program and recorded songs for two small companies, including "Swing Wide Your Gate of Love" and "Whoa Sailor." This led to a contract with Capitol in 1947 and a hit record with "Humpty Dumpty Heart." Hank's band the Brazos Valley Boys evolved into a full western-swing conglomerate over the next two or three years. While much of his fame rested on "The Wild Side of Life," Thompson had plenty of additional hit records, including "Rub-a-Dub-Dub" and "Wake Up Irene," that went to number one and numerous other high-ranking standards, such as "Yesterday's Girl," "The Blackboard of My Heart," "Honky-Tonk Girl," "Squaws Along the Yukon," "A Six Pack to Go," and a 1961 revival of Jack Guthrie's "Oklahoma Hills." After departing from Capitol in 1965, he signed with Warner Brothers and then Dot, having several hits on the latter label, such as "On Tap, in the Can, or in the Bottle," but none with the impact of his earlier efforts. Except for a brief stint with the *Grand Ole Opry* in 1949, Thompson generally had minimal contact with Nashville until after he went with Dot. All of his Capitol sides were recorded in either Texas, California, or at live venues in the Far West. His Warner Brothers and earliest Dot sessions were also made in California. In recent years, he has continued to play live shows from his home in Texas, but not as much as in his prime years.

Recommended Recording: Hank Thompson & His Brazos Valley Boys, Bear Family BCD 15904, 1996 (twelve-CD set containing all 323 Capitol recordings).

Travis, Merle (1917–1983). Merle Travis made a number of significant contributions to country music. He ranks as an important singer and songwriter but is probably best-known as an innovative finger-picking guitarist. While elements of the Travis style came from other western Kentucky musicians, such as Mose Rager, Ike Everly, Kennedy Jones, and Arnold Schultz, it was Merle who made it known to the wider musical world. Travis himself worked an apprenticeship as a member of Clayton McMichen's Georgia Wildcats and with a WLW Cincinnati-based band called the Drifting Pioneers before going to California, where he signed with Capitol Records in the spring of 1946. His first release, "Cincinnati Lou," and "No Vacancy" both gained hit status. Songs like "Divorce Me C.O.D." and "So Round, So Firm, So Fully Packed" each spent several weeks at number one.

Hit songs to the contrary, Merle Travis gained more fame for his guitar work and song writing. The latter included such songs associated with coal mining like "Dark as a Dungeon," "Over by Number Nine," a rewrite of "Nine Pound Hammer," and especially "Sixteen Tons," which became a huge hit for Tennessee Ernie Ford some years after Merle first wrote it. While none of his guitar tunes became major hits, they had considerable impact within the industry and influenced other guitar pickers, such as Chet Atkins. Travis also did session work with just about every Capitol artist who recorded in California, so much in fact that he had no releases under his own name from 1956 until 1961. After leaving Capitol in the early 1970s, he made an album with Chet Atkins and later recorded for CMH Records. He spent his last years living in Oklahoma.

Recommended Recording: Guitar Rags and a Too Fast Past, Bear Family BCD 15637, 1994 (containing all recordings through 1955).

Travis, Randy (b. 1959). If Ricky Skaggs personified the neotraditional movement in country music in the early 1980s, Randy Travis (born Randy Traywick) assumed that role in the latter part of the decade. A soft-spoken North Carolinian, Travis put together a string of hit records that led to two CMA Male Vocalist of the Year awards. Brought up in a family that appreciated what has come to be called "classic country" music, Travis had some rocky moments in adolescence but ultimately settled into a more stable existence under the guidance of Lib Hatcher, operator of a Charlotte nightclub where Travis played regularly and who eventually became his manager and spouse. Travis came to Nashville in 1981 and sang in clubs until finally landing a contract in 1985 with Warner Brothers Records, where his first release cracked the charts and another number, "1982," became a hit. "On the Other Hand" and "Diggin' Up Bones" both reached number one in 1986, and Travis gained star status.

Travis joined the *Grand Ole Opry* cast in December 1986 and had ten more top hits in the next five years, with "Forever and Ever, Amen" and "Hard Rock Bottom of Your Heart" ranking as the most successful. In addition, his first two albums, *Storms of Life* and *Always & Forever*, sold three and five million, respectively. He also did a quality theme album of new western-flavored songs, *Wind in the Wire*, and appeared in a number of motion pictures.

Recommended Recordings: Greatest Hits, Volume One, Warner Brothers 45044, 1992; *Greatest Hits, Volume Two*, Warner Brothers 45045, 1992; *Wind in the Wire*, Warner Brothers 45319, 1993.

Tubb, Ernest (1914–1984). When Ernest Tubb hit the country music world with a string of hits in the early 1940s, he soon became the prototype for what was becoming known as the honky-tonk style of country music.

Characterized by fiddle, steel guitar, an electric lead guitar, and identifiable vocal inflections, Tubb became an institution in the music. He had not always been such. As a poor rural youth growing up in Texas, the man who became known as the "Texas Troubadour" started out emulating Jimmie Rodgers, and only after developing his own style did he have much success.

Ernest Tubb struggled on a variety of Texas radio stations, endeavoring to make a living with music. He recorded for Bluebird in 1936 and 1937, but his early releases sold poorly. Signing with Decca in 1940, he had a minor hit with "Blue Eyed Elaine" and a major one with "I'm Walking the Floor over You" in 1941. After that, the hits came regularly for the next twenty years. He appeared in a couple of motion pictures in 1942 and joined the *Grand Ole Opry* cast in February 1943. Some of his other well-known numbers include "Soldier's Last Letter," "Rainbow at Midnight," "Are You Waiting Just for Me," "It's Been So Long Darling," and "Waltz Across Texas" (said to be President George W. Bush's favorite). With his band the Texas Troubadours, Tubb toured regularly for some 150 to 200 dates per year until a bout with emphysema finally forced his retirement in 1982. He became widely known and respected for his loyalty to fans and for helping young artists get started in the business. His Nashville-based Ernest Tubb Record Shop became and remains one of the best-known retail outlets for country phonograph records.

Recommended Recordings: Walking the Floor over You, Bear Family BCD 15688, 1995 (eight-CD boxed set containing 1936–1946 material); *Let's Say Goodbye Like We Said Hello*, BCD 15498, 1991 (five-CD set containing 1947–1953 recordings); *Country Music Hall of Fame Series*, MCAD 10086, 1990 (good sampler of Decca material).

Twain, Shania (b. 1965). The phenomenal success of Shania Twain (born Eileen Edwards) in album sales in the mid-1990s made country music history. Her second Mercury album, *The Woman in Me*, had sold over nine million copies by the end of 1997, making her by far the all-time top-selling female vocalist in the field. Her other albums also proved to be top sellers as well. This seemed like the culmination of a rags-to-riches story for the young Canadian singer who had experienced her share of challenging moments in her youth spent largely in the somewhat remote town of Timmins, Ontario.

Born in Windsor, Edwards moved to Timmins when her mother remarried, and Edwards subsequently took the name of her stepfather, Jerry Twain, an Ojibwa Indian. In her teens, she got some good experience on Canadian television but had to temporarily return home to support and rear younger siblings after 1987, when her parents were killed in an automobile accident. During this time, she sang in a local resort. This probably delayed her entry onto the national scene, which occurred after she came to Nashville in 1991. Signing with Mercury, her first album and singles attracted some attention, but two music videos caught the eye of producer John "Mutt" Lange, who saw star quality and not only took over production of her next album but also became her husband in December 1993. The next album resulted in spectacular sales and yielded four number one hits, including her first, "Any Man of Mine," as well as four lesser chart makers. Three additional albums have kept Twain in the limelight as a top star. Through 2000, her biggest hits have been "Love Gets Me Every Time" in country and "From This Moment On" with Bryan White, which climbed to number four on the pop listings. Some have held that Twain's music is too much in the pop-rock category, but a recent joint appearance with Dolly Parton on the *Oprah Winfrey Show* demonstrated that she could sing country-style music as well as anyone when properly presented.

Recommended Recordings: The Woman in Me, Mercury CD 314 522886, 1995; *Come on Over*, Mercury 314 536003, 1997.

Wagoner, Porter (b. 1927). Missouri-born Porter Wagoner, known as the "Thin Man from West Plains," emerged as a major country star of the 1960s and 1970s, partly on the strength of several hit RCA Victor recordings, *Grand Ole Opry* membership, and, perhaps most of all, because of his status as the first country music star to hit big with a syndicated TV program. Growing up in southern Missouri and reared on country sounds, Wagner formed his first band before he was out of his teens, had a program on a local radio station beginning in 1950, and moved on to regional powerhouse KWTO in Springfield in 1951. The Porter Wagoner Trio, which also included Don Warden and Speedy Haworth, toured the Ozark region and signed with RCA Victor in 1952. Wagoner had his first hits in 1954 and 1955 with "Company's Comin'" and "A Satisfied Mind," respectively.

Wagoner was an early regular on the *Ozark Jubilee* but moved to Nashville in 1956 and joined the *Grand Ole Opry* in February 1957. His syndicated TV show began in 1960 and ran for twenty-one years. He added vocalist Norma Jean (Beasler) and comedian Speck Rhodes to his entourage as well as a quality band—the Wagonmasters—that came to include such figures as Buck Trent, Mack Magaha, and George McCormick, of which each made something of a name for themselves in their own rights. Norma Jean left the show in 1967, was replaced by Dolly Parton, who had become a bigger star than Wagoner by the time she left the program in 1974. At its peak, the show was aired on nearly 100 stations and had about three million weekly viewers. It undoubtedly aided Wagoner's popularity, and he enjoyed such hit records as "Misery Loves Company," "Green Green Grass of Home," "The Carroll County Accident," and "The Cold Hard Facts of Life." In addition, he and Parton had several successful duets beginning with "The Last Thing on My Mind" in December 1967. He left RCA Victor in 1980 and after a pair of minor hits with Warner Brothers in the early 1980s vanished from the charts, but he remained a key figure at the *Opry* and something of a senior statesman following the death of Roy Acuff.

Recommend Recording: The Thin Man from the West Plains, *1952–1962*, Bear Family BCD 15499, 1993 (four-CD boxed set).

Wakely, Jimmy (1914–1982). Jimmy Wakely was one of the better-known Hollywood singing cowboys, starring in a series of twenty-eight films for

Monogram Pictures in the late 1940s. While his films never posed a major threat to either Gene Autry or Roy Rogers, his recording career was quite successful, particularly in the 1944–1951 era. Arkansas-born and Oklahoma-reared, from 1937 Wakely played on radio in Oklahoma City, where the Jimmy Wakely Trio, which also included Johnny Bond and Scotty Harrell, earned sufficient stature to go in 1940 to Hollywood, where they became regulars on Gene Autry's CBS Network program, *Melody Ranch*. Wakely began recording on Decca in 1940.

While his movie series was running, Jimmy Wakely began recording for Capitol Records and turned out such number one hits as "One Has My Name (the Other Has My Heart)," "I Love You So Much It Hurts," and his duet with Margaret Whiting, "Slipping Around," which spent seventeen weeks at the top and three at that position on the pop listings. Several of his other songs made the top ten. His voice was sufficiently smooth to send several songs to the pop top forty. In the waning days of network radio, Wakely had a program from 1952 to 1957 and came to own the shows, from which he later issued a series of albums on his own Shasta label. He continued touring into his later years, sometimes with son John and daughter Linda Lee. He also hosted a deejay program on Armed Forces Radio in his later years.

Recommended Recordings: Vintage Collections, Capitol CD 7243, 1996; *The Very Best of Jimmy Wakely*, Varese Sarabande 302 066 134-2, 2000 (Shasta masters).

Walker, Frank (1889–1963). As a businessman who played a key role in phonograph records, Frank Walker spent several years each with Columbia, RCA Victor, and M-G-M, making significant contributions in music to each label and helping to make stars of figures as diverse as blues queen Bessie Smith and such country figures as Charlie Poole, the Skillet Lickers, and Hank Williams. Born and reared in upstate New York, Walker had early experience in banking prior to navy service in World War I. He joined Columbia in 1921 and during his years with the company created both the 14,000 D blues series and the 15,000 D hillbilly series. Major artists in the latter included Poole, Riley Puckett, Clayton McMichen, and Gid Tanner. Through much of the 1930s, Walker headed RCA's budget-priced Bluebird label and in August 1945 was hired to start the record division of M-G-M. Although M-G-M recorded many country artists during the decade that Walker managed the label, the only real star that the firm produced in that period was Hank Williams. Walker retired in 1956 but stayed on as a consultant from his home in Queens, New York, until his death.

Wells, Kitty (b. 1919). Kitty Wells (born Muriel Deason) ranked as the first female country performer to attain true stardom as a solo performer. One of the few country performers actually born in Nashville, in 1937 she married country singer Johnnie Wright, who was half of the duo of Johnnie and Jack. She performed as the female singer with their entourage through the 1940s on a variety of southern radio stations, taking her stage name from the old sentimental ballad "Sweet Kitty Wells." Her initial recordings for RCA Victor in 1949 earned her little attention, but in May 1952, she cut an answer to Hank Thompson's current country hit "The Wild Side of Life" entitled "It Wasn't God Who Made Honky Tonk Angels" for Decca. It became a number one hit for six weeks and launched a solo career that earned her the nickname "Queen of Country Music."

Although some of Kitty Wells's other early hits were also answer songs, such as "Paying for That Back Street Affair" and "Hey Joe," most were not. Her other high-ranking hits included "Heartbreak, U.S.A.," "Makin' Believe," "Searching," and "Whose Shoulder Will You Cry On." Many of her songs reflected a female point of view, although—unlike those of a later generation—often that of a victim of masculine insensitivity. Wells also had some notable duets with Red Foley, such as "One by One" and "As Long As I Live." She remained supreme as the leading female performer of the 1950s, although by the 1960s younger women, such as Patsy Cline, Wanda Jackson, Loretta Lynn, Norma Jean, and Dottie West, began to offer serious competition. Kitty continued to tour with Johnnie and Jack and after 1963 with just Johnnie Wright, who astutely managed her career. She remained a regular on the country charts with Decca through 1972 and spottily thereafter through the remainder of the decade. With advancing age, the Wrights curtailed their appearances.

Recommended Recordings: The Queen of Country Music, Bear Family, BCD 15638, 1992 (four-CD boxed set containing 1949–1958 recordings); *Country Music Hall of Fame Series*, MCA CD 10081, 1991 (good sampler of her best work).

Williams, Hank (1923–1953). Hank Williams (born King Hiram Williams) probably ranks as the best-known figure in country music history. In the years following World War II, he achieved stardom as a singer and even more acclaim as a songwriter. Unfortunately, a number of personal problems contributed to an early death and legendary status before the Alabama native reached the age of thirty.

Williams spent his childhood in various small towns in south Alabama, moving in 1937 to Montgomery, where his mother operated a boarding house. He played on local radio and spent World War II alternating between work in the Mobile shipyards and performing on WSFA. His original songs had attracted some attention. Fred Rose first became interested in his compositions as a vehicle for Columbia artist Molly O'Day and signed Williams to an Acuff-Rose writing arrangement and to record for Sterling Records in 1946. The next year Williams signed with M-G-M, where his song "Move It on Over" reached number four in 1947. In August 1948, Williams relocated to KWKH in Shreveport and the *Louisiana Hayride*. While there his version of "Lovesick Blues" took off and became a major hit—sixteen weeks at the top in country and number twenty-four on the pop charts—in 1949 and got him a move to Nashville and the *Grand Ole Opry*. For the next three years, Williams was highly successful and had several top hits, including "Long Gone Lonesome

Blues," "Why Don't You Love Me," "Cold, Cold Heart," "Moanin' the Blues," "Hey Good Lookin'," and the Cajun-flavored "Jambalaya." Several others made the top ten, and he had a series of somewhat morbid numbers released under the name "Luke the Drifter." However, in 1952 his personal life began to unravel, and in August he was fired from the *Opry* and returned to Shreveport. He died enroute to a performance on New Year's Eve, but his legend continued to grow and he had four posthumous number one hits—most notably, "Kawliga" and "Your Cheatin' Heart." Most of his recordings have remained in print in one form or another, and son Randall Hank (b. 1949), who is known as Hank Williams, Jr., attained country stardom in his own right. Numerous artists in the country and pop fields have continued to record his songs.

Recommended Recording: The Complete Hank Williams: Deluxe Edition, Mercury 314 536 077-2, 1998 (ten-CD boxed set).

Wills, Bob (1905–1975). A 1975 tribute song by country "outlaw" Waylon Jennings titled "Bob Wills Is Still the King" pretty much said it all as far as western swing music is concerned. Texas fiddler Bob Wills along with his band the Texas Playboys dominated that field through the music's heyday and remained much revered afterward. Wills and vocalist Milton Brown could be termed the prime creators of the style during their days with the Light Crust Doughboys, but the style really began to emerge when each created his own band. Brown's early death left Wills as the surviving founder and stylist, although there were several good groups in Texas and Oklahoma. The first Wills band started in Waco late in 1932 and worked briefly in Oklahoma City but did not really achieve popularity until settling in at KVOO in Tulsa in February 1934. They began recording for the American Record Corporation in 1935. The Texas Playboys included such key musicians as Leon McAuliffe on steel guitar, Eldon Shamblin on lead guitar, Jesse Ashlock on fiddle, Al Stricklin on piano, and Tommy Duncan as lead vocalist. When horns were added, the band had as many as sixteen members. Their music was intended for dancing, and they played regularly at many of the big dance halls throughout the region, being especially known for their frequent appearances at Cain's Dancing Academy in Tulsa. While "New San Antonio Rose" constituted their best-known number, the Texas Playboys had numerous hits to their credit, including "Time Changes Everything," "Take Me Back to Tulsa," "Trouble in Mind," "Home in San Antone," and "Roly Poly." In 1940, Bob and five band members appeared in the Tex Ritter film *Take Me Back to Oklahoma* and later made several pictures with Russell Hayden.

When World War II broke out, several band members, including Wills briefly, entered military service, and after his 1943 discharge, Wills reorganized the Texas Playboys in California. Later bands had mostly different personnel, and in 1947, Wills left Columbia Records for M-G-M, where the band's biggest hit was "Faded Love" in 1950. Bob later had bands that recorded for Decca and

Liberty. After 1964, he led bands composed mostly of studio musicians and Texas Playboy reunion collections. He suffered from both heart problems and strokes toward the end, at a time, ironically, when western swing interest was beginning to experience a resurgence.

Recommended Recordings: San Antonio Rose, Bear Family BCD 15933, 2000 (ten-CD boxed set containing all ARC/Columbia recordings); *The King of Western Swing*, Living Era CD, AJA 5250, 1998 (good sampler of Columbia material); *Milk Cow Blues*, Blue Moon BMCD 3065, 1997 (good sampler of Tiffany Transcription material from 1946 to 1947).

Wiseman, Lulu Belle (1913–1999) and Scotty (1909–1981). From the mid-1930s through the 1950s, Lulu Belle and Scotty reigned as the leading husband-wife duo in country music. A pair of North Carolina mountain folk who met in Chicago, the duo gained their greatest fame on the *National Barn Dance* and other programs at WLS radio. Scott Wiseman attended college at Fairmont State in West Virginia, where he also appeared on the local station WMMN before going to Chicago. Lulu Belle (born Myrtle Cooper) moved with her parents to Evanston, Illinois, and in 1932 began performing on the *Barn Dance*, where John Lair gave her the name "Lulu Belle" and initially matched her with Red Foley in duets prior to Scotty's arrival on the program. The two married on December 13, 1934, and reigned as the "sweethearts of the *Barn Dance*" for the program's duration, except for a brief period when they went to WLW Cincinnati before returning to Chicago.

Lulu Belle and Scotty were essentially radio stars, and to the surprise of many, Lulu Belle won the title "Radio Queen" in a national contest sponsored by *Radio Guide* in 1936, outpolling several movie stars who had network programs. Over the years, the twosome also had featured roles in seven motion pictures and made numerous recordings for Bluebird (Scotty only), the American Record Corporation, Vogue, and Mercury. Their best-known songs, some composed by Scotty, included "Remember Me," "Good Old Mountain Dew," "Homecoming Time in Happy Valley," "Have I Told You Lately That I Love You," and numerous novelty numbers. After their retirement to Spruce Pine, North Carolina, they periodically recorded albums for such companies as Starday, Birch, and Old Homestead. Albums were also compiled from their radio transcriptions. After Scotty's death, Lulu Belle remarried and passed away some thirteen years later.

Recommended Recording: Lulu Belle & Scotty: Early & Great, Old Homestead OHCD 168, 1999.

Wiseman, Mac (b. 1925). Malcolm "Mac" Wiseman, known as the "Voice with a Heart," has enjoyed a long and durable career in country and bluegrass music without ever becoming a superstar. A native of the Shenandoah Valley of Virginia, Wiseman built up a repertoire of old songs and gained early radio experience in such locales as Harrisonburg, Bristol, and Knoxville, sometimes working as a featured performer with Buddy Starcher, Molly O'Day, Bill

Monroe, and the Flatt and Scruggs team. His first opportunity to make solo recordings came with the new Dot label in 1951. Most of his earlier recordings were with bluegrass accompaniment, although Wiseman never considered himself exclusively a bluegrass vocalist.

After recording several numbers with Dot in the early 1950s that became bluegrass standards, including his theme " 'Tis Sweet to Be Remembered," "I Wonder How the Old Folks Are at Home," "I'll Still Write Your Name in the Sand," and "Goin' Like Wildfire," Wiseman switched to a more country-oriented approach and had his biggest hit with a folksy version of "Jimmy Brown, the Newsboy," a number often associated with bluegrass. For a time, he worked as an executive with Dot and lived on the West Coast but then came back to Nashville and began recording for Capitol, again doing both bluegrass and country material. Still later, he based himself at WWVA Wheeling and then came to Nashville and signed with RCA Victor, having a modest hit with "Johnny's Cash and Charlie's Pride" and recording three albums with Lester Flatt. Later in the 1970s, he went with CMH and recorded bluegrass material both by himself and with the Osborne Brothers. Since then, he has continued to play bluegrass festivals and to adapt to whatever his audience seems to favor, be it bluegrass, country, or folk.

Recommended Recordings: 'Tis Sweet to Be Remembered, Bear Family BCD 15976, 2003 (six-CD boxed set containing 1951–1964 recordings); *Mac Wiseman: Early Dot Recordings*, County CCS-Cd-113, 1992 (good sampler).

Wynette, Tammy (1943–1998). For a time in the late 1960s and early 1970s, Tammy Wynette (born Virginia Wynette Pugh) shared honors with Loretta Lynn and Dolly Parton as the three great female superstars of the country music world. Recurring health and personal problems perhaps prevented her from maintaining the longevity and staying power of the other two, yet she managed to prove herself a tough survivor under often adverse circumstances. A native of Itawambi County, Mississippi, she came from a working-class background, married prior to her high school graduation, and trained as a beautician. Wynette came to Nashville as a twenty-three-year-old divorcée to try her luck at a musical career.

After several rejections, she signed with Epic and had modest success with her first release, "Apartment #9," and a hit with her second release, "Your Good Girl's Gonna Go Bad." A string of number one hits followed, including "I Don't Wanna Play House," "Take Me to Your World," "D-I-V-O-R-C-E," and "Stand By Your Man," the latter also registering high on the pop charts. From February 1969 until 1975, she was married to George Jones, and their stormy marriage produced several duet hits, including "We're Gonna Hold On," "Golden Ring," "We're Not the Jet Set," and "Two Story House." She continued to score well on the listings through the 1970s and into the 1980s, although not as often as in her peak years. Wynette finally found some stability with her fifth marriage to producer George Richey from 1978, but health problems plagued her later years.

Recommended Recording: Tammy Wynette: 16 Biggest Hits, Columbia CK 69437, 1998.

Yoakam, Dwight (b. 1956). Although born in tradition-music rich Pike County, Kentucky, and reared in the Appalachian-migrant city of Columbus, Ohio, Dwight Yoakam became the leading figure on the West Coast country scene from the mid-1980s. After failing to make much impact in Nashville, Yoakam headed for California in 1978, where he finally began to make an impression on the club scene and cut a six-number effort for Oak Records in 1984, which was later picked up by Reprise in 1986 with additional songs added. The album contained two hits, "Guitars, Cadillacs" and a revival of Johnny Horton's 1956 hit "Honky-Tonk Man," and ultimately sold over a million copies. Although somewhat apart from the neotraditional efforts of artists based in Nashville, such as Ricky Skaggs, Randy Travis, and George Strait, Yoakam's music fit well into the same mold.

Later albums in the 1980s, *Hillbilly DeLuxe* and *Buenas Noches from a Lonely Room*, also sold over a million each. The latter contained "Streets of Bakersfield" with additional vocal by Buck Owens and gave Yoakam his first actual number one hit. He had another in February 1989 with "I Sang Dixie." Through 1994, the Kentucky-born Californian had fourteen numbers in the top ten; thereafter his chart ratings declined, but his albums continued to do quite well. In addition, Yoakam had some acting credits in motion pictures.

Recommended Recordings: Guitars, Cadillacs, Etc., Etc., Reprise 25372, 1986; *Hillbilly DeLuxe*, Reprise 25567, 1987.

Young, Faron (1932–1996). Emerging to national prominence from the stage of the *Louisiana Hayride* in 1953, Faron Young remained a significant figure on the country scene for nearly three decades. Born in Shreveport and reared on a nearby farm, Young's first recordings appeared on the Philadelphia-based Gotham label, and he signed with Capitol early in 1952. Military service intervened, and he spent much of the next two years making recruiting transcriptions for the U.S. Army. Meanwhile, his fourth single, "Goin' Steady," reached number two on the charts early in 1953. He left the army in November 1954, just as "If You Ain't Lovin' (You Ain't Livin')" was attaining hit status, and a few months later in 1955, "Live Fast, Love Hard, Die Young" provided the young veteran with his first number one hit.

Like many other honky-tonk country singers, Young found the going tough during the rockabilly era, but he ultimately recovered with hits like "Alone with You" and "Country Girl" in 1958 and 1959, respectively. In 1961, he had one of his biggest hits with "Hello Walls," which also ranked high on the pop charts. Switching to Mercury, Faron had another hit with "The Yellow Bandana" in 1963 and steadily had songs on the charts for fifteen years, with "Wine Me Up" in 1969 and "It's Four in the Morning" in 1971 being the most memorable. His later chart efforts with MCA and Step One were less successful. Apparently despondent and encountering serious health problems, Young took his own life at age sixty-four.

Recommended Recordings: Faron Young: The Classic Years, 1952–1962, Bear Family BCD 15493, 1990 (five-CD boxed set); *Live Fast, Love Hard*, Country Music Foundation CMF-020D/S 21-18678, 1995 (good sampler of Capitol sides).

Selected Bibliography

BOOKS

Allen, Bob. *George Jones: The Life and Times of a Honky Tonk Legend.* New York: Birch Lane Press, 1994.

Amburn, Ellis. *Dark Star: The Roy Orbison Story.* New York: Lyle Stuart/Carol, 1990.

Artis, Bob. *Bluegrass.* New York: Hawthorn Books, 1975.

Atkins, Chet. *Country Gentleman.* Chicago: Henry Regnery, 1974.

Black, Bob. *Come Hither to Go Yonder: Playing Bluegrass with Bill Monroe.* Urbana: University of Illinois Press, 2005.

Bond, Johnny. *The Tex Ritter Story.* New York: Chappell Music Co., 1976.

Bronner, Simon J. *Old-Time Music Makers of New York State.* Syracuse, NY: Syracuse University Press, 1987.

Brooks, Tim, and Earle Marsh. *The Complete Directory to Prime Time Network and Cable TV Shows.* 8th ed. New York: Ballantine Books, 2003.

Brown, Maxine. *Looking Back to See: A Country Music Memoir.* Fayetteville: University of Arkansas Press, 2005.

Bufwack, Mary A., and Robert K. Oermann. *Finding Her Voice: The Saga of Women in Country Music.* New York: Crown, 1993.

Campbell, Archie. *An Autobiography.* Memphis, TN: Memphis State University Press, 1981.

Cantwell, David, and Bill Friskics-Warren. *Heartaches by the Number: Country Music's 500 Greatest Singles*. Nashville, TN: Vanderbilt University Press, 2003.

Cantwell, Robert. *Bluegrass: The Making of the Old Southern Sound*. Urbana: University of Illinois Press, 1984.

Caress, Jay. *Hank Williams: Country Music's Tragic King*. New York: Stein & Day, 1979.

Carlin, Bob. *String Bands in the North Carolina Piedmont*. Jefferson, NC: McFarland, 2004.

Carlisle, Dolly. *Ragged but Right: The Life & Times of George Jones*. Chicago: Contemporary Books, 1984.

Cash, Johnny. *Man in Black*. Grand Rapids, MI: Zondervan Publishing, 1975.

Cohen, Norm. *Folk Music: A Regional Exploration*. Westport, CT: Greenwood Press, 2005.

———. *Long Steel Rail: The Railroad in American Folksong*. Urbana: University of Illinois, 1981.

Cooper, Daniel. *Lefty Frizzell: The Honky Tonk Life of Country Music's Greatest Singer*. Boston: Little, Brown, 1995.

Cusic, Don. *Eddy Arnold: I'll Hold You in My Heart*. Nashville, TN: Rutledge Hill Press, 1997.

Daniel, Wayne. *Pickin' on Peachtree: Country Music in Atlanta*. Urbana: University of Illinois Press, 1990.

Dawidoff, Nicholas. *In the Country of Country: People and Places in American Music*. New York: Pantheon Books, 1997.

Dempsey, John Mark. *The Light Crust Doughboys Are on the Air: Celebrating Seventy Years of Texas Music*. Denton: University of North Texas Press, 2002.

Denisoff, R. Serge. *Waylon: A Biography*. Knoxville: University of Tennessee Press, 1983.

Ellison, Curtis W. *Country Music Culture: From Hard Times to Heaven*. Jackson: University Press of Mississippi, 1995.

Escott, Colin. *Hank Williams: The Biography*. Boston: Little, Brown, 1994.

———. *Roadkill on the Three-Chord Highway: Art and Trash in American Popular Music*. New York: Routledge, 2002.

Escott, Colin, and Kira Florita. *Hank Williams: Snapshots from the Lost Highway*. New York: DaCapo Press, 2001.

Fleischhauer, Carl, and Neil V. Rosenberg. *Bluegrass Odyssey: A Documentary in Words and Pictures*. Urbana: University of Illinois Press, 2001.

Flippo, Chet. *Your Cheatin' Heart: A Biography of Hank Williams*. New York: Simon and Schuster, 1981.

Garbutt, Bob. *Rockabilly Queens*. Toronto: Ducktail Press, 1979.

Ginell, Cary. *Milton Brown and the Founding of Western Swing*. Urbana: University of Illinois Press, 1994.

Ginell, Cary, and Kevin Coffey. *Discography of Western Swing and Hot String Bands, 1928–1942*. Westport, CT: Greenwood Press, 2001.

Goldrosen, John. *The Buddy Holly Story*. 2nd rev. ed. New York: Quick Fox, 1979.

Gray, Scott. *On Her Way: The Shania Twain Story*. New York: Ballantine Books, 1998.

Green, Archie. *Only a Miner: Studies in Recorded American Coal Mining Songs*. Urbana: University of Illinois Press, 1972.

Green, Douglas B. *Country Roots: The Origins of Country Music*. New York: Hawthorn Books, 1976.

———. *Singing in the Saddle: The History of the Singing Cowboy*. Nashville, TN: Vanderbilt University Press, 2002.

Griffis, Ken. *Hear My Song: The Story of the Sons of the Pioneers*. Los Angeles: John Edwards Memorial Foundation, 1977.

Guralnick, Peter. *Last Train to Memphis: The Rise of Elvis Presley*. Boston: Little, Brown, 1994.

———. *Lost Highway: Journeys and Arrivals of American Musicians*. New York: Random House, 1979.

Hagan, Chet. *Country Music Legends in the Hall of Fame*. Nashville, TN: Thomas Nelson Publishers, 1982.

———. *Grand Ole Opry*. New York: Henry Holt, 1989.

Hall, Wade. *Hell-Bent for Music: The Life of Pee Wee King*. Lexington: University Press of Kentucky, 1996.

Haslam, Gerald W. *Workin' Man's Blues: Country Music in California*. Berkeley: University of California Press, 1999.

Hemphill, Paul. *Lovesick Blues: The Life of Hank Williams*. New York: Viking Press, 2005.

———. *The Nashville Sound: Bright Lights and Country Music*. New York: Simon and Schuster, 1970.

Hopkins, Jerry. *Elvis: A Biography*. New York: Warner Brothers, 1972.

———. *Elvis: The Final Years*. New York: St. Martin's Press, 1980.

Jensen, Joli. *The Nashville Sound: Authenticty, Commercialization, and Country Music*. Nashville, TN: Vanderbilt University Press, 1998.

Jones, George. *I Lived to Tell It All*. With Tom Carter. New York: Villard, 1996.

Jones, Louis M. *Everybody's Grandpa: Fifty Years Behind the Mike*. With Charles K. Wolfe. Knoxville: University of Tennessee Press, 1984.

Jones, Loyal. *Minstrel of the Appalachians: The Story of Bascom Lamar Lunsford*. Boone, NC: Appalachian Consortium Press, 1984.

———. *Radio's "Kentucky Mountain Boy" Bradley Kincaid*. 2nd ed. Berea, KY: Berea College Appalachian Center, 1988.

Jones, Ramona. *Make Music While You Can: My Story*. Madison, NC: Empire, 1999.

Kennedy, Rick. *Jelly Roll, Bix, and Hoagy: Gennett Records and the Birth of Recorded Jazz*. Bloomington: Indiana University Press, 1994.

Kienzle, Rich. *Southwest Shuffle*. New York: Routledge, 2003.

Kingsbury, Paul, ed. *The Encyclopedia of Country Music*. New York: Oxford University Press, 1998.

Koon, Bill. *Hank Williams: So Lonesome*. Jackson: University Press of Mississippi, 2001.

Laird, Tracey E. W. *Louisiana Hayride: Making Music on the Shores of the Red River*. New York: Oxford University Press, 2004.

Lewis, Myra. *Great Balls of Fire: The Uncensored Story of Jerry Lee Lewis*. With Murray Silver. New York: Quill Press, 1982.

Logan, Horace. *Elvis, Hank, and Me: Making Musical History on the Louisiana Hayride*. New York: St. Martin's Press, 1998.

Lovullo, Sam, and Marc Eliot. *Life in the Kornfield: My 25 Years at Hee Haw*. New York: Boulevard Books, 1996.

Lyle, Katie Letcher. *Scalded to Death by the Steam*. Chapel Hill, NC: Algonquin Books, 1984.

Malone, Bill C. *Country Music, U.S.A.* 2nd rev. ed. Austin: University of Texas Press, 2002.

———. *Don't Get Above Your Raisin': Country Music and the Southern Working Class*. Urbana: University of Illinois Press, 2002.

———. *Singing Cowboy and Musical Mountaineers: Southern Culture and the Roots of Country Music*. Athens: University of Georgia Press, 1993.

———. *Southern Music/American Music*. Lexington: University Press of Kentucky, 1979.

McCloud, Barry, et al. *Definitive Country: The Ultimate Encyclopedia of Country Music and Its Performers*. New York: Perigee Books, 1995.

McNeil, William K., ed. *Encyclopedia of American Gospel Music*. New York: Routledge, 2005.

Meade, Guthrie T., Jr. *Country Music Sources: A Biblio-Discography of Commercially Recorded Traditional Music*. Chapel Hill, NC: Southern Folklife Collections, 2002.

Miller, Zell. *They Heard Georgia Singing*. Macon, GA: Mercer University Press, 1996.

Montana, Patsy. *The Cowboy's Sweetheart*. With Jane Frost. Jefferson, NC: McFarland, 2002.

Morrison, Craig. *Go Cat Go! Rockabilly Music and Its Makers*. Urbana: University of Illinois Press, 1998.

Nash, Alanna. *Dolly*. Los Angeles: Reed Books, 1978.

Nassour, Ellis. *Patsy Cline*. New York: Tower Books, 1981.

O'Neal, Bill. *Tex Ritter: America's Most Beloved Cowboy*. Austin, TX: Eakin Press, 1998.

Perkins, Carl, and David McGee. *Go Cat Go: The Life and Times of Carl Perkins*. New York: Hyperion, 1996.

Peterson, Richard A. *Creating Country Music: Fabricating Authenticity*. Chicago: University of Chicago Press, 1997.

Piazza, Tom. *True Adventures with the King of Bluegrass*. Nashville, TN: Vanderbilt University Press, 1999.

Porterfield, Nolan. *Jimmie Rodgers: The Life and Times of America's Blue Yodeler*. Urbana: University of Illinois Press, 1992.

———, ed. *Exploring Roots Music: Twenty Years of the JEMF Quarterly*. Lanham, MD: Scarecrow Press, 2004.

Pugh, Ronnie. *Ernest Tubb: The Texas Troubadour*. Durham, NC: Duke University Press, 1996.

Rhodes, Don. *Ramblin' Rhodes: Collected Columns*. Hartwell, GA: North American Publications, 1982.

Rosenberg, Neil V. *Bluegrass: A History*. Urbana: University of Illinois Press, 1985.

Rothel, David. *The Singing Cowboys*. New York: A. S. Barnes, 1978.

Russell, Tony. *Country Music Records: A Discography, 1921–1942*. New York: Oxford University Press, 2004.

Schlappi, Elizabeth. *Roy Acuff: The Smoky Mountain Boy*. Gretna, LA: Pelican, 1993.

Shelton, Robert, and Burt Goldblatt. *The Country Music Story*. Indianapolis, IN: Bobbs-Merill, 1966.

Smith, Richard. *Can't You Hear Me Callin': The Life of Bill Monroe, Father of Bluegrass*. Boston: Little, Brown, 2000.

Snow, Hank. *The Hank Snow Story*. With Jack Ownbey and Bob Burris. Urbana: University of Illinois Press, 1994.

Stamper, Pete. *It All Happened in Renfro Valley*. Lexington: University Press of Kentucky, 1999.

Streissguth, Michael. *Eddy Arnold: Pioneer of the Nashville Sound*. New York: Schirmer Books, 1997.

———. *Voices of the Country: Interviews with Classic Country Performers*. New York: Routledge, 2004.

Tichi, Cecilia. *High Lonesome: The American Culture of Country Music*. Chapel Hill: University of North Carolina Press, 1994.

Tinsley, Jim Bob. *For a Cowboy Has to Sing*. Orlando: University of Central Florida Press, 1991.

———. *He Was Singin' This Song*. Orlando: University Presses of Florida, 1981.

Tosches, Nick. *Country: The Biggest Music in America*. New York: Dell, 1977.

———. *Hellfire: The Uncensored Story of Jerry Lee Lewis*. New York: Dell, 1982.

———. *Unsung Heroes of Rock 'n' Roll*. New York: Charles Scribner's Sons, 1984.

Townsend, Charles. *San Antonio Rose: The Life and Music of Bob Wills*. Urbana: University of Illinois Press, 1976.

Tribe, Ivan M. *Mountaineer Jamboree: Country Music in West Virginia*. Lexington: University Press of Kentucky, 1996.

———. *The Stonemans: An Appalachian Family and the Music That Shaped Their Lives*. Urbana: University of Illinois Press, 1993.

Tribe, Ivan M., and John Morris. *Molly O'Day, Lynn Davis and the Cumberland Mountain Folks: A Bio-Discography*. Los Angeles: John Edwards Memorial Foundation, 1975.

Whitburn, Joel, comp. *Top Country Albums, 1964–1997*. Menomonee Falls, WI: Record Research, 1997.

———. *Top Country Singles, 1944–2001*. Menomonee Falls, WI: Record Research, 2002.

White, John I. *Git Along Little Dogies: Songs and Songmakers of the American West*. Urbana: University of Illinois Press, 1975.

Whiteside, Jonny. *Ramblin' Rose: The Life and Career of Rose Maddox*. Nashville, TN: Vanderbilt University Press, 1997.

Wiggins, Gene. *Fiddlin' Georgia Crazy: Fiddlin' John Carson, His Real World, and the World of His Songs*. Urbana: University of Illinois Press, 1987.

Williams, Roger M. *Sing a Sad Song: The Life of Hank Williams*. 2nd ed. Urbana: University of Illinois Press, 1981.

Wolfe, Charles K. *Classic Country: Legends of Country Music*. New York: Routledge, 2001.

———. *A Good-Natured Riot: The Birth of the Grand Ole Opry*. Nashville, TN: Vanderbilt University Press, 1999.

———. *In Close Harmony: The Story of the Louvin Brothers*. Jackson: University Press of Mississippi, 1996.

———. *Kentucky Country: Folk and Country Music of Kentucky*. Lexington: University Press of Kentucky, 1996.

———. *Tennessee Strings: Country Music in Tennessee*. Knoxville: University of Tennessee Press, 1977.

Wolfe, Charles K., and James E. Akenson. *Country Music Goes to War*. Lexington: University Press of Kentucky, 2005.

Wolfe, Charles K., and Ted Olson, eds. *The Bristol Sessions: Writings about the Big Bang of Country Music*. Jefferson, NC: McFarland, 2004.

Wright, John. *Traveling the High Way Home: Ralph Stanley and the World of Traditional Bluegrass Music*. Urbana: University of Illinois Press, 1993.

Zwisohn, Laurence J. *Loretta Lynn's World of Music*. Los Angeles: John Edwards Memorial Foundation, 1980.

Zwonitzer, Mark. *Will You Miss Me When I'm Gone?: The Carter Family and Their Legacy in American Music*. With Charles Hershberg. New York: Simon and Schuster, 2002.

JOURNALS AND MAGAZINES

For full citations of individual articles, check individual chapter endnotes.

Banjo Newsletter

Bluegrass Now

Bluegrass Unlimited

Country America

Country Music

Country Song Roundup

Cowboy Songs

JEMF Quarterly

Journal of American Folklore

Journal of Country Music

The Journal of the American Academy for the Preservation of Old-Time Country Music

Mountain Broadcast and Prairie Recorder

Muleskinner News

Music City News

National Hillbilly News

Old-Time Herald

Old Time Music

Pickin'

Western Clippings

Western Folklore

LINER NOTES AND BOOKLETS THAT ACCOMPANY RECORD SETS

Liner Notes and booklets that accompany anthologies and boxed sets or recordings vary from virtually worthless to excellent. Those booklets (sometime full-length hardbound books) that accompany Bear Family recordings are especially informative and often written by top scholars in the field, such as Charles Wolfe and Kevin Coffey. Those that have proven useful to this study are cited in the chapter endnotes with author credits.

Index

About the Author

IVAN TRIBE is Professor of History in the Social Science Department at University of Rio Grande.